Steve—my friend and cam——
co-laborer — thank you for your
Interest in my book. I hope you enjoy
it!   —Jeff Taylor   9-20-06

Where Did the Party Go?

Bill Ducker
March 2009

Where Did the Party Go?

WILLIAM JENNINGS BRYAN,

HUBERT HUMPHREY,

AND THE

JEFFERSONIAN LEGACY

Jeff Taylor

University of Missouri Press
Columbia and London

Library of Congress Cataloging-in-Publication Data

Taylor, Jeff, 1961–
Where did the party go? : William Jennings Bryan, Hubert Humphrey,
and the Jeffersonian legacy / Jeff Taylor.
p.   cm.
Summary: "Using a twelve-point model of Jeffersonian thought, Taylor
appraises the competing views of two Midwestern liberals, William
Jennings Bryan and Hubert Humphrey, on economic policy, foreign
relations, and political reform to demonstrate how the Democratic party
lost its place in Middle America"—Provided by publisher.
Includes bibliographical references and index.
ISBN-13: 978-0-8262-1659-5 (hard cover : alk. paper)
ISBN-10: 0-8262-1659-5 (hard cover : alk. paper)
ISBN-13: 978-0-8262-1661-8 (pbk. : alk. paper)
ISBN-10: 0-8262-1661-7 (pbk. : alk. paper)
1. Democratic Party (U.S.)—History.   I. Title.
JK2316.T39 2006
324.2736—dc22
2006005919

Designer: Stephanie Foley
Typesetter: Crane Composition, Inc.
Printer and binder: Thomson-Shore, Inc.
Typeface: Bembo

The University of Missouri Press offers its grateful acknowledgment to
an anonymous donor whose generous grant in support of the publication of outstanding dissertations has assisted us with this volume.

Frontispiece photos: William Jennings Bryan, courtesy of the Library of
Congress; Hubert H. Humphrey, courtesy of the U.S. Senate
Historical Office.

For permissions, see p. 373

CONTENTS

PREFACE

Hubert Horatio Humphrey was my first political hero. My earliest memories of him are from my childhood in the late 1960s. My mom seemed to have favorable feelings toward him. During my prepolitical years, I tended to confuse Hubert Humphrey with Herbert Hoover and J. Edgar Hoover. By 1972, I knew who the man was, and I favored him for president during the Democratic primaries. Perhaps it was a geographic thing: I grew up in Iowa and Minnesota was a neighboring state. But I must have been attracted to his personality as well. He was energetic and a vocal critic of Nixon as Watergate began to unfold. He seemed to say what he felt, without regard for political niceties. During this "mod" period of popular fashion, Humphrey wore wide ties and colorful shirts, which seemed to make him a little cooler in my eyes. When Humphrey lost the 1972 nomination, I was one of only two students in my sixth grade class to support McGovern in the fall. Along with Benjamin Franklin, Thomas Jefferson was my favorite Founding Father. I admired his range of talents, love of writing, personality of quiet strength, appreciation for science, and reputation as a man of the people. Following in the footsteps of my father and grandfather, I possessed deep-rooted populist instincts. Jefferson and Jackson had always been my favorite presidents. That is why I was a Democrat, and my parents' distrust of Nixon reinforced my partisanship.

By 1975, I had become acquainted with conservative populist writing, and I grew to despise limousine liberalism. Unfortunately, my hero Humphrey was one of the preeminent examples of that ideology. I went on to embrace other contemporary politicians with equal affection and respect. They were, by default, conservative populists because I was not aware of the existence of liberal populists. Ten years later I returned to the Democratic Party for a hero, one that was long since deceased. William Jennings Bryan was a man who embodied both my political and religious views. He was a liberal populist—and not one of those phony liberals who talks about serving the common people and then drinks champagne with the powers-that-be. Bryan was not just about the Cross of Gold speech and the *Scopes* trial. There was a lot more to him. Like Humphrey, he was a neighbor. My grand-parents had lived near Omaha. A decade after discovering Bryan, I was doing graduate work on his career and on Humphrey's.[1] Two decades later, this book is being published. Despite their differences with each other and despite certain weaknesses in each man, I will always have a fondness for Humphrey and Bryan because they were genuine statesmen. They were more honest than most politicians and sincere in their desire to make the world a better place through politics. Good intentions are not enough, and motivations can be mixed, but sincerity is praiseworthy, even when sincerely wrong.

Everyone has a perspective or bias from which she or he views events and the world. Mine is evident in this book. I am a populist. My readers may not be. If so, perhaps you believe Hamilton had a superior ideology in compar-ison to Jefferson, or at least had some stronger points. Perhaps you believe the Democratic Party was correct in discarding traditional tenets as circum-stances changed. Perhaps you will agree with me that the party should at least be honest about its changed nature.

It is easy for populists to romanticize the common people. I think most average Americans have populist instincts and would do a better job of rul-ing than the class that largely occupies the seats of power. Unfortunately, the average American also has a short attention span, an aversion to facing unpleasant realities, and a tendency to be distracted by bread and circuses. He or she knows little about the political process and pays undue deference to authority figures. Journalist H. L. Mencken had a wonderful ability to see through the cant of the leading politicians of his day, but he sank into mis-anthropy and elitism as he watched the masses routinely vote so many self-serving phonies into high office. He became antidemocratic because he could not reconcile popular sovereignty with popular stupidity. I understand the dilemma, but I still think that majority rule is the best form of govern-ment available at this time. What is the alternative? Minority rule. That con-tradicts my innate sense of fairness. The common people are far from perfect, but in a nonangelic world, it is safest to disperse power as widely as possible.

This is a study of Jeffersonianism, including its ideological tenets and philosophical underpinnings. There are many conflicting theories about Jefferson's political thought, presidential record, personal life, and historical legacy. I urge readers to keep an open mind and allow room for divergent points of view. The realm of political philosophy, ideology, and partisanship is fraught with controversy, emotion, and long-standing assumptions. Although clear differences of viewpoint exist among historians, political scientists, and active citizens, it is still worthwhile to consider new ideas and a range of theories.

The political ideas of Thomas Jefferson serve as a point of departure for this book. Whether Jefferson's ideology is labeled as *liberalism, populism, libertarianism,* or *agrarianism,* it has distinctive traits, many of which are generally agreed upon and have played an important role in the development of the Democratic Party. Using Jefferson as an exemplar, or a measure, I examine the contrasts between two liberal champions of the twentieth-century Democratic Party: William Jennings Bryan and Hubert Humphrey. Bryan and Humphrey were quite similar in many ways: both were Democrats, both were midwesterners, both had outgoing personalities, both were orators, both have been linked by many historians to Franklin Delano Roosevelt, and both have places in the pantheon of American liberalism. Despite these similarities, the overall contrast between Bryan and Humphrey is stark. Bryan and Humphrey responded to Jefferson's influence in varying ways, and their weighty dissimilarities come from contrasting responses to the claims of Jefferson and his ideological allies in the early days of the republic.

This book examines the philosophy and ideology of liberalism in Jefferson's day and shows how liberalism changed from the period of Bryan, 1885–1925, to the period of Humphrey, 1938–1978. Since I am interested in the content of the ideological theory, I have chosen the purest possible exponents and practitioners of liberalism. Some may wonder why President Woodrow Wilson has not been selected as the exemplar of early twentieth-century Democratic liberalism. Despite his reforming and moralizing reputation, the depth and sincerity of Wilson's liberalism have been seriously called into question by contemporaries and historians.[2] Even among those who take liberal professions of faith by Wilson at face value, it is almost universally conceded that Bryan was more liberal than Wilson. This may be because Bryan did not have to put his idealistic utterances to the test as president of the United States or because he was genuinely more radical than the expositor of the New Freedom. Regardless of the explanation, Bryan is widely viewed as the preeminent example of early twentieth-century liberalism within the Democratic Party and as a forerunner of Franklin Roosevelt and the New Deal.

Balance demanded that I select two nonpresidents as the exemplars of Democratic liberalism, but the case for excluding Oval Office occupants can be made on other grounds as well. John Kennedy had a relatively undistinguished congressional career before he entered the White House and was viewed with suspicion by most liberals when he was running for the 1960 Democratic presidential nomination. Despite his record of support for the New Deal and the Fair Deal, most liberals also had misgivings about Lyndon Johnson in 1960. Humphrey was seen as much more liberal than Kennedy and Johnson. Two-time Democratic presidential nominee Adlai Stevenson was the other favorite of liberal purists in 1960. Stevenson would be a suitable exemplar but his career in national politics did not have the longevity of Humphrey's—he entered the national limelight in 1952 and died in 1965. Vice President Henry Wallace, another favorite of post–New Deal liberals, had an even briefer career in the national political spotlight, and his liberalism is called into question by strange inconsistencies, including simultaneous Communist and Wall Street domination of his 1948 presidential campaign.[3]

Humphrey seems to be the most suitable exemplar of Democratic liberalism during the 1938–1978 period. He was a founder of Americans for Democratic Action (ADA), was made famous by his championing of a strong civil rights plank at the 1948 Democratic National Convention, and was widely perceived as the most liberal candidate for the Democratic presidential nomination during the 1960 primary season. Humphrey was attacked by the New Left, the Counterculture, and some ADA liberals in the 1960s because of his public stance on the Vietnam War, but by 1976 he was seen as the "great white hope" by many liberals within the party.

Given the "great men of history" theoretical inclination of most scholars, most U.S. presidents have received their fair share of scholarly studies, and that is another reason I have not chosen presidents such as Wilson, Kennedy, or Johnson. There is a dearth of ideological examinations of Bryan and Humphrey; they have been the subjects of some fine biographical studies but have not received the attention they deserve in terms of ideological commitment and influence. What exists for Bryan tends to be old; what exists for Humphrey tends to be narrowly focused on his civil rights record. The new book *A Godly Hero: The Life of William Jennings Bryan,* by Michael Kazin, is a major work by a gifted historian, but it is primarily a biography and mistakenly identifies Bryan as an ideological precursor of Franklin Roosevelt.

This book makes an original and valuable contribution to the discourse of American history and political science. The transformation of Jefferson's legacy has not been adequately examined by historians or political scientists. There is no comprehensive look at Jefferson's ideology or its transmutation within the Democratic Party during the critical years between the careers of Bryan and Humphrey. Jeffersonian profiles by historians such as Dumas Malone, Merrill Peterson, and Noble Cunningham include information about Jefferson's political thought, but they are essentially biographies that say very little about his influence on twentieth-century American ideology. Peterson's *The Jeffersonian Image in the American Mind* is an exception because it goes beyond biography to help us understand Jefferson's ideological legacy and includes a useful discussion of the link between Jefferson and Bryan. It does not, however, mention Humphrey. Of course, there are scholarly works that mention Jefferson's influence on various modern Democrats, but these allusions tend to be rather brief.

Some scholars have pointed to differences between the old progressives of the 1900s and the new liberals of the 1930s. Nonetheless, there is no consensus among historians, and many have emphasized ideological continuity between the two groups. When changes in liberalism have been studied, they have usually been cast in terms of individual personalities and social conditions, rather than in terms of ideology. Furthermore, scholars have not clearly defined *Jeffersonianism*. This being the case, it is not surprising that the specifics of the post–New Deal change in liberalism have not been clearly identified. Plus, the implications of the change have not been pursued with any degree of depth. While some attention has been given to these ideological developments, they have heretofore received piecemeal and passing treatment rather than comprehensive and sustained treatment. *Where Did the Party Go?* covers modern Democratic liberalism with the breadth and depth the subject deserves.

This book has special relevance today as we witness a revival of interest in Thomas Jefferson, experience the centenary of Bryan's three presidential campaigns, and seek to understand popular discontent with the nation's political elite. The 2004 election demonstrated a growing emphasis on moral values in American politics. Jefferson was a moralistic politician with a relatively low level of compromise when it came to public policy. This emphasis on public morality and commitment to principle was adopted by a young William Jennings Bryan. Grounded in a different tradition, Hubert Humphrey tended toward an economic emphasis in which materialism trumped moralism. Sociopolitical "salvation" was cast in secular terms, with welfare programs and economic growth taking center stage. Humphrey was a pragmatist who embraced compromise. He disliked idealists who "try to make politics into a religion" and boasted that he wasn't "pure" because he was willing to settle for half a loaf. This strain of pragmatic, trimming, nonmoralistic politics can be seen in other recent Democratic leaders—from Michael Dukakis's claim that the 1988 election was about competence not ideology to John Kerry's general agreement with the economic and foreign policy aims of the Bush administration, even though he disagreed with the means. Campaign trail invocations of God by such Democrats strike most people as stilted and calculated. This was not the case with Jefferson and Bryan. A closer look at their tradition may say something about the Democratic Party's current lack of appeal to Middle America.

For many Americans, a commitment to moral values trumps economic well being, in theory if not in practice. Many believe that elites in George-town, Manhattan, and Hollywood exist in a stratosphere beyond morality, where power and money are the primary aims of their lives and careers. It is assumed that these elites see the masses as ignorant, provincial, and super-stitious. Thomas Frank's insightful book *What's the Matter with Kansas?* uses one state as a case study to show how, in his view, many average Americans vote against their own economic interests because they are attracted by the moralistic rhetoric of Republicans and repelled by modern Democratic ten-dencies. Unlike the book you are about to read, *Kansas* examines the mod-ern populist vs. elitist milieu by focusing on conservatism, not liberalism. In his conclusion, Frank makes the seemingly obvious but usually ignored observation that "somewhere in the last four decades liberalism ceased to be relevant to huge portions of its traditional constituency, and we can say that liberalism *lost* places like Shawnee and Wichita with as much accuracy as we can point out that conservatism won them over."[4] He does not delve into the history of Democratic liberalism to explain this loss, but he does accu-rately identify the tendencies of the Democratic Leadership Council (DLC) as a contemporary reason for this shift of heartland voters from Democratic liberalism to Republican conservatism. Despite his own populist instincts and criticism of DLC corporatists, Frank is essentially a Humphrey Demo-crat, not a Bryan Democrat: he defines traditional Democratic liberalism as "equality and economic security" and uses FDR as a measure of real liber-alism.[5] This may be a limitation of perspective, but Frank's book deserves to be hailed as a classic treatment of modern American ideology.

Since the 1940s, millions of traditional Democrats have stopped voting for the Democratic Party. The trend has accelerated since the 1970s. Where did the party faithful go? Many went to the Republican Party, some became Independents, and a few began voting for third parties. Why did they leave? Most probably felt that the party of Jefferson, Jackson, and Bryan left them.

ACKNOWLEDGMENTS

I want to thank my parents, Jim and Judy, as well as my brother Greg and sister Julie. I am indebted to my earliest political mentors: Glenn Taylor, Vince Mart, and Helen Rasdal. Many of my college friends provided insight and example. I appreciate my friends in Missouri and Minnesota for the moral support, interesting discussions, and shared campaigns. The members of my graduate committee, especially Richard Hardy, Paul Wallace, and Arthur Kalleberg, inspired me as a student and as a scholar. Cornboy mates and political allies Fritz and Kelly DeBrine have been with me through good times and bad. I would like to thank Steve Higgins for converting my old Mac files and Jon Benson for his help with indexing and translating. Comments from manuscript readers have strengthened this book considerably. John Rensenbrink, Karl Trautman, and Bill Kauffman merit specific gratitude. Beverly Jarrett, Jane Lago, Karen Renner, Beth Chandler, Susan King, and the entire team at University of Missouri Press have been wonderful. Thank you Shirley, for the love, support, and title. This book is dedicated to Shirley, William, and Jane. Κυριε ευχαριστω σοι

Where Did the Party Go?

CHAPTER 1

Introduction

What Is Liberalism?

Liberal is frequently used in American political discourse but is rarely defined. It serves as shorthand for a series of positions on controversial issues. Largely left unexamined is the ideology underlying these positions. The origin, content, and transmutation of American liberalism merit examination and understanding. Liberalism's strange ideological transformation, or ideological alchemy, began in the early 1910s and was virtually complete by the early 1940s. The "lowly" thought of Jefferson was discarded in favor of the exalted, gold-plated thought of Hamilton.[1] The content of liberalism changed dramatically while the name remained the same. This has led to misunderstanding and confusion by political scientists, historians, politicians, and voters. Another word for this perplexing process might be *paradiastole,* a Hobbesian term indicating a transvaluation of values or a redefinition of vices as virtues and vice versa.

Classical liberalism is associated with the natural rights political theory of John Locke and the laissez-faire economic theory of Adam Smith. This study focuses on *modern liberalism, progressive liberalism,* or *left-liberalism.* Early proponents of this ideology accepted some elements of classical liberalism while infusing their political thought with humanitarianism and egalitarianism. The word *liberal*—in its modern, progressive sense—came into widespread use during the 1930s, but it was used on occasion during the Progressive Era to describe populists and progressives, muckrakers and mavericks. In fact, it was used by Thomas Jefferson himself in 1824 to describe his own ideology.[2]

Early American liberals included sociopolitical radicals involved in the

American Revolution, opponents of the proposed U.S. Constitution, or Anti-Federalists, and founding members of the Democratic-Republican Party. Among the more prominent adherents of this ideology were Samuel Adams, Patrick Henry, Robert Yates (Brutus), Thomas Paine, John Taylor, George Clinton, and John Randolph. But preeminent among these men in fame, influence, and power was Thomas Jefferson; he was the exemplar of exemplars, the model democrat. The twelve main tenets of Jefferson's political thought, or *Jeffersonianism*, are: democracy rather than aristocracy, political decentralization, strict constructionism, opposition to banking, legislative preeminence vis-à-vis executive, suspicion of the judiciary, protection of civil liberties, ethnic inclusiveness, frugal spending, low taxation, pacifism, and isolationism. These tenets are not accidental or arbitrary, discrete or dated public policy positions, and they possess a natural interconnectedness. Jefferson may not have been a systematic political philosopher, but he had a sincere regard for the aspirations of the vast majority of Americans, an intuitive understanding of human beings, and a mind capable of both logic and vision when it came to government.

The word *ideology,* when used in this book, refers to a coherent, systematic set of beliefs about government and politics. While the political thought of Jefferson will be used to measure subsequent versions of liberalism, it should be clearly understood that the term *Jeffersonianism* does not signify merely the ideology of one individual; rather, it signifies the ideology of early American liberals. The ideology bears the name of Jefferson only because he was its greatest expositor and practitioner. Having established Jeffersonianism as the basis of American liberalism and having traced this ideology from the early days of the republic through the Jacksonian, antebellum, and Gilded Age eras, this book explores the influence of Jeffersonianism on Democratic Party liberalism during two forty-year periods, from 1885 to 1925, and from 1938 to 1978. The emphasis is on two exemplars of twentieth-century Democratic Party liberalism: William Jennings Bryan (1860–1925) as the representative of pre–New Deal liberalism and Hubert Horatio Humphrey (1911–1978) as the representative of post–New Deal liberalism. Throughout this work, the thoughts and actions of these two individuals will be examined in relation to the twelve tenets of Jeffersonianism.

The ideology of liberalism was not confined to the Democratic Party. During the twentieth century, Republican figures as disparate as Robert La Follette, Theodore Roosevelt, Wendell Willkie, Thomas Dewey, and Nelson Rockefeller were described as liberals. Unfortunately, an analysis of both major U.S. political parties would be unwieldy. The Democratic Party is the logical choice for this work since Jefferson is usually acknowledged as its principal founder. While the Republican Party would be expected to contain substantial Hamiltonian influence because of its roots in the Federalist and Whig parties, Democratic Party figures throughout the past two hundred years have paid homage to Jefferson and might be expected to embrace his ideology.

Transcendence of Ideology

What about the timelessness of Jeffersonian liberalism? Is the twelve-tenet model a valid yardstick for twentieth-century liberalism? Are principles enunciated in the context of the preindustrial, recently independent, and globally isolated America of the late 1700s relevant to the modern America of the early and mid-1900s? Yes, ideology is time transcendent. The meaning of the words associated with a particular ideology may change, and social circumstances are bound to change over time, but the ideology itself does not change. The objective existence of ideas is both a Platonic and a Judeo-Christian concept.[3] Whether deemed natural or supernatural, first principles are viewed as not being socially derived. While used in the context of earthly society, they have real existence beyond this context. This is true of ideas relating to the sphere of politics. This view does not deny the importance of history. Public policy specifics emanating from first principles change over time as warranted by changing historical conditions. Political thought is not static, but its underlying ideas are time transcendent. The transcendent nature of ideology has been recognized by historians such as Staughton Lynd and Howard Zinn.[4]

Ideas that are primarily religious, moral, or ethical—Ten Commandments, Sermon on the Mount, Tao—make claims not only of time transcendence but of place transcendence.[5] It could be argued that the application of political ideas is limited by the fact that they are first enunciated in the context of a specific place with its own social contract and political culture. Thus, for example, principles that apply to American politics may not apply to Thai politics. This argument can be challenged on the grounds that it ignores Euro-American global hegemony during the past two centuries. More important, it ignores the bond of human nature that transcends nationality. Political ideas are also usually linked to religious-moral-ethical ideas. Opposition to banking, one of the seemingly less universal tenets of Jeffersonianism, did not spring up merely because of the rising capitalist threat to American agrarianism or because of the controversy over the Bank of the United States. It was an elaboration of Aristotelian and biblical warnings against usury (lending money at interest).[6]

Jefferson recognized that "differences of circumstance" between nations "furnish differences of fact whereon to reason, in questions of political economy, and will consequently produce sometimes a difference of result." While believing that human laws and institutions are changeable, he also thought that there are some natural political principles, the foundational one being the conflict between democracy and aristocracy. Three centuries earlier, pioneer political scientist Niccolò Machiavelli made the exact same point.[7] Even if we accept the argument that political ideas are not place transcendent, this does not mean that tenets set forth in the U.S. of the 1790s are not relevant to the U.S. of the 1890s and beyond. The principles of the Declaration of Independence are still widely revered, despite its antiquated list of grievances against King George III and the fulfillment of its immediate purpose. The Constitution is still in effect; its spirit is still cited even by those who ignore its letter. There is no reason to believe that the twelve Jeffersonian tenets are an inappropriate measure of ideology since they are being applied in the same national context in which they were first presented. When it comes to foundational ideas concerning politics, applicability may vary from time to time and from place to place while validity remains constant.

Despite the many changes that occurred in the United States during the nineteenth century, Jeffersonianism continued to flourish throughout the period. It was viewed as a viable ideology for at least one hundred years after the death of Thomas Jefferson. The assumption that it somehow suddenly became obsolete during a fifteen-year period, from 1925 to 1940, seems dubious. If Jeffersonianism was time transcendent for a century, why did it lose this attribute in the space of little more than a decade? The answer is: it didn't. Jeffersonianism is not an ideological dodo bird. It still exists. Today, the ideology may not wield much power on the national political stage, but thousands if not millions of Americans consider themselves to be Jeffersonians. More to the point of this study, post–New Deal liberals claimed to be in the same ideological stream as pre–New Deal liberals, a stream that can be called nothing else but Jeffersonian. Thus, Jefferson's political thought was relevant in the 1940s and continues to possess utility in the twenty-first century.

CHAPTER 2

Jefferson and Early American Liberalism

Jefferson as Primary Exemplar

The essence of liberalism consists of a genuine respect and concern for the thoughts and feelings of the common people. Liberalism is opposed to special privileges for the rich and powerful and committed to freedom, justice, and peace. Liberalism as thus defined is a wide stream of ideology that includes an assortment of populists, progressives, and pacifists. In America, this type of ideology can be traced back to colonial sources such as John Wise, Roger Williams, Anne Hutchinson, William Penn, James Oglethorpe, and John Woolman. The Iroquois League also played an important but indirect role in the development of liberal ideology in America.

In some ways, American liberalism was refined and expanded over the course of the nineteenth and twentieth centuries. Perhaps most notably, it developed a greater awareness of the importance of racial justice and gender equality. Nonetheless, the basic tenets of liberalism were in place by the late eighteenth century. Thomas Jefferson was liberalism's most prominent champion in the realm of electoral politics. When Jefferson was running for president in 1800, his platform consisted of eight main planks: democracy rather than aristocracy, states' rights, lower government spending, lower taxes, trade with all nations but political alliances with none, no standing army in peacetime, protection of civil liberties, and ethnic inclusiveness.[1] He advocated legislative preeminence as early as 1776, favored strict construction of the Constitution and expressed hostility toward banks as early as 1791, and opposed judicial tyranny after 1801. These twelve concepts form the basis of a model for the study of early American liberalism.

Despite some inconsistencies and mixed motivations, liberals such as Jefferson, Robert Yates, Thomas Paine, Patrick Henry, Samuel Adams, John Taylor of Caroline, John Randolph of Roanoke, and George Clinton attempted to protect the interests of two groups largely unrepresented by government: the small farmers (yeomen) and the urban workers (artisans and mechanics). During the period from 1801 to 1809, some of these men were more Jeffersonian than Jefferson himself. As president, Jefferson made occasional compromises of principle, but these should not be allowed to compromise the ideological standard set during the Adams administration. Jefferson's failings to be true to his core beliefs or to be consistent in the face of political pressures should not lower the bar. Jeffersonianism was no mere product of one man's mind or career. It is a time-transcendent set of interconnected political ideas that can also be called early American liberalism, populism, libertarianism, or agrarianism. It is important to not lose sight of this fact. Jefferson's ideology is far bigger than his foibles as a man and politician. Jefferson is the primary exemplar of this ideology not because he created it or was its purest exponent but because he was its most influential advocate.

Jefferson was the most important founder of the Democratic Party. Party members were commonly referred to as "Jeffersonians," "Democrats," or "Republicans," thus the "Democratic-Republican" label used by historians. Yates, Paine, Adams, Taylor, Randolph, and Clinton were associated to varying degrees with the party of Jefferson. While these men differed with Jefferson on some issues or areas of emphasis, the twelve tenets of Jeffersonianism largely encompass the political views of these and other early American liberals. This chapter focuses on Jefferson, but the singular focus should not be misunderstood. Early American liberalism was not a capricious or accidental outgrowth of one man's personality and experience. It was an ideology held and espoused by many.

By examining the views of Jefferson in relation to these twelve policy areas, it will be possible to establish the nature of early American liberalism. Having done this, I will use this depiction of ideology as a measure of liberalism in connection with parties and politicians from 1830 to the present. This study will first attempt to establish a standard by which claims of liberalism may be judged. For each issue, the viewpoint of early American conservatism will be summarized before moving on to that of Jefferson. There was not a consensus in American politics regarding these issues. The views of Jefferson and his political associates represent a distinct ideology, one that can be clearly distinguished from that of Alexander Hamilton and his allies.

Thomas Jefferson (1743–1826) was a lawyer and plantation owner who served in the Virginia legislature during the 1760s and 1770s. In 1776, he wrote the Declaration of Independence and three years later drafted the Act for Establishing Religious Freedom for the state of Virginia. Jefferson was governor of Virginia from 1779 to 1781. He was elected to the Continental Congress in 1783 and was named minister to France in 1785. In 1789, Jefferson became the nation's first secretary of state. Weary of his personal and ideological rivalry with a fellow cabinet member, Secretary of the Treasury Alexander Hamilton, Jefferson resigned in 1793. Jefferson was vice president of the United States from 1797 to 1801, and he served two consecutive terms as president from 1801 to 1809. He was "uneasy about his own presidency" because of the compromises he made during his eight years in office.[2] After leaving the presidency, Jefferson fathered the modern Library of Congress and played a leading role in founding the University of Virginia. *Notes on the State of Virginia,* published in 1784, was Jefferson's only original full-length book. His public papers and personal letters serve as the main sources of his political thought. Jefferson's words and deeds have inspired countless liberals, agrarians, populists, advocates of liberty, and independent thinkers.

Democracy

The form of government created by the United States in 1789 was not a democracy. The framers of the Constitution understood the distinction between a democracy and a republic. Most of them utterly rejected the former, having fear of and contempt for direct rule by the masses. John Adams, the first vice president and second president of the United States, believed democracy to be "the most ignoble, unjust and detestable form of government."[3] Most of the Founding Fathers were elitists who preferred monarchy or aristocracy. They thought democracy was chaotic and dangerous and disdainfully referred to it as "mobocracy." Thus, they created a republic, or "mixed constitution." A republic includes components of each of the three traditional types of government: monarchy, aristocracy, and democracy. The framers of the Constitution established a monarchic component (president), aristocratic components (Supreme Court and Senate), and a democratic component (House of Representatives). Despite this concession to democracy, the House is an example of "representative democracy," not classical democracy. In a representative democracy, the people do not make the decisions themselves, and the House is merely one half of one branch, or one-sixth of the government. Operating in this context, the political parties of

the early republic either emphasized the Constitution's monarchic and aristocratic aspects (Federalists) or democratic aspects (Democratic-Republicans).
Many who belonged to the two parties wished to change the document to
bring it more nearly into line with the form of government they favored.

Secretary of the Treasury and Federalist Party leader Alexander Hamilton
was committed to government by the elite. At the Constitutional Convention in 1787, he advocated the creation of an American monarchy. In reference to the legislative branch, he told convention delegates,

> All communities divide themselves into the few and the many. The first
> are the rich and well-born, the other the mass of the people. . . . The
> people are turbulent and changing; they seldom judge or determine
> right. Give, therefore, to the first class a distinct, permanent share in the
> government. They will check the unsteadiness of the second . . . Can a
> democratic assembly, who annually revolve in the mass of the people, be
> supposed steadily to pursue the public good? Nothing but a permanent
> body can check the imprudence of democracy.

A decade earlier, he had written, "When the deliberative or judicial powers
are vested wholly or partly in the collective body of the people, you must
expect error, confusion, and instability." He considered most people "very ill
qualified to judge for themselves what government will best suit their peculiar situations," and he dismissed traditional, Athenian-style democracies by
saying that they "never possessed one feature of good government."[4] As a
protégé of George Washington, and in-law of a wealthy family, Hamilton
was at the center of wealth and power. He believed "that no government
could endure which did not identify its interests with the interests of property and wealth." Hamilton's fiscal policies were designed to "attach the
powerful interests of banking and commerce to the government and to
make them the controlling element." The Federalist Party of Hamilton and
John Jay, of Washington and John Adams, of John Marshall and Charles
Pinckney, "found its chief strength among merchants and financial speculators, whose support for the new government it sought to assure by policies
which would afford them pecuniary advantage."[5]

Secretary of State and Democratic-Republican Party leader Thomas Jefferson believed that people are "naturally divided into two parties: 1. Those
who fear and distrust the people . . . 2. Those who identify themselves with
the people, have confidence in them." Whether the two parties are called
"Liberals and Serviles, Jacobins and Ultras, Whigs and Tories, Republicans
and Federalists, Aristocrats and Democrats, or by whatever name you please,"

he maintained that "they are the same parties still, and pursue the same object."[6] Jefferson's thoughts and actions were amazingly democratic. The truth of this statement can be seen when one considers the aristocratic context in which he lived: Jefferson's mother was from the distinguished Randolph family and his colleagues were the Founding Fathers. Historian Claude Bowers comments, "From the Randolphs he probably inherited his love of beauty, his fondness for luxury, but they failed utterly to transmit to him any aristocratic notions of government. There was a reason—his father was a middle-class farmer." Jefferson believed in a "natural aristocracy" based on virtue and talent, not on family birth or land wealth. He was an enemy of "artificial aristocracy." From the dawn to the twilight of his political career, Jefferson attempted to serve the common people. In colonial Virginia, he allied himself with Patrick Henry as a "champion of the backwoodsmen" in opposition to the wealthy tidewater families who maximized power and profit under British rule. In his draft of the Virginia constitution of 1776, Jefferson tried to create a more equitable distribution of land in the state. His attempt to abolish primogeniture, a law whereby the eldest son inherited all the land, was "the first effective blow at the landowning aristocracy of Virginia." Despite being a plantation owner himself, Jefferson was not blind to the injustice of the situation in Virginia and elsewhere. In 1785, he wrote, "I am conscious that an equal division of property is impracticable, but the consequences of this enormous inequality producing so much misery to the bulk of mankind, legislators cannot invent too many devices for subdividing property."[7]

After the American Revolution, Jefferson did not move toward conservatism, as was the case with former allies Patrick Henry and John Adams. Instead, he joined Thomas Paine in becoming "the most consistent revolutionary of all the Founding Fathers, so consistent that he was for years denounced by many as an anarchist and a Jacobin."[8] During the 1780s a reaction against radical change and popular government developed among the nation's leading patriots, and they began to resemble the royal authorities they had cast off a decade earlier. In 1786, an uprising known as Shays' Rebellion was launched by poverty-stricken farmers in western Massachusetts. Led by Revolutionary War veteran Daniel Shays, the men took up arms and marched against the state government to press their demands of currency reform, lighter taxation, and suspension of mortgage foreclosures. Government troops crushed the rebellion, but it raised the specter of mobocracy, which, in turn, became a motivating factor in the effort by conservatives to discard the Articles of Confederation in favor of a much stronger type of government. In November 1787, Jefferson's liberalism was evident in his comments about the rebellion:

... Can history produce an instance of rebellion so honorably conducted? I say nothing of its motives. They were founded in ignorance,
not wickedness. God forbid we should ever be twenty years without
such a rebellion. . . . What country can preserve its liberties, if its rulers
are not warned from time to time, that this people preserve the spirit of
resistance? Let them take arms. The remedy is to set them right as to
facts, pardon and pacify them. What signify a few lives lost in a century
or two? The tree of liberty must be refreshed from time to time, with
the blood of patriots and tyrants. It is its natural manure.[9]

While serving as members of President Washington's cabinet, Hamilton
and Jefferson came to epitomize conservatism and liberalism. Hamilton's financial policies favored the wealthy merchants and manufacturers of the
Northeast, while Jefferson was more interested in serving the small farmers
of the South and West. Having been only recently freed from the yoke of a
king, possessing political leaders who had lived under royal rule for most of
their lives, and operating under a newly created system of government,
Americans feared that Federalist leaders might try to restore monarchy in
the United States. This fear was granted plausibility by the Federalists' an-
tipathy toward popular government, their attraction to power and appreciation for splendor, and their adoration of England. In his important January
26, 1799, letter to Elbridge Gerry, Jefferson declared that he was opposed to
"monarchising" the Constitution "by the forms of its administration, with a
view to conciliate a first transition to a President and Senate for life, and
from that to an hereditary tenure of these offices, and thus to worm out the
elective principle." During the 1800 campaign, Jefferson supporters asserted,
"There is a monarchical party in the United States, and . . . Mr. Hamilton
and Mr. Adams belong to that party." The two parties represented starkly different visions: aristocracy (if not monarchy) vs. democracy. Federalists attacked Jefferson with great vehemence, and the ideological shift in policy
resulting from his victory explains references to "the Revolution of 1800."[10]
    In his first inaugural address, Jefferson made plain his belief in majority
rule with minority rights: "All, too, will bear in mind this sacred principle,
that though the will of the majority is in all cases to prevail, that will, to be
rightful, must be reasonable; that the minority possess their equal rights,
which equal laws must protect, and to violate which would be oppression."[11] President Jefferson chose Governor George Clinton of New York to
be his running mate in the 1804 election. As governor, Clinton "led the
small farmers year after year in the adoption of tax laws that helped the
farmer and brought anguished howls from the merchants." In 1810, Jefferson

wrote, "I have been ever opposed to the party so falsely called Federalists, because I believe them desirous of introducing into our government authorities hereditary or otherwise independent of the national will." He explicitly rejected government by an aristocracy founded on wealth and birth. According to Jefferson, "The influence over government must be shared among the people. If every individual which composes their mass participates in the ultimate authority, the government will be safe; because the corrupting of the whole mass will exceed any private resources of wealth." Writing to F. A. Van der Kemp in 1812, he argued that popular control of government was necessary to prevent oppression of the mass and "perpetuation of wealth and power" in the hands of the few. Living in a day when the banking system in America was being nurtured by the federal government, Jefferson feared "the growth of a capitalistic class." Similarly, he did not believe that government should foster commerce. Jefferson "accepted the tariff of 1816 on the ground that political independence demanded economic independence," but Jeffersonians, before the passage of this import tax and since, have usually opposed protective tariffs and other government efforts to intervene on behalf of business. Jefferson himself had earlier opposed a Federalist-inspired tariff because he "dreaded the power of capitalism."[12]

Jefferson's definition of a pure republic was identical to that of classical democracy: "A government by its citizens in mass, acting directly and personally, according to rules established by the majority." He argued that "such a government is evidently restrained to very narrow limits of space and population. I doubt if it would be practicable beyond the extent of a New England township." In Jefferson's opinion, the people choosing representatives to legislate, execute, and judge on their behalf and as they desire is "the nearest approach to a pure republic, which is practicable on a large scale of country or population." He maintained, "The full experiment of a government democratical but representative was and is still reserved for us." Jefferson rejected property as a qualification for voting. In 1800, he contended that he had always been in favor of universal suffrage. In an 1816 letter to John Taylor, Jefferson lamented the fact that "one-half of our brethren who fight and pay taxes, are excluded, like Helots, from the rights of representation, as if society were instituted for the soil, and not for the men inhabiting it." He continued,

> Governments are more or less republican, as they have more or less of
> the element of popular election and control in their composition; and
> believing, as I do, that the mass of the citizens is the safest depository of
> their own rights and especially, that the evils flowing from the duperies

of the people, are less injurious than those from the egoism of their agents, I am a friend to that composition of government which has in it the most of this ingredient.

Jefferson told Samuel Kercheval, "I am not among those who fear the people. They, and not the rich, are our dependence for continued freedom." In 1824, he endorsed a draft constitutional amendment before Congress providing for popular election of the president. Ten days before his death, Jefferson wrote, "The general spread of the light of science has already laid open to every view the palpable truth, that the mass of mankind has not been born with saddles on their backs, nor a favored few booted and spurred, ready to ride them legitimately, by the grace of God."[13]

Decentralization

Alexander Hamilton supported "strong government based on political and fiscal centralization." He was an important advocate of centralization both before and after adoption of the U.S. Constitution. It is not surprising that he was a vigorous critic of the Articles of Confederation. Charles Wiltse noted that "Hamilton, under the influence of the two political theorists most distasteful to Jefferson, Hobbes and Hume, was frankly the champion of the leviathan state. . . . Weakness and decentralization were to him intolerable."[14] In contrast, liberals have traditionally been suspicious of highly centralized government because it tends to be directed by distant elitists and administered by remote bureaucrats. In their view, neither the elitists nor the bureaucrats are responsive to the actual needs and desires of ordinary citizens.

Thomas Jefferson supported adoption of the Constitution, but he was never a supporter of great centralization. According to Wiltse, "If Jefferson had been slow to approve the constitution, it was because he feared its centralization of power would rob the common man of his liberty." In a November 1787 letter to John Adams, Jefferson wrote, "I think all the good of this new constitution might have been couched in three or four new articles, to be added to the good, old and venerable fabric, which should have been preserved even as a religious relique." Two years later, he expressed to Francis Hopkinson a stronger support for the document:

> You say that I have been dished up to you as an anti-federalist, and ask me if it be just. . . . I am not of the party of federalists. But I am much farther from that of the anti-federalists. I approved, from the first mo-

ment, of the great mass of what is in the new Constitution . . . What I
disapproved from the first moment also, was the want of a bill of rights
. . . I disapproved, also, the perpetual re-eligibility of the President.

When he was writing his autobiography in 1821, Jefferson maintained his
belief that the Constitution was an improvement over the Articles of Confederation.[15]

Unlike the Anti-Federalists, Jefferson believed that it was possible for representative democracy to function in a large geographic area. "I suspect that
the doctrine," he wrote, "that small States alone are fitted to be republics,
will be exploded by experience . . . Perhaps it will be found, that to obtain
a just republic (and it is to secure our just rights that we resort to government at all) it must be so extensive as that local egoisms may never reach its
greater part." In this instance, Jefferson's embrace of Enlightenment philosophy, with its emphasis on reason and progress, may account for his refusal to
emulate the skepticism of Anti-Federalists, many of whom were committed
to theologically orthodox Christianity, with its emphasis on sin and regress.
Regardless of its source, Jefferson's initial optimism regarding a large republic was somewhat diminished during the presidency of John Adams. His belief in decentralization was strengthened by the heavy-handedness of the
federal government. In 1798, Jefferson secretly penned a series of resolutions
endorsing state nullification of federal laws. When enacted by the Kentucky
legislature, these resolutions became known as the Kentucky Resolutions.
According to the resolutions, "whensoever the general government assumes
undelegated powers, its acts are unauthoritative, void, and of no force." They
asserted that "the government created by this compact was not made the exclusive or final judge of the extent of the powers delegated to itself . . . each
party [to the compact] has an equal right to judge for itself as well of infrac-
tions, as of the mode and measure of redress." Preparing to run for president,
in 1799, Jefferson wrote, "I am for preserving to the States the powers not
yielded by them to the Union . . . I am not for transferring all the powers of
the States to the General Government."[16]

While Jefferson supported states' rights and nullification, he was not an
enthusiast of sectionalism or secession. He resisted secession on practical, not
theoretical, grounds, and his letters on the subject reveal mixed emotions.
Writing in 1816 to William Crawford, he conceded the right of secession:
"If any state in the Union will declare it prefers separation . . . to a continuance in Union . . . I have no hesitation in saying, 'let us separate.'" Still, he
considered the Missouri Compromise of 1820 to be a "fire-bell in the
night" and the death "knell of the Union" because it represented growing
sectionalism. He viewed this development with great regret. It is important

to note that the "Principles of '98" were not the exclusive property of slavery advocates as the nineteenth century unfolded. Echoing Jefferson's rejection of a consolidationist, or unitary, interpretation of the Constitution, many New England Federalists favored secession during the War of 1812. In a lesser-known instance, in 1859, the Wisconsin legislature endorsed the Kentucky and Virginia Resolutions. This was a rejection of the Fugitive Slave Act and an outgrowth of abolitionist defiance of the federal government and its proslavery policies.[17]

The Tenth Amendment to the Constitution provides that the "powers not delegated to the United States by the Constitution, nor prohibited by it to the States, are reserved to the States respectively, or to the people." By the early 1820s, it was clear that this amendment was being largely ignored by all three branches of the federal government. Not only was the Supreme Court refusing to uphold the Tenth Amendment, but it was handing down rulings that curbed the power of states to make decisions for themselves. Jefferson believed that a constitutional amendment to limit the power of federal judges was needed. As he wrote in his autobiography, "There was another amendment [to the Constitution], of which none of us thought at the time [1787–1789], and in the omission of which, lurks the germ that is to destroy this happy combination of National powers . . . and independent powers in the States." He called federal judges "sappers and miners" who were "steadily working to undermine the independent rights of the States, and to consolidate all power in the hands of that government in which they have so important a freehold estate." Jefferson maintained,

> It is not by the consolidation, or concentration of powers, but by their distribution, that good government is effected. Were not this great country already divided into States, that division must be made, that each might do for itself what concerns itself directly, and what it can do so much better than a distant authority. . . . Were we directed from Washington when to sow, and when to reap, we should soon want bread.[18]

Jefferson's commitment to states' rights emanated from his commitment to individual rights. He wished to "secure the sphere of the state against the encroachments of the federal authority" because he deemed "the small unit better adapted to preserve the liberty of individuals, and more likely to promote their happiness." Jefferson believed in minimalistic government, and he envisioned a land populated by self-governing individuals. In 1801, during his first inaugural address, he called for "a wise and frugal government, which shall restrain men from injuring one another, which shall leave them otherwise free to regulate their own pursuits of industry and improvement, and shall not take from the mouth of labor the bread it has earned." For Jefferson, this was "the sum of good government." An opponent of monopoly, he realized that government would invariably favor one interest over another if it was intimately involved in the economy. If this were to occur, it would violate his belief in "equal rights for all, special privileges for none."[19] Thus, he recommended a laissez-faire approach to economics.

It is a relatively small step from the decentralized democracy of Thomas Jefferson to the individualistic anarchy of Henry David Thoreau. Noam Chomsky asserts that "Jefferson's concept that the best government is the government which governs least or Thoreau's addition to that, that the best government is the one that doesn't govern at all, is one that's often repeated by anarchist thinkers through modern times." Jefferson's type of democracy was not far from anarchy. In a 1787 letter, he wrote,

> I am convinced that those societies (as the Indians) which live without government, enjoy in their general mass an infinitely greater degree of happiness than those who live under the European governments. Among the former, public opinion is in the place of law, and restrains morals as powerfully as laws ever did anywhere. Among the latter, under pretence of governing, they have divided their nations into two classes, wolves and sheep. . . . [Their societies are characterized by] the general prey of the rich on the poor.

According to Richard Matthews, "In regard to communitarian anarchism, Jefferson's repeated use of the American Indian as an edifying countercultural example of how men can live in a community without the need for formal government is demonstrative of his anarchist tendency." Jefferson admired *Enquiry Concerning Political Justice,* which was written by anarchist William Godwin in 1793. When Jefferson's political opponents accused him of being an anarchist, there was a kernel of truth in the charge. As Henry Silverman points out, Jefferson "contributed ideas which have become important parts of the libertarian ethic."[20]

Construction of the Constitution

Arguing for a broad interpretation of the Constitution, loose constructionists such as Alexander Hamilton relied heavily on article I, section 8 of the document, the "necessary and proper clause." In their hands, it became an "elastic clause" possessing limitless flexibility. Strict constructionism entailed literal interpretation of the Constitution. For liberals, strict construction was linked to concepts such as fidelity and fairness.

As a wartime governor of Virginia, Thomas Jefferson's "scrupulous observance of the constitutional limitations upon the executive might have been anticipated by anyone familiar with the workings of his mind." To him, "fundamental law was not so sacred that it could not be changed," but until it was, "it stood as an expression of the public will and could not be challenged by a particular official." As a member of President Washington's cabinet, Jefferson opposed the creation of the Bank of the United States and a number of other extraconstitutional measures devised by Hamilton. He was the most influential advocate of strict constructionism during the first few decades of the republic, arguing that "though written constitutions may be violated in moments of passion or delusion, yet they furnish a text to which those who are watchful may again rally and recall the people; and they fix too for the people the principles of their political creed." In the Kentucky Resolutions, Jefferson asserted that the necessary and proper clause was being interpreted by the federal government in such a way that it was leading to "the destruction of all limits prescribed to their power by the constitution." "Words meant by that instrument to be subsidiary only to the execution of the limited powers," he wrote, "ought not to be so construed as themselves to give unlimited powers, nor a part to be taken so as to destroy the whole residue of the instrument." In 1803, Jefferson stated,

> When an instrument admits two constructions, one safe, the other dangerous, the one precise, the other indefinite, I prefer that which is safe and precise. I had rather ask an enlargement of power from the nation, where it is found necessary, than to assume it by a construction which would make our powers boundless. Our peculiar security is in the possession of a written Constitution. Let us not make it a blank paper by construction.

Jefferson recognized that he was exceeding the powers granted to the president by the Constitution when he supported the Louisiana Purchase. Lacking specific constitutional authorization to agree to such a land acquisition, he drew up an amendment to make provision for it, but his friends in the cabinet and the Senate rejected this approach as untenable. Thus, with mixed feelings, he submitted the treaty to Congress. While conceding that Jefferson was going beyond the written Constitution, Charles Wiltse makes a distinction between the president's decision and that of Chief Justice John Marshall in *McCulloch v. Maryland:* "Jefferson was not construing, but transcending, the constitution for the public good, and the means were at hand for the public to accept or reject his judgment. Marshall was subverting the constitution for an end which he knew in advance the people would reject were they given the opportunity."[21]

Despite a few instances of personal compromise, Jefferson's support for literal interpretation of the Constitution had important ramifications not only during his presidency but also during some succeeding presidencies. Although unable to prevent the creation of a central bank in 1791, Jefferson played an indirect role in its destruction two decades later. When renewal of the charter for the Bank of the United States was brought up in the Senate, with President James Madison's support, the vote turned out to be a tie. Before casting the deciding vote, Vice President George Clinton, an Anti-Federalist who had been Jefferson's vice president during his second term, said, "In the course of a long life, I have found that government is not to be strengthened by the *assumption* of *doubtful* powers, but a *wise* and *energetick* execution of those which are *incontestable;* the former never fails to produce suspicion and distrust, whilst the latter inspires respect and confidence." Clinton voted against the renewal, and the bank was killed. Jefferson believed that "real friends of the constitution in its federal form, if they wish it be immortal, should be attentive by amendments to make it keep pace with the advance of the age in science and experience." While not averse to formally changing the Constitution, he opposed changing it through tricks of interpretation. Referring to written constitutions, in 1824, he declared, "We consider them not otherwise changeable than by the authority of the people, on a special election of representatives for that purpose expressly; they are until then the *lex legum*."[22]

Banking

Liberals have traditionally been suspicious of, if not hostile toward, banking. This tradition stretches back to Hebrew society, which prohibited lending money with interest attached. In addition to forbidding usury, the Old Testament contains general warnings against exploiting and oppressing the poor and the weak. The New Testament includes the story of Christ driving the money changers out of the temple. Christ told his disciples to give freely to those who request material assistance and to not expect to be paid back. In American history, early conservatives were not constrained by antibanking sentiments rooted in the Judeo-Christian tradition. The Federalist Party was the champion of bankers and the promoter of early capitalism.[23]

As early as 1800, Thomas Jefferson opposed political centralization partly because it served as "an augmentation of the field" for stockjobbing and speculating. When the idea was first advanced by Alexander Hamilton, Secretary of State Jefferson and his followers, opposed creation of the Bank of the United States on both constitutional and economic grounds, and liberals made an unsuccessful attempt to kill the proposal in Congress. The Constitution did not authorize the creation of a national bank, and Jeffersonians viewed it as a monopoly designed to benefit wealthy and powerful men. In a 1792 letter to President Washington, Jefferson condemned "the creation of ten millions of paper money, in the form of bank bills now issuing into circulation." He specifically objected that "the ten or twelve per cent. annual profit paid to the lenders of this paper medium" was being "taken out of the pockets of the people, who would have had without interest the coin it is banishing," that "all the capital employed in paper speculation" was "barren and useless, producing, like that on a gaming table, no accession to itself, and is withdrawn from commerce and agriculture, where it would have produced addition to the common mass," and that it nourished "in our citizens habits of vice and idleness, instead of industry and morality." Finally, he protested that a "corrupt squadron of paper dealers" was aiding the "monarchical federalists" in Congress. Referring to the national bank, in 1803, President Jefferson told Secretary of the Treasury Albert Gallatin, "Now, while we are strong, it is the greatest duty we owe to the safety of our Constitution, to bring this powerful enemy to a perfect subordination . . . The first measure would be to reduce them to an equal footing only with other banks, as to the favors of the government." In 1815, he castigated "banking mania" and called bankers a "traitorous class."[24]

Jefferson opposed reestablishment of the Bank of the United States in 1816, declaring that "like a dropsical man calling out for water, water, our deluded citizens are clamoring for more banks, more banks. . . . We are now taught to believe that legerdemain tricks upon paper can produce as solid wealth as hard labor in the earth." That same year, in a letter to John Taylor, he posited, "The system of banking we have both equally and ever reprobated. I contemplate it as a blot left in all our Constitutions, which, if not covered, will end in their destruction . . . I sincerely believe, with you, that banking establishments are more dangerous than standing armies." Jefferson warned that banks were "raising up a monied aristocracy in our country." In 1825, he referred to those who "look to a single and splendid Government of an aristocracy founded on banking institutions and moneyed corporations, under the guise and cloak of their favoured branches of manufactures, commerce and navigation, riding and ruling over the plundered ploughman and beggared yeomanry."[25]

Legislature and Executive

Legislative preeminence vs. executive power is an old and controversial idea. It played a role in the colonies' decision to separate from Great Britain and was the focus of one of the important political debates during the Articles of Confederation era. State constitutions drawn up during the Revolutionary War "placed final power in the legislatures and made the executive and judicial branches subservient to them." The situation was deplored by members of the old colonial aristocracy and by the new elite of the revolutionary era, but these groups were unable to restore executive control at the state level during the 1780s. Federalists preferred executive and judicial rule over legislative rule partly because they recognized the legislature as the most democratic branch of government. In his opening speech at the Philadelphia convention, Edmund Randolph reminded his aristocratic colleagues that "our chief danger arises from the democratic parts of our constitutions . . . None of the [state] constitutions have provided a sufficient check against the democracy." The debate on adoption of the U.S. Constitution "was white-hot because for a moment in history self-government by majorities within particular political boundaries was possible. Those majorities could do what they wanted, and some of them knew what they wanted. Democracy was no vague ideal, but a concrete program."[26]

Alexander Hamilton favored a national executive chosen for life: "Starting from the premise of Hobbes that the sovereign must be absolute, he discards the republican form because it 'does not admit of vigorous execution.' . . . The monarch 'ought to be hereditary, and to have so much power that it would not be his interest to risk much to gain more.'" The struggle between legislative power and executive power continued in the period following adoption of the Constitution. Hamilton's party

> endeavored to increase the powers . . . of the executive branch at the expense of the legislative. Distrusting and fearing the people as "a great beast," it looked for the coming of a "crisis" when, through military dictatorship, popular licentiousness might be curbed and the "frail and worthless fabric" of the Constitution might be replaced by a more "energetic" government after the pattern of the English monarchy.

While Hamilton was unable to bring about the creation of a literal American monarchy, the nation "has had no stronger or more farsighted champion of executive authority." He opposed the idea of presidential term limits in *Federalist Paper* No. 72.[27]

While serving as governor of Virginia during the Revolutionary War, Jefferson did not attempt to expand the powers of the executive and refused to resort to illegal or arbitrary methods even during British invasion of the state. He was "passionately hostile to autocracy at the close of his own executive experience, just as he was before it began." His proposed Virginia constitution gave responsibility for military affairs to the legislature rather than to the governor. The Declaration of Independence's indictment of King George III included the charge, "He has dissolved Representative Houses repeatedly, for opposing with manly firmness his invasions on the rights of the people." Despite his criticism of the British monarch's actions against the British legislature, Jefferson later considered one weakness of the Articles of Confederation to be its lack of separation of legislative and executive powers. He viewed the creation of an executive branch as a needed improvement. He did, however, see some danger in the executive as proposed by the Constitutional Convention. In letters to John Adams and James Madison, Jefferson decried the absence of presidential term limits: "Once in office, and possessing the military force of the Union, without the aid or check of a council, he would not be easily dethroned, even if the people could be induced to withdraw their votes from him. I wish that at the end of the four years, they had made him forever ineligible a second time." Jefferson told Madison, "The second feature I dislike, and strongly dislike, is the abandonment, in every instance, of the principle of rotation in office, and most particularly in the case of the President." When adopting the Constitution, New York recommended an amendment prohibiting a third term for the president, a move supported by Governor George Clinton. In the early 1820s, Jefferson himself wrote, "Should a President consent to be a candidate for a third election, I trust he would be rejected, on this demonstration of ambitious views."[28]

Referring to the need for a bill of rights in the Constitution, Jefferson wrote in 1789, "The executive, in our governments, is not the sole, it is scarcely the principal object of my jealousy. The tyranny of the legislatures is the most formidable dread at present, and will be for many years. That of the executive will come in its turn." He did not see an immediate threat to civil liberties from the executive branch because he trusted George Washington, and he saw little support for monarchical government. During the next decade, his attitude changed as a result of the monarchical tendencies of Hamilton, Adams, and other Federalist leaders. During Washington's presi-

dency, Jefferson was alarmed by "Hamilton's enthusiastic affirmation of presidential power." Jefferson's opposition to executive usurpation of legislative
power was a plank in his presidential campaign platform. In 1799, he declared, "I am for preserving to . . . the legislature of the Union its constitutional share in the division of powers . . . I am not for transferring all the
powers . . . to the executive branch."[29]

From 1801 to 1809, as president of the United States, Jefferson had an opportunity to put his theories into practice on a national scale. He was "reluctant to interfere with the prerogatives of Congress. . . . When U.S. Navy
ships fought against pirates in the Mediterranean, Jefferson—recognizing
that the Constitution gave Congress alone the power to declare war—
ordered the Navy to engage in defensive actions only until Congress autho-
rized offensive measures." This initial attack on American ships by Tripoli
occurred in 1801. During his remaining years in office, President Jefferson
"continued to resist the temptation to enlarge the idea of defensive war." In
1805, faced with Spanish incursions into Louisiana, he announced, "Considering that Congress alone is constitutionally invested with the power of
changing our condition from peace to war, I have thought it my duty to
await their authority for using force. . . . The course to be pursued will require the command of means which it belongs to Congress exclusively to
yield or to deny." Jefferson faithfully executed the congressional will when
the use of military force was denied. Despite widespread encouragement, he
refused to run for a third term, declaring, "I should unwillingly be the person who, disregarding the sound precedent set by an illustrious predecessor,
should furnish the first example of prolongation beyond the second term of
office." Jefferson viewed a representative legislature as one of the two "essen-
tials constituting free government," the other being a bill of rights. In 1816,
he referred to the House of Representatives as the "purest republican feature
in the government." The Senate, he said, was "equally so the first year, less the
second, and so on," the executive "still less, because not chosen by the people
directly," and the judiciary "seriously anti-republican, because for life."[30]

Judiciary

Alexander Hamilton viewed the U.S. Supreme Court as undemocratic.
He considered this to be a positive trait, and he maintained that the judiciary
could be an "excellent barrier to the encroachments and representations of
the representative body." A proponent of judicial review, Hamilton assisted
in the creation of "a check upon democracy and localism by means of an
organ of government not subject to popular control." He was an enthusiastic

proponent of anything that extended the powers of the federal courts.[31] Conversely, liberals have traditionally been suspicious of the judicial branch. They argued that it is the most undemocratic branch of the federal government because the justices are appointed for life, are accountable to no one after they are confirmed, and are able to overturn decisions made by the two elected branches of government while these branches have no power to overturn Court decisions.

As a democrat, Jefferson favored popular election of judges and believed the power of the Supreme Court should be curbed by limiting its members to six-year terms. As he noted, "It is a misnomer to call a government republican, in which a branch of the supreme power is independent of the nation." During his first year in office, President Thomas Jefferson urged the repeal of the Judiciary Act, which had established additional federal courts. In 1803, his suspicions about the Supreme Court were only heightened with the handing down of *Marbury v. Madison.* In this opinion, penned by Chief Justice John Marshall, a Federalist, the Court gave itself the power to declare laws passed by Congress unconstitutional. Jefferson believed that this new power of judicial review "arrogated far too much power" to the Court. According to Noble Cunningham Jr., "Jefferson's hostility toward the court would become more manifest as time passed. At this time his opposition to Marshall was more on political than constitutional grounds."

Throughout the rest of his presidency and beyond, Jefferson continued to try to limit the powers of the Court. In 1807 and 1808, he saw to it that a constitutional amendment was introduced making it possible for federal judges to be removed by a joint action of the president and Congress. The amendment was defeated both times. In 1820, he told William Jarvis that to consider the Supreme Court justices as the final arbiters of constitutional questions is "a very dangerous doctrine indeed, and one which would place us under the despotism of an oligarchy." Jefferson's criticism of the judiciary was not confined to the federal courts. He also questioned the nature of local courts: "The [federal] Judiciary [is] seriously anti-republican, because for life . . . Add to this the vicious constitution of our county courts (to whom . . . nearly all our daily concerns are confided), self-appointed, self-continued, holding their authorities for life."[32]

Civil Liberties

Claude Bowers describes the period in America from 1798 to 1801 as the "Reign of Terror." In comparison to the Robespierre era in France, this is an obvious exaggeration, but it does point to a disturbing time in American history. During these years, the Federalist Party controlled the presidency, both houses of Congress, and the Supreme Court. The "terror" was legally sanctioned by the Alien and Sedition Acts. The Sedition Act of 1798—passed by Congress, signed by Adams, and supported by Hamilton—was intended to "crush the opposition press and silence criticism of the ruling powers."[33]

Thomas Jefferson was a moralist and Deist, but his views on theology and on state-sponsored religion engendered some suspicion and abuse. He advocated freedom of conscience and separation of church and state throughout his life. One of Jefferson's proudest accomplishments was his sponsorship of the landmark 1786 Virginia statute for establishing religious freedom. He initially opposed adoption of the Constitution until a bill of rights, with a provision for religious freedom, was added. After the Constitution was adopted, he continued to encourage James Madison to arrange for congressional passage of the Bill of Rights.

The phrase *separation of church and state* is not found in the Constitution itself: a Supreme Court opinion handed down many years later linked it to the establishment clause of the First Amendment, which is how it gained the force of law. The credit or blame for introducing the phrase into the nation's vocabulary is often given to Jefferson. In 1802, President Jefferson declared in a letter to a group of Baptists in Danbury, Connecticut:

> Believing with you that religion is a matter which lies solely between man and his God; that he owes account to none other for his faith or his worship; that the legislative powers of the government reach actions only, and not opinions, I contemplate with sovereign reverence that act of the whole American people which declared that their legislature should "make no law respecting an establishment of religion, or prohibiting the free exercise thereof," thus building a wall of separation between Church and State.

While not an orthodox Christian, Jefferson was no atheist or advocate of a religion-free nation. He closed his letter by writing, "I reciprocate your kind prayers for the protection and blessing of the common Father and Creator of man."[34]

The Baptists who wrote to Jefferson disagreed with his interpretation of the New Testament—he rejected miracles and anything else that offended his sense of reason—but they liked his political stance on religious liberty because they were a minority. In Connecticut, Congregationalism was the official religion. Congregational ministers were supported by tax dollars and church members were given special privileges unavailable to Baptists and other citizens. Jefferson may have been borrowing his separation terminology from Roger Williams, the founder of Rhode Island and an early Baptist minister. Williams was an evangelical Christian who did not want the government to support churches because he believed alliances between the church and the state corrupted the church.

In November 1798, Jeffersonians in Dinwiddie County, Virginia, adopted resolutions that "serve as an example of the public statement of Republican arguments against Federalist policies, which Republicans made the principal issues of the election of 1800." They described the Sedition Act as "a daring and unconstitutional violation of a sacred and essential right" and called freedom of the press "the great bulwark of liberty" that "can never be restrained but by a despotic government." Outraged by the Alien and Sedition Acts, Vice President Jefferson was the driving force behind the Kentucky and Virginia Resolutions. In 1799, he wrote, "I am . . . for freedom of the press, and against all violations of the Constitution to silence by force and not by reason the complaints or criticisms, just or unjust, of our citizens against the conduct of their agents." Some historians contend that President Jefferson was not as consistent in his support for civil liberties as citizen Jefferson.[35] While the contention may be true, it does not negate the existence of the civil libertarian tenet of early American liberalism. Jefferson's failure to live up to the standards of liberalism he helped to create does not invalidate the standards themselves.

Ethnic Groups

The Constitution, written and adopted by Federalists, protected the slave trade for another twenty years and sanctioned the existence of slavery through the three-fifths compromise. Alexander Hamilton is sometimes viewed as an antislavery influence in early American history because he made statements about the moral wrongness of slavery and because he belonged to a manumission society. But this is not the full story. Hamilton, who lived in the North, "held slaves throughout his life" and "was no enemy of slavery in the South; he upheld the three-fifths rule and deplored the injection of the slavery issue into the debates in Congress." Federalist Party leaders failed not only to make any serious attempts to liberate African Americans but were hostile toward voluntary immigrants, particularly those from Ireland and France. In 1798, Congress enacted the Alien Act, with the support of President John Adams. The law was passed at a time when war with France seemed imminent. In 1799, Hamilton complained that Adams was not enforcing the Alien Law, and he wondered why the alien enemies of the Federalists had not been deported. During the 1804 campaign, Federalists opposed President Jefferson's immigration policies. Hamilton warned against "a too unqualified admission of foreigners to an equal participation in our civil and political rights."[36] Hamilton's attitude was ironic, since he himself was a foreigner, having been born in the British West Indies. Early American conservatives had little time for those who did not speak English and did not profess either Episcopal or Congregational religion. Conversely, numerous compromises and inconsistencies notwithstanding, early American liberals advocated ethnic inclusiveness.

Thomas Jefferson addressed the subject of ethnic inclusiveness in all its fullness, including Native Americans; German, Irish, French, Scotch-Irish, and Jewish immigrants; and enslaved Africans. To some degree, Jefferson respected Indians and admired their anarchistic governance. He was revolted by the way his fellow Americans casually slaughtered them. During his second inaugural address in 1805, he said,

> The aboriginal inhabitants of these countries I have regarded with the commiseration their history inspires. Endowed with the faculties and the rights of men, breathing an ardent love of liberty and independence, and occupying a country which left them no desire but to be undisturbed, the stream of overflowing population from other regions directed itself on these shores; without power to divert, or habits to contend against, they have been overwhelmed by the current, or driven before it.

Despite considerable friendliness toward and respect for Indians, Jefferson's attitude was also ethnocentric and paternalistic. He attempted to prevent bloodshed between the United States and the Indian nations, but as president he "committed the federal government to promote future removal of the Creek and the Cherokee from Georgia" and thought that Indians living in "civilized" areas of the nation should move to the newly obtained Louisiana Territory.[37]

As the author of Virginia's statute for religious freedom, Jefferson was a longtime opponent of established churches. While this stand alienated many English members of the two colonial-era state churches, the Congregational Church and the Church of England, it appealed to many non-English immigrants. In the early 1780s, Jefferson warned that large-scale "importation

of foreigners" could threaten the nation's homogeneity of political principles. He was, however, far from being a xenophobe. Jefferson believed that
the Alien Law "was aimed at his own friends, especially Volney, Albert Gallatin, and the Polish patriot Thaddeus Kosciusko. He watched in sorrow as
resident Frenchmen, fearing imprisonment, signed up in droves for passage
back to Europe." Federalists detested Irish immigrants even more than they
did French immigrants. This hatred was partly "a by-product of the Federalist partiality for England" and partly because the revolutionary instincts of
the Irishmen "took them in a body into the Jeffersonian Party, of which
they became the shock troops in many parts of the country." During the
1800 campaign, Federalists warned that victory by Jefferson would result in
a civil war, which would be initiated by Frenchmen and Irishmen: "The
refuse of Europe who have fled from the pillory and the gallows, and are
here stirring up revolution . . . [will] rush from their lurking places, whet
their daggers, and plunge them into the hearts of all who love order, peace,
virtue, and religion."[38]

After the Federalists snubbed him, former speaker of the house Frederick
Muhlenberg of Pennsylvania led German Americans into the Jeffersonian
camp. His brother, Congressman Peter Muhlenberg, a Democratic-Republican, had long been an Anti-Federalist and a Jeffersonian. Both brothers
supported Jefferson's presidential candidacy in 1800. Resentment among
German immigrants in the Muhlenbergs' home state had been brewing for
a few years. In 1798 and 1799, these immigrants participated in a short-lived
rebellion, led by John Fries, to protest the raising of taxes on land, houses,
and windows by Federalist leaders. During the 1800 campaign, Jeffersonians
asked Germans, "Why should you hear any more of the Alien Law?" Members
of predominantly German religious groups were told that President Jefferson would promote "the *equal Brotherhood* of the Moravian, the Mennonist,
and the Dunker." Jeffersonians in New Jersey accused Federalists of attacking Jefferson because he was not "willing that the *Quaker,* the *Baptist,* the
Methodist, or any other denomination of Christians, should pay the pastors
of other sects," and because he did not "think that a catholic should be ban-
ished for believing in transubstantiation, or a jew, for believing in the God of
Abraham, Isaac, and Jacob." Jefferson supported religious freedom and social
equality for Jews. In his first message to Congress on December 8, 1801,
President Jefferson encouraged immigration, saying, "I cannot omit recommending a removal of the laws on the subject of naturalization. . . . Shall
oppressed humanity find no asylum on this globe?"[39]

Despite his inclination to suspect a natural inferiority of blacks and his
status as a slaveholder, racial justice was a component of Jefferson's vision of

ethnic inclusiveness. In 1770, he served as lawyer for a mulatto slave seeking freedom. In this case, he unsuccessfully argued that "under the law of nature, all men are born free, and every one comes into the world with a right to his own person." In the mid-1770s, he denounced slavery as "an infamous practice" and insisted that its abolition was "the great object of desire" in the American colonies. In the Declaration, Jefferson accused King George of waging "cruel war against human nature itself, violating its most sacred rights of life and liberty in the persons of a distant people who never offended him, captivating and carrying them into slavery in another hemisphere" and of "suppressing every legislative attempt to prohibit or to restrain this execrable commerce." These words were omitted by the Continental Congress. Jefferson also drafted an amendment for the Virginia legislature that would have emancipated all slaves born after passage of the act. With no hope of adoption, the amendment was not introduced. He supported legislation "pushed by the Quakers and passed in 1782 which permitted private manumission [emancipation] by individual masters."[40]

Jefferson's strongest condemnation of slavery is in his *Notes on the State of Virginia:*

> In the very first session held under the republican government, the assembly passed a law for the perpetual prohibition of the importation of slaves. This will in some measure stop the increase of this great political and moral evil, while the minds of our citizens may be ripening for a complete emancipation of human nature. . . . There must doubtless be an unhappy influence on the manners of our people produced by the existence of slavery among us. The whole commerce between master and slave is a perpetual exercise of the most boisterous passions, the most unremitting despotism on the one part, and degrading submissions on the other. . . . I tremble for my country when I reflect that God is just; that his justice cannot sleep forever.

In 1787, Jefferson congratulated Edward Rutledge on passage of a state law ending the slave trade: "This abomination must have an end. And there is a superior bench reserved in heaven for those who hasten it." In 1791, he wrote to Benjamin Banneker, a black man, "Nobody wishes more than I do to see such proofs as you exhibit, that nature has given to our black brethren, talents equal to those of the other colors of men, and that the appearance of a want of them is owing merely to the degraded condition of their existence, both in Africa and America." During the 1800 presidential campaign, Federalists warned that if Jefferson was elected, blacks in the South, "'tools with which Jacobinism delights to work,' would revolt and 'lay waste the fair fields of our southern brethren,' implying that Jefferson himself would lead the slave insurrections." Despite the mixed signals sent by his own lifestyle and his nonaggressive attitude toward abolition in his home state, Jefferson's antislavery words had an effect on Democratic-Republicans throughout the nation. During his first term in the White House, one Jeffersonian newspaper declared, "Slavery should be abolished. The New Jersey House has voted its abolition." At least one scholar has accused Jefferson the slave owner of preferring "a Napoleonic colony to a black republic in the Caribbean." In 1801, President Jefferson supposedly gave Emperor Napoléon Bonaparte a secret go-ahead to reconquer Santo Domingo (Haiti) after a revolution led by Toussaint-L'Ouverture. This version of history relies on an account of the dealings of a French diplomat in Washington, who may or may not have conveyed accurate information from French minister Talleyrand to Jefferson and vice versa. We know Jefferson refused to give aid to French troops when they tried to reconquer the island. We do not know why. During his retirement years, Jefferson continued to favor gradual emancipation of American slaves. Of the hundreds of slaves he himself owned, Jefferson freed only three during his life and five at his death.[41]

William Cooper Jr. and Thomas Terrill point out that the "most visible antislavery spokesmen in the Revolutionary South" were Virginians such as Thomas Jefferson, George Mason, Richard Henry Lee, and Patrick Henry. Mason, Lee, and Henry became prominent Anti-Federalists. Jefferson, of course, became the leader of the Democratic-Republicans. Such men "agonized over the fundamental contradiction between their deep belief in liberty and their possession of human slaves. . . . Despite their conviction that slavery was an unmitigated evil . . . they led no crusade against that special horror. Very few of them even emancipated their own slaves." After questioning the motives of antislavery slave owners and noting the lack of major efforts to end the institution, Cooper and Terrill argue that "one can draw two conclusions from the evidence. No doubt can exist about the genuineness of the intellectual and spiritual turmoil caused by the clash between slavery and liberty; and that turmoil engendered no significant alteration in slavery in Virginia."[42]

While some historians condemn Jefferson as a hypocrite or opportunist in regard to slavery, others are more understanding toward the contradictions of his life. Charles Wiltse wrote, "He could not have freed his own slaves, even had he wished to, because he was in debt during most of his life, and the law would not allow him to deprive his creditors of that security." Wiltse also argues that there was "no place in the southern system for a free negro; and in most of the northern states, they were forbidden to live at all."

He concludes by saying, "The Ordinance of the Northwest Territory, from Jefferson's hand, prohibiting slavery in any of the states that might be made from it after 1800, is further testimony to his sincerity in the cause of abolition." As Noble Cunningham contends,

> To the twentieth-century mind Jefferson's views on race stand in contrast to the liberal stance that he took on most of the major issues of the day; yet his repeated condemnation of the institution of slavery and his insistent arguments that steps must be taken to bring it to an end placed him in advance of most—but far from all—eighteenth-century persons.

Referring to Jefferson's 1814 letter to Edward Coles, in which he answers the rhetorical question, Are you right in abandoning this property? with a not-at-this-time answer, Richard Matthews perceptively comments, "Although he shows a concern for the plight of blacks, Jefferson's wording of the question, which equates men with property, shows how he was never really able to transcend his own cultural history."[43] This failure to transcend should be neither minimized nor exaggerated.

Allegations of a sexual relationship between Thomas Jefferson and Sally Hemings shed more heat than light on the questions of his slavery philosophy and legacy. Nonetheless, given the level of recent publicity, the controversy must at least be mentioned. In 1802, the embittered and disreputable James Callender first accused Jefferson of fathering a child with his slave Sally. The charge was largely forgotten until the 1974 publication of Fawn Brodie's *Thomas Jefferson: An Intimate History*. As the subtitle implies, Brodie attempted to delve into Jefferson's private life—most notably, into his reputed sexual relationship with Sally Hemings. Unfortunately, Brodie often lapsed into historical conjecture and psychological guesswork. Her unorthodox approach and questionable conclusions produced a book that was popular among nonacademics but widely dismissed by scholars. Most historians rejected her theory concerning Jefferson and Hemings. In the late 1990s, a DNA study of some Hemings descendants was conducted by a team of geneticists. But the widely reported commentary on the study published in the journal *Nature* mischaracterized the DNA results. The historian cowriting this article seemed motivated at least partly by a desire to excuse the sexual and legal misconduct of the then-current White House occupant.[44]

In an interesting and underreported twist, the DNA tests essentially disproved any genetic tie between Jefferson and the focus of the original Callendar allegation: Sally Hemings's son Thomas Woodson. Thus, the entire

"Jefferson in Paris loving young Sally" story is shown to be fictional. The tests established that Eston Hemings, another son of Sally, was almost certainly fathered by a Jefferson male, but they could not tell us which Jefferson male. Testing indicated that his father was one of about two dozen Jefferson males living in Virginia in 1808. Historical evidence and oral history of the Eston Hemings family suggest that Thomas Jefferson's younger brother Randolph Jefferson was most likely the father of Eston Hemings. It is also possible that Eston was fathered by one of Randolph's sons, and that other children of Sally Hemings were fathered by one or more nephews of Thomas Jefferson during visits to Monticello. Regardless of the truth concerning Sally Hemings, we know that Jefferson had a reputation for being opposed to the practice of miscegenation (interracial marriage and bearing of children).[45] If he did have such a relationship with Hemings, it could make him seem more sinful and tarnished, more passionate and enlightened, or more abusive and hypocritical, depending on one's perspective. This debate may be nothing more than an interesting diversion, since the scant evidence we have is inconclusive.

Sociologist James Loewen calls "the open white supremacy of the Democratic Party" for the century after Jefferson's death his "political legacy to the nation." The historical record is not so simple and not so unflattering to Jefferson. The most famous advocate of slavery during the nineteenth century was John Calhoun of South Carolina. He was a man who filled numerous roles: congressman, secretary of war, vice president, senator, secretary of state, and presidential candidate. Having failed to gain the presidency as a National Republican centralizer, Calhoun eventually became a staunch defender of states' rights, but this defense was apparently motivated by factors quite different from those that motivated Jefferson. Rather than being motivated by concern for popular control of government, Calhoun seemed to be primarily interested in protecting slavery and advancing his own career. Unlike Jefferson, Calhoun glorified slavery, championed aristocracy, supported central banking, and embraced militarism. Calhoun espoused Hamiltonian economics, received the support of many former Federalists when he ran for president in 1824, assisted the Whig Party in the mid-1830s, and repeatedly tried to thwart leading Jeffersonians within the Democratic Party.[46] An aristocrat and slavocrat, Calhoun was not a democrat and not a follower of Jefferson.

Slavocracy was an ideology of most large-scale planters in the Old South. It viewed slavery as an integral and beneficial part of southern culture. Far from seeing slavery as an immoral institutional or necessary evil, as did many of the southern Founding Fathers, this ideology touted African enslavement

as a positive good ordained by God and nature. Slavocrats rejected the principle of rule by the common people. This was a repudiation of Jeffersonianism since support for democracy is the most important of its tenets and the
one from which the others are largely derived. Instead, slavocrats emphasized social hierarchy and patrilineal aristocracy. Rhetorical honor was paid
to the man of Monticello while his political principles were pressed into the
service of slavery and other aspects of a sanctified southern tradition. In
1848, Calhoun specifically criticized Jefferson for holding "an utterly false
view of the subordinate relation of the black to the white race in the
South." According to Calhoun, Jefferson's proposition that all men are created equal contained "not a word of truth in it" and eventually produced
"poisonous fruits." In complete contrast to Jefferson, Calhoun had contempt
for the concept of natural rights.[47]

Calhoun was a remarkable politician and authentic intellectual, but he
was also an ambitious man whose career was marked by a gigantic flip-flop
from nationalism to sectionalism. The scent of opportunism is discernible.[48]
Some knowledgeable and politically astute admirers of Calhoun would disagree with this assessment, but it has been widely believed since the 1820s
for good reason. It is not just a slander concocted by abolitionists or consol-
idationists but has a real basis in history. Political Johnnies-come-lately
should be viewed with some suspicion, especially when their conversions
coincide with presidential ambitions. Even if Calhoun's belated embrace of
states' rights was principled, it does not mean that this embrace was inspired
by an affinity for the thought of Jefferson and other early American liberals.

Calhoun's ideological heirs—men like Oscar Underwood, Joseph Robinson, and Walter George—were aristocratic Bourbons. They were not small-d
democrats, such as Thomas Watson, Benjamin Tillman, and Theodore Bilbo.
Both sides took white supremacy for granted. The former evoked Jefferson's
name when it was convenient, but their careers were marked by economic
self-interest and alliance with Wall Street Republicans at the national level.
The latter were far more consistent Jeffersonians despite their overt racism.
The legislative records of the Bourbons "suggest that their ultimate principle was not the Democratic party, ideological conservatism, or states' rights,"
but rather the maintenance of the social and economic arrangements that
provided them with great personal benefit.[49] They were heirs of the plantation system and friends of urban commerce, as opposed to the small farming
tradition of "rednecks" and "peckerwoods."

The most famous political defenders of slavery and states' rights during
the antebellum period—namely, Calhoun, John C. Breckinridge, Jefferson
Davis, and Alexander Hamilton Stephens—are problematic because their

link to Jefferson is questionable at best. Jefferson's principled support for states' rights and real, if personally inconsistent, opposition to slavery have been maligned by a largely imagined link to later southern leaders. These men were far more committed to political aristocracy, extensive landholding, and human bondage than was Jefferson. In these men, the ideas undergirding the "Revolution of 1800"—democracy, individualism, human freedom, near pacifism, liberty of conscience, and republican simplicity—were either absent or transformed into means for a far different end, the preservation of a plantation-dominated society built on slave labor. All kinds of justifications or rationalizations were brought forth to defend the southern status quo, from passages in the Bible to criticism of wage slavery in the North, but these had little to do with Jefferson.

Following Calhoun, Davis "rejected the individualistic heritage of Jefferson and Jackson for an ideal of an organic slaveholding community." This ideal included disparagement of majoritarianism and southern yeomanry. In the end, for Davis, it also included an open embrace of political centralization as president of the Confederate States of America (CSA). For instance, the CSA constitution did not explicitly allow secession, the executive branch was strengthened, conscription was forced on southerners, and constitutional rights were suspended.[50] Jeffersonian principles to which lip service had long been paid fell one after another as political power and its slave-owning companion were threatened by federal troops. In contrast to Jefferson's hostility toward incipient capitalism and its industrial trappings, Davis and Breckinridge were boosters of the early railroad business and its dependence on government largesse. Support for internal improvements was an important component of National Republican and Whig ideology. It violated Jeffersonian support for laissez-faire economics and frugal government. Today it would be considered a type of corporate welfare, something beloved by chamber of commerce members who object to high government spending and taxing except when they themselves benefit directly from the revenue. It is also telling that while Jefferson attempted to promote the Quaker system of peace, Calhoun, Davis, and Breckinridge each served as a secretary of war.

Those looking for southern political figures who represented aspects of Jeffersonian thought that were neglected or rejected by their more famous contemporaries could consider Robert Jefferson Breckenridge, Thomas Hart Benton, Francis P. "Frank" Blair and his sons, Frank Jr. and Montgomery, or B. Gratz Brown. These men represent another side of the South—learned and strong-willed but far more emancipationist and egalitarian than usually described.[51] It must be stressed, however, that genuine support for slavery did not exclude genuine support for decentralization and democracy. Not all support for nullification or secession was opportunistic, and not all Confederate ideology was un-Jeffersonian. Many southerners throughout history have honestly held Jeffersonian views even if they did not follow the Virginian in every particular. Jeffersonians within the Democratic Party of the 1840s included admirers not only of Martin Van Buren but also of John C. Calhoun. Their ranks included both Barnburners of the North and fire-eaters of the South. Each group of rank-and-file Democrats represented different—and sometimes conflicting—aspects of Jefferson's legacy.[52]

The proslavery Democratic leaders of the 1850s, including Presidents Franklin Pierce and James Buchanan, were far more influenced by the votes of southern slave owners and dollars of northern capitalists than by the writings of Jefferson. Senator Charles Sumner denounced a comparable political situation within the Whig Party, calling it a conspiracy between "the lords of the lash and the lords of the loom." Incidentally, Sumner's father was "an ardent Jeffersonian, at a time when only Federalism was respectable in Massachusetts." When antislavery Democrats and Conscience Whigs formed the Free Soil Party in 1848, Sumner supported Martin Van Buren for president on that ticket. Van Buren was a disciple of Jefferson and the political ally of Andrew Jackson. Sumner placed the Declaration of Independence on equal or higher footing with the Constitution.[53]

The center of American wealth and power during the nineteenth century was a continuation of the eighteenth-century center. It was led by the ideological heirs of Alexander Hamilton, not Thomas Jefferson. This center supported the continuance of slavery. During the 1850s and 1860s, there was "a striking genealogical continuity between former Federalists and proslavery leaders." The membership roll of the Society for Promoting National Unity, a proslavery organization formed in 1861, "reads like an inclusive listing of the long-entrenched governing elite of New England and the North." Below the Mason-Dixon Line, there was a similar phenomenon. Alexander Hamilton Stephens, vice president of the Confederate States of America, had previously been a Whig member of Congress. A member of the monied elite of Georgia, he opposed the Jackson and Van Buren administrations. According to Stephens, slavery—not states' rights—was the cornerstone of the Confederacy. In his famous 1861 speech, he declared,

> The prevailing ideas entertained by him [Thomas Jefferson] and most of the leading statesmen at the time of the formation of the old constitution were that the enslavement of the African was in violation of the laws of nature, that it was wrong in principle, socially, and morally, and

politically. . . . Our new Government is founded upon exactly the opposite idea. Its foundations are laid, its cornerstone rests upon the great
truth that the Negro is not equal to the white man, that slavery, subordination to the superior race is his natural and moral condition.[54]

Thus, we have testimony from a key source that the Confederacy was based
on the *opposite* of Jefferson's thought. The four southern states that publicly
declared the causes of secession—South Carolina, Georgia, Mississippi, and
Texas—each identified opposition to their commitment to slavery as the
main reason for leaving the union. As the Mississippi secession convention
put it up front: "Our position is thoroughly identified with the institution of
slavery—the greatest material interest of the world."[55]

In addition to the distinctly un-Jeffersonian nature of many prominent
slavocrats during the pre-1866 period, we should not overlook the role
played by Jefferson's criticism of slavery and championing of liberty. His belief in states' rights served as a subterfuge for proslavery and prosegregation
forces after his death, but his declaration that "all men are created equal" and
"endowed by their Creator with certain unalienable rights" was an even
more powerful inspiration for antislavery and antisegregation forces. This
book gives the question of Jefferson and slavery extended treatment not because ethnic inclusiveness outweighs other tenets of his thought, but because his supposed views and legacy in this area have been unfairly used to
discredit Jeffersonianism as a whole.

Spending

Extensive government is expensive government. Alexander Hamilton was
a practitioner of "big government." While Secretary of State Jefferson had a
staff of less than ten, Secretary of the Treasury Hamilton "had over a hundred men working for him in New York, and additional excisemen all over
the nation." To pay for large government expenditures, Federalists relied on
substantial borrowing and heavy taxation. Hamilton, "Father of the National
Debt," condoned deficit spending and believed that a national debt can be a
"national blessing."[56] In contrast, a low level of government spending is a
traditional tenet of American liberalism. This belief in the desirability of low
spending goes hand in hand with an aversion to the existence of a national
debt and the levying of heavy taxes.

The party of Thomas Jefferson championed fiscal responsibility, which
was linked to the ideal of republican simplicity. In 1797, Jefferson advocated

a constitutional amendment to remove from the federal government the power to borrow money. The following year, the Jeffersonians of Dinwiddie County, Virginia, declared that "every expense not absolutely necessary ought to be avoided." They expressed opposition to increasing the national debt on the grounds that "the only proper way to raise money for national purposes, is by taxes, duties, excises and imposts, and that the power of borrowing money, ought not to be exercised except in cases of absolute necessity." In 1799, Jefferson declared, "I am for a government rigorously frugal and simple, applying all the possible savings of the public revenue to the discharge of the national debt; and not for a multiplication of officers and salaries . . . and for increasing, by every device, the public debt." During the 1800 campaign, Jeffersonians promised "Reduced Public Salaries, and a system of economy and care of the public money." Jefferson embraced neither a tax-and-spend policy nor a borrow-and-spend policy. Rejecting the notion that a public debt is a public blessing, President Jefferson balanced the federal budget and substantially reduced the national debt. When running for reelection in 1804, he pointed to his record of "simplicity and frugality in government." When he retired in 1809, Jefferson could be satisfied in the knowledge that $33.5 million of the national debt had been eliminated during his eight years in office.[57]

Taxation

Like the British monarchy during an earlier period, the Federalist Party was known for imposing a high level of taxation on Americans. Alexander Hamilton's support for excise taxes helped to bring about the Whiskey Rebellion in 1794. Taxes levied by the Federalists for a planned war against France brought about the Fries Insurrection in 1799.[58] In contrast, low taxation is a traditional tenet of American liberalism. It is based on respect for individual liberty and concern for the well-being of the common people.

Thomas Jefferson alluded to oppressive taxation in the Declaration. Its indictment of King George included the charge, "He has erected a multitude of New Offices, and sent hither swarms of Officers to harass our people, and eat out their substance." Jefferson was unhappy with the tax policies of the Washington and Adams administrations. He joined John Taylor in opposing the Hamilton-sponsored "carriage tax" in 1794. In 1799, Jefferson criticized "the vexations of the stamp act," "the disgusting particularities of the direct tax," and "taxes of ten millions now paid by four millions of people, and yet a necessity, in a year or two, of raising five millions more for annual expenses."

During the 1800 campaign, Jeffersonians promised to reduce taxes, and after winning the White House, they "reduced and abolished until they cut the direct and internal revenue taxes and duties down almost to the vanishing point." At the close of 1801, President Jefferson noted that collection of all internal taxes had been suspended and the tax collectors dismissed. When he ran for reelection, he pointed out that taxes had been reduced during his first term. After his reelection, in his second inaugural address, he stated,

> The suppression of unnecessary offices, of useless establishments and expenses, enabled us to discontinue our internal taxes. . . . The remaining revenue on the consumption of foreign articles, is paid cheerfully by those who can afford to add foreign luxuries to domestic comforts . . . It may be the pleasure and pride of an American to ask, what farmer, what mechanic, what laborer, ever sees a taxgatherer of the United States?

In 1810, Jefferson declared that Federalists "always consume the public contributions and oppress the people with labor and poverty." He looked forward to the day when the small farmer would "see his government supported, his children educated, and the face of the country made a paradise by the contributions of the rich alone, without his being called on to spare a cent from his earnings."[59]

Military

During the last two decades of the eighteenth century, Alexander Hamilton was "the personification of American militarism." His role models were famed military leaders. He called Julius Caesar the "greatest man that ever lived." He was inspired by the conquests of Napoléon Bonaparte. He was aide-de-camp to George Washington during the Revolutionary War and looked to him as a father figure for years thereafter. During the war, Hamilton possessed "ardor for military glory." The Constitution, largely written and adopted by Federalists, allowed the existence of a standing army in peacetime. Amidst talk of a war with England in 1794, Hamilton warned against going into battle without adequate preparation. While not advocating immediate war, he "urged Congress to create an army of 25,000 men (later reduced to 15,000), to hold 80,000 militia in readiness for any eventuality, to build a navy, fortify the harbors, impose higher taxes and invest the President with adequate powers to deal with the national emergency."

Amidst talk of a war with France in 1797, he "urged that the army be increased to 25,000 men; that a strong force of artillery and cavalry be raised; that the frigates be rushed to completion; that the defenses of American harbors be restored; that American merchantmen be armed; and that a system of naval convoys in the West Indies be instituted."[60]

Hamilton played an important role in creating the martial tone of the Adams presidency. Employing a strategy subsequently used by militarists throughout American history, he wanted to wage war in 1798 but wanted France to make the first strike since the American people disapproved of an offensive war. He viewed war as a means of protecting commerce, creating an empire, and uniting the people in support of the government. Envisioning "a truly American patriotism that would defend American interests from attack from every quarter," Hamilton wanted the nation to pursue this course even if it meant going to war against France and England at the same time. When an army was raised in 1798 in preparation for war against France, Washington was appointed commander in chief and Hamilton was named second in command with the rank of major general. Washington allowed Hamilton to take charge of the troops and to make detailed plans for the army. The Hamiltonian wing of the Federalist Party unsuccessfully demanded war in 1799.[61]

Thomas Jefferson was "essentially a man of peace." He was uninterested in military glory and suspicious of professional soldiering. The Declaration's indictment of King George includes the charges, "He has kept among us, in times of peace, Standing Armies without the Consent of our legislatures. He has affected to render the Military independent of and superior to the Civil power." In 1788, Jefferson suggested to Madison that a constitutional bill of rights should include a prohibition on peacetime standing armies. In the late 1790s, Jeffersonians in Congress "opposed everything that tended to strengthen the armed forces of the United States." In 1798, the Jeffersonians of Dinwiddie County, Virginia, declared that "regular armies, except in case of an invasion, or the certain prospect of an invasion, are not only highly detrimental to the public welfare, but dangerous to liberty." They opposed great naval armament "because it enlarges still more the fund for increasing executive influence: because the expense is incalculable . . . because this country cannot hope to protect its commerce by a fleet . . . or to guard from invasion a coast fifteen hundred miles in extent." In 1799, Jefferson asserted,

> I am for relying, for internal defence, on our militia solely, till actual invasion, and for such a naval force only as may protect our coasts and

> harbors from such depredations as we have experienced; and not for a
> standing army in time of peace . . . nor for a navy, which, by its own ex-
> penses and the eternal wars in which it will implicate us, will grind us
> with public burthens, and sink us under them.

That same year, in letter to Edmund Pendleton, he criticized "the additional
army without an enemy, and recruiting officers lounging at every court-
house to decoy the laborer from his plough, a navy of fifty ships, five millions to be raised to build it." Instead of a standing army and navy, he
believed that the male citizens of the nation should be classified and trained
for possible military service in the event of war.[62]

During his first term as president, Jefferson "reduced the military establishment to a mere police force of 2,500 officers and men." He "distinguished himself from other leaders of his time not only by his dislike of war
as a profession but also by his obstinate pursuit of other means to obtain political ends." Responding to an informal declaration of war by the pasha of
Tripoli in 1801, President Jefferson reluctantly sent the navy to the coast of
North Africa, but this was the exception rather than the rule. During the acquisition of the Louisiana Purchase, Jefferson's negotiators peacefully bro-
kered a deal for the land at a time when Federalists were clamoring for a war
against France. He chose to negotiate with rather than fight with American
Indian tribes and was able to avert war with England. After the deadly surprise attack on the *Chesapeake* by the English in 1807, there was a clamor for
war, but Jefferson did not wish to involve America in the ongoing conflict
between England and France. Faced with "a choice of war, submission, or
some form of commercial pressure," he asked Congress to supplement its
nonimportation act with a blanket embargo on the departure of ships from
American harbors. According to Claude Bowers, Jefferson's embargo was
"the first valorous attempt of an American statesman to find, in economic
pressure, a substitute for war."[63]

President Jefferson did pursue some policies "hardly consistent with his
individualist, pacifist philosophy." During the Embargo Act period, he cau-
tiously moved in the direction of military preparedness and eventually asked
for a substantial increase in the size of the regular army. While in the White
House, he oversaw the creation of a military academy, an idea previously
championed by Hamilton and opposed by Jefferson. An academy at West
Point, New York, was created by the Military Peace Establishment Act of
1802. Jefferson's motives for establishing West Point "have never been convincingly explained," but most scholars believe that he wished to create a
school to emphasize science rather than the classics and to train engineers

for the new nation. Theodore Crackel, a scholar affiliated with the so-called military-industrial complex, asserts that President Jefferson's military policies were demagogic and motivated by partisanship rather than by suspicion of standing armies and desire for economical government. Crackel's thesis is unconvincing. Jefferson was a practical politician, but he was not a demagogue. Throughout his life, he showed a genuine commitment to liberty, economy, and peace. As a former president, Jefferson opposed the War of 1812 before its declaration. In 1811, he wrote,

> Peace, then, has been our principle, peace is our interest, and peace has saved to the world this only plant of free and rational government now existing in it. . . . However, therefore, we may have been reproached for pursuing our Quaker system, time will affix the stamp of wisdom on it and the happiness and prosperity of our citizens will attest its merit. And this, I believe, is the only legitimate object of government and the first duty of governors, and not the slaughter of men and devastation of countries placed under their care in pursuit of a fantastic honor unallied to virtue or happiness; or in gratification of the angry passions or the pride of administrators excited by personal incidents in which their citizens have no concern.

In June 1822 Jefferson remarked to John Adams, "I hope we shall prove how much happier for man the Quaker policy is, and that the life of the feeder is better than that of the fighter."[64]

Foreign Policy

Imperialists believe that the American government should protect what it considers to be the national interest, even if that means getting involved in conflicts around the globe. They also maintain that it is the government's duty to spread our political and economic systems to other countries, by force if necessary, and that the United States should lead the world. The Federalists were the original American imperialists. Being Anglophiles, they looked to Great Britain as the role model for American foreign policy. Federalists desired strong financial and political ties to England and an economy based on overseas trade. Power needed to be concentrated in a strong federal government, so that the nation could speak with one voice to the governments of other nations. A strong military was needed to protect the interests of American bankers and businessmen. An admirer of Caesar and Napoleon, Alexander Hamilton desired an imperialistic foreign policy for the new nation. In 1799, Major General Hamilton "was a man who dreamed dreams, and in his imagination he was already leading his army into Louisiana, the Floridas and points south. 'We ought,' he said, 'to squint at South America.'" The ideological division in early American public policy is clear: "Hamilton longs for empire, opulence, and glory for the nation, whereas Jefferson seeks virtue, freedom, and happiness for the social individual." Hamilton was "very opportunistic about international diplomacy" and distrusted "moralizing in foreign policy."[65]

Isolationists believe in national self-determination and argue that the American government should be predominantly concerned about the needs and desires of its own citizens. They do not believe our government should be involved in every conflict around the globe or attempt to control the governments of other nations. The Anti-Federalists and Democratic-Republicans were the original American isolationists. They championed decentralized politics and agrarian-based economics. They believed that America should not have a standing army, and that our government should stay out of Europe's continual bloodshed. They called for friendship with other nations but nonalliance with other governments.

Isolationists are often characterized as provincial bumpkins, but this characterization hardly fits the nation's premier isolationist. Jefferson was a diplomat and a student of language, science, and philosophy. Cosmopolitan in outlook, he nonetheless opposed national involvement in overseas political and military conflicts. Referring to a 1791 controversy about the West Indies, he stated, "If there be one principle more deeply rooted than any other in the mind of every American, it is, that we should have nothing to do with conquest." In 1798, the Jeffersonians of Dinwiddie County, Virginia, proclaimed their opposition to "an alliance with any nation on earth" and to "the practice of maintaining ministers resident in foreign countries." The following year, Jefferson wrote, "I am for free commerce with all nations; political connection with none; and little or no diplomatic establishment. And I am not for linking ourselves by new treaties with the quarrels of Europe; entering that field of slaughter to preserve their balance." Democratic-Republicans criticized Federalists for establishing "Quixotish embassies to the Turks, the Russians, Prussians, and Portuguese" rather than following George Washington's maxim "Not to intermeddle with European politics." In his first inaugural address, President Jefferson urged "peace, commerce, and honest friendship with all nations, entangling alliances with none." He held this view throughout his life. Jefferson's support for the Monroe Doctrine was expressed in an 1823 letter to the president: "Our first and fundamental maxim should be, never to entangle ourselves in the broils of

Europe. Our second, never to suffer Europe to intermeddle with cis-Atlantic affairs."[66]

Using the word *isolationism* to describe Jefferson's foreign policy is an oversimplification. Setting aside the negative images with which it is saddled due to seventy years of imperial propaganda, the term is still problematic because it does not express the full range of Jefferson's thought. In addition to the obvious forswearing of entangling alliances, Jeffersonian isolationism involved support for a republic rather than an empire, for national sovereignty, for ethical conduct, for human rights, and for popular control of foreign policy. These five beliefs were causes, components, or concomitants of isolationism. Jefferson "vigorously rejected the view that only individuals are bound by a moral code, and that nations are free to act in accordance with self-interest without any restraints." In 1789 he told James Madison, "I know but one code of morality for men, whether acting singly or collectively. He who says I will be a rogue when I act in company with a hundred others, but an honest man when I act alone, will be believed in the former assertion but not in the latter." Despite his belief in the importance of moral conduct in foreign relations, Jefferson was not naive in his view of the world, and he had a realistic assessment of foreign governments. In 1812, Jefferson condemned both the French and British governments for trying to "draw to themselves the power, the wealth and the resources of other nations." Three years later, he called Napoléon "the wretch . . . who has been the author of more misery and suffering to the world, than any being who ever lived before him. After destroying the liberties of his country, he has exhausted all its resources, physical and moral, to indulge his own maniac ambition, his own tyrannical and overbearing spirit." He did not, however, have a favorable view of the British government and other opponents of Napoléon. Jefferson condemned the imperialism of all the leading countries of Europe: "The will of the allies? There is no more moderation, forbearance, or even honesty in theirs, than in that of Bonaparte. They have proved that their object, like his, is plunder."[67]

Isolationism is a problematic word. It is an epithet. It is anachronistic when applied to Jefferson and fails to indicate the full range of thought involved. Admittedly, it is a flawed term, but it may be the best term available. *Noninterventionism* is a nondefinition that merely calls attention to another undefined term, the word *continentalism* never caught on after being proposed by scholar Charles Beard, and *neutrality* is too vague. To some, *isolationism* may imply ostrich-like, willful ignorance of the rest of the world, but this was never the case with its most famous practitioners. The isolation is not one of intellect, trade, or travel but one of entangling alliances, military conflict, and imperial domination. For isolationists, national self-determination for colonies and national sovereignty for America are closely related principles emanating from a common source: a commitment to democracy, freedom, and decentralization. Isolationism is the foreign policy of traditional liberals. As Robert Morss Lovett noted in 1924,

> It is historically characteristic of governments devoted to conservative measures and the maintenance of the *status quo* in domestic affairs to develop an aggressive policy in foreign affairs, and similarly for governments whose chief outlook is toward the progressive improvement of existing conditions to seek to disembarrass themselves from the complications of foreign policy.[68]

This progressive tradition was first manifested in power through the presidency of Thomas Jefferson.

Isolationism may be an unfortunate term in some ways, but it describes a real, deep, and honorable tradition in American politics. Before the 1930s, the ideological underpinning of America's approach to the world lacked a distinct label because it was simply accepted as traditional U.S. foreign policy. In his 1776 pamphlet *Common Sense,* Thomas Paine wrote, "As Europe is our market for trade, we ought to form no partial connection with any part of it. It is the true interest of America to steer clear of European contentions." In his 1796 Farewell Address, George Washington noted, "The great rule of conduct for us, in regard to foreign nations, is in extending our commercial relations, to have with them as little political connection as possible. . . . It is our true policy to steer clear of permanent alliances with any portion of the foreign world." The Independence Day speech of Secretary of State John Quincy Adams in 1821 indicated that isolationism was still taken for granted twenty-five years later. Referring to America, he reminded the House of Representatives, "She has abstained from interference in the concerns of others, even when conflict has been for principles to which she clings . . . She goes not abroad, in search of monsters to destroy. She is the well-wisher to the freedom and independence of all. She is the champion and vindicator only of her own." The Monroe Doctrine acted as an isolationist bulwark for many years, until it was corrupted by the Theodore Roosevelt Corollary (1904) and virtually set aside by Woodrow Wilson and Franklin Roosevelt. According to this doctrine,

> In the wars of the European powers in matters relating to themselves we have never taken any part, nor does it comport with our policy to

do so. . . . It is impossible that the allied powers [of Europe] should extend their political system to any portion of either [American] continent without endangering our peace and happiness; nor can anyone believe that our southern brethren, if left to themselves, would adopt it of their own accord. . . . It is still the true policy of the United States to leave the [Latin American] parties to themselves, in hope that other powers will pursue the same course.

In opposing the annexation of Santo Domingo (Dominican Republic) in 1870, Senate Foreign Relations Committee chairman Charles Sumner (R-MA) argued that Caribbean islands "should not be absorbed by the United States, but should remain as independent powers, and should try for themselves to make the experiment of self-government. . . . To the African belongs the equatorial belt and he should enjoy it undisturbed."[69] Things began to change dramatically in 1898. With the annexation of Hawaii and the Spanish-American War, we were well on our way to becoming an empire with extensive political and military ties to the rest of the world. As a result, traditional foreign policy fell into disfavor among U.S. elites and was eventually disparaged by the dismissive term *isolationism*.

CHAPTER 3

Competing Philosophies: Hamilton vs. Jefferson

Foundation of Ideology

Jeffersonianism can be summed up by the twelve tenets already introduced: democracy rather than aristocracy, political decentralization, strict
constructionism, opposition to banking, legislative preeminence in relation
to the executive branch, suspicion of the judiciary, support for civil liberties,
ethnic inclusiveness, frugal spending, low taxation, pacifism, and isolationism. Any study of American liberalism would be incomplete, however, without an examination of the emphases and assumptions underlying these
ideological tenets. Philosophy transcends politics: it emanates from and has
an influence on religion and morality, psychology and sociology, worldview
and lifestyle. When philosophy is squeezed into the political realm, the resulting shape is ideology.

The philosophical evolution of twentieth-century American liberalism
involves eight pairs of contrasting emphases: ideology vs. pragmatism, commitment vs. compromise, populism vs. elitism, morality vs. economics, common good vs. special interests, agrarian vs. urban, left vs. center, and radical
vs. respectable. No value judgment is implied by the terminology used to
examine the emphases, and examples from two of the pairs should prove this
point. *Commitment* can be equated with standing firm for a righteous cause
or with unproductive obstinacy, and *compromise,* with a cornerstone of democratic politics or with political apostasy. *Populism* can be equated with
being a friend of the people or with being a self-seeking demagogue, and
elitism, with the pursuit of excellence or with hostility toward democracy.

Ideology vs. Pragmatism

Thomas Jefferson was not the sole founder of the Democratic-Republican Party, but for years he served as its primary ideological exponent and electoral champion. Despite his key role in the development of the party that rallied around him during the Washington years and accepted his leadership during the Adams years, Jefferson is sometimes thought of as a nonpartisan statesman. This image is partly a result of the conciliatory tone of his first inaugural address, in which Jefferson sought to reassure the many Americans who despised and feared him: "Let us, then, fellow citizens, unite with one heart and one mind. . . . Every difference of opinion is not a difference of principle. We have called by different names brethren of the same principle. We are all republicans—we are federalists." While Jefferson was certainly extending an olive branch to those who had opposed his election, it would be going too far to interpret this passage as a denial of the continued existence of distinct ideologies in America. The next line of his speech makes it clear that he was narrowly construing the words *republican* and *federalist:* "If there be any among us who would wish to dissolve this Union or to change its republican form, let them stand undisturbed as monuments to the safety with which error of opinion may be tolerated where reason is left free to combat it." If desire to preserve the union of states and belief in representative government are the definitions being used, then the vast majority of Americans were both federalists and republicans. Jefferson's subsequent reference to those who "fear that a republican government cannot be strong" could have been a veiled rebuttal of the monarchism of some Federalist leaders.[1]

According to Albert Jay Nock, "no man ever drew a clearer picture of economic motive in party affiliation" than Jefferson did. Jefferson declared that the Federalist Party consisted of "old refugees and Tories," "British merchants residing among us," "American merchants trading on British capital," "Speculators, and holders in the banks and public funds," "Officers of the Federal Government," "Office-hunters, willing to give up principles for places," and "Nervous persons," while the Democratic-Republican Party consisted of "the entire body of landholders" and "the body of labourers, not being landholders, whether in husbanding or the arts."[2] Jefferson's recognition of the existence of important ideological differences remained a lifelong trait.

James Monroe, a protégé of Jefferson, was elected president in 1816. Despite their longstanding friendship, Jefferson rejected the compromising, bipartisan spirit of Monroe's "Era of Good Feelings." In 1822, Jefferson wrote, "You are told that there are no longer parties among us; that they are all now amalgamated; the lion and the lamb lie down together in peace. Do not believe a word of it. The same parties exist now as ever did." The following year, he asserted, "The Federalists . . . have given up their name . . . and have taken shelter among us and under our name, but they have only changed the point of attack." To Henry Lee, Jefferson declared,

> I am no believer in the amalgamation of parties, nor do I consider it as either desirable or useful for the public; but only that, like religious differences, a difference in politics should never be permitted to enter into social intercourse . . . In that form, they are censors of the conduct of each other, and useful watchmen for the public. Men by their constitutions are naturally divided into two parties: 1. Those who fear and distrust the people . . . 2. Those who identify themselves with the people, have confidence in them."

Whether called liberals and serviles, Jacobins and ultras, Whigs and Tories, Republicans and Federalists, or aristocrats and democrats, Jefferson saw a substantive difference in ideology between the two parties. It was not just a matter of competence or style, but of underlying differences in thought and commitment. Andrew Jackson and Martin Van Buren continued the Jeffersonian tradition of ideological politics. Alexander Hamilton represented a pragmatic, nonideological approach to politics that can be contrasted not only with Jefferson's approach but also with John Adams's. Henry Clay exemplified the pragmatic approach during the 1820s, 1830s, and 1840s.[3]

Commitment vs. Compromise

Commitment is an outgrowth of ideology; compromise is an outgrowth of pragmatism. While ideologues may cut corners here and there in recognition of political realities, they strive to stay faithful to planned ends and means. While pragmatists understand the need to have desired goals, they often compromise to get things done. In American politics, pragmatism has long been dominant, thus accounting for the widespread use of maxims such as "Politics is the art of the possible" and "Politics is the art of compromise." Ideologues counter by pointing out that compromise may be a product of self-interested ambition rather than of an altruistic desire to get half a loaf when a whole loaf is unattainable.

Thomas Jefferson was willing to compromise on occasion, but his political career was, on balance, characterized by commitment. It would have been far easier for him to have thrown in his lot with the incipient Federalist Party while serving as secretary of state under President Washington. If he had been willing to stick more closely to the political principles of Washington and the majority of his cabinet, he undoubtedly would have avoided most of the abuse he received at the hands of leading merchants, financiers, clergymen, educators, and politicians. His membership in the Randolph family, service to the state of Virginia, authorship of the Declaration of Independence, diplomacy in Paris, and friendship with Washington would have been highlighted, rather than accusations of anarchism and atheism. Jefferson fulfilled most of his campaign promises during his eight years in the White House. While a few notable compromises were made, he remained committed to the ideological tenets outlined in his January 26, 1799, letter to Elbridge Gerry.[4]

Populism vs. Elitism

The Greek word for "people" is *demos;* in Latin it is *populus.* Democracy is the form of government in which the people control society, and populism is the philosophical value that supports the rights, aspirations, and power of the people. In a democratic government, the common people rule, and populists support rule by the common people. Populism is an integral part of Jeffersonianism. Thomas Jefferson identified with the people and had confidence in them. He viewed landholders and laborers as his natural political allies. Jefferson recognized the existence of a "natural aristocracy" of virtue and wisdom, but he was not—despite his own great intelligence and learning—an advocate of intellectual or academic elitism. "State a moral case to a ploughman and a professor," he declared, and "the former will decide it as well, and often better than the latter, because he has not been led astray by artificial rules."[5]

Elitism is the philosophical value that supports the rights, aspirations, and power of a select group of people. Rather than supporting democracy—in the traditional, direct, rule-by-the-common-people sense of the word—elitists support less popular forms of government such as monarchy, autocracy, oligarchy, aristocracy, and plutocracy. Elitists do not trust the common people, believing that a relatively small group of individuals must manage society because the masses do not understand what is best for them and the world. Elitists are willing to take on the burden of leadership, and they, at least in ostensibly democratic nations, prefer to use the word *serve* rather than the word *rule.* Elitists are condescending if not contemptuous in their relations with the common people. Alexander Hamilton is the archetypical elitist in American politics.

Morality vs. Economics

There has always been tension between morality and economics in American political life. While most Americans accept the nation's economic system and its attendant doctrines, there are built-in conflicts between GDP and GOD that produce cognitive dissonance if not conscious dichotomy. Morality is not the same as religion, but most citizens identify with the Judeo-Christian tradition. Despite many clerical attempts to sanctify the American economic system, there are portions of the Bible that critique the system: injunctions against usury, greed, selfishness, and materialism. An assessment of Democratic liberals can be made partly on the basis of how much they emphasize morality or religion in their own lives, whether they take a moralistic approach to politics, and the degree to which they emphasize economic issues.

Early American liberalism was highly moralistic. Most Anti-Federalists were suspicious of commerce and luxury, of self-interest and capitalism. They championed religion, virtue, morality, and commonwealth. Samuel Adams emphasized morality amidst the growing prosperity of New England. Adams, Patrick Henry, and many other Anti-Federalists were orthodox Christians whose political careers were heavily influenced by their religious beliefs. Thomas Jefferson was a Deist, or Unitarian, who rejected some of the so-called irrational tenets of historic Christianity, but he had a keen sense of morality. In *Notes on Virginia,* he pointed to what he saw as a conflict between morality and manufacturing:

> Corruption in morals in the mass of cultivators [farmers] is a phenomenon of which no age nor nation has furnished an example. It is the mark set on those, who, not looking up to heaven, to their own soil and industry, as does the husbandman, for their subsistence, depend for it on casualties and caprice of customers. Dependence begets subservience and venality, suffocates the germ of virtue, and prepares fit tools for the designs of ambition.

Analyzing Jefferson's political philosophy, historian Richard Matthews contends, "The spread of capitalism across the continent, together with the enlargement of the state, sets Hamilton's imagination ablaze with visions of glory. . . . Hamilton longs for empire, opulence, and glory for the nation, whereas Jefferson seeks virtue, freedom, and happiness for the social individual." The yeomen and mechanics who supported early American politicians such as Jefferson, Samuel Adams, Patrick Henry, and George Clinton defined success as competence, independence, and morality, not as wealth and fame.[6]

Common Good vs. Special Interests

The debate over whether democracy works better when the common good is emphasized or whether it works better when special interests are emphasized has been taking place in America since the eighteenth century. Thomas Jefferson and John Taylor advocated common good governance, while James Madison and John Adams advocated special interest governance. Madison, Adams, and other early proponents of pluralistic democracy insisted that they were not promoting political favoritism or unfairness when arguing for governance on the basis of what we would call today socioeconomic classes or interest groups. Borrowing from Plato, they argued that order or interest had something to contribute to society and would derive appropriate benefits from the state if a proper equilibrium was maintained.[7] A democratic balance would result if all of the specific groups of citizens had opportunities, at various points in time, to influence the political process. Because of the presence of countervailing forces, no particular group would dominate. At the same time, the involvement of special interests would serve as a check on tyranny by an unreasoning majority. In the 1950s, this view of pluralistic democracy replaced the traditional academic view of classical democracy as the prevalent model for American political scientists.

Rather than emphasizing the role of special interest groups, Jefferson, Taylor, and other appreciators of classical democracy argued that it hinged on the totality of individual voters. Jefferson's view of democracy may have been influenced by the writings of philosopher Jean-Jacques Rousseau, who advocated popular sovereignty and direct democracy and upheld the notion of the "general will." The general will considers only common interests, not special interests. Rousseau opposed representative democracy because he believed it leads to the decay of the general will by magnifying voters' private interests. The Puritan, Quaker, and Moravian traditions in America, which emphasized the common good, may have also influenced Jefferson.

Jefferson's view of the common good was summed up in the expression "Equal rights for all; special privileges for none." This maxim was often used by Andrew Jackson, William Jennings Bryan, and other classical democrats. Jefferson was a staunch opponent of monopoly, and he understood that only government had the ability to create monopolies through its use of law and force. If the state became involved in economics, religion, and other private matters, it would invariably favor one interest over another, thus granting a special privilege if not creating a full-blown monopoly.[8]

Agrarian vs. Urban

Thomas Jefferson's philosophy was agrarian in nature. His most famous tribute to farmers is in his *Notes on Virginia:* "Those who labor in the earth are the chosen people of God, if ever He had a chosen people, whose breasts He has made His peculiar deposit for substantial and genuine virtue. It is the focus in which He keeps alive that sacred fire, which otherwise might escape from the face of the earth." Jefferson believed strongly in the agrarian lifestyle because it promotes self-sufficiency rather than dependency. Self-sufficiency is a key component of democracy, decentralization, and a number of other Jeffersonian tenets. Noting that nonfarmers depend on the "casualties and caprice of customers," Jefferson wrote, "Dependence begets subservience and venality, suffocates the germ of virtue, and prepares fit tools for the designs of ambition."[9]

Jefferson is known for his disparaging attitude toward city dwellers. In *Notes on Virginia,* he declared, "While we have land to labor [as farmers] then, let us never wish to see our citizens occupied at a workbench, or twirling a distaff. Carpenters, masons, smiths, are wanting in husbandry; but, for the general operations of manufacture, let our workshops remain in Europe." His desire to have more land in the West for farmers was one reason he agreed to the Louisiana Purchase, despite constitutional scruples. Jefferson's much-quoted words concerning the urban masses suggest a pronounced antiurban bias: "The mobs of great cities add just so much to the support of pure government, as sores do to the strength of the human body. It is the manners and spirit of a people which preserve a republic. A degeneracy in these is a canker which soon eats to the heart of its laws and constitution."[10]

While Jefferson's preference for farming is clear, his hostility toward urban workers and opposition to manufacturing should not be exaggerated. *Notes on Virginia* was written relatively early in his political career. During his three

campaigns for president, Jefferson received considerable support from the laboring class in the eastern cities. In Baltimore, for example, most white men
and many black men were mechanics, and in the late 1790s, they played an
important role in building the Democratic-Republican Party in Maryland.
Much the same can be said for other urban areas. Jefferson began to look fa-
vorably on the idea of American factories even before the War of 1812. As
early as 1791, he openly endorsed the idea of the nation gradually moving
into manufacturing. One final point must be made concerning Jefferson's
agrarianism. While he was a relatively wealthy Virginia farmer himself, Jefferson was a champion not only of large-scale planters but also of small
farmers.[11]

Left vs. Center

In this study, *Left* is used broadly to include republicanism, democratism,
egalitarianism, populism, socialism, progressivism, liberalism, and humanitarianism. American liberalism shifted from the Left to the Center during the
first half of the twentieth century. Thomas Jefferson and other early American liberals belonged to the Left of their day. Robert Yates was on the losing
side not only in the eighteenth-century debate over adoption of the Constitution but in the history books, where *The Federalist Papers* are cherished
and the Anti-Federalist papers are not. After his *Common Sense* acclaim
faded, Thomas Paine turned into a very controversial figure: he was imprisoned in France, he publicly criticized George Washington, and he disputed
the claims of established theology. John Taylor was associated with the Tertium Quids, a radical minority within the Democratic-Republican Party.
George Clinton, Samuel Adams, Patrick Henry, and other prominent liberals were either not invited to the Constitutional Convention or chose to
stay away.

The term *Left,* in its ideological sense, has its origins in the location of
seats in the French National Assembly of 1789. It was not used in the context of early American politics, but Jefferson was, by the standards of his day,
what we would now call a leftist. Despite his Randolph lineage, plantation
ownership, and public offices, Jefferson was not ideologically in the Center.
His views were out of the mainstream of prominent political and economic
thought. Jefferson approved of the initial phase of the French Revolution
because of its emphasis on republicanism, constitutionalism, and civil liberties.[12] While he later rejected the revolutionary despotism of Robespierre
and military despotism of Bonaparte, he supported the Left over the Right

during the tumult of the late 1780s. His Francophone and Jacobin views marked him as a dangerous man in the eyes of many Americans. He was not alarmed by Shays' Rebellion in Massachusetts. Although Jefferson supported replacement of the Articles of Confederation, he was not present at the Constitutional Convention and had some serious objections to the finished product. He was a high-ranking member of the Washington administration, but he did not belong to the political faction that developed around the first president. In contrast to most of the Founding Fathers, Jefferson was a populist, decentralist, and abolitionist. In an era of growing capitalism and government involvement in the economy, Jefferson remained an agrarian and laissez-faire advocate until his death in 1826.

Jefferson stood apart even from other national leaders of the Democratic-Republican Party, and this is further evidence that he was on the Left rather than in the Center. His friends and presidential successors, James Madison and James Monroe, did not closely follow his policies. Historian Richard Matthews contends that Madison's concept of property, man, government, and society was closer to Hamilton's than to Jefferson's. Madison began his national career as a coauthor, with Hamilton and Jay, of *The Federalist Papers.* President Madison pursued the expansionistic War of 1812 against Jefferson's advice. After the war ended, his administration was characterized by nationalism, centralization, and loose construction of the Constitution. In the mid-1810s, Madison's legislative agenda was distinctly Hamiltonian in nature. He called for an increase in the size of the military, direct internal taxation, higher government salaries, aid to manufacturers, and creation of a new national bank. In his final annual message to Congress in December 1816, Madison argued for the creation of a system of roads and canals, a change of the federal judiciary along lines previously advocated by Federalists, and the establishment of a national university in Washington.[13]

While Madison had major ideological differences with Jefferson from the start, Monroe apparently compromised his original beliefs once he reached the White House. He was, in some respects, a protégé of John Taylor. An Anti-Federalist, Monroe spoke against adoption of the Constitution at Virginia's ratifying convention in 1788. He was supported for president in 1808 by John Randolph of Roanoke and some other Tertium Quids because he was viewed as more Jeffersonian than Madison. After becoming president in 1817, Monroe led New Republicans such as John Quincy Adams, John Calhoun, and Henry Clay in pursuing policies that were "far closer to Federalist economics" than to the Democratic-Republican laissez-faire of Jefferson. Monroe had ties to New York City business figures that were uncharacteristic of Virginia Democrats of his day. His wife, Elizabeth Kortright, was a daughter of a wealthy merchant and a sister-in-law of businessman Nicholas Gouverneur. John Jacob Astor was a friend of and money lender to Monroe. Federalists generally supported Monroe during his two terms in the White House. Leaders of the Federalist Party were pleased that "the party which had displaced it, and which had the popular prejudice in its favor, should gradually assume its principles, which were the original principles of our government." They were pleased that the Democratic-Republican Party was no longer "anti-commercial" and "anti-naval," but rather an "unsubstantial spectre of our former enemy." Retired president Jefferson rejected the compromising, bipartisan spirit of President Monroe's Era of Good Feelings.[14] The most prominent Jeffersonian purists of the nineteenth century were Martin Van Buren and William Jennings Bryan. Neither was able to retain his grip on the reins of the Democratic Party. Van Buren knew the party had slipped into less Jeffersonian hands in 1844. Bryan unwittingly assisted the transfer of power in 1912.

Radical vs. Respectable

Early American liberals were often marginalized and denounced as radicals by the Center. When he was running for president in 1800, Jefferson was called an atheist and an anarchist. Some citizens reportedly hid their Bibles after he was elected because they were afraid of a reign of terror under his presidency. Of course, as author of the Declaration of Independence and friend of George Washington, Jefferson was not a complete outcast, and many Americans discounted Federalist warnings as mere campaign rhetoric. While some of the criticism was just a cynical attempt to scare voters, some of it was grounded in a real distinction between the Left and the Center. It is for good reason that historian Richard Matthews refers to "the radical politics" of Jefferson.

Decades between Jefferson and Bryan

Andrew Jackson the popular hero and Martin Van Buren the party manager worked together to construct the modern Democratic Party and to bring about presidential election victories in 1828, 1832, and 1836. Despite having very different personalities, both men were liberals. During the 1820s, Jackson succeeded Jefferson as the leading spokesman of liberalism in the United States. Old Hickory was a committed follower of the Sage of

Monticello. Jackson did, however, set aside three of the twelve tenets of Jefferson's political thought: he believed in executive preeminence (at least in his own case), he had no evident qualms about the enslavement of African Americans and oppression of Native Americans, and he was militaristic. According to Charles Beard, Jackson, "a representative of the agrarian South and West, ardently supported by the working classes in the East, took his place firmly in the left wing of the party started by Jefferson. His position with respect to the main Federalist institutions and articles of political faith makes this evident beyond argument." Shortly before his death, Jackson wrote a private letter that praised "the economy and simplicity of our republican institutions and the plainness of our republican citizens," referring to the latter as "the great laboring and producing classes, that form the bone and sinew of our confederacy." Associated at various times with the so-called Bucktail, Locofoco, and Barnburner wings of the Democratic Party in New York, Martin Van Buren always belonged to the wing most committed to the principles of Thomas Jefferson. Van Buren stood "squarely in the Old Republican tradition" of Jefferson, Taylor, Randolph, and Macon when it came to states' rights, strict construction, and frugal government. He possessed an "unquenchable animosity towards 'the money power.'"[15]

Jackson shared Jefferson's agrarianism and expanded Jefferson's concept of democracy. Jackson and his supporters, many of whom were uneducated, plainspoken backwoodsmen "out West," advocated giving more power to the common people. Jacksonians "feared that Hamiltonian men of business controlled and directed the [John Quincy] Adams administration to advance their economic interests. 'Contending as we are against wealth & power,' said a future member of Jackson's cabinet, 'we look for success in numbers.'" From the 1820s to the 1840s, the Democratic Party engaged in a principled struggle with the Whig Party, which had succeeded the Federalist Party as the political bastion of special privilege. Jacksonians criticized the monied aristocracy and its hirelings in government. The most radical, or liberal, members of the Democratic Party were the urban workers in the East who belonged to the workingmen's associations and the Locofoco faction during the 1820s and 1830s.[16]

By the late 1840s, the liberal nature of the Democratic Party had become seriously compromised by the proslavery sentiments of a substantial portion of its members. The most prominent and powerful proslavery Democrats were not Jeffersonians. The ideology of John C. Calhoun and other slavocrats has already been noted. Despite being northern Democrats, President Franklin Pierce and President James Buchanan were supporters of slavery. Bankrolled by August Belmont of the House of Rothschild and possessing

close ties to other big businessmen, Pierce and Buchanan cannot be accu-
rately described as Jeffersonians when they entered the White House.[17]
Other loyalties had weakened Pierce's record of Jeffersonian fidelity by 1852.
Buchanan was even further removed from Jefferson. When he began his political career, he belonged to the party founded by Hamilton. Buchanan was
elected to the state legislature and to the U.S. House of Representatives as a
Federalist.

During the Jacksonian and antebellum eras, the stream of Jeffersonianism
was advanced through a number of prominent individuals. Liberals during
this period included many noted literary men and social reformers. They
were democrats, decentralists, pacifists, abolitionists, and feminists. Liberal
statesmen and politicians during this period tended to be advocates of
democracy, friends of labor, champions of freedom, and defenders of states'
rights. Some were opponents of slavery who supported the Free Soil Party
in 1848. Proponents of honest governance, many supported the Liberal Republican Party in 1872. Jeffersonianism was maintained within the Democratic Party by individuals such as Andrew Jackson, John Randolph, Thomas
Ritchie, Martin Van Buren, William Leggett, Silas Wright, Thomas Hart
Benton, Frank Blair, and John Hale. Whigs and Republicans influenced by
Jefferson's authorship of the Declaration and by his example of placing the
public good above private gain included Charles Sumner, George Julian,
Horace Greeley, Charles Francis Adams, Lyman Trumbull, and Carl Schurz.

Seven eventful decades passed between the death of Jefferson in 1826 and
the nomination of Bryan in 1896. The two major political parties became
ideological battlegrounds, with liberal Jeffersonian and conservative Hamiltonian factions coexisting uneasily at times and engaging in open warfare at
other times. *Plutocracy,* which means rule by the wealthy, is a variety of aristocracy. While slavocracy and plutocracy were distinct tendencies within the
Democratic Party, they were not antagonistic tendencies. On the contrary,
they often worked hand in hand. August Belmont of New York City was
linked to the slaveholding aristocracy through his wife's uncle, Senator John
Slidell of Louisiana. After serving as a financial patron of Pierce and
Buchanan, Belmont went on to sponsor Senator Stephen Douglas of Illinois
and Senator Thomas Bayard of Delaware and to serve as chairman of the
Democratic National Committee from 1860 to 1872. Belmont, William B.
Astor, and Moses Taylor were among the Hamiltonian influences in the
Democratic Party during the Gilded Age. President Grover Cleveland came
out of this East Coast, plutocratic tradition. The Republican Party was
formed in 1854 by a coalition of principled abolitionists, pragmatic politicians, and powerful businessmen. A widespread shift occurred within the

party from equality and morality toward wealth and power during and after the Civil War. Many Democrats in the tradition of Jefferson and Jackson had joined the Republican Party in the 1850s because they disliked the proslavery tilt of the Democratic Party and its domination by wealthy interests. Many of these antislavery, prodemocracy Republicans left the GOP during the 1870s and 1880s as the party weakened its support for black civil rights and became overtly dominated by high financiers and railroad tycoons. Many of these disillusioned Republicans joined newly created political parties such as the Prohibition Party, Greenback-Labor Party, People's (Populist) Party, and Silver Republican Party.

CHAPTER 4

Bryan, Humphrey, and Their Ideological Descent

Two Individuals

William Jennings Bryan of Nebraska and Hubert Horatio Humphrey of Minnesota are the quintessential liberals of Democratic Party politics of the past one hundred years. Bryan served as a U.S. representative and secretary of state, and he was a three-time Democratic presidential nominee. Humphrey was mayor of Minneapolis, U.S. senator, four-time presidential candidate, vice president of the United States, and Democratic presidential nominee.[1]

For the sake of fair ideological comparison, it is important that Bryan and Humphrey be on equal footing, in terms of background, fame, power, influence, and circumstance. Equivalence can be seen by looking at specific traits. Both Bryan and Humphrey had fathers who served in the state legislature, both settled as young men in Republican states, both were midwesterners, both were Democrats, both were associated with powerful third parties in their states, both were members of Congress, both possessed sanguine temperaments, both were noted orators, both were repeat presidential candidates, both were presidential nominees of a major party, and both were high officials in a presidential administration.

Unlike Jefferson, Bryan and Humphrey were not important original thinkers. Instead, they were mainly popularizers. They used their positions as high officials of the U.S. government to popularize ideas associated with their respective versions of liberalism. Perhaps more important, they used the platform provided by a presidential candidacy to spread their messages. The years 1925 and 1978 have been chosen as the closing dates for the two time

57

periods being studied because Bryan died on July 26, 1925, and Humphrey died on January 13, 1978. Each death symbolized the passing of a political era.

Bryan's Descent

It is useful to consider the claims and evidence of ideological descent for the two exemplars and their supporters. The purpose of this study is to ascertain the influence of Jeffersonianism on Democratic Party liberalism as expressed through Bryan and Humphrey. The logical place to start is with their words and actions in relation to Jefferson and his political successors, as well as Hamilton and his heirs.

The Populists, whose presidential nominee Bryan endorsed in 1892 and whose national banner Bryan carried in 1896, "used Jefferson's philosophy and principles of government to develop their criticism of existing government and to outline their concept of its proper alternative." Throughout his long political career, Bryan was inspired by and indebted to Jefferson. When he contemplated Jefferson, "it was with the veneration usually accorded to saints." As early as 1880, he declared, "Against Hamilton and the followers of Hamilton, the Democratic party has raised and will forever raise, its voice." Referring to the Sage of Monticello, the Great Commoner wrote, "His culture connected him with the educated and the refined, and yet his creed and principles made him the comrade and work fellow of the people." Bryan drew a clear distinction between "Jeffersonian Democrats" such as himself and "Republican allies who masquerade as democrats."[2]

In 1899, Congressman William Sulzer (D-NY), a Bryan supporter, noted the Jeffersonian nature of Andrew Jackson, including his belief in "our cardinal principle of special privileges to none, equal opportunities for all." With Bryan's continual enunciation of this cardinal principle and his championing of democracy, it is not surprising that he was often compared to Jackson. As Bryan was preparing for his second run for the White House, Governor John Peter Altgeld (D-IL) said, "This country needs more Andrew Jacksons, and the people believe that they have found one in William J. Bryan." In his influential book *The Promise of American Life,* Herbert Croly wrote this concerning Bryan: "He can, perhaps, be best understood as a Democrat of both Jeffersonian and Jacksonian tendencies, who has been born a few generations too late. He is honestly seeking to deal with contemporary American political problems in the spirit, if not according to the letter, of traditional democracy."[3]

While Bryanism was primarily inspired by the liberal tradition within the Democratic Party, it was to a lesser extent inspired by the stream of Jeffersonianism flowing through nineteenth-century abolitionists, Conscience Whigs, and early Republicans. Bryan's father, Silas Bryan, supported Horace Greeley for president in 1872. Senator Lyman Trumbull (R-IL) was a major influence on the young Bryan. A friend of Silas Bryan, Trumbull hired William as a clerk for his law office in 1882. Trumbull, who joined the People's Party in 1894, was "the sponsor and preceptor" of Bryan's "social idealism."[4] Abolitionist William Lloyd Garrison influenced Leo Tolstoy's thinking in regard to nonviolence; Tolstoy, in turn, was a major influence on Bryan.[5] Despite important differences of ideology between Thomas Jefferson and Abraham Lincoln, Populists and Bryan Democrats often praised the two men in the same breath. Lincoln was far more Jeffersonian in reputation than in reality, but reputation was enough to attract Jacksonian Democrats such as Peter Cooper and James Weaver to the early Republican Party. Over two hundred delegates at the 1900 Silver Republican National Convention had voted for Lincoln in 1860. These delegates hailed Lincoln in the party platform as "the great interpreter of American history and the great apostle of human rights and of industrial freedom." The Silver Republicans joined the Democrats and fusion Populists in nominating Bryan for president. Bryan approvingly quoted Lincoln's reputed statement, "The Republican party believes in the man and the dollar, but in case of conflict it believes in the man before the dollar" and cited Lincoln's warning about an attempt to put "capital upon an equal footing with labor."[6]

Liberal third parties of the Gilded Age also played a role in the ideological development of Bryanism. When Silas Bryan unsuccessfully ran for Congress in 1872, he was endorsed by the Greenback-Labor Party. The elder Bryan was "interested in the economic activities of the new Greenback party, which was one of the first to consider the currency problem as the basis of economic inequality." In 1892, William Jennings Bryan supported the presidential candidacy of Populist nominee—and 1880 Greenback nominee—James Weaver, and Weaver subsequently became a key supporter of Bryan's presidential campaigns.[7]

Humphrey's Descent

In assessing the ideological nature of mid-twentieth-century Democratic liberalism, it is important to consider the extent to which Hubert Humphrey was influenced by Jefferson and other nineteenth-century liberals, and by Bryan and other early twentieth-century liberals. Humphrey had no understanding of or sympathy for the position of the Anti-Federalists. Calling the adoption of the Constitution "inherently wise, moral, and in our self-interest," and noting that it was ratified by a narrow margin in New York and Virginia, he wondered how "so many virtuous and intelligent men" could have been "so wrong in 1788." As Humphrey was growing up, his father read to him the writings of Thomas Jefferson and Thomas Paine. In his master's thesis, Humphrey contended that the philosophy behind the New Deal was "essentially Jeffersonian."[8] Humphrey was personally devoted to the New Deal throughout his life, so it is fair to conclude that he saw his own philosophy as "essentially Jeffersonian." According to close Humphrey ally Senator Paul Douglas (D-IL), Thomas Jefferson and Abraham Lincoln were the two preeminent American heroes of midcentury Democratic liberals in Congress, with Andrew Jackson, Woodrow Wilson, and Franklin Roosevelt ranking just below them. Despite professed reliance on Jefferson by Humphrey and his supporters, Jefferson's name was rarely invoked by Humphreyites, in comparison to Bryanites. In 1952, Humphrey called Alexander Hamilton a great statesman. Lyndon B. Johnson, a friend and mentor of Humphrey, was distinctly un-Jeffersonian. Historian Arthur Schlesinger Jr. wrote the book on Vital Center ideology. While not personally close, Humphrey was ideologically close to Schlesinger, a strong Hamiltonian.[9]

Humphrey "placed the New Deal in the direct line of developments from Jefferson through Jackson to Populism, Progressivism, and Wilson's 'New Freedom.'" Humphrey's thesis and Douglas's assessment notwithstanding, there was little detectable influence by Andrew Jackson on Humphrey or on his supporters. With the obligatory exception of Abraham Lincoln, Humphreyites were not greatly influenced by abolitionists, Conscience Whigs, or early Republicans. Humphrey's father was "spiritually" a "descendant of the Populists." Humphrey was born and raised in South Dakota, a prairie state in which People's Party presidential nominees were strong in 1892 and 1896. He saw many of the policies and programs of the New Deal foreshadowed by Populist platforms. Humphrey placed himself in "the progressive-populist-liberal-reformist tradition." As Humphrey was growing up, William Jennings Bryan was a great hero in his household. Humphrey's father, a small businessman in a Republican state, became a Democrat after hearing Bryan speak. Impressed with the Cross of Gold speech Bryan gave at the 1896 convention, Hubert Humphrey Sr. read the words to young Hubert. Many biographers and commentators have compared Humphrey to Bryan; both have been seen as prairie populists who championed progressive reform. Some of Humphrey's supporters also had clear links to Bryan—Senator Paul

Douglas supported Bryan in 1908 and Senator Adlai Stevenson III was a great-grandson of his 1900 running mate.[10]

Hubert Humphrey's biographers have long placed him in the midwestern liberal tradition of Republican senator Robert La Follette of Wisconsin and his ally Senator George Norris of Nebraska. In his autobiography, Humphrey noted the influence of progressive Republicanism in South Dakota during his early years. He identified Senators La Follette, Norris, Peter Norbeck, Charles McNary, William Borah, and Hiram Johnson as men who "spoke for agrarian America and added a distinctly dissident strain to the Republican party." In 1939, Humphrey praised La Follette in his master's thesis. Two decades later, Humphrey announced his candidacy for president. Referring to this announcement, James Reston of the *New York Times* commented, "Old Bob LaFollette and William Jennings Bryan would have loved it . . . He is . . . an authentic son of the old agrarian reformers."

A few of Humphrey's supporters were tied to La Follette in closer ways. In the late 1930s and early 1940s, Senator William Benton (D-CT) was associated with Philip La Follette and Robert La Follette Jr. through the National Progressives of America and the America First Committee. Senator Douglas also provided Philip La Follette with some contacts as he worked to create a national progressive party. La Follette Sr. and Norris were the two senators who, "in the whole history of the Senate," Douglas most admired.[11] There was a significant link between Humphrey and Norman Thomas. Thomas was a longtime Socialist Party leader who supported La Follette in 1924. Many of La Follette's 1924 supporters, in turn, voted for Thomas on at least one of the six occasions he ran for president. Paul Douglas supported Thomas in 1928 and 1932. Max Kampelman, who went with Humphrey to Washington and became his legislative assistant, supported Thomas in 1948. In the late 1940s, Humphrey became one of Thomas's friends. In May 1964, he praised Humphrey, calling him "the type of Democrat I like and one who would be a Socialist if he got to England." Thomas campaigned and voted for Johnson-Humphrey in 1964. Shortly before his death in 1968, Thomas endorsed Humphrey for president.[12]

The relationship between La Follette supporters and Humphrey supporters was not a completely positive one. There are various interactions that indicate at least some level of discontinuity between La Follette and Humphrey. In the early 1940s, Reinhold Niebuhr resigned from the Socialist Party, denounced Norman Thomas as a "utopian," and became an admirer of Franklin Roosevelt. Niebuhr and Humphrey were both founders of Americans for Democratic Action, a procapitalist, pro-Cold War group, and were both supporters of Truman rather than Thomas in the fall of 1948.

Despite Thomas's friendship with Humphrey, Humphrey was ideologically much closer to Niebuhr than to Thomas. While Thomas ended up casting his vote for Humphrey in 1968, he had earlier supported a stop-Humphrey coalition at the Democratic convention.[13] In his autobiography, Humphrey said that it was "fortunate for America" that Senator Robert Taft of Ohio was not the 1952 Republican presidential nominee, calling him a representative of "shallow partisanship." Although Taft was viewed as one of the nation's preeminent conservatives throughout his years in the Senate, his ideology had more in common with La Follette's than with that of the standpatters who opposed La Follette. The reactionary Republicans of La Follette's day—including Robert Taft's father, President William Howard Taft—were Hamiltonian in ideology and personified the wealth-and-power Establishment. Senator Taft was an anti-Establishment politician with decided Jeffersonian leanings. He viewed himself as more genuinely liberal than Wendell Willkie or Harold Stassen. In contrast to most Republican presidential contenders, Robert Taft was a spokesman for Main Street and rural America, not for Wall Street and corporate America.[14] In the early 1950s, Humphrey's close political friend Paul Douglas frequently led Senate forces promoting policies that Taft opposed as militaristic and imperialistic. Douglas's veering away from a La Follette-style foreign policy during the 1950s and 1960s was perhaps foreshadowed by an earlier turning away in domestic policy. During the 1930s, Douglas was one of the New Deal intellectuals who "derided as nostalgic folly the Jeffersonian ideal of a nation of small farmers and shopkeepers." Douglas scoffed at La Follette's supposedly antiquated 1924 platform.[15]

Wisconsin attorney general Bronson La Follette, a grandson of Robert La Follette, supported Eugene McCarthy against Humphrey in 1968 and John Lindsay against Humphrey in 1972. Referring to Wisconsin, Carl Solberg noted, "Of all the fifty states, none was more consistently unrewarding to Humphrey."[16] While La Follette's Wisconsin shared a progressive tradition with Humphrey's Minnesota, it repeatedly rejected him in Democratic presidential primaries—going for Kennedy in 1960, McCarthy in 1968, and McGovern and Wallace in 1972. Humphrey blamed his defeats on Republican crossover voting in the open primary, but a more accurate explanation likely involves Wisconsin's traditional preference for isolationism over imperialism. This partly explains the Republican presidential primary victories of Norris in 1928 and 1932, Borah in 1936, MacArthur in 1944, and Taft in 1952. More recent examples of Wisconsin's isolationism are Governor Jerry Brown's strong showing in the 1992 Democratic primary and the voting record of Democratic senator Russell Feingold, who has opposed the North

American Free Trade Agreement, the General Agreement on Tariffs and Trade/ World Trade Organization, the Bosnian troop deployment, a huge 1998 appropriation for the International Monetary Fund, the Kosovo bombing campaign, the 2002 Department of Defense Appropriations Act, and Iraq War.

In his autobiography, Humphrey acknowledged that the traditional agrarian populists within the Minnesota Farmer-Labor Party opposed fusion with the Democratic Party:

> It is ironic that the legitimate heirs to the Farmer-Labor tradition, opposed to the fusion, were not in power within the Farmer-Labor party. The left-wing group that had parasitically attached itself to that tradition like a lamprey on a lake trout was in power, and unity had become a religion with them. They twisted and turned according to the demands of the Soviet line.

Significantly, Humphrey worked with the Marxist bloc within the Farmer-Labor Party to bring about fusion in 1944, thereby running roughshod over the "legitimate heirs" of Minnesota populism. Humphrey voted against former governor Hjalmar Petersen, leader of the traditional, populist wing of the FLP, in the 1942 gubernatorial election. Humphrey remembered his 1948 senatorial campaign in this way: "Outside the university area within the Twin Cities, we largely depended on the cleaned-up labor movement, and outstate we found farmers and farm co-operative leaders who were not aligned with the more radical agrarian traditions." As with the Democratic-Farmer-Labor (DFL) merger, Humphrey's first senatorial campaign represented a discontinuity with La Follette, who was certainly aligned with the radical agrarians of Minnesota. Decades after the fact, Senator Eugene McCarthy (DFL-MN) acknowledged that Humphrey's domestic and foreign policies represented a major departure from the tradition of the Non-Partisan League and the Minnesota Farmer-Labor Party.[17]

While Humphrey and his supporters drew to some extent upon the Populist Democracy tradition of Bryan and the Progressive Republican tradition of La Follette, they were far more indebted to two other twentieth-century political traditions: Vital Center Democracy and Middle Way Republicanism. A word of explanation is necessary concerning this book's seemingly anachronistic use of the terms *Vital Center* and *Middle Way*. Popularized by Arthur Schlesinger Jr., the first term was used to designate the postwar Democratic liberalism of Harry Truman and Americans for Democratic Action. The second term was associated with the moderate Republicanism of

Dwight Eisenhower and Republican Advance. I use these terms to refer not only to Truman and Eisenhower but also to political antecedents possessing essentially the same ideology. Thus, Woodrow Wilson and Franklin Roosevelt are referred to as Vital Center Democrats and Theodore Roosevelt and Wendell Willkie are referred to as Middle Way Republicans. There are two reasons for the appropriateness of such use. The first is related to the nature of semantic shorthand: historians routinely apply labels to persons, events, and trends after the fact (e.g., Civil War, World War I, Progressive Era). While such application is technically anachronistic, it is usually helpful and often unavoidable. The second, and more important, reason for applying *Vital Center* and *Middle Way* to the likes of Woodrow Wilson and Theodore Roosevelt is that they actually possessed these ideologies. It is wrong to think that Truman-era Democratic liberals and Eisenhower-era Republican liberals sprang into existence out of nothing. There were three main differences between the New Deal of Franklin Roosevelt and the Vital Center of Truman: the Vital Center tried to adapt to material abundance rather than scarcity, it largely discarded rhetoric critical of big business, and it turned away from the Popular Front to anti-Communism and the Cold War.[18] These differences were more stylistic than substantive.

There was a postwar economic boom in the 1920s as a result of the European conflict and of government-business confluence. Wilsonian, self-described progressive Democrats such as James Cox, John Davis, and Al Smith were supporters of the bipartisan political-economic status quo that maintained affluence for many Americans until the stock market crash of 1929. Wilson's opposition to big business was always more rhetorical than real. The domestic suppression of civil liberties during the Cold War was prefigured by the Red Scare. Like Schlesinger and Truman, Wilson was an ideological centrist. He rejected both the Bryan populists, La Follette progressives, and Debs socialists of the Left and the shortsighted, plainspoken, union-breaking, domestic-oriented, laissez-faire industrialists of the Right.[19] By the late 1930s, Franklin Roosevelt set aside the New Deal and concerns about domestic unemployment in favor of an imperialistic foreign policy and its attendant open embrace of corporate wealth.[20] There is a direct line of ideological descent from Wilson through FDR to Truman. Vital Center champions Humphrey and Schlesinger each authored scholarly tributes to Roosevelt and his programs. There was nothing terribly new about the Vital Center of the late 1940s: it was mostly a repackaging of image to fit new sociopolitical conditions. In fact, faced with a tough election in 1948, Truman fell back on anti-Wall Street rhetoric that had supposedly been rendered obsolete by World War II, widespread affluence, and the drive for economic growth.[21]

The Middle Way of Eisenhower emphasized voluntarism, harmony of social interests, expert knowledge, and government-business partnership. Historian Robert Griffith contends, "Eisenhower's vision of a corporate commonwealth did not, of course, originate with him. Indeed, variations of this concept—with its emphasis on organization, cooperation, and social harmony—go back at least to the Progressive era." Griffith cites as forerunners of the Middle Way such corporate liberals as members of the National Civic Federation, businessmen Bernard Baruch and Gerard Swope of the War Industries Board, Herbert Hoover with his associative state, advocates of welfare capitalism during the 1920s, and pro-Roosevelt big businessmen associated with the Business Advisory Council. He argues, "Common to all of these activities was an attempt to fashion a new corporate economy that would avoid both the destructive disorder of unregulated capitalism and the threat to business autonomy posed by socialism." Theodore Roosevelt and his political allies were centrist expositors of enlightened conservatism. Wendell Willkie and Thomas Dewey represented the same belief system in the 1940s.[22] Vital Center, Middle Way, NATO liberalism, Cold War liberalism, and other labels associated with the Power Elite's postwar bipartisan consensus described an ideology that was the latest variant of corporate liberalism.[23]

Hubert Humphrey Sr. became a Democrat because of William Jennings Bryan, but Woodrow Wilson was his idol. In his autobiography, Hubert Humphrey declared, "Wilson was my boyhood hero, and the hero of my father's adult life." In his master's thesis, Humphrey saw Wilson's New Freedom as a forerunner of his beloved New Deal. Just before his vice-presidential term ended in 1969, Humphrey asked outgoing President Johnson to nominate him as a trustee of the newly created Woodrow Wilson International Center for Scholars. Johnson went even further by nominating him as the first board chairman.[24] Political scientist R. Jeffrey Lustig posits that the tenor of Wilson's career before the 1912 campaign "had always been closer to Hamilton's thinking than to Jefferson's." Historian Gabriel Kolko maintains that President Wilson's reliance on Jeffersonian doctrine was "more verbal than genuine." Sociologist E. Digby Baltzell points out that Wilson "always called himself a Federalist in private." Before making his decision to run for president in 1912, Wilson was an overtly anti-Bryan Democrat. He voted against Bryan in 1896, expressed the hope in 1907 that Bryan would be "knocked into a cocked hat," and refused to speak on the same platform with Bryan in 1908. According to Kolko, Wilson was used by "Eastern conservative Democrats" to eliminate the threat of Bryan being nominated in 1912; Wilson's nomination and election "represented the triumph of Eastern

Democracy over Bryanism." Wilson's 1912 and 1916 campaigns were largely financed by Wall Street and its corporate offspring. Although Bryan served as Wilson's initial secretary of state, he resigned in 1915 because he opposed the president's prowar policies. In 1921 he declined to raise funds for the Woodrow Wilson Foundation, saying that he could not "endorse with enthusiasm" Wilson's entire record.[25]

Hubert Humphrey Sr. viewed Democratic governor Al Smith of New York as "a progressive who would be a fine President for the people." Humphrey Sr. was not the only self-professed liberal to support Smith for president in 1928, but most liberals were unenthusiastic about the tweedledee-tweedledum nature of the Hoover-Smith contest, in terms of substance, not style. Al Smith's personal ethnoreligious tolerance, dependence on urban political machines, support for social welfare programs, use of populist campaign rhetoric, and reliance on big business to finance his campaigns foreshadowed Hubert Humphrey's type of liberalism. Despite his eventual reputation for liberalism, Smith compiled a conservative record as a state legislator and governor. Alton Parker, Bryan's nemesis at the 1904 and 1912 conventions, supported Smith's campaign for the 1924 Democratic presidential nomination. While Bryan backed William Gibbs McAdoo for president in 1924, Smith ran against McAdoo and supported Oscar Underwood, another old Bryan foe, when his own campaign ran out of steam at the convention. Bryan opposed the nomination of Smith not only because of his support for liquor manufacture and his ties to the corrupt Tammany Hall machine, but also because he was "for Wall Street." Following his nomination in 1928, Smith appointed John Raskob—an executive for DuPont and General Motors and registered Republican—to be his campaign manager and chairman of the Democratic National Committee. During the 1930s, Smith criticized FDR for being too liberal. As a front man for the plutocratic American Liberty League, Smith proclaimed that he would not let socialists "march under the banner of Jefferson, Jackson or Cleveland."[26] It is significant that Smith chose to include Grover Cleveland, the political archenemy of Bryan, in the Democratic Party pantheon.

Franklin Delano Roosevelt was perhaps the preeminent ideological inspiration and practical role model for Hubert Humphrey and Humphrey supporters. In the 1930s, Humphrey "fell in love" with Roosevelt—a man his father "worshiped." His master's thesis was a tribute to Roosevelt that made plain Humphrey's devotion to the policies of New Deal liberalism. Throughout the 1950s, Senator Humphrey fought to protect and extend Roosevelt's legacy. Roosevelt's widow, Eleanor, encouraged Humphrey to run for the 1960 presidential nomination. In his speech at the dedication of the William Jennings Bryan memorial statue in Potomac Park, President Roosevelt called attention to Bryan's sincerity, saying it "served him so well in his lifelong fight against sham and privilege and wrong." A classic example of Machiavelli's "fox," Roosevelt was known for his insincerity, albeit, according to his admirers, with the best of reasons and for the noblest of goals.[27] The difference between Bryan and Roosevelt went beyond personality or strategy. It had an ideological dimension, which is why Bryan and Roosevelt were so often engaged in opposing activities during the dozen years they shared the national political stage.

Roosevelt supported McKinley over Bryan in the 1900 election. A "big navy" enthusiast, Roosevelt was always more of a militarist than Bryan. Roosevelt favored U.S. entry into World War I while Bryan resisted it. Unlike Bryan, Roosevelt never repudiated the person or policies of Woodrow Wilson.[28] Roosevelt supported Herbert Hoover for the 1920 Democratic presidential nomination while Bryan dismissed Hoover and boosted Senator Robert Owen (D-OK). Senator Hiram Johnson (R-CA) was condemning Hoover as a front man for J. P. Morgan and Company at the same time Roosevelt was declaring, "He is certainly a wonder, and I wish we could make him President of the United States. There could not be a better one." Roosevelt agreed to be James Cox's running mate in 1920; Bryan gave only tepid support to the Cox-Roosevelt ticket because of Cox's opposition to Prohibition and support for plutocracy. Roosevelt was a leading supporter of Al Smith for president at the 1920, 1924, and 1928 conventions; Bryan consistently opposed Smith. In 1924, Roosevelt "personally admired" John W. Davis and supported his election in the fall. Bryan supported Davis after he chose his brother, Governor Charles Bryan (D-NE), as his running mate, but he had earlier denounced Davis as a possible nominee because he was J. P. Morgan Jr.'s attorney and had been bitterly disappointed when Charles decided to accept the vice-presidential nomination. Millions of liberal Democrats followed the lead of Senator Burton Wheeler (D-MT), who decided to support La Follette because the Democratic Party had gone to Wall Street for its presidential nominee. When, in December 1924, Roosevelt issued a call for a national Democratic Party strategy session, he was planning to exclude Bryan from the proposed conference while inviting Cox and Davis to participate. In March 1925, the Bryan brothers announced at a press conference in New York City that they were opposed to Roosevelt's proposed unity meeting and that they did not see eastern Democrats playing a significant role in future party affairs.[29]

In the late 1920s, Governor Franklin Roosevelt "seemed to many progressives to be at one with the conservative northeasterners who had taken the party over; he was a New Yorker, a Manhattan lawyer, and to all appearances a close ally of Al Smith." He was the scion of an aristocratic family doubly linked to the very wealthy Astor family, and his foreign policy views reflected his ties to Wall Street. Always an imperialist, Roosevelt was a strong supporter of the League of Nations and the World Court. His thinking was to a large extent influenced by leaders of the Council on Foreign Relations, an organization founded in 1921 by a group of international investment bankers and others friendly to big business. Before being elected governor, Roosevelt had been a Wall Street financier involved with a number of speculative international enterprises, and his 1928 and 1930 gubernatorial campaigns were largely funded by big bankers and big businessmen.[30]

Despite his conservative record, FDR gained the support of liberals in 1932 by moving toward public control of water power, by publicly distancing himself from Tammany Hall, by criticizing John Raskob, by setting aside his enthusiasm for the League of Nations, by giving his "forgotten man" speech, and by having Al Smith as a primary opponent. Although there were some encouraging appointments and proposals in the early years of his presidency, many traditional liberals had serious doubts about President Roosevelt by 1937 and were openly hostile toward his administration by 1940.[31] They viewed his domestic and foreign policies as a repudiation of the kind of liberalism exemplified by Jefferson, Jackson, Sumner, Bryan, and La Follette. During his twelve years in office, FDR became the measure of all things liberal. *Newsweek,* for example, became known as a liberal magazine because of its New Deal sympathies despite the fact that it was published by corporate multimillionaires such as Vincent Astor and W. Averell Harriman.[32] Liberals who retained Jeffersonian ideals instead of embracing Rooseveltian ideals became known as conservatives, despite their continued opposition to Hamiltonian conservatism. Years later, Burton Wheeler, a Bryan Democrat who was La Follette's 1924 running mate on the Progressive-Socialist ticket, commented,

> During World War II, the practice of pasting on political labels became ridiculous. To the "liberals," it didn't matter how reactionary you were on domestic issues. If you were an "interventionist," that is, pro-war, you were automatically welcomed with open arms as a "liberal." . . . Some of the most conservative senators embraced FDR's policies— and immediately were called liberals. Then there was Wendell Willkie, the Wall Street private power advocate, who had fought against the Utility Holding Company Act of 1935; he joined Roosevelt when he couldn't lick him, and was hailed for his "liberal" views. On the other hand, when lifelong progressives like myself opposed intervention, as we always had previously, we were denounced for having deserted liberalism.[33]

In his autobiography, Governor Philip La Follette (Pr-WI) recalled a White House meeting with Roosevelt after the 1936 election:

> The genial mask dropped as he said, "Phil, there have always been poor people; there always will be. Be practical!" . . . I knew then what I had only feared before: Roosevelt had no more real interest in the common man than a Wall Street broker. He was playing the same kind of game as Big Business, only he sought, got, and intended to keep *power,* rather than money.[34]

As a result of their rejection of the version of liberalism espoused and practiced by the president, many longtime liberals—Charles Bryan, Upton Sinclair, Huey Long, Thomas Gore, William Murray, Bronson Cutting, Hiram Johnson—were the targets of public criticism, patronage denials, and electoral opposition by the White House. There were, of course, some traditionally liberal public officials—Josephus Daniels, George Norris, Harold Ickes, Fiorello La Guardia, Thomas Amlie—who continued to support Franklin Roosevelt throughout his presidency and, in turn, received warm treatment by his administration. Senator Robert La Follette Jr. (Pr-WI) was close to the president from 1933 to 1941 before finally breaking with him over foreign policy differences. Individuals such as Daniels and Norris seem to have been the exception rather than the rule. Most early congressional opponents of the New Deal were "essentially Jeffersonian Democrats" who "sought to recreate Jefferson's vision of America: a rural nation of independent yeomen, a small government which left people alone." A good example of this Jeffersonianism was Congressman George Huddleston (D-AL), a strong Bryan supporter who became a strong Roosevelt opponent. Historian Wayne Cole asserts that the anti-FDR isolationists of the late 1930s and early 1940s embraced the entire Jeffersonian creed.[35]

What explains Jeffersonian hostility toward the chief executive who led the party of Jefferson, laid claim to the mantle of Bryan, denounced economic royalists, and proclaimed himself a liberal? According to historian Merrill Peterson, Alexander Hamilton was "the true father of the New Deal." Peterson argued that the New Deal "killed the Jeffersonian philosophy as a recognizable and usable tradition in American government and politics." Historian Lee Benson recognized that the Whig Party of Webster came closer to being a nineteenth-century forerunner of the New Deal than did the Democratic Party of Van Buren. Other political analysts also recognized the essentially anti-Jeffersonian nature of Franklin Roosevelt's administration and the type of liberalism it spawned. In 1960, Stewart Alsop wrote, "If the word 'liberal' means anything these days, it means an internationalist and a big-government man." More recently, Murray Rothbard referred to "the gigantic welfare-warfare state brought to us by the New Deal and its heirs." Post-World War II politics in America has been dominated by a bipartisan consensus that favors "central government control over diverse states, provinces, or regions" and "a permanent policy of massive global intervention by the United States." Joseph Sobran put it succinctly: "Roosevelt's twin legacy is centralized government and permanent militarism. You are supposedly 'liberal' or 'conservative' according to which part of this legacy you prefer." Gore Vidal declared, "With Franklin Roosevelt, the words 'liberal' and 'conservative' were reversed. Because, during the short-term New Deal, he had made some liberal reforms (Social Security), he was thought to be liberal, but at heart he was a traditional Eastern conservative, with a love of foreign wars." According to historian Samuel Francis, in the 1940s liberalism

> "turned into a form of conservatism," . . . Liberal intellectuals . . . began to reformulate liberalism in a way that muted the radical, progressivist, egalitarian, and utopian premises . . . "Consensus liberalism"—what the New Left later called "corporate liberalism" because of its positive and uncritical concept of corporate capitalism—in fact reflected the new position and power of the managerial elite and the mass organizations it controlled. . . . Liberalism endorsed and rationalized the evolution of the "Imperial Presidency" that presided over the regulatory and interventionist bureaucracy, the globalist diplomacy, and the military managers of the mass state.[36]

Certainly FDR was and remains a beloved figure for many Americans. It is his Jeffersonian image, not his Hamiltonian record, that engenders that love.

Henry Wallace was one of Hubert Humphrey's heroes during his early years as a politician. Humphrey supported Wallace for renomination as vice president at the 1944 Democratic National Convention. He later recalled, "No man seemed more closely aligned with the Midwest, with the Populist liberals, Farmer-Laborites, Non-Partisan Leaguers, and ardent New Dealers than Wallace." Harry Truman was nominated instead. After the 1944 election, Humphrey wrote to Wallace, expressing disappointment that he had not been appointed secretary of state and pledging support for a Wallace presidential candidacy in 1948. By the time that election rolled around, Humphrey had turned against Wallace and was supporting the retention of Truman in the White House. Humphrey shared with Wallace a personality trait that greatly affected his political career: the desire to be loved, or at least liked, by everyone. Despite their reputations as bleeding-heart liberals, Wallace and Humphrey were both practitioners of pragmatic politics.[37]

As a member of the Democratic Party, Hubert Humphrey was more influenced by Vital Center Democracy than by Middle Way Republicanism, but the latter tradition did play a role in his political thought and practice. Middle Way Republicanism was the GOP's version of corporate liberalism. Middle Way Republican leaders in the 1940s included Thomas Dewey, Earl Warren, Harold Stassen, and Wendell Willkie. Willkie was a Democrat at the time his name was first mentioned for the 1940 Republican presidential nomination. If Willkie was a liberal Democrat when he sought the 1940 Republican nomination, he was a liberal in the tradition of Woodrow Wilson and Al Smith, not of William Jennings Bryan.[38] Likewise, if his nomination represented a triumph for liberal Republicanism, it was a triumph for Theodore Roosevelt liberalism, not for Robert La Follette liberalism.

After Willkie was nominated for president, *Life* magazine ran a puff piece on his triumph at the GOP convention. According to the magazine, for once the Republican delegates "obeyed not the party bosses but the will of the people." "Within the Party," the article read, "the Willkie victory marked a final ascendancy of . . . progressive leadership over the stand-pattism of the Old Guard." Yet even this slanted news story contained a hint of discongruity. Robert Taft was portrayed as a candidate of the "old bosses," but his attack on Willkie as a "Wall Streeter" was also noted. What was "stand-pattism" within the Republican Party if not devotion to Wall Street? How could Willkie simultaneously be the vanquisher of "stand-pattism" and the champion of Wall Street? Willkie's drive for the nomination was immeasurably helped by support he received from Wall Street-controlled newspapers and magazines. The mainstream media portrayed Willkie as a reluctant, homespun man from Indiana, not as an ambitious New Yorker linked to high society and economic power.[39]

Willkie attempted to gain the support of traditional liberals in the Midwest and West. Despite such attempts, the ideological heirs of La Follette viewed Willkie with a skeptical if not hostile eye. Congressman Usher Burdick (R-ND) declared,

> We Republicans in the West want to know if Wall Street, the utilities, and the international bankers control our party and can select our candidate? I believe I am serving the best interests of the Republican Party by protesting in advance and exposing the machinations and attempts of J. P. Morgan and the New York utility bankers in forcing Wendell Willkie on the Republican Party.

Traditional liberal Republicans who had endorsed Willkie in 1940 turned completely against him in 1941 as he became an open advocate of U.S. involvement in World War II and an overseas emissary for Franklin Roosevelt.[40]

In his master's thesis, Hubert Humphrey called the Theodore Roosevelt of 1912 an "early New Dealer." He liked the positive-state approach of Roosevelt and the Progressive Party platform. In 1940, Humphrey voted for Wendell Willkie for president, Harold Stassen for governor, and Joseph Ball for senator. Stassen and Ball supported Willkie for the GOP presidential nomination. Despite his Democratic upbringing and admiration for FDR, in 1942, Humphrey told Congressman-elect Walter Judd (R-MN) that he was a Republican. Humphrey's mayoral campaign literature in 1943 included a photograph of him reading Willkie's book *One World*. In the mid-1940s, he considered running for office as a Republican when the Cowles publishing group offered to support him if he would do so.[41] Humphrey was supported by many "Stassen Republicans" during his years as mayor of Minneapolis. Throughout the 1940s, Willkie and Humphrey were similar in their emphases on internationalism and civil rights.

Humphrey tended to pattern his political career after less genuine liberal icons— Woodrow Wilson, Al Smith, Franklin Roosevelt, Wendell Willkie— rather than after more devoted and sincere liberal icons—William Jennings Bryan, Richard Pettigrew, William Stone, Burton Wheeler. A model created by political analyst Dwight Macdonald is illustrative of the different types of liberals. In 1948, Macdonald named three types of liberals: nineteenth-century liberals, who were "dangerous men, devoted to high ideals and willing to challenge established institutions"; early twentieth-century liberals, who were "increasingly ineffectual, mildly benevolent figures, trying to straddle the basic issues"; and mid-twentieth-century liberals, who exemplified "the liberal *realpolitiker,* the 'social engineer' who Gets Things Done and thinks in terms of efficient conduct of modern mass-society." Thomas Paine is an example of the first group, Oswald Garrison Villard, an example of the second, and Henry Wallace and Fiorello La Guardia are examples of the third. According to Macdonald, the first type was "principled and effective," the second, "principled and ineffective," and the third, "unprincipled and effective."[42]

If Macdonald's model is valid, then Wallace, one of Hubert Humphrey's seminal ideological inspirations and political role models, was unprincipled, thereby inferior in liberalness to Paine, a leading Jefferson supporter, and Villard, a leading La Follette supporter and eventual admirer of Bryan. Macdonald believed that Bryan was, in comparison to Wallace, the more consistent liberal and the more genuine populist.[43] Vice President Wallace and Mayor La Guardia were associated with the Republican Party early in their careers, but they became staunch supporters of President Franklin Roosevelt. As noted above, FDR was probably Humphrey's preeminent ideological inspiration and practical role model. To a large extent, ideological ancestry explains important differences between pre–New Deal and post–New Deal liberalism.

CHAPTER 5

Modern Philosophy 101

APPROACH, FIDELITY, AND POWER

Ideology vs. Pragmatism

To say that a political figure is nonideological does not mean, of course, that the person lacks an ideology. What a person chooses not to say or not to emphasize says something important about him or her. When the word *ideologue* has a negative connotation in political life—as it does in the United States—people who create and flourish in such an atmosphere do not want to be thought of as having an ideology. Yet they do. To be proudly pragmatic is to make an ideological statement. Most often, it is to reject the ideological Right and the ideological Left in favor of the ideological Center.[1] What is the content of Centrism? At its core, it is not as mushy as it seems. It may be the realpolitik of Machiavelli, it may be an unspoken but unwavering devotion to international monopoly capitalism, or it may be something else. But whatever it is, there is certainly an ideological dimension to nonideological politics. If pragmatism does not mean the actual absence of ideology, what does it mean? It means—for whatever reasons—that the ideology of the pragmatist is not brought to the forefront. It exists, but it generally stays out of sight. It also involves the idea that the end justifies the means. Results are what count, winning is essential, a premium is placed on flexibility, and competence is deemed more important than creed. The pragmatist is often guided more by personality than by philosophy. Pragmatists tend to deny or discourage the role of ideology in interparty contests (between parties) and intraparty contests (within parties).

William Jennings Bryan was a "practical ideologue." He was a relatively successful politician who understood what it takes to win nominations and elections. He was willing to cut corners at times to be successful, but his career was grounded on principle, and he remained generally faithful to this foundation. In his famous Cross of Gold speech at the 1896 Democratic National Convention, Bryan declared that "principles are eternal." Possessing an ideological and moralistic perspective, he "perceived the jumbled landscape of contentious politics not as a sprawling, confused canvas where meaning was difficult to untangle, but a scene that was stark and precise and readily interpreted." His electoral defeats in 1896 and 1900 did not change his attitude toward the principles of liberalism. Distinguishing between the liberal Democrats who stood on the fundamental principles of the Democratic Party as contained in the 1900 Kansas City platform and the conservative Democrats who opposed the platform, Bryan asserted that the former had "fixed principles," stated them "without ambiguity," and invited "judgment upon them"; the latter sanctimoniously spoke in generalities and uttered platitudes but refused to "put their principles into concrete form" or "outline a plan" for dealing with the political problems of the day. Before the 1904 convention, he announced,

> I want my party to write an honest platform, dealing candidly with the questions at issue; I want it to nominate a ticket composed of men who conscientiously believe in the principles of the party as enunciated, and then I want the party to announce to the country, "These are our principles; these are our candidates. Elect them and they will carry out the principles for which they stand; they will not under any circumstances betray the trust committed to their keeping."

During a 1908 meeting with southern Democrats who objected to his adoption of "impossible" issues, Bryan exclaimed, "Win! Win! That's it! You want to win! You would sacrifice principle for success. I would not. . . . I intend, if I am the candidate, that the principles shall be preserved."[2]

Bryan believed that interparty contests should be waged on the basis of ideology. Speaking abroad, he declared,

> Jefferson said that there were naturally two parties in every country—a democratic party and an aristocratic party . . . Go into any country in Europe, and you will find a party of some name that is trying to increase the participation of the people in the government, and you will also find a party of some name which is obstructing every step toward popular government.

Instead of trying to make the Democratic Party so much like the Republican Party that it would get a few Republicans by mistake, Bryan wanted to make it so different from the Republican Party that it would get those "who turn from the mammon-serving leaders of that party and seek a party that puts the man before the dollar."[3]

Bryan also maintained that intraparty contests should be waged on the basis of ideology. Throughout his political career, he drew a clear distinction between democrats and plutocrats within the Democratic Party. Warning against the type of harmony promoted by conservative Democrats, in 1901, Bryan wrote, "No process has ever been discovered for welding together into one harmonious party men who differ in conviction and desire the triumph of opposite principles." A decade later, he warned House Speaker Champ Clark (D-MO) that when he boasted of trying to get conservatives and progressives together he was overlooking the fundamental difference "between those who have three times defeated the party and those who have supported it." Bryan predicted that the Wall Street crowd would be at the 1912 Democratic convention "ready to sell harmony at wholesale at the regular price, namely the betrayal of the public."[4]

Liberals in the Vital Center and Middle Way traditions have an ideology even if it is undefined or unacknowledged. It includes but is not limited to pragmatism. Famed Florentine diplomat Niccolò Machiavelli was a student, advocate, and practitioner of pragmatic politics. William Allen White noted the occasional Machiavellianism of Theodore Roosevelt and Woodrow Wilson. Franklin Roosevelt has been compared to Machiavelli's Prince.[5] Given his generally straightforward and principled approach to politics, few would accuse Bryan of being Machiavellian, or credit him with being the same, if the term is equated with astuteness and efficiency.

Woodrow Wilson was Hubert Humphrey's first political hero. Referring to Wilson, historian Ronald Schaffer wrote,

> An aura of idealism enveloped him, and his advisors understood that when they wanted to bring up some practical policy, it was wise to frame it in principled arguments; yet he operated in a highly pragmatic way, shifting positions when it was expedient to do so, deceiving his listeners at times, acting, in other words, like a normal politician.

Franklin Roosevelt was Humphrey's political hero during his early adult years. FDR was clearly a pragmatist. Humphrey approvingly noted that in attacking the Depression, the New Deal was not "bound by any creed or 'party line,'" but rather, in part, "adopted the trial-and-error method." Roosevelt replaced the Democratic Party's traditional commitment to specific Jeffersonian tenets with "a shapeless Progressive synthesis accenting a pragmatic approach to grave national problems." In 1936, Walter Lippmann noted that there were no great issues separating Roosevelt and Landon. The sound and fury associated with FDR's denunciation of economic royalists and his rivals' denunciation of socialism evidently signified little or nothing. By this time, many liberals in the Bryan-La Follette tradition were concerned about the expediency of President Roosevelt and his supporters. For example, John Haynes Holmes wrote, "If we are looking for the bankruptcy of liberalism, . . . here it is. . . . I find scarcely a trace of principle or idea. . . . I discover no clear cut philosophy of life." A decade later, Dwight Macdonald observed,

> A "liberal" used to be one who favored the spread of liberty: freedom of thought, more humane economic arrangements, the "popular" cause in general against kings or bankers or governments. Today it has become one who favors the extension of governmental authority for reasons of efficiency, especially in wartime. The modern liberal generally calls himself a "progressive," a semantically interesting shift from a term which implies *values* to a term which implies *process*.[6]

Franklin Roosevelt's ideological successors within the Democratic Party extended his pragmatic legacy throughout the 1940s and 1950s. Referring to "the ideological divisions within the government and the electorate" in the mid-1950s, Senator Barry Goldwater (R-AZ) recalled, "The two camps were labeled 'conservative' and 'liberal.' To my mind, this convenient categorization concealed more than it revealed. Many of the New Deal-Fair Deal men in government were virtually devoid of philosophical commitment. They simply asked, 'What's in it for me?'" Referring to the Eisenhower "Right" and the Stevenson "Center," sociologist C. Wright Mills commented at the time, "Public relations fills any need for 'ideology,' and public relations are something you hire. Just now, the elite of wealth and power do not feel in need of any ideology." Political scientist Rick Tilman contrasted Mills with the Roosevelt-Truman-Stevenson-Humphrey stream of liberalism within the Democratic Party:

> It is interesting to note that Arthur Schlesinger, Jr.'s "vital center," which prides itself on being "pragmatic," failed to recognize pragmatism in the American tradition in Mills' thought. One reason for this oversight is that "pragmatism" has come to mean little more than opportunism, and since Mills' politics was obviously not based on expediency the pragmatic residues in his thought have largely escaped the notice of political centrists.

Tilman placed Mills in the American radical tradition of Thomas Jefferson and Thomas Paine, Eugene Debs and Norman Thomas.[7]

Bryan and Humphrey were both outgoing, talkative men, but there was a marked contrast in their utterances: Bryan's words were full of emotion and reason, but Humphrey's were almost pure emotion. Bryan named names and set forth logical arguments; Humphrey spoke in generalities with little logic. Humphrey had a master's degree in political science and became vice president of the American Political Science Association long after receiving his degree. Despite his educational achievements and professional affiliations, Humphrey was not an intellectual or even a man of ideas. A friendly biographer of Humphrey wrote,

> He reads quite a bit, but swiftly and in a fragmentary, journalistic way, reports, magazines, and sometimes a topical book of the hour. He does not read long books for work or for play . . . He likes action. . . . In general he never seems to enjoy being alone, he never says he is looking forward to a quiet time in which to read and think over some report. . . . He does not seem to be interested in constructing a philosophy of government.[8]

In 1965, a reporter pointed out, "In reality, Humphrey is an untheoretical man. His philosophy of government is close to the ground, emotional rather than intellectual." At the same time, another friendly biographer remarked that Humphrey's "courage is not a sort of rigid devotion to doctrine, exemplified to some extent by such men as William Jennings Bryan and Robert La Follette; he is far more practical and politically sensitive than either of those progressives." Biographer Carl Solberg also drew a distinction between Bryan and La Follette on the one hand and Humphrey on the other: "He differed from his great midwestern predecessors, outsiders all their lives . . . By the ingratiating force of his personality, Humphrey carried his Progressive principles into the mainstream of American politics. . . . He was a pragmatic Progressive." Bryan also possessed an ingratiating personality, so Humphrey's "likeability quotient" was not the key difference. The key difference was Humphrey's pragmatism. His pragmatic approach to politics has been recognized by friends, enemies, and scholars alike.[9]

Humphrey's pragmatism was clearly indicated by his writings and actions throughout his long career. In 1939, he wrote,

> Governments are not thought out in abstraction but spring from practical needs and if they are to endure they must meet the requirements of practice. In other words, the final test of good government is the pragmatic test. . . . To condemn or praise New Deal programs by a simple comparison with the days of 1800 is neither scientific nor reasonable.

The traditional agrarian populists within the Minnesota Farmer-Labor Party opposed fusion with the Democrats during the 1940s. These Farmer-Laborites "were honest, progressive, principled people who thought of the Democratic party as being one of patronage only and without real ideology." Humphrey, who admired President Roosevelt for his lack of ideology, was a prime mover behind the DFL merger. Humphrey was also involved in the 1948 effort by Americans for Democratic Action (ADA) to find an alternative to President Truman for the Democratic presidential nomination. A Humphrey biographer noted that the dump-Truman movement was about style and viability, not ideology: "The product of Missouri's Pendergast machine, Truman, in the eyes of the ADA, just didn't have the grace or the charisma of an FDR. Even more important, he was considered a dead duck with the voters." In a 1955 article for *American Scholar*, Humphrey contended that the "liberal approach must be experimental, the solution tentative, the test pragmatic" and that "no particular manifestation of our basic social institutions is sacrosanct or immutable."[10]

Humphrey's assessment of why he lost the 1960 West Virginia primary to John F. Kennedy is instructive. In his autobiography, he explains, "I was whipped not only by money and organization but, more particularly, by an extraordinary man. Jack Kennedy was at his best in West Virginia, and his best was without equal. . . . He brought at least a ray of sunshine and glory and glamour into that gloomy, gray atmosphere. He brought hope to people who had none." Issues had nothing to do with the West Virginia campaign: it was a case of politics being devoid of substance. Humphrey gives us a personality-driven analysis. We might conclude from his words that Marlon Brando or Marilyn Monroe could have contributed as much to the lives of West Virginians had they and their entourages spent some time in the state. Senator Humphrey approved of President Kennedy's pragmatic approach to public policy.[11]

Although he called himself a liberal, Humphrey was an advocate of contentless ideology. In 1964, he defined "the liberal approach" as an "informed, common-sense, and compassionate approach." According to Humphrey, American liberalism "is, basically, an attitude toward life rather than a dogma—characterized by a warm heart, an open mind, and willing hands." In the midst of a defense of big business, he declared, "It is high time that the traditional hostility between the intellectuals on the one hand and [corporate] management on the other was ended. Doctrinaire thinking has no place in the vital and proliferating society of the 1960's."[12] Not surprisingly, *Fortune* saw in Humphrey an example of "a replacement of ideology by pragmatic economics." In the early 1960s, one biographer noted, "There is a feeling that the glibness and superficiality that his critics believe to be characteristic of Humphrey's views are also related to opportunism and to a basic political drive to take advantage of first one thing and then another." Vice President Humphrey's conduct in 1968 was widely seen as illustrative of this pragmatism and opportunism. Carl Solberg commented, "It was ironic—and it must be said, pitiable—that in the period from [Robert] Kennedy's death to the [Democratic national] convention in August, this most voluble of American politicians had almost nothing to say about the issues that troubled his fellow citizens most. As he himself said, he 'ducked and bobbed.'"[13]

As he makes clear in his 1976 autobiography, Humphrey retained his pragmatism to the end of his long career. According to Humphrey, "The American people are not dogmatists or doctrinaire, but pragmatists. Ideology is foreign to most Americans." While rejecting "vacuous expediency," he also rejected ideological "rigidity." On the one hand, Humphrey acknowledged some value to the existence of political ideologues, calling them "irritating but indispensable"; on the other hand, he made clear that he thoroughly disliked them. Toward the end of the book, he summed up his viewpoint by saying, "It is a fact of American life that politics is not a static discipline. It shifts and alters its preoccupations to correspond with new ideas, new events, and new perceptions in the greater society that surrounds it. And that is as it should be." Noting the "unusual closeness and collaboration" between President Carter and Senator Humphrey in 1977, one analyst found it strange that Humphrey, "an exuberantly outspoken ideological liberal," and Carter, a "pragmatic and purposefully non-ideological outsider," became allies.[14] The explanation is rather simple. Humphrey had always been exuberant, but he had never been ideological. This is why he could so easily work with the pragmatic and nonideological Carter.

One aspect of pragmatism is the practice of being guided more by personality than by philosophy. Humphrey was guided by his heart, not by his mind. For Bryan, liberalism was a type of ideology, whereas for Humphrey, liberalism was a type of personality or emotion. Humphrey equated it with sympathy or niceness. A difference in substance can even be detected in the nicknames widely ascribed to the two politicians: the "Great Commoner" referred to Bryan's populism, and the "Happy Warrior," to Humphrey's personality. More than useful, it is necessary to spend some time dealing with the psychology and feelings of Hubert Horatio Humphrey because his political philosophy was, to a large extent, subsumed within his personality. According to his close friend Edgar Berman, Humphrey "was governed by his heart rather than his head." Throughout the 1960s and 1970s, Humphrey was the nation's premier "bleeding-heart liberal." Berman noted that Humphrey was "unashamed of his love, his compassion, and his interest in people."[15]

Humphrey's politics of personality produced some incongruent results. Humphrey "hated dispute, strife, and personal confrontation of any kind. Even in language he hated violence and vulgarity." Despite this personality trait, Humphrey was an enthusiastic supporter of every U.S. war from 1938 to 1978. If Humphrey had relied more on reason and less on emotion, he might have produced policy positions more consistent with his personal character. There are other indications that Humphrey's disinterest in ideology adversely affected his political stature. Despite his reputation as a great orator, Humphrey's speech in favor of sustaining President Truman's veto of the 1950 Internal Security Act was bombastic and jumbled. It reads like an emotional outburst without reason or order. Similarly, when Humphrey responded to incisive and well-documented criticism of the 1974 Foreign Assistance Act by a fellow liberal Democrat, his words were evasive, simplistic, and blustery. All of his "by golly," "good grief," "it's great," and "pleased as punch" utterances could lead one to suspect that there was a sort of intellectual flabbiness to Humphrey that was not present in Bryan.[16] Although we must also acknowledge the possible influence of Minnesota colloquialism, Humphrey's quaintly colorful language may have reflected his penchant for emotion rather than ideology. Bryan's thought has been criticized for being unoriginal, rooted in religion, and stuck in the past, but it was thought nonetheless. In contrast, Humphrey's words give the impression of almost pure feeling—with thought, inferior or otherwise, being noticeably absent.

In his autobiography, Humphrey bemoaned the fact that the "Eisenhower years were not filled with fun and laughter" because they were dominated by "serious businessman types." The accent was on the seriousness, not on the business ties, of Eisenhower's appointees. The "serious businessman types" were not criticized for sucking democracy and justice out of Washington; they were criticized for sucking fun and laughter out of Washington. Referring to Humphrey in 1959, a biographer wrote, "His close associates say, 'It would be more fun to live in the United States if he were President.'" It is difficult to imagine close associates of Bryan saying this in 1895. In 1964, Humphrey declared, "I was thinking how lucky we are to be Democrats. Look at the fun we have. Look at the joy we have. Look at the spirit we have!" When he announced his candidacy for president in 1968 amidst America's war divisiveness, racial strife, and cultural turmoil, he called for "the politics of happiness" and "the politics of joy." Reacting to the shooting of Robert F. Kennedy, Humphrey said, "This horrible business just takes all the fun out of politics." For a happy warrior who practiced "the politics of joy," politics was more a matter of personality and pleasure than ideology and issues. After losing the 1968 election to Richard Nixon, Humphrey told a friend, "Imagine Nixon, the president of the United States—no warmth, no spirit, no heart. I guess I've let everybody—a whole nation—down." Humphrey's revulsion at the thought of Nixon in the Oval Office was cast in terms of personality, not ideology. It was not that Nixon was too pluto-cratic, too militaristic, too imperialistic; rather, it was that Nixon was too cold, too stolid, too miserly. Humphrey was plagued by self-doubt and guilt when he reflected on the 1968 election results. "He was haunted by those who voted against him, but forgot the almost equal number who voted for him. . . . Over and over again, he talked about his 'friends' who had denied him their support."[17] For Humphrey, everything was personal; everything was about friendship. Humphrey's response to his 1968 defeat can be con-trasted with Bryan's reaction to Democrats who deserted the ticket in 1896. Rather than taking the defections personally, Bryan recognized that Demo-cratic Party supporters refused to vote for him because they were closer in ideology to McKinley or Palmer. Rather than engaging in self-pity, Bryan publicly condemned the apostasy of Cleveland Democrats.

In a personal sense, it appears that Humphrey was a somewhat weak and self-absorbed man. He "could never stand even insinuations of unfairness about himself," "couldn't stand not to be loved," and "abhorred strained re-lations." In his speeches and writings, Humphrey condemned his political opponents for being mean, not for being plutocratic or ideologically wrong. In the late 1940s, Humphrey's pro-Truman stance turned left-wing mem-bers of the Minnesota Democratic-Farmer-Labor Party "meanly against" him, and when he helped to found Americans for Democratic Action, their "meanness boiled into hate." Conservative Republicans in the U.S. Senate in the late 1940s and early 1950s were "critical and cynical," nurtured "a nega-tivism in politics that brought forth the worst in people," and were respon-sible for a "miasma of meanness." Nearly all of the Republican senators were either "lackluster or mean." Humphrey decried the "meanness" of the Mc-Carthy Era. Years after the fact, he disagreed with the suggestion that it would have been politically wise to have broken with President Johnson in 1968, saying, "Johnson could be very mean if he wanted to be." When asked in 1975 why he was still regarded as a viable presidential candidate after his 1968 and 1972 defeats, Humphrey responded, "I've never hated people. I've never indulged in any mean, nasty attacks on even my Republican friends. I really believe that sowing of seed is coming home in the harvest. There's a lot of goodwill."[18] According to Humphrey, his personality was the key to his political viability. Ironically, despite Humphrey's almost obsessive dislike and fear of nasty people, he was supported for president in 1968 by President Lyndon Johnson and Mayor Richard Daley—who were hardly considered nice people—and in 1968, 1972, and 1976 by Congressman Wayne Hays (D-OH)—who was long known as the meanest man in Congress.

After his 1968 election loss, Humphrey "could not shake the bleak thoughts of a nonpolitical future." He felt that he had fallen "into the seventh circle of Dante's hell reserved for dispossessed politicians."[19] Humphrey's seemingly self-pitying, self-absorbed reaction can be contrasted with Bryan's following his 1896, 1900, and 1908 losses. After his 1900 defeat, Bryan took it upon himself to found *The Commoner*, an ideological magazine designed to help him stay in touch with his supporters and publicize the issues of the day. After his 1968 defeat, Humphrey accepted a public relations job with an encyclopedia company owned by his friend Senator William Benton. He had no constituency with which to work or burning issues to advance. Humphrey did make a political comeback by running for the Senate in 1970 and for president in 1972, but his initial reaction was telling.

All successful politicians possess a certain degree of egotism and an inflated sense of self-importance. William Jennings Bryan was no exception to this rule. Hubert Humphrey's self-absorption was perhaps more apparent because he did not possess the ideological commitment of Bryan. Lacking an explicit commitment to ideology, Humphrey's public preoccupation with his own feelings and his own goodness stand out in bold relief. He had a curious way of referring to himself in the third person. He was constantly in need of personal positive reinforcement from others, and if he did not receive it, he resorted to self-congratulation. Humphrey once angrily told an unfriendly newspaper publisher that he only wished that his paper had Minnesota "as much at heart" as he did. During the 1968 campaign, a black man from a poor part of Philadelphia clasped Humphrey's hand and slowly said, "Mr. Humphrey, you're the only hope we have. If you don't make it, we got no chance at all." Humphrey responded, "I've never let you down yet, and I don't intend to start now. Be of good cheer, my friend; we're going to do it together." When he returned to his limousine, the vice president of the United States said, "Dear God, I wish Lyndon Johnson, Gene McCarthy, and all those college professors were on the street to hear that one. . . . I have to win if for no other reason than for those people. . . . Do you think Mr. Nixon has any plans for that man's problems?"[20] Humphrey's messianic interaction with the desperate man, his unawareness of the incongruity of the savior of the poor returning to a luxurious automobile to be whisked away to the next fundraising dinner or photo opportunity, and his flattered and self-righteous response to the incident are revealing of his character.

Criticizing the press for misconstruing the phrase *the politics of joy* in Humphrey's 1968 announcement speech, his close friend Edgar Berman wrote, "If they didn't know he was aware of the world's misery, who did? Remedying it was his benchmark for twenty years in the Senate. Who could have been more upset by the deaths of Martin Luther King or Bobby, or the war?"[21] Berman's comments are revealing and seem to reflect Humphrey's own megalomania. It is possible that an impoverished black person in the South was more upset by King's death than was Humphrey, an affluent white person in the North. It is conceivable that Ethel Kennedy was more upset by Kennedy's death than was Humphrey, one of Bobby's political opponents throughout the 1960s. It is likely that the parent of a dead soldier was more upset by the war than was Humphrey, a consistent public supporter of American involvement in Vietnam who had no large personal stake in the war other than his own political career. It is interesting that "remedying misery" is viewed as Humphrey's main contribution in the Senate, not "fighting for justice" or "pushing for democracy." Again, we see the emotional, nonideological nature of Humphrey's politics. Misery is a feeling, not an issue or a principle. Humphrey sounds like a glorified social worker, a social worker with access to the U.S. Treasury and the world's media. He seems to have been more of a do-gooder than a progressive of the type inhabiting the Senate chambers in 1918. Often derided as a bleeding-heart liberal, Humphrey may have been more of a bleeding heart than a liberal. Time and time again, Humphrey's bleeding heart led him to turn his back on liberal principles. Unfortunately, Humphrey's heart often bled for himself. His strong need to be liked by everyone—including the rich and powerful—often led him to reluctantly kowtow to Lyndon Johnson and other representatives of the rich and powerful even at the expense of the poor and weak. If we assume the most liberal of intentions in Humphrey's case, it must still be said that his voracious need for social acceptance was his Achilles' heel. Since he spent most of his adult life as a leading politician, Humphrey's hunger for acceptance was usually satisfied by high-ranking government officials, big businessmen, and military officers far removed from the lives of most Americans. This being the case, it is not surprising that Humphrey often went along with illiberal initiatives pushed by the "big boys" while simultaneously maintaining his liberal reputation by supporting multitudes of government programs designed to help the "little people." If the illiberal nature of an initiative was widely recognized, Humphrey justified his action by saying that he would be unable to do the latter if he did not first do the former. In other words, if he did not do whatever it took to gain office, he would be unable to help people.

Pragmatists tend to deny or discourage the role of ideology in interparty contests. This was the case with Humphrey and his political allies. Despite the hardcore liberal, if not socialist, reputation of Americans for Democratic Action, the words of ADA founders such as Arthur Schlesinger Jr. and Humphrey make clear that ADA liberals did not see party politics in ideo-

logical terms. Schlesinger "asserted that fundamental differences in tempera-
ment and interest divide people into liberal and conservative camps"; para-
phrasing Emerson, he believed that humankind is "divided between the
Party of Conservatism and the Party of Innovation, between the Past and
the Future, between Memory and Hope." Innovation is a trait, the future is
a time, and hope is an attitude. None of these characteristics of liberalism are
ideological in nature. According to Berman, Humphrey

> believed that Americans wanted to be tied to an ideology—and that's
> what parties stood for. He would jokingly cite the fundamental differ-
> ences between Democrats and Republicans. "The Democrat fights for a
> chicken in every pot and has fun doing it; the Republican wants only
> Lobster Cardinal for his friends and neighbors and always looks like he's
> bilious."[22]

Despite Berman's mention of ideology as the basis of political parties, the
ideological tenets cited by Humphrey are not very ideological. The first
tenet—a chicken in every pot vs. lobster cardinal for his friends and
neighbors—is ideological in a superficial way if it is ideological at all. It is
an endorsement of the welfare state, but this endorsement could be reduced to what is really only a personality trait (generosity vs. selfishness).
The second tenet—having fun vs. looking bilious—is a personality trait
(cheerfulness vs. dourness). Assuming Berman's words are representative of
Humphrey's basic views, for Humphrey, the essence of the struggle between liberals/Democrats and conservatives/Republicans consisted of generosity and cheerfulness vs. selfishness and dourness. He saw no need for
party battles if members on both sides of the aisle were welfare statists who
treated people nicely. In this way, Humphrey was a leading advocate of a
bipartisanship of the Center.
   Humphrey was a Republican in 1940. He approvingly noted that the
"outstanding factor" of the Republican and Democratic platforms that year
"was not their opposition in principles of public policy, but their essential
agreement." In his autobiography, Humphrey praised President Eisenhower
for helping to defuse "the explosive nature of American politics" by rising
above "rabid" partisanship. He praised Senator Lyndon Johnson for rising
above partisanship during the Eisenhower years, noting that he "tried to co-
operate with the President on international affairs and even to work with
the Administration on domestic issues where that was possible." Schlesinger
endorsed John Kennedy for the 1960 Democratic presidential nomination after
Adlai Stevenson declined to enter the primaries. During the fall campaign, the

historian wrote *Kennedy or Nixon: Does It Make Any Difference?* in an attempt to dispel "the favorite cliché of 1960"—that there was little difference between the two candidates and the two parties. Stephen Depoe commented, "Schlesinger's analysis of the two candidates reflected an interest more in style than in substance. . . . Most of the book delved into the personalities of the two candidates. Frankly, it was true that Nixon and Kennedy differed little on the substantive issues." CBS commentator Eric Sevareid noted at the time that Nixon and Kennedy were both "sharp, opportunistic, devoid of strong convictions and deep passions, with no commitment except to personal advancement."[23] Although Humphrey had opposed Kennedy during the 1960 primaries, he was a devoted supporter after the election.

Schlesinger and Humphrey approved of continual cooperation between the two major political parties and believed that both parties should be led by centrists of goodwill, so voters would end up with a good candidate regardless of which party they chose to support. This view is unlike the view of Jefferson and Bryan, who maintained that the two parties should be quite distinct to give voters a clear and contrasting choice between liberals and conservatives. Political analyst Kevin Phillips, a present-day Jeffersonian, comments,

> America's political duopoly has another unique characteristic that makes little sense to politicians elsewhere—frequent bipartisanship. Hallowed in the United States, the practice is observed in few other countries, except in wartime, because those party structures pivot on deep philosophic and interest-group differences. . . . [Bipartisanship in the U.S. frequently involves] a suspension of electoral combat to orchestrate some outcome with no great public support but a high priority among key elites. . . . Bipartisanship is too often a *failure* of the party system—a failure of both political responsibility and of representative government—and not a *triumph*.[24]

Pragmatists also tend to deny or discourage the role of ideology in intraparty contests. The existence of Humphrey and Kennedy "fraternities" within the Democratic Party is one sign of the absence of ideology in intraparty contests. The groupings are called *fraternities* because they are not schools of thought. They are products of personal electoral rivalry, loyalty based on friendship, and stylistic differences. The Humphrey and Kennedy fraternities arose out of the 1956 contest for the Democratic vice-presidential nomination. In virtually every presidential nomination contest since that time, one or more representatives from each fraternity have been major candidates. Thus, we have seen men like Humphrey, Muskie, Jackson, Clinton,

Gore, and Lieberman run against men like the Kennedy brothers, McGovern, Shriver, Dukakis, Bradley, and Kerry. Both fraternities are dominated by pragmatists who are ideological centrists. The only real ideological conflicts within the Democratic Party since the 1960s have involved insurgent efforts by conservative Jeffersonians and liberal Jeffersonians.

Commitment vs. Compromise

As a practical ideologue, William Jennings Bryan made occasional compromises. Referring to the demoralization of ideals in the realm of politics, Bryan said, "Instead of asking 'Is it right?' we are tempted to ask 'Will it pay?' and 'Will it win?' As a result the public conscience is becoming seared and the public service debauched." Bryan was willing to engage in minor retreats to win a victory at a later time. He recognized the reality of political compromise, but instead of making him more moderate in his positions, it made him more radical. He often told his wife, "All progress comes through compromise; not a compromise of principle, but an adjustment between the more radical and the less radical positions. If I begin far in advance, when the compromise is made, our position will be much ahead of the place I would have secured by a less advanced standpoint." Mrs. Bryan adds, "And he would take the extreme stand, submitting to misunderstanding and ridicule for the sake of the compromise which would be most advantageous to the cause." In 1901, Bryan wrote, "Those who fight for principle may mourn over a defeat, but their purpose is not shaken because they are doing what they believe they ought to and find their reward in the consciousness of duty done."[25]

Bryan rejected "the nonmoral, nonreligious styles of thought" that "value compromise and consensus." According to political scientist Louis Koenig, Bryan's beliefs included "a hard core held with closest tenacity; an intermediate region, important, vigorously asserted, and to a degree open to compromise; and a peripheral region deemed of minor importance and readily available for compromise." Koenig adds that the third, readily compromisable region was "virtually nonexistent" because "few beliefs were peripheral with Bryan." Following Bryan's nomination by Democrats in 1896, leading party members wanted John McLean of Ohio to be his running mate. Believing that McLean represented the forces of organized wealth, Bryan flatly rejected the idea, saying, "If that man is nominated for vice president I would decline the nomination for the presidency. I would not run on a ticket with that man." Bryan refused to be moved on the subject and the leaders were forced to choose a different vice-presidential candidate. Campaigning in 1896, Bryan said, "One of the papers said that I 'lacked dignity.' I have been looking into the matter, and have decided that I would rather have it said that I lacked dignity than have it said that I lack backbone to meet the enemies of the Government who work against its welfare in Wall street." Bryan refused to set aside his support for free silver and opposition to trusts to gain the support of industrialist Andrew Carnegie for a 1900 campaign stressing anti-imperialism while minimizing socioeconomic issues. Possessing an unusual "loyalty to past promises," he "found altering any of his public positions almost impossible."[26]

Bryan's actions as a member of the Resolutions Committee of the 1904 Democratic National Convention demonstrate his tendencies toward ideological, committed politics rather than pragmatic, compromising politics. He stood firm in defense of the controversial planks of the 1896 and 1900 platforms, despite strong opposition from a majority of committee members, including old friends and allies. During his seconding speech for Senator Francis Cockrell (D–MO) at the St. Louis convention, Bryan said, "You may dispute whether I have fought a good fight, you may dispute whether I have finished my course, but you cannot deny that I have kept the faith." Bryan resolutely opposed the nomination of ultimate nominee Alton Parker, and he campaigned only minimally for Parker in the fall. He believed that the Democratic Party "must stand for democratic ideals and it must apply democratic principles to all questions regardless of the prospect of temporary victory or the danger of temporary defeat." In the fall of 1908, Bryan was told by conservative Democrats during a private dinner "that New York, and thus the White House, would be his if the business interests were assured that he would name friendly men like George Gray to fill Supreme Court vacancies." Bryan politely refused to give such an assurance. The next day, Josephus Daniels was told that Bryan had "defeated himself" by refusing to go along with the offer.[27]

When Bryan did occasionally make substantial compromises of principle, those compromises were usually linked to his sense of partisanship. From 1896 to 1912, he was the leader of the national Democratic Party, and he took his role seriously. He understood that many party leaders were more plutocratic than democratic. He did not hesitate to denounce prominent conservative Democrats by name, but he retained a sense of loyalty to the party. For this reason, he made some notable compromises during his career. Bryan was not as pure as many leaders of the People's Party desired. He accepted support from the corrupt Tammany Hall machine in New York City. He sometimes supported ideologically acceptable Democratic candidates against prominent liberal Republican officeholders. He collaborated with President Wilson on a number of illiberal measures while heading the State Department. He campaigned for conservative John W. Davis in the fall of 1924 despite being much closer in ideology to third-party candidate Robert La Follette (in fairness, the presence of brother Charles Bryan on the Democratic ticket probably accounts for Bryan's active participation). When Bryan died, liberal Senator George Norris (R-NE) praised a number of aspects of Bryan's life but was critical of his partisanship. During the first decade of the century, Bryan said, "It is more important that reform shall be secured than that those reforms shall come through any particular party." He did not always act in accordance with these words that urged support for principle above party, but on some important occasions he practiced what he preached. For example, Bryan sat out general election campaigns when his party nominated conservatives Cleveland in 1892 and Cox in 1920. Despite his latter-day affluence and the conservative turn of his party and the nation as a whole, Bryan remained a strong liberal during the 1920s.[28]

While Bryan tended to have an either/or mentality, Hubert Humphrey had a both/and mentality. Political scientist G. Theodore Mitau points out, "Despite instances of rhetorical extremes and not infrequent hyperbole, Humphrey was in some ways the most political of men, comfortable with compromise and moderation. Unlike so many earlier voices of Midwest populism . . . Humphrey's brand of politics stressed coalition-building and consensus." As mayor of Minneapolis in the mid-1940s, Humphrey was known for "negotiation and conciliation" rather than "rigid decisions" and "frontal attacks." According to biographer Michael Amrine, the great difference between young Bryan and young Humphrey is that the latter came to "understand the realities of American politics as distinguished from the debater's dream of 'the forces of evil' being overcome by the golden voices of prophets of the people."[29]

In 1959, Amrine noted, "Senator Humphrey's slogan, sometimes used in campaigns, has been, 'He gets things done.' Humphrey will often 'compromise' in the sense that he would rather see only a part of some program implemented than none of it. But his purpose is to get something done." Humphrey was a "strong believer in compromise." As he explained,

> Liberals sometimes demand a purity of performance which I couldn't honestly give. Compromise isn't a dirty word, and it isn't a sellout—you don't have to sacrifice your principles. Frequently, it's the only way to get things done. Even a Republican can see that, unless you're the winner, all or nothing isn't as good as fifty-fifty.

In his autobiography, Humphrey praised compromise and warned of the dangers that can accompany "self-righteous" commitment: "Compromise is not a dirty word. . . . In a democratic, pluralistic society, legislation ought to be a compromise of differing points of view, of different interests." He thought that "to make losing a habit in the name of moral principle or liberal convictions is to fail to govern and to demonstrate the incapacity to persuade and convince and to develop a majority." As a senator, Humphrey found that one "can end up with nothing two ways: by being so rigid that the entire legislation is lost, or so flexible that your opponents gut the bill." Recommending "strong and sensible arguments" coupled with "a responsible compromise," Humphrey argued, "It is better to gain a foot than to stand still, even when you seek to gain a mile." He recognized the unhappiness this approach produced among some members of his liberal base: "When a liberal senator adopts this approach, he is bound to engage the wrath and disdain of some of his fellow liberals, particularly in the intellectual community. There are those people who feel that any compromise is a sell-out."[30] Humphrey dismissed these liberal critics for their lack of practicality, experience, and common sense.

One biographer of Humphrey wrote, "He takes great risks only when great challenges or his basic convictions are involved. . . . He is willing to stand alone, to endure the indifference of others to causes which command his attention, and to risk even the mockery of a prevailing public attitude." Humphrey's "courageous" civil rights speech at the 1948 Democratic National Convention is cited as an example of Humphrey's willingness to "advocate forcefully a position even when he fully understands the extent to which that advocacy will endanger his own popularity or political future."[31] While it is true that on rare occasions he took positions from which he refused to move, according to Amrine, Humphrey's political career from the beginning was marked by compromise. He cannot with justification be pointed to as an example of a political risk taker. Even at the 1948 convention, Humphrey did not stand alone: he was supported by Americans for Democratic Action, by big city bosses, and by a majority of the delegates. His actions may have incurred the momentary displeasure of President Truman, but they also had attendant benefits for both Humphrey and the Democratic Party. Humphrey's actions propelled him into the national spotlight, and the Democratic Party was able to undercut the appeal of Henry Wallace. Even if the 1948 speech is granted as an example of a purely risk-filled, uncompromising incident, it is difficult to think of many other examples of commitment in Humphrey's career that exposed him to indifference, mockery, or danger. When his actions produced such a reaction, it usually emanated from ideologues who were dismissed as extremists, radicals, and the lunatic fringe by Humphrey and his allies.

Biographer Allan Ryskind points out that Humphrey proved himself "a remarkably resourceful politician" during his first term in the U.S. Senate. He entered Congress with a reputation for being a "flaming radical," an "enemy of Dixie," and an opponent of President Truman; such attributes "may have been useful in gaining him a seat in the U.S. Senate, but they seemed hardly likely to promote his political career once he was there." The Democratic Party in the Senate was controlled by Truman and the southern Bourbons. Unlike many of the body's most prominent liberals, Humphrey "was not left out in the cold when it came to shaping Democratic policy. He seriously coveted power and developed the knack of obtaining it." He "became Truman's most fervent supporter and legislative ball carrier" and a friend of the southern leaders. Throughout the 1950s, Humphrey did not "seriously buck the Democratic leadership when he served in the Senate." In 1975, when Humphrey was asked about attacks on him for being a compromiser, he responded, "Once in a while you run into this new breed, and they try to make politics into a religion. Some of these people think I'm always selling out because I'm perfectly willing to take half a loaf. . . . Well, I'm not pure. My name is not Ivory Soap. It's Hubert Humphrey. I try to get things done."[32]

According to Martin Luther King Jr., "The ultimate measure of a man is not where he stands in moments of comfort and convenience, but where he stands at times of challenge and controversy." Humphrey's commitment to principle tends to compare unfavorably with Bryan's in the context of challenging and controversial times. Opposed to President Wilson's prowar policy, Secretary of State Bryan resigned from the administration. Supposedly opposed to President Johnson's prowar policy, Vice President Humphrey did not break with the administration. Instead, he relied on the president to gain his party's presidential nomination.

There were significant differences between Bryan and Humphrey in their relations with presidents who belonged to their own party. In 1968, Allan Ryskind observed, "It is a curious fact of life that Humphrey—known for his deep liberal convictions—has never had a serious public dispute with a Democratic President since he came to the Senate." Bryan had serious public disputes with Democratic presidents Cleveland and Wilson. He supported Weaver over Cleveland in 1892, criticized Cleveland throughout his second term, and defied Cleveland at the 1896 convention. Bryan and Cleveland continued to publicly oppose one another until the latter's death in 1908. Serving as a loyal follower of a seemingly sadistic president,

Humphrey's conduct as vice president was viewed by many political insiders as pathetic if not contemptible. Humphrey was a Johnson apologist. He "made all sorts of excuses" for the president's coerciveness, deviousness, and broken promises.[33]

Referring to Humphrey in 1968, Charles Garrettson asserted, "He could have considered William Jennings Bryan's justification for resigning as secretary of state (namely, as a protest over Woodrow Wilson's commitment to entering World War I), yet the circumstances were drastically different— Bryan was not, in this case, an elected official." Actually, it was not a "drastically different" circumstance since the vice president is basically a tagalong. Despite being formally elected by the electoral college, Humphrey owed his office to Johnson, not to the American people. There was precedent for a vice-presidential resignation: John Calhoun resigned in 1832 over differences with Andrew Jackson. If Humphrey felt strongly about Johnson's Vietnam policy and Johnson's demeaning treatment of the vice president, there was another option available to him besides resignation. He could have publicly repudiated Johnson and fought for the presidential nomination on the strength of his own twenty-five-year record. Explaining one of his many carefully worded statements on the Vietnam War, in September 1968, Humphey told a friend, "Johnson is a vindictive man. I know what he's done to me, but he could do worse. You have to be practical and examine what we'd lose if he isn't handled with kid gloves. One state—Texas—could do it, and Nixon would be president. Then where would we be?" In 1921, Bryan refused to serve on a committee to raise funds for a foundation created to honor the late President Wilson because he could not "endorse with enthusiasm" Wilson's entire record. In 1974, Humphrey paid tribute to the late President Johnson with gushing words of praise.[34]

What accounts for Humphrey's embrace of compromise as a political strategy? On a philosophical level, he believed that the give-and-take of politics required one to compromise to get half a loaf. There were also personal reasons that may partly explain his willingness to compromise on so many occasions. In the case of Bryan, his personal religion—with its moral absolutes and dichotomous, good vs. evil perspective—helps to explain his strategy of commitment. For Humphrey, personal ambition, optimism, and need may help to explain his strategy of compromise. All politicians are ambitious, and Humphrey was no exception. In his autobiography, he wrote, "By 1948, newspapers in Minnesota had begun to describe me as ambitious, as though it were a sin. . . . While many things remained to be done in Minneapolis, I began to feel restricted, limited to a local scene when my own interests were increasingly national." Actually, he was feeling "restricted" as early as 1945. During his first month as mayor, Humphrey told his uncle,

To me, public life and political activities are the very essence of a full life. I think that I thrive on it. . . . To be Mayor of Minneapolis surely is not the highest accomplishment that one could desire but I do feel that it is a first step and if successfully handled can lead to greater and better accomplishments. . . . It is within the realm of possibility to make a name for oneself as Mayor.

Ambition apparently played a role in Humphrey's desire to conciliate the powers-that-be. He realized that he had to go along to get along if he wanted to move up the political ladder. This strategy carried him to the U.S. Senate, the Senate majority whip position, the vice presidency, and the Democratic presidential nomination. Another possible explanation for Humphrey's willingness to compromise was his optimism. Humphrey described himself as "a born optimist."[35] He may have been willing to accept half a loaf instead of holding out for a full loaf because he genuinely believed he would be able to get a full loaf in the future.

Possessing a great need to be liked and appreciated, Humphrey's compromising served to prevent and assuage unpleasant personal interaction. In November 1955, Humphrey wrote an amazing letter to Senate majority leader Lyndon Johnson. While Johnson was away from the Senate recovering from a heart attack, Humphrey told the press that he would oppose one of Johnson's legislative priorities—a bill to end the regulation of natural gas. Johnson called Humphrey and demanded to know what was going on. Afterward, Humphrey wrote, "I really hope, Lyndon, what I said did not upset you. I praised Lyndon Johnson . . . But you've got to leave me a little room on the gas bill. I'm learning a great deal from you. You're the one teacher who makes a fellow like what he's being taught. Hurry up and get back to Washington. I'm lonesome." It is unimaginable that Bryan would have written such a letter to a conservative Democratic leader. In contrast to Humphrey's response, an old Farmer-Labor friend advised Humphrey, "Don't you cut, shuffle or deal with that son of a bitch, he's owned lock, stock and barrel by Texas oil and gas interests."[36]

Populism vs. Elitism

Deeply committed to democracy, William Jennings Bryan was a quintessential populist. According to biographer Louis Koenig, "No other political leader, not even [Theodore] Roosevelt, was on such continuous and intimate terms with a vast national following. In fact, no other American political figure, before or since Bryan's time, has enjoyed such a relationship."[37]

Like Andrew Jackson, Bryan possessed a "distrust of the expert" and a "reliance upon the average citizen to run the government." He was an implacable foe of "elitist snobbishness," and the feeling was mutual. One biographer noted that "academicians, professional economists, and the more serious journals almost unanimously opposed Bryan's free silver position" in the 1890s. Although he was a college graduate, attorney, and savvy politician, his "political endeavors sometimes appeared unsophisticated. Moral certitude left him poorly read in the growing literature of the social sciences and his arguments unfettered by its findings."[38] Bryan's homespun mannerisms, championing of the common people, advocacy of free silver, serving of grape juice on diplomatic occasions, and literal interpretation of the Bible evoked ridicule and scorn from the political, economic, cultural, and educational elites of his day.

Because he was a friendly man from the Midwest with no great personal wealth, the eastern press depicted Hubert Humphrey as a prairie populist when he made his first serious bid for the presidency in 1960. As he was growing up, Humphrey was certainly exposed to the ideology of the Populist Party and William Jennings Bryan through his father. Humphrey was also exposed to other, less populistic influences—namely, Woodrow Wilson and Franklin Roosevelt, two of his father's political heroes. Wilson was an Ivy League professor and president, who donned the cloak of the common man relatively late in life. He was closely connected to the nation's economic elite. Referring to Wilson, scholar Ronald Schaffer noted, "In private, he was a snob, bored by the ordinary citizens of his country. He told his fiancée during his first term that the great majority of people who came to his office . . . and most American voters were 'not of our kind.'" In this, as in so many other ways, Wilson was distinctly different from Bryan. In the mid-1910s, Wilson pulled a reluctant if not resistant nation into World War I. Not surprisingly, wartime brought greater centralization and authoritarianism to the United States. Schaffer commented, "One of the paradoxes of America's war for democracy is that so many of the people who participated in it, whether conservative businessmen, liberal politicians, or social reformers, thought of themselves as an elite and acted as such, trying to shape the attitudes and behavior of common men and women."[39]

In 1964, Humphrey approvingly quoted Franklin Roosevelt's 1938 statement that American liberals have always "believed in the wisdom and efficacy of the will of the great majority of the people, as distinguished from the judgment of a small minority of either education or wealth." Actually, Roosevelt was famous for his reliance on intellectuals and academics, a fact that Humphrey himself acknowledged in his master's thesis: "The New Deal has placed considerable responsibility and faith in this trained personnel. The Chief Executive and his department heads have relied on experts to an unprecedented extent in the formulation of legislation and policy." FDR was a Wall Street financier during the 1920s who remained on close terms with a number of leading bankers and brokers throughout the 1930s. He publicly opened the gates of his administration to big banking and big business in the early 1940s.[40] Like Wilson, who was one of his mentors, Roosevelt pulled a reluctant if not resistant nation into a world war years before Pearl Harbor.[41] Also like Wilson, FDR was something of a snob. When his political manager, James Farley, complained to Eleanor Roosevelt that he was never invited to private functions with the president, she responded, "Franklin is not at ease with people not of his own class."[42] Despite his populist campaign rhetoric, there is every reason to believe that Roosevelt did, in fact, pay inordinate attention to small minorities of education and wealth.

The political heirs of Franklin Roosevelt shared his elitist tendencies. Henry Wallace served as secretary of agriculture and vice president under Roosevelt and was another hero of young Humphrey. In the late 1940s, journalist Dwight Macdonald contrasted the genuine populism of Bryan with the false populism of Wallace: "Wallace's audience is drawn from liberals who are economically well off and culturally sophisticated. For them, populism is, culturally, a phony way of making a connection with the inarticulate masses . . . and, politically, a way to engage in world power-politics under attractive slogans." Lyndon Johnson, a loyal New Dealer, was Humphrey's longtime political sponsor. Johnson had humble origins and a down-to-earth style, but his ideology was in the southern Bourbon tradition, not the Populist tradition. Macdonald, Harry Elmer Barnes, and other political analysts with an affinity for traditional liberalism were critical of what they viewed as the pragmatic, bureaucratic, undemocratic, and militaristic legacy of New Deal liberalism.[43] This was not a populist milieu. The adoption of so-called totalitarian traits by latter-day liberals was eventually rationalized for them by James Burnham in his 1941 book *The Managerial Revolution*. Barnes pointed out that those belonging to the liberal managerial elite described by Burnham were at the core of the Vital Center described in Arthur Schlesinger Jr.'s 1949 book. Stephen Depoe wrote,

> It may be noted that Schlesinger's use of history has often resembled what he has termed "exculpatory history," historical arguments presented to justify or maintain existing power arrangements. A bias toward the status quo is intrinsic to Schlesinger's belief in the tides of national politics. While Schlesinger's definitions of "liberal" and "conservative"

have been grounded in varying attitudes toward change, government, and the public interest, Schlesinger has placed both perspectives within a "vital center" of political action. Within this vital center, political conflict is contained. Both sides maintain a respect for the political process and an elitist preference for rationality and expertise over emotion and mass participation.

According to Depoe, Schlesinger became even more supportive of the socioeconomic status quo during the 1950s when he set aside economic class as a basis for distinguishing liberalism from conservatism. Depoe also pointed to Schlesinger's attacks on radical groups and ideas that threaten the stability of the two-party system and his "constant call for the emergence of heroic liberal leadership" as ways in which he has used his historical writings to defend the existing political system. If the American political system is dominated by a power elite, as is suggested by some scholars, Schlesinger's defense of the status quo amounts to a defense of the Power Elite. Schlesinger's hostility toward ideology and hostility toward populism converge in his history: "Schlesinger has at times elevated the means of obtaining and keeping power for liberals over the ends of using political power for the benefit of dispossessed or marginalized groups."[44] Humphrey was a leading member of the elitist-leaning Vital Center movement.

   With Wilson and Roosevelt serving as his two main political inspirations, it is perhaps not surprising that Humphrey adopted an elitist perspective despite his prairie populist upbringing. As a graduate student at the University of Minnesota, "Humphrey drew upon [John] Dewey to give coherence to the prairie pragmatism he had already learned in Doland [South Dakota]. He latched on to the 'experimentalism' of Dewey's thought." Throughout his career as a political leader, Humphrey referred again and again to the American "experiment," as though the land were a giant laboratory and the citizens were subjects in a scientific study. There is a degree of elitism and paternalism inherent in such a perspective. If his own words are to be believed, Humphrey's political career was largely based on a desire for cosmic recognition and a paternalistic attitude that mistook decentralization for helplessness:

> You know, when I was a young man in South Dakota, everything— everyone—even the state itself seemed so anonymous. I always felt— gosh, I'll live and die out here and nobody'd ever know that I ever was. I had to get out. But it wasn't only that. I just thought that somebody should know what all those good people are all about. Who's going to help them with their problems if no one knows they're here?

Apparently it did not occur to Humphrey that the people "out here"—a phrase which might imply an East Coast frame of reference—might have the ability and desire to help themselves. While Humphrey worried that no one knew the people in South Dakota existed, presumably the people recognized their own existence and the value of their lives—apart from any potential validation or recognition by wealthy or powerful people in New York or Washington. Humphrey's assessment of why he lost the 1960 West Virginia primary has already been mentioned. It reveals an unintentionally condescending attitude toward the people of West Virginia.[45]

Humphrey was often dismissed by critics as a do-gooder. In terms of public policy, there is a difference between doing good for others and restraining those who do evil. The latter approach is a Jeffersonian, negative-state approach. Although the former approach has the appearance of being more humanitarian, it can also be interpreted as elitist and paternalistic. In many cases, the do-gooder acts without the request of or even against the will of the "do-goodee." Toward the end of his life, Humphrey told a friend, "You know—my life—I don't think I would have changed one snip of it"; reconsidering, he said, "No, I wouldn't say that; I'd have liked to see if I could run this country."[46] Humphrey's choice of words is revealing. He said that he would like to have seen if he could have run the country, not that he would have liked to have served the people as president.

A biographer noted Humphrey's ever-present tendency to "move toward, rather than against, the power center." Humphrey was usually moving toward the Power Elite and away from the common people. After losing a race for mayor of Minneapolis in 1943, Humphrey decided to run again in 1945. He recalled,

> In the intervening time, I had turned my attention to understanding the people behind the structure, those who caused government to operate. I followed local news more closely than before, figuring out who the real leaders were in the city—in more current terms, "defining the power structure." Then I set out to meet them—bankers, publishers, businessmen of other sorts—and at the same time I strengthened my association with labor.

It is interesting that Humphrey came to recognize the existence of a power elite in his city and then decided to court its favor. He chose to seek its support rather than to oppose as plutocrats the city's "real leaders" or to expose the undemocratic nature of the shadowy people who "caused government to operate." Humphrey's early experience with power politics may help to explain why he opposed the traditional agrarians within the Farmer-Labor Party in the mid-1940s, the Mississippi Freedom Democratic Party in the mid-1960s, the New Left and Counterculture in the late 1960s and early 1970s, and the right-to-life movement in the mid-1970s. "Antagonism to mass movements and to social change that escapes the control of privileged elites is . . . a prominent feature of contemporary liberal ideology," and Humphrey was no exception to this rule.[47]

Political scientist Thomas Dye welcomes elite rule in the United States because it is enlightened and humane. According to Dye, the primary values of the Power Elite are "a concern for liberal reform and social welfare, an interest in problems confronting the poor and blacks, a desire to educate the ignorant and cure the sick, and a willingness to employ governmental power to accomplish these ends."[48] How noble and altruistic! A more realistic assessment of the situation would acknowledge the powerful role of self-interest, especially a self-interest expressed in monetary terms since the Power Elite is dominated by capitalists for whom profit—not humanitarianism—is the bottom line.

When thinking about becoming Lyndon Johnson's running mate in 1964, Humphrey told friends, "Look, I'm a poor man. I don't have rich friends. I come from a small state. I just can't do it on my own. The only way I can become president is first to become vice president." Humphrey did have at least a few rich friends, but what does his statement tell us? It tells us that Humphrey recognized the key role played by wealth in national politics and that he saw no way to gain entrance to the White House except on the shoulders of a man who had long been perceived as illiberal. This was not the approach of Bryan. In 1896, Bryan was not personally wealthy and had few wealthy friends, but he sought the presidency despite his realization that the monied interests would be against him. He was not elected, but he was nominated three times and made respectable showings in the general elections. Humphrey began his Senate career as a vigorous midwestern rabble-rouser. By 1968, Humphrey had "changed as he reached for the heights—affable, cheerful, voluble as ever but indubitably rounded and smoothed by the years of proximity to power and wealth." Referring to Humphrey and the Vietnam War in 1968, Hays Gorey commented, "The man who in 1948 had so courageously moved his party toward 'a necessary goal' by taking on what he termed 'the Establishment' was, in the 1960's, part of the Establishment and unable to bring himself to defy it." In direct contrast, Bryan was a radical, anti-Establishment politician even during his last years.[49]

Humphrey's attitude toward the presidential campaigns of Alabama's Democratic governor George Wallace is instructive. Humphrey's abhorrence of Wallace's racism was logical and liberal, but Humphrey went further than this: he could see nothing of redeeming value in the Wallace campaigns. Referring to 1968, Humphrey wrote, "The tragedy for our campaign resulting from the Wallace incursion was not simply the loss of votes; it was the atmosphere of heightened hostility and anger in the country, the irritability and the grating antagonisms." Some obvious questions arise in connection with Humphrey's words: Did Wallace cause the hostility and anger? Or did he merely provide a safe outlet for expressing it? Although Humphrey saw nothing good in the Wallace campaign, there were elements to it that could, in theory, be appreciated even by conscientious liberals: the nonviolent way of letting off social steam, the added electoral choice, the example of grassroots politics. In fact, another 1968 candidate did exactly that. Dick Gregory, a prominent black activist, praised the Wallace campaign for injuring the two-party system and increasing citizen awareness. Gregory said this after criticizing the Humphrey campaign for being an undemocratic creation of discredited party bosses! Reflecting on Wallace's 1972 campaign, Humphrey was willing to concede the "limited validity" of Wallace's message insofar as it "reflected a strong public undercurrent of dissatisfaction with the whole economic and social system." Nonetheless, Senator Humphrey viewed Governor Wallace as a threat to what he considered "the essence of the American experiment: goodwill, conciliation, justice for all." Writing in 1971, political analyst Kevin Phillips—a man who disagreed with Wallace on a number of things—predicted that a Wallace 1972 campaign would "drive the fashionable Establishment nuts with his gutsy populist attacks on the left-wing media, Harvard disarmers, foundation limousine liberals, fat cat labor leaders, and the presidential candidates who cultivate them." As a part of the Establishment, Humphrey was unable to appreciate Wallace's populist appeal—which existed quite apart from his support for segregation and opposition to busing. In 1972, Humphrey could speak with facility to the leaders of interest groups within the Democratic Party, but he had little to say to the common people of the United States.[50]

Despite having long since lost his reputation as a prairie populist, Humphrey made occasional overtures to America's growing populism. In the mid-1970s, he wrote, "A kind of elitism, a professional governmental snobbishness, has grown as bureaucracy has expanded and government programs increased."[51] Humphrey sometimes criticized the federal bureaucracy, but he rarely criticized elitism in the executive, legislative, or judicial branches. He did not speak out against political elitism or condemn economic elitism. Humphrey's silence on these subjects can be contrasted with the words of some of his fellow Democratic presidential contenders—Governor Wallace, Senator George McGovern, and Governor Jerry Brown—during the 1970s.

By the mid-1960s, Hubert Humphrey was associated with limousine liberalism, the prevailing ideology of Manhattan and Hollywood, Palm Springs and Beverly Hills, Aspen and Capitol Hill. The inconsistency if not hypocrisy of limousine liberalism has been noticed by conservative writers such as Mary Davison, Gary Allen, and Joseph Farah. Many Americans believe there is something deeply hypocritical and demagogic about liberal politicians such as Nelson Rockefeller and Edward Kennedy freely spending the hard-earned money of other people for poverty programs while keeping their own unearned riches safely tucked away in personal property, real estate, bank accounts, and tax shelters. In the early 1970s, the mayor of Camden, New Jersey, responded to Kennedy's comments concerning a city poverty program by saying, "It is difficult to imagine Senator Kennedy having any interest in Camden's poor while he vacations on the ski slopes of Switzerland, the winter playground of the jet set and the fashionable European hideway of millionaires." Conservative criticism of privileged-and-professional concern for the poor found a spokesman in the electoral arena when Governor Wallace ran for the 1972 Democratic presidential nomination. Wallace declared,

> Strangely enough, many of the super-rich in this country also believe in socialism. They set up tax-free foundations which promote socialist programs with the taxes they evade, and then arrange to tax the working man to pay for those programs. Such limousine "Liberals" are not humanitarians. If they were they would lead by example and divide their own wealth instead of hiding it in tax shelters while they promote an ever-increasing tax burden on the middle class.[52]

Millions of "Wallace Democrats" left the Democratic Party during the 1970s partly because they perceived it as a party that sanctimoniously seized their income without a genuine concern for others. These working-class and middle-class voters became known as "Reagan Democrats."

Many liberals at the grassroots level agree with conservative criticism of national pillars of official concern. They are sensitive to the dangers of hypocrisy and co-optation. They want themselves and others not only to "talk the talk" but also to "walk the walk." In 1992, Governor Jerry Brown repeatedly pointed out the dichotomy between what his intraparty rivals were saying in public and how they were raising their money in private. Many liberals oppose the materialism inherent in the limousine liberal version of *Lifestyles of the Rich and Famous.* Attracted to a relatively simple, down-to-earth lifestyle, they try to practice the saying "Live simply that others may simply live."

Liberals in the New Left and Counterculture traditions argue that truly helping the poor is not high on the Democratic Party's list of priorities because the party is dominated by big business and wealthy people. According to such liberals, lower-class Americans and middle-class Americans are pawns to be used and symbols to be exploited by the upper-class Americans who control the party. In 1974, Mary Meehan, a three-time supporter of Senator Eugene McCarthy for president, wrote an article calling into question the validity of a liberalism shaped by wealthy and dynastic candidates: "A political party's dependence on money and family fame is plainly undemocratic. . . . Besides, wealthy liberals are isolated from the everyday life of most Americans. . . . Noblesse oblige has tried to speak for such people, but it has failed. It is time that they speak for themselves."[53] Thinking of the 1970s, if Humphrey did not like populism from the Right, he could still have embraced populism from the Left. He did not.

Democrats who had supported the presidential campaigns of Hubert Humphrey and his ideological colleagues Senator Edmund Muskie (D-ME) and Senator Henry Jackson (D-WA) took the lead in forming organizations designed to oppose the influence of liberal populists within the party. The Coalition for a Democratic Majority, founded in 1972, stood opposed to the "New Politics" exemplified by the campaigns of Eugene McCarthy in 1968 and George McGovern in 1972.[54] The Democratic Leadership Council, founded in 1985, stood as a counterweight to the grassroots 1984 and 1988 campaigns of Jesse Jackson. During the 1992 primary season, notable Humphreyites Senator Paul Simon (D-IL) and Senator Tom Harkin (D-IA) campaigned in Wisconsin against Jerry Brown on behalf of Bill Clinton, a man in the Humphrey tradition who chaired the DLC.[55] While Clinton and his DLC associates were often called "Centrist Democrats" or "New Democrats," Democrats associated with the CDM became known as *neoconservatives.* There was little difference between CDM adherents and DLC adherents. They were enemies of populism, egalitarianism, and isolationism. The most notable difference between the two groups was that the DLC was largely populated by southern politicians, while the CDM's most prominent spokespersons were eastern intellectuals. Many neoconservatives joined the Republican Party during the 1980s, but others—including Daniel Patrick Moynihan and Ben Wattenberg—remained within the Democratic Party. In 1979, analyst Kevin Phillips contended that neoconservatism "is profoundly elitist, and tends to look down its urbane Eastern nose at the populist politics" of the New Right. By the early 1990s, ideological heirs of Humphrey were ascendant in both major parties, but they faced populist opposition from the McGovern-Jesse Jackson-Brown wing of the Democratic Party and the Goldwater-Helms-Buchanan wing of the Republican Party.[56]

CHAPTER 6

Modern Philosophy 102

FOUNDATION, FOCUS, RESIDENCE, SPECTRUM, AND STATUS

Morality vs. Economics

William Jennings Bryan was an evangelical Christian. He was affiliated with the Social Gospel movement but was a fundamentalist rather than a modernist when it came to biblical authority and interpretation. The combination of theological conservatism with political liberalism may strike the modern reader as strange, but it was not so unusual in the nineteenth and early twentieth centuries. It was exemplified by Charles Finney in America, Catherine Booth in England, and Charles Péguy in France. According to Walter Rauschenbusch, one of the leaders of the Social Gospel movement, "The spiritual force of Christianity should be turned against the materialism and mammonism of our industrial and social order." Calling it "Applied Christianity," Bryan shared this perspective. Historian Gary Gerstle calls Bryan a "moral reformer"; historian Paolo Coletta refers to him as a "political puritan."

Bryan's allies, the Populists, were a highly moralistic political group, and he infused the Democratic Party with this same energy during his years of dominance from 1896 to 1912. Louis Koenig notes, "To Bryan, political issues were always moral issues, and politics was a battleground of moral struggles." Between his second and third nominations, Bryan said, "Our fight must be made upon a moral plane, for we seek justice. Our people must appeal to the conscience of the country, and that conscience awakened will sweep everything before it." It was during this period that Bryan began appearing each summer on the Chautauqua lecture circuit. Chautauqua audiences were "religious-minded, agrarian masses who hated 'Wall Street'

(Eastern monopoly capitalism) and detested the sophisticated, irreligious culture of the Eastern seaboard." Emphases on morality and economics are outgrowths of populism and elitism, respectively. Populists tend to focus on people and their relationship with God—a relationship possessing egalitarian availability—while elitists tend to focus on wealth. Bryan "was more than a progressive politician"; he was a "lay prophet of the social gospel" who "emphasized the relationship between ethics and economics."[1]

When the Silver Republicans met to nominate Bryan for president in 1896, the man who placed his name in nomination said, "The time has come to determine whether this nation is ruled by an Almighty Dollar or by an Almighty God." Bryan believed in the biblical statement "The love of money is the root of all evil." In 1901, he attacked the worship of mammon: "It is the overweaning desire to get rich that so absorbs the attention of many that they have no time left for the discharge of civic duties; it is the same thirst for wealth which perverts party organizations, corrupts officials and rushes nations into wars of conquest." Bryan condemned plutocracy for, among other things, "making a mockery of morals." He said, "I am convinced that we have all given relatively too much time to the consideration of the pecuniary features of public questions, and too little time to the consideration of the moral principles, which underlie all questions." Bryan viewed the rampant consumerism, materialism, and commercialism of the 1920s as signs of moral and cultural decline.[2] The essence of Bryan's critique of big business was moral, not economic. He was demanding an upholding of justice, not a redistribution of wealth. During the 1910s and 1920s, enlightened conservatism and welfare capitalism—including such things as corporate public relations, philanthropy by rich individuals, a growing middle class, and crumbs being thrown to the downtrodden by those dining at the table of the privileged—answered some of the economic objections to big business, but they did nothing to address the moral objections.

As evolutionary biologist Stephen Jay Gould has noted, Bryan opposed Darwinism on both theological and sociopolitical grounds. He linked the detrimental social effects of Darwin's theory to the might-makes-right philosophy of Friedrich Nietzsche. He believed that such thinking served not so much as an explanation for injustice but more as an excuse, particularly in the areas of harming the weak and waging war. This violated his belief in the Sermon on the Mount and his appreciation for the thought of Tolstoy. Bryan's support for democracy was another important element in his opposition to Darwinian evolution. He believed that parents, the vast majority of whom were professing Christians, should be able to control what was taught to their children in local public schools. The lengthy closing statement he was planning to make at the *Scopes* trial in Dayton, Tennessee, in 1925 was entitled "Who Shall Control?"[3] Incidentally, the play and film *Inherit the Wind* that features Bryan under a fictionalized name is full of historical inaccuracies and has slandered the real Bryan for generations. He is portrayed as an ignorant, rude, and self-righteous fanatic. Given this reputational context, the first thing that strikes a reader when approaching the writings of Bryan is the surprising degree of intelligence and knowledge to be found. Contrary to expectations, he was a man of reason as well as faith.

A historical episode recounted by Ronald Schaffer nicely illustrates the contrasting attitudes toward morality exhibited by pre-New Deal liberals and post-New Deal liberals:

> [During World War I, the U.S. Army] made prophylactic instruction and treatment available to all troops. Secretary of the Navy [Josephus] Daniels, however, forbade the use of prophylactic kits on the ground that using it "would tend to subvert and destroy the very foundations of our moral and Christian beliefs and teachings with regard to these sexual matters." But when Daniels was out of his office, at [Raymond] Fosdick's suggestion Assistant Secretary of the Navy Franklin D. Roosevelt signed an order providing for prophylactic treatment.[4]

The relevance of this story becomes apparent when one considers that Josephus Daniels had been a supporter of Bryan since 1896 and was his closest friend in the Wilson cabinet. Roosevelt went on to become president of the United States; Fosdick became president of the Rockefeller Foundation. Roosevelt was a political inspiration for both Hubert Humphrey and Nelson Rockefeller. Humphrey and Rockefeller are the purest examples of midcentury liberalism in their respective parties. Government distribution of condoms is a minor but good example of the ongoing struggle between moralistic and nonmoralistic forces in American politics. This struggle has been highlighted more recently in controversies over sex education and condom distribution in schools. One of the arguments used on behalf of school condom distribution is that the prevention of teen pregnancies will reduce the amount of tax dollars spent on welfare programs. The same argument has been used to advocate for subsidized abortion for poor women. As is often the case, economics is pitted against morality.

It has been argued that Hubert Humphrey was, like Bryan, in the Social Gospel tradition, but in Humphrey's case the emphasis on Christian morality was, for the most part, one generation removed. Humphrey's father was an adherent of Applied Christianity. Unlike Bryan, Humphrey was not an evangelical Christian. Based on Humphrey's own words, we can conclude that he was not a Christian in any traditional sense of the word. In 1950, Dwight Macdonald included Humphrey in his critique of "the dominant non-religious social tendency in this country." When he was nearing the end of his life, Humphrey told a close friend, "I'm not a church-going Christer, but I do have a feeling for nature or God or whatever. I've been a realist, and I don't have redemption fantasies, dreams of heaven or reincarnation. . . . If I have any real faith it's in man and man's nature, and to me that's enough." Like Bryan's Nebraska, Humphrey's Minnesota is—according to Daniel Elazar's political culture model—a moralistic state. In fact, according to Ira Sharkansky's scale, Minnesota is the most moralistic state in the nation. William Lee Miller wrote, "No one represented the moral legacy of American progressive politics in mid-century in so pure and consistent a way, with so warm an appreciation from those who shared those political purposes, as Hubert Humphrey."[5] He rightfully places Humphrey above Truman, Stevenson, Kennedy, and Johnson in this regard.

Humphrey *was* a moralist, but his moralism was cast in distinctly economic terms, and morality was thus subordinate to economics. He was firmly in the tradition of corporate liberalism. During the first quarter of the twentieth century,

> the corporatist model of society replaced the pluralistic model as the American dream became ever more rooted in material betterment rather than in political ideals. . . . Corporatism promised an ever-expanding pie for all classes of society and a virtual guarantee of middle-class status for whites who persisted long enough in one locale or occupation. Economic growth was the sine qua non of the corporatist model . . . Americans gradually came to accept the idea that mass production required advanced industrial organization, albeit under the eye of government. Bigness became a way of life in the new, immensely prosperous America.

Bryan disapproved of this crucial change in the content of liberalism; Humphrey approved. In approving of corporatism, Humphrey was following in the footsteps of his heroes Woodrow Wilson and Franklin Roosevelt. In his master's thesis, Humphrey quoted Louis Hacker on the New Deal:

> Our state has become transformed almost overnight. Formerly, it concerned itself almost exclusively with the civil administration and national defense, and when it intervened in other realms it for the most part acted in the capacity of umpire between equals. . . . Today, however,

the state is operating to defend the underprivileged, to increase the national income, and to effect a more equitable distribution of that income among the various categories of producers. . . . Our state, in
short, has become the capitalist state, where only yesterday it was the
laissez-faire or passive state; it protects the young, weak and aged; it con-
structs and operates plants, and it buys and sells goods and services, lends
money, warehouses commodities, moves ships and operates railroads.

Humphrey condoned this change from a laissez-faire economy to state capitalism, which was labeled *fascism* by some New Deal critics.[6] It is important
to note Hacker's change in governmental analogy from "umpire" (fair play
= morality) to "capitalist" (economics).

Biographer Michael Amrine wrote, "There is a firm moralistic tone in
this thesis on the New Deal, as there is in many of Humphrey's major efforts
to define his philosophy." Referring to the New Deal, Humphrey contends,

Coupled with an intuitive desire for a change there was an awakening
desire for more idealism in our economic life. . . . The sense of empti-
ness that came with the collapse of business values stimulated a spiritual
or idealistic awakening that demanded recognition in social and economic planning. Nothing was more logical than the development of
some sort of "New Deal" economics, set in a framework of a new idealism, a "reorientation of economic purpose on a broader and less selfish basis, for really universal not merely individualistic welfare."

Humphrey alludes to a spiritual awakening, but he casts this awakening in
economic terms. It has nothing to do with spirituality as generally defined—God or religion or morals or freedom or fraternity. It has to do with
money. It is a more equitably distributed materialism with the federal government acting as the distributor. Elsewhere in his thesis, Humphrey made
his econocentric perspective even more explicit, declaring, "The problem of
modern democracy is intrinsically an economic one. It may be fairly stated
thus: Can the flagrant inequality of possessions and of opportunity now existing in a democratic state be corrected by democratic methods?"[7] So, for
Humphrey, the question was not, Who rules? but rather, Can we keep our
economic system afloat by using our traditional political system? Democracy was placed in the service of capitalism, but it was a modified form of
democracy—more pragmatic, more technocratic, more statist.

Humphrey was a strong supporter of Democratic administrations from
the 1930s to the 1970s—all of which placed a higher value on economics
than morality. In the mid-1950s, historian Richard Hofstadter contrasted the

"moral absolutes" of the Progressive movement with the New Deal: "While something akin to this was by no means entirely absent from the New Deal, the later movement showed a strong and candid awareness that what was happening was not so much moral reformation as economic experimentation." Four decades later, historian Gary Gerstle disagreed with Hofstadter's characterization of the New Deal as amoral, but he agreed that it largely set aside Progressive concerns in favor of an emphasis on economics: "Missing from the New Deal was the Progressive preoccupation with individual virtue and vice. Progressives had been intent on reforming individuals and improving character."[8] It should be understood that while the New Deal distilled the moralism of the Progressive Era into economic terms, New Deal economics were tame in comparison to the economics espoused by Bryan, La Follette, and their ideological heirs. The New Deal was devoid of the radicalism of the Progressive Era. FDR opposed vigorous enforcement of the Sherman Anti-Trust Act, the remonetization of silver, restructuring of the Federal Reserve System, the Townsend Plan, Huey Long's share-the-wealth idea, and Upton Sinclair's EPIC. For this reason, some Bryan-La Follette liberals supported the Union Party presidential candidacy of Congressman William Lemke (R-ND) in 1936, while others voted for Socialist Party nominee Norman Thomas.

President Harry Truman's acceptance speech at the 1948 Democratic National Convention is an indication that corporate liberalism continued to wield power during the Fair Deal years. When he turned to domestic issues, to the record of his party, Truman defined those issues and that record in economic terms—citing the income of farmers and laborers and saying that each bloc of voters would be "ungrateful" if it failed to vote for him. The postwar era was marked by an emphasis on economic growth. A culture of abundance and affluence was facilitated by planned obsolescence, mass advertising, and easy credit. The American people were encouraged to exercise an idolatrous devotion to economic growth. *Democracy* and *freedom, progress* and *success,* the *American Dream,* became virtual synonyms for the ownership of property, acquisition of wealth, and purchase of consumer goods. For the minority of Americans who stayed true to the moralistic tradition of puritans and populists, of anabaptists and anarchists, *growth* and *opportunity* were codewords for gold and greed, for mammon and materialism. During the 1950s, there was a general consensus between the leadership of the two major political parties on domestic policy and foreign policy. The Cold War undercut liberal criticism of social inequality and material prosperity undercut liberal criticism of big business. Democratic and Republican leaders agreed on the ends of American life: anticommunism and economic growth.[9]

Hubert Humphrey and his three-time choice for president, Adlai Stevenson, were committed to these two goals.

Early in his Senate career, Humphrey "appeared to turn all issues into moral issues." This emphasis faded as he moved into the center of senatorial power during the 1950s. Humphrey strongly believed in the importance of the nation's economic growth. In the 1950s and 1960s, he equated a growing gross national product (GNP) with growing liberalism and social justice. Humphrey's growth liberalism included encouragement for big business because he believed that as the GNP rose, the lives of all Americans—rich and poor—would get better. Humphrey compared this to a pie growing larger and larger. "Enlarged-pie economics" was a midcentury version of what liberals would later decry as trickle-down economics when implemented by the Reagan administration in the 1980s. Economic growth was the cornerstone of John F. Kennedy's New Frontier. When Kennedy talked about "getting the country moving again," he was referring to economic growth, not moral growth. Humphrey was a key senatorial supporter of President Kennedy as he promoted growth by filling his administration with big businessmen and pushing for a tax cut that disproportionately helped corporations and wealthy individuals. In 1964, Humphrey wrote, "The American economic republic is the remarkable achievement of free men working together in a political democracy." This suggests that capitalism is the wonderful end and democracy is merely a means. The following year, he told the U.S. Chamber of Commerce, "The Great Society only has meaning in the context of an expanding economy."[10] The primacy of economics in Humphrey's thinking is apparent in this statement.

The corporate liberals or establishment liberals of the 1960s had a seemingly contradictory approach toward economics. On the one hand, they publicly downplayed or denied class differences and the power of corporate wealth. On the other, they possessed a worldview that was more materialistic than moralistic and that assumed popular discontent could be assuaged by the application of dollars. In contrast to the bipartisan Power Elite, the Goldwater campaign and the New Left emphasized morality in politics.[11] Both accused the Establishment of believing that everything and everyone had a price, and that injustice should be addressed by throwing money at problems.

There were, of course, some important differences between populist conservatives and populist liberals. Goldwater supporters were suspicious of big business but accepted the legitimacy of capitalism. Advocates of hyperindividualism, they championed the myth of the self-made man and had material affluence as one of their goals. The New Left and Counterculture had a more radical critique of society. Members of these movements were interested in individual rights but were equally interested in commonwealth. They tended to reject the consumer society, in theory, if not practice. While the morality of Goldwaterites emanated from the Judeo-Christian tradition, that of New Leftists and Counterculturists often came from Enlightenment humanism, Eastern religion, or Earth spirituality.

George McGovern was one of Humphrey's leading opponents for the 1972 Democratic presidential nomination. Attempting to take advantage of the discontent felt by students, peace activists, feminists, black power advocates, and environmentalists, McGovern developed a reputation as a radical, anti-Establishment leftist, yet he was firmly in the Kennedy mainstream of the Democratic Party. While McGovern did not belong to the New Left or Counterculture himself, he received substantial support from members of those movements, and he conducted a moralistic campaign reminiscent of them. In contrast, Humphrey's 1972 campaign was a traditional growth liberalism effort. He tried to stop McGovern during the California primary with an attack appealing to voters' economic self-interest.[12]

Common Good vs. Special Interests

William Jennings Bryan was a classical democrat. In word and deed he was a champion of small farmers, urban laborers, and small businessmen. To him, these were not special interest groups; their needs and desires exemplified the common good because they were at least 90 percent of the population. In the view of Bryan, special interests—notably the economic elite and its political handmaidens—tried to divide and conquer this 90 percent. In 1896, the Great Commoner was the presidential nominee of the People's Party. Given this combination, it is not surprising that Bryan claimed to be an advocate for the common people. Populists emphasized the common people and their common interests. According to historian Chester McArthur Destler, "Populism was but an extreme projection of the Jeffersonian creed. Antimonopolism was the dynamic element in Populism." The preamble of their 1892 Omaha platform called for the establishment of "equal rights and equal privileges" for all the men and women of the United States.[13]

Classical democrats in the 1890s were politically hindered by effective use of the divide-and-conquer strategy of the Power Elite of their day. According to political scientist E. E. Schattschneider, "the displacement of conflicts is a prime instrument of political strategy." In *The Semisovereign People,* he wrote, "The use of racial antagonism by southern conservatives [plutocrats] to keep poor whites in line or the use of a sharply sectional alignment to destroy the radical agrarian movement in the 1890s illustrates the use to which the strategy can be put." Turn-of-the-century plutocrats used racism as an instrument to divide poor whites from poor blacks and sectionalism to divide populist southerners from populist northerners.[14] In these cases, appeals were made to citizens on the basis of special interest, not the common good. If the majority of the people who were socially and economically oppressed had joined hands, they might have been able to overturn the power of the economic elite and its political hirelings.

When Bryan read in the preamble of the U.S. Constitution that the federal government was created partly to "promote the general welfare," he saw a call to promote the common good. He did not see a call to promote the welfare of specific groups or to redistribute wealth. Bryan did not favor class legislation because he viewed that as the granting of special privilege. Instead, he favored identical distribution of rights and fair application of laws. For Bryan, this was equality and justice. In 1893, he asserted that the war cry of the common people was "equality before the law." Congressman Bryan opposed repeal of the purchasing clause of the Sherman Silver Purchase Act because repeal represented an attempt by corporations and banks to gain "special legislation, favors, privileges, and immunities." Bryan invoked the Jeffersonian maxim "Equal rights for all; special privileges for none" in his 1896 and 1900 acceptance speeches. This was one of his bedrock principles throughout his political career. In 1900, he said, "Whenever government comes into contact with the citizen, whenever the citizen touches the government, then all must stand equal before the law, and there must be no high, no low, no rich, no poor."[15]

In an 1899 speech, Bryan called for the abolition of monopolies, but said he was not yet ready to call for the abolition of all private corporations, only harmful, monopolistic ones. When asked if his position was also applicable to rich individuals such as John D. Rockefeller, Bryan replied, "We have not reached a point yet where an individual has been able to do harm, and, in my judgment, if we would abolish those laws that grant special privileges and make some men the favorites of the government, no man, by his own brains and muscle, could ever earn enough money to be harmful to the people." Bryan later said,

> The democratic party does not expect to destroy poverty . . . The democratic party is protesting against those things which interfere with the natural distribution of rewards and punishments. It is protesting against legislation which gathers from millions in order to give an undeserved advantage to hundreds, or at most, thousands. . . . Equality in rights does not mean equality in possessions or equality in enjoyment.

Bryan was *not* an early advocate of the welfare state created by politicians like FDR and Humphrey. His concern for the common people—many of whom were relatively poor—did not include using the federal government to solve their poverty problems. He believed in a laissez-faire economy through which industry, thrift, cordiality, and honesty would be naturally rewarded. He objected to governmental favors that interfered with this natural order, and he opposed "ship-subsidy grabbers," "trust magnates," and other members of "the privilege-hunting and favor-seeking class" who acquired wealth through exploitation and governmental favoritism.[16]

Hubert Humphrey followed in the Samuel Gompers/Norman Thomas tradition of special interest liberalism, not the Bryan/La Follette tradition of common-good liberalism.[17] An adherent of pluralistic democracy, Humphrey saw interest groups as beneficial, not divisive. His faith in a multiplicity of special interests may partly account for his faith in big government. As Theodore Lowi argued, "Since the days of Madison the pluralist view has been that there is nothing to fear from government so long as many factions compete for its favor." According to Louis Hacker, the New Deal was a political program "in behalf of agricultural landlords and big commercial farmers, organized trade unionists, and overseas investors and speculators." In 1939 Humphrey added, "For it is these groups that reap the bounteous benefits of the profit system and demand its maintenance." It is interesting to note that small farmers, small businessmen, and nonunion laborers were largely ignored by the New Deal. Humphrey acknowledged that FDR's policies helped big farmers and big businessmen more than their small counterparts, but he believed this was necessary and helpful in order to stop the Depression.[18]

In his master's thesis, Humphrey succinctly summarized his position on the common good vs. special interests debate by explaining and endorsing the New Deal approach:

> One would not be in error in stating that for the New Dealers the essence of a liberal society is that it makes the common good available not only to a privileged class but to all in so far as the capacity of each permits him to share it. . . . Freedom or liberty does not consist only in the absence of restraint but also in a positive power or capacity of doing or enjoying something worth doing or enjoying. . . . Thus in the attempt to reform and regulate the economic organization of the American community, the New Deal has sought to equalize privileges by curbing here and adding there.[19]

Instead of promoting the common good, the New Deal was favoring special interests in the name of the common good. Instead of equality for all and special privileges for none, it was special privileges for some to achieve equality for all. These seemingly subtle shifts represented a major departure from the earlier tradition of common-good liberalism. While Bryan believed that government should be neutral, Humphrey believed that government should be a philanthropist.

Although he approved of governmental favoritism, at times Humphrey sounded like a traditional liberal in attacking wealthy special interests. During the debate over the 1950 tax bill, he asked himself, "Were those tax policies fair? Did they fall unjustly on those least able to pay? Did they reach properly those best able to pay? Were there special privileges being granted to some that were not available to others? Could these special privileges be justified as in the national interest?" Referring to the New Deal and the Fair Deal, he said, "The people are beginning to express themselves and as they express themselves the few and the privileged who have looked upon political activity and politics as their business and only their business are fighting to maintain their power and positions of privilege." Attacks on wealthy special interests were prominent during the Truman years, but Humphrey never lost his belief in government as arbiter of rival voting blocs. He was an advocate of a mixed economy. In 1964, he wrote,

> I should prefer to call it the "balanced economy." In such an economy, where big business and small, capital and labor, factory farmer and family farmer all have roles to play, there will of course be conflicts and struggles for advantage . . . But, within a context of over-all growth policies set by the government, these are conflicts that can be resolved, to the benefit of all and to the actual detriment of none.[20]

Humphrey apparently wanted a system of special privileges for *all*. While in theory this may have been useful in moving toward social equality, in practice some special interests proved to be more special than others.

In the 1960s, a radical political movement arose that challenged the type of interest group politics supported by Humphrey. Members of the New Left wanted to "erase the special interests that stand between the people and the general will." An opponent of the New Left, Humphrey retained his traditional approach of courting interest groups. Referring to his 1972 presidential campaign, Theodore White observed, "Humphrey had dealt always in the structured systems of power where friendly leaders could deliver what tradition or loyalty had long since packaged—unions, ethnic blocs, farm groups, big-city machines."[21] Humphrey could not connect with "the unorganized." His 1972 campaign can be contrasted with the grassroots, unorganized nature of the George McGovern and George Wallace campaigns.

Agrarian vs. Urban

William Jennings Bryan was a preeminent representative of agrarianism. He was, first and foremost, an eloquent voice of rural and small-town America. An heir and enlarger of the agrarian revolt of the Gilded Age, Bryan was a friend of farmers. Whether living in Illinois, Nebraska, District of Columbia, or Florida, he remained true to his vision of a farm-based society. Bryan believed that farm life is superior to city life for a number of reasons: it is a more independent way of living, requires less capital to begin work, cultivates hospitality and generosity, emphasizes the true basis of rewards, and produces informed and independent voters. He also thought that it is a more healthful lifestyle that allows for increased parental influence and for the entire family to work together. He liked that the habits of daily living on a farm and the skills necessary for farm life are easily acquired. He later added three more reasons: contact with nature encourages belief in God, dependence on Mother Earth means the farmer is neither a parasite nor a pilferer, and the work schedule shields the young from those who profit from commercialized nighttime vices.[22]

Because of his commitment to rural life, Bryan looked to the noneastern regions of the nation for the bulk of his political support. It was difficult for Bryan to look kindly upon the East. The East was not only urban based but was the home of America's economic and intellectual elites. In his Cross of Gold speech at the 1896 convention, he proclaimed,

> Ah, my friends, we say not one word against those who live upon the Atlantic coast, but the hardy pioneers who have braved all the dangers of the wilderness . . . are as deserving of the consideration of our party as any people in this country. . . . You come to us and tell us that the great cities are in favor of the gold standard; we reply that the great cities rest upon our broad and fertile prairies. Burn down your cities and leave our farms, and your cities will spring up again as if by magic; but destroy our farms and the grass will grow in the streets of every city in the country.[23]

In stark contrast to Grover Cleveland's three campaigns, Bryan carried no eastern state in his three runs for the White House.

President Woodrow Wilson, an urban easterner, was reelected in 1916. Some believed that Bryan's campaigning on behalf of Wilson was the single most important factor in the Democratic victory. According to Bryan, the election had been won "BY THE WEST AND SOUTH WITHOUT THE AID OR CONSENT OF THE EAST. The scepter has passed from New

York, and this is sufficient glory for one year." In December 1916, Bryan told a Democratic audience,

> I love the South and the West, and the ideals to which they are attached; but I would do injustice to the East if I told you that the people of the South and West were at heart different from the people of the other sections of our country. . . . In the East, the common man is over-shadowed by concentrated wealth so that he has not the freedom of expression or action that he has in the West, and then, too, he is the victim of a press that publishes truth by accident and falsehood by consistently cultivated habit.

Later in the speech, he said, "The great wet cities were willing to turn this government back to the predatory interests, and it was left to the prohibition states of the West and South to save the Party and the nation from the wet cities of the East."[24]

In the 1920s, party nominees rejected the western-southern strategy in favor of an eastern-southern strategy because their "ideology reflected the concerns of urban finance capitalism rather than those of western rural activism." James Cox, James Davis, and Al Smith exemplified this orientation during the 1920s; Franklin Delano Roosevelt continued the pattern in the 1930s. Bryan opposed eastern influence within the Democratic Party until his last breath. In December 1924, he announced, "The only hope of national success for the Democratic Party lies in a union between the producers of the South and West against the predatory corporations that dominate the politics of the Northeast. . . . In 1916 we won without the aid of the East, and we must win without its aid in 1928."[25]

While the Grange, Farmers Alliance, People's Party, and other groups of agrarian reform during the Gilded Age have received much attention as examples of grassroots liberalism, Chester McArthur Destler points to the importance of urban centers in the political radicalism of this period. The Populists had an agrarian base, but they made overtures to organized labor and had sympathy for urban workers.[26] Bryan was primarily a candidate of the farms and towns of rural America, but he did have some backing in the cities. He was supported by some urban politicians—beyond his on-again, off-again relationship with the Tammany Hall machine in New York—including John Peter Altgeld of Chicago, Isidor Rayner of Baltimore, James O'Gorman and William Sulzer of New York City, James Reed of Kansas City, and David Walsh of Boston. Mayoral candidate Henry George of New York supported Bryan in 1896.

Bryan made a bid for the support of organized labor in the close of his Cross of Gold speech:

> Having behind us the producing masses of this nation and the world, supported by the commercial interests, the laboring interests, and the toilers everywhere, we will answer their demand for a gold standard by saying to them: You shall not press down upon the brow of labor this crown of thorns, you shall not crucify mankind upon a cross of gold.

Samuel Gompers of the American Federation of Labor, James Sovereign of the Knights of Labor, John McBride of the United Mine Workers, Eugene Debs of the American Railway Union, and Edward Keating of the Railway Brotherhoods were among the union leaders who supported Bryan for president in 1896. Despite his efforts, Bryan's agrarian background and emphasis on silver apparently hurt him among laborers and city dwellers. McKinley did better than Bryan in every important urban center. While Bryan was undoubtedly disappointed by his failure to pry eastern laborers away from the GOP in the numbers for which he had hoped, he did receive the votes of many urban workers. Regardless of how much support he received from their members in 1896, Bryan was a lifelong supporter of many measures desired by labor unions, such as standard working hours, collective bargaining, and labor injunction relief. Secretary of State Bryan kept in close touch with Gompers during the early years of the Wilson administration, and he played a role in exempting labor unions from the Clayton Antitrust Act.[27]

Like Bryan, Hubert Humphrey was raised in the rural Midwest. The two men had, however, quite different presidential role models: Bryan looked to Thomas Jefferson and Andrew Jackson above all others, while Humphrey looked to Woodrow Wilson and Franklin Roosevelt. Bryan's models were exponents of agrarian liberalism; Humphrey's models represented urban liberalism. World War I helped to plant the seeds of destruction for family farming through the proliferation of modernization, expertization, agribusiness, and government domination. Bryan resisted U.S. entry into the war; Wilson encouraged it. While he had small-town roots in South Dakota, during the 1940s, Humphrey was mayor of Minneapolis, the nation's fourteenth largest city. Americans for Democratic Action, the interest group cofounded by Humphrey, was from its inception dominated by urbanites and easterners.[28] Midwesterner Humphrey was the exception, not the rule.

Referring to the Eisenhower administration of the 1950s, Humphrey later wrote,

One need not yearn for an impossible dream of Jeffersonian yeomen tilling the fields to feel that agriculture was still basic to a healthy economic system in modern America. Farmers were leaving the farms by the millions for a number of reasons, some inexorable and impossible to change, but others amenable to change by government policies. . . . For virtually every day that Ezra Benson served in the Cabinet, I rose in the Senate to condemn his policies, to suggest alternatives, and to make him a political issue. I drew vivid word pictures of people driven off the farm into a slum of city misery. I attacked the Eisenhower-Benson policies not only to change them, but to make clear the political issue for the 1956 and 1958 elections.[29]

Thinking in pragmatic and economic terms rather than ideological and moral terms, Humphrey rejected the Jeffersonian vision. His candid admission of mixed motives is also interesting. In 1959, Humphrey said that the democratic processes had not yet recognized the "growing urbanization of America" and thus the "great urban majority" in the nation did not have proper representation in state legislatures and Congress. Humphrey tried to make the problems of the cities a major theme of his 1960 presidential campaign. Despite Humphrey's membership in the elite Americans for Democratic Action and his emphasis on urban problems, some members of the Establishment looked upon his presidential candidacy with skepticism because of the East's traditionally dismissive attitude toward the Midwest.[30]

Humphrey was able to make a smooth transition from intraparty rival to legislative champion in relation to John F. Kennedy. Historian Wayne Cole observed, "*Insofar as they reflected urban interests and values,* President John F. Kennedy and his Democratic administration had more in common with Federalist Alexander Hamilton than with Thomas Jefferson." As Senate majority whip in the early 1960s, Humphrey was a loyal and enthusiastic supporter of President Kennedy and the New Frontier. Between 1958 and 1967, employment on farms—as a percentage of overall American employment—fell from 8.5 to 4.8 percent. In contrast, white-collar employment and service employment rose, and blue-collar employment fell by less than one percent during this period. This shift away from farming occurred under Presidents Eisenhower, Kennedy, and Johnson. Humphrey thoroughly supported the domestic policies of Kennedy and Johnson. During the Eisenhower years, he joined other Democrats in demonizing Secretary of Agriculture Ezra Taft Benson, but his opposition was as much partisan as ideological. While mourning the migration from farm to city, Humphrey suggested programs to ameliorate urban problems and virtually declared the inevitability of agrarian numerical decline.[31] The policies he backed under Democratic presidents encouraged continuation of the decline.

In a 1964 book, Humphrey wrote that he believed that the federal government needed to ensure "the survival of the family farm in the face of a trend toward large-scale 'factory' farming." A decade later, he argued that people living in rural towns and small cities could act as a countervailing force to the bigness of modern American society. He defined his legislative vision in these terms: "It was a vision of an urban, industrial America with attractive and varied alternatives, with people living near the land, in towns; of small businesses healthy and profitable and immediate, as a slight antidote to the massive concentration of business wealth."[32] Humphrey added that his vision was "impossible and irrelevant" without positive action by the federal government. Humphrey's expressions of concern about social bigness and corporate power are ironic since he had done so much over the decades—through his rejection of antimonopolism, embrace of corporate liberalism, and insistence that political power must be centralized in Washington—to help bring about these very conditions.

Members of the Counterculture of the late 1960s and early 1970s were more consistently Jeffersonian in their approach. Unapologetic agrarians, they believed that government worked in concert with corporations to destroy traditional American values such as freedom, community, thrift, and harmony with nature. They advocated going "back to nature" and getting "back to the land." Far from arguing the impossibility and irrelevance of social change without federal government direction, they created their own rural communes. Humphrey's response during this period was much different. He remained a champion of agribusiness. From the days of the Grange and Non-Partisan League, the millers, bankers, and railroad tycoons headquartered in Minneapolis had been infamous for their exploitation of family farmers. Despite their illiberal reputations, these forces developed a close relationship with Humphrey. He relied on support from Pillsbury, General Mills, Peavey, Minneapolis and St. Louis Railroad, Cargill, American Milk Producers, Inc., Archer Daniels Midland, and similar companies from the start of his career to its close. This crowd had little in common with the small independent farmer of the Jeffersonian tradition. Not surprisingly, in a poll of Iowa voters taken in April 1976, Humphrey fared far better among metropolitan dwellers than among farm dwellers.[33] Although he was from a farm state, Humphrey had extensive ties to urban constituencies. Famous for his pro-civil rights speech at the 1948 Democratic National Convention, he was an eloquent defender of equality for blacks. An opponent of anti-Semitism and champion of Israel, Humphrey was a favorite of Jewish Americans. He welcomed ethnic diversity and supported liberalized immigration laws.[34] Humphrey cultivated relationships with the Congress of Industrial Organizations (CIO) and other labor unions while he was running for and serving as mayor of Minneapolis. He supported legislation favored by organized labor throughout his Senate career. James Hoffa, president of the Teamsters union, supported Humphrey's presidential campaign during the 1960 primary season, perhaps partly out of hatred for the Kennedys. United Auto Workers president Walter Reuther favored Humphrey for the 1960 and 1964 vice-presidential nominations. Humphrey became more intimate with "Big Labor" after befriending AFL-CIO president George Meany in 1964. Meany strongly supported Humphrey for the 1964 vice-presidential nomination and the 1968, 1972, and 1976 presidential nominations. I. W. Abel, president of the United Steelworkers, also favored Humphrey for president in 1968, 1972, and 1976.[35]

Left vs. Center

Political scientist Anthony Downs argues that "most voters are massed" in the ideological Center rather than on the Left or the Right.[36] His scale does not take into account the populist and elitist distinction that cuts across liberal and conservative lines. The traditional linear scale does not adequately measure and depict ideology. It may be more useful to think of the Left and the Right as two components of populism, with elitism residing in the Center. The political spectrum may be linear, but it is not a straight line. It is shaped like a horseshoe. We usually think of America and Asia as being quite far apart, but they are actually divided by the narrow Bering Strait. Similarly, Left and Right are located at the ends of the spectrum separated by a relatively small distance containing contentious but secondary issues that divide modern liberals and conservatives. Despite some obvious differences in perspective and emphasis, the populist Left and populist Right are ideological cousins and natural allies in the struggle against the elitist Center. This can most often be seen with overarching issues associated with democracy, community, and foreign policy.

According to Downs's Median Voter Theory, the two major political parties keep moving toward the Center to appeal to the median voter. If we accept the premise that the Center represents the Power Elite, then we can say that someone like David Rockefeller is the median voter. With this version of the Median Voter Theory, the bell curve represents the quantity of wealth and power, not the quantity of voters. The two major parties stay close to the Center not because most of the voters reside there, but because most of the wealth and power reside there. The quantity of voters and the quantity of money and power are in an inverse relationship. Most citizens cast their vote for one or another of the major parties despite the parties' centrism, not because of it. Downs asks if "indifferent voters [are] equally pleased by all parties or equally repelled by them." The latter seems to be the answer. If the two major parties reside in the Center of wealth and power, but the majority of voters do not reside there, it is not surprising that only half of the eligible voters decide to cast ballots in presidential elections. When people feel unrepresented year after year—regardless of which party is in the White House or controls Congress—many eventually give up in disgust or despair.[37]

Populism split in the late 1930s in response to Franklin Roosevelt's co-optation and changing of the word *liberalism*. Roughly speaking, populists who valued justice more than freedom remained liberals; populists who valued freedom more than justice became conservatives. Before this time, populism was synonymous with liberalism, which was committed to both social fairness and individual liberty. In the pre–New Deal days, elitists were conservatives. By the early 1940s, many populists who remained committed to an antistatist domestic policy and anti-imperialist foreign policy were being called conservative, even though the Jeffersonian conservatism of Robert Taft and his allies was quite distinct from the older Hamiltonian conservatism. Throughout the twentieth century, the ideological Center has been based in Wall Street. Just as the Bank of the United States symbolized the center of wealth and power for the first third of the nineteenth century, the international investment banks and corporate law firms of Wall Street have epitomized the dominant force in American economic and political life during the past one hundred years. Companies linked to Wall Street through stock ownership and legal services are giant, global corporations. The public policy positions of the Fortune 500 have been expressed through centrist groups such as the National Civic Federation, Conference Board, Council on Foreign Relations, Business Advisory Council, Committee for Economic Development, U.S. Chamber of Commerce, and American Enterprise Institute.[38]

Distinct from the robber barons of the Gilded Age, the corporate liberals of the Progressive Era were so-called enlightened conservatives because they muted their elitist rhetoric and came to terms with some of the social realities of their day. According to historian Gabriel Kolko, they saw potential benefits in a partnership between big business and big government.[39] Corporate liberals, or centrists, rejected a laissez-faire economy in favor of state capitalism. They were favorable toward regulation by the federal government

because it was an alternative to antitrust enforcement and supplanted super-
vision by more liberal state governments, and because the regulatory agencies could be hijacked, and thus turned into corporate helpers rather than
corporate watchdogs. Centrists advocated overseas military involvement and
the exporting of capitalism. They embraced Keynesian economics rather
than a simple and frugal government. They were willing to establish friendly
relations with organized labor because a partnership meant that the unions
would have a stake in the capitalist system and because American Federation
of Labor leaders supported the corporate-inspired foreign policy of contin-
ually expanding markets and military protection of overseas investments.
These policies were explored by the Wilson and Hoover administrations and
institutionalized by the Franklin Roosevelt administration. In the 1960s and
1970s, business conservatives of the Center—as opposed to value conservatives of the Right—supported the welfare state at home and détente abroad.
During the past seven decades, liberal Jeffersonians on the Left and conservative Jeffersonians on the Right have attempted—when they have not been
fighting each other over hot-button, polarizing issues—to thwart the bipartisan consensus of Hamiltonians in the Center.[40]

William Jennings Bryan was thrice nominated for the highest office in
the land by one of the nation's major political parties, but he remained on
the fringe of wealth and power. Friend and foe acknowledged the leftward
tilt of Bryan's thought. Even when they criticized him for his obsession with
silver or for political ineffectiveness, nonfusion Populists and Independence
Party supporters did not question the genuineness of his commitment to the
liberalism of Jefferson. Bryan was not a socialist, but Eugene Debs, who
went on to become the five-time presidential nominee of the Socialist Party,
supported Bryan for president in 1896. Bryan was often denounced as a socialist by his political enemies. While he rejected socialism as a system of political thought, Bryan was no red-baiter. In 1906, he wrote, "There should be
no unfriendliness between the honest individualist and the honest socialist;
both seek that which they believe to be best for society. The socialist, by
pointing out the abuses of individualism, will assist in their correction."
When Bryan was a presidential candidate, the contrast between the Democratic and Republican nominees was stark. There was no mistaking the attitude of Wall Street toward Bryan and vice versa. In the area of foreign
policy, as a quasi pacifist and anti-imperialist, Bryan swam decidedly upstream within the context of sociopolitical trends. His conflict with the
Center did not end with the crusade for free silver or with his last presidential bid in 1908. Bryan was still a leftist in the 1920s, as Lawrence Levine's
book clearly shows.[41]

Hubert Humphrey was a centrist from the beginning to the end of his political career. He was a founder of Americans for Democratic Action and a recipient of praise from Arthur Schlesinger Jr. Schlesinger's Vital Center stood in contrast to the reputed failures of the Right and the Left. Before *The Vital Center's* publication in 1949, some of its material appeared in the *New York Times Sunday Magazine* under the title "Not Left, Not Right." For Schlesinger, the Right consisted of business-dominated politicians and activists. Kenneth Wherry was an example. The Left consisted of progressive politicians and activists. Henry Wallace was an example. The Center consisted of liberal politicians and activists. Harry Truman was an example. Schlesinger asserted that the Right turns to fascism in its crisis of despair and the Left turns to communism, while the Center remains true to democracy and freedom. For Schlesinger, New Dealers were in some sense members of the Left. They were part of a doing, pragmatic, democratic Left tradition rather than a wailing, dogmatic, totalitarian Left tradition. According to Schlesinger, the formation of ADA in 1947 marked "perhaps as much as anything the watershed at which American liberalism began to base itself once again on a solid conception of man and of history." In *The Vital Center's* acknowledgments, he noted the influence of his fellow ADA founders: "They have helped to mold the general direction of my thinking and to renew in me the conviction that American liberalism has a bright future." Although he embraced liberalism and was willing to place his ideology within the framework of a noncommunist Left, Schlesinger's liberalism was centrist, not leftist in nature. He believed that American politics should be about "reasoned discourse and gradualism" rather than "utopian idealism or radical protest." In the late 1940s, Schlesinger and his allies castigated members and friends of the Communist Party of the USA (CPUSA), despite having openly collaborated with them in the Popular Front during the years of U.S. participation in World War II. Vital Centrists rejected not only American Stalinists but also liberals in the Jeffersonian tradition who opposed big business, refused to endorse American militarism and imperialism, wanted to move quickly on black civil rights, and upheld civil liberties for leftists. Senator Glen Hearst Taylor (D-ID) was clearly not a Communist, but he was subjected to a large amount of abuse for his public positions even before joining Henry Wallace on the Progressive Party ticket in 1948.[42]

Throughout his political career, Humphrey was viewed by the Right as a man of the Left. Humphrey was actually a lifelong spokesman for the Center, but his supposed leftism had some basis in fact. During World War II, "Uncle Joe" Stalin was the Vital Center's friend abroad and his CPUSA admirers were its friends at home. In 1944 the Communist Party endorsed

FDR for a fourth term. That same year, Humphrey sided with a "parasitic" procommunist group against traditional agrarian populists in pushing for fusion of the Minnesota Farmer-Labor Party and the Democratic Party. Mayor Humphrey courted procommunists within the state's CIO until March 1947. At that time, he unleashed an attack on the "Communists and their supporters" within the Democratic-Farmer-Labor Party (DFL) at an ADA-sponsored rally in Minneapolis. The party line of the Vital Center had changed. World War II was over; the Cold War was beginning. Humphrey urged "true liberals, true Democrats and true Farmer-Laborites" to recapture the DFL and proclaimed, "If I have to choose between being called a Red-baiter and a traitor, I'll be a Red-baiter." In June 1947, he said, "These people headed by Elmer Benson are trying to wreck the party, and if they don't succeed one way they will try another. . . . I am among those who helped shape the Democratic-Farmer-Labor Party and I am interested only in seeing that it stimulates action toward good government." Humphrey was taking an interesting stance. A Republican less than five years before this, he was now reading lifelong Farmer-Laborites out of the party. Considering Humphrey's own collaboration with quasi and actual Communists, his much-publicized attack may have had something to do with personal political rivalry at the state level and Cold War politics at the national level. The following year, former Governor Elmer Benson (FL-MN) supported Henry Wallace for president, while Humphrey backed Harry Truman. Benson was no Communist; he had roots in the Prohibition Party and was a La Follette supporter in 1924.[43] Benson's radicalism was of the homegrown American type, not the Moscow variety.

Humphrey's alliance with Reds in the mid 1940s branded him thereafter as a leftist in the eyes of Taft Republicans. It is important to understand, though, that throughout the decade, the traditional agrarians within the Farmer-Labor Party were more radical and more truly leftist than were the Communist sympathizers. The latter group was seeking a more popular vehicle than the CPUSA through which to work in Minnesota. It had no deep commitment to the Jeffersonianism of the FLP. The nonideological, opportunistic nature of the Red bloc can be seen in its 1939–1941 flip-flops on U.S. involvement in World War II (changes in party line reflecting changes in Kremlin foreign policy). In addition to his brief involvement with DFL Reds, Humphrey was viewed throughout his career by value conservatives as a "socialist," "pinko," or "procommunist" because of his support for the welfare state, the United Nations, and East/West trade and disarmament. The system of state capitalism underlying the social welfare programs of the Roosevelt, Truman, Kennedy, and Johnson administrations was actually a product of the Center and conflicted with the traditional economics of the American Left. Likewise, simultaneous empire-building and détente-pursuing was the foreign policy of the Center, not the Left.[44]

Since American liberalism shifted from Left to Center during the twentieth century, it was not incongruous for Humphrey to call himself a liberal while at the same time identifying himself with the ideological center. Mid-century, the word *liberal* was a popular term, and Vital Center Democrats did not hesitate to apply the label to themselves. Invoking the names of Thomas Jefferson and Andrew Jackson, Harry Truman publicly depicted the 1948 campaign as "A Year of Challenge: Liberalism or Conservatism." In a speech on the Senate floor in 1957, Humphrey remarked, "Insofar as I am sorry for anything, it is not because I am a liberal, but it is because I am not more liberal than I am." In 1964, he declared that he was "proud to be a modern American liberal."[45] The word *modern* should not be overlooked—this qualifier signified, among other things, the historical shift from Left to Center. Humphrey retained a liberal self-designation even in the mid-1970s, when the label was beginning to wane in popularity because it conjured up images of oppressive regulation, bloated bureaucracy, high taxation, and self-seeking special interest groups.

While consistently linking himself to the liberal label of New Deal fame, Humphrey tried to make clear that his liberalism was of the nonradical, nonextreme variety. Throughout his life, he "shied away from political polarities." Humphrey was no leftist during his undergraduate days at the University of Minnesota in the late 1930s. One professor remembers Humphrey as "a liberal Democrat willing to find the middle every time." In this, as in so many other aspects of his career, Humphrey was emulating his hero, Franklin Roosevelt. According to historian Barton Bernstein, FDR "explored the narrow center" and most of his New Deal colleagues were fellow "doctrinaires of the center." Arthur Schlesinger Jr., expositor of Vital Center Democracy, was also influenced by President Roosevelt, as well as by theologian Reinhold Niebuhr. Niebuhr was also a major influence on Humphrey and a supporter of his 1960 presidential campaign. Humphrey joined with Schlesinger, Niebuhr, Eleanor Roosevelt, and other centrists in founding Americans for Democratic Action. He served as chairman of the Minnesota chapter of ADA in 1947, chairman of ADA from 1949 to 1950, and vice chairman of ADA from 1950 to 1964. Positioned in the center between Henry Wallace liberals and Strom Thurmond conservatives, President Truman was able to defeat Thomas Dewey in 1948 despite the fractured condition of the Democratic Party. After the election, Humphrey was asked if ADA had been right in trying to dump Truman from the Democratic ticket.

He replied, "I think we were dead wrong." ADA dissatisfaction with Truman was about style and electability, not ideology. In the late 1940s and early 1950s, Senator Humphrey identified himself as a "Truman Democrat" and, initially, supported Truman for renomination against the more liberal Senator Estes Kefauver (D-TN).[46] Humphrey later supported ADA-affiliated Governor Adlai Stevenson (D-IL) for the 1952 nomination.

After Stevenson decided to sit out the 1960 presidential primaries, Arthur Schlesinger Jr. cast his lot with John Kennedy. As a White House aide during the Kennedy years, Schlesinger "attempted to defend the administration against attacks from what he viewed as the 'Radical Right' and the 'New Left' elements of the American political spectrum." As the Senate majority whip, Humphrey served a similar role. After Kennedy's death, the new chief executive continued the Vital Center tradition. In a May 1964 letter, Humphrey wrote, "President Johnson right now has universal acceptance—he occupies the center." When accepting the 1964 vice-presidential nomination, Humphrey said, "I believe in the two-party system, but there must be two responsible parties . . . It is imperative that the leadership of the great parties move within the mainstream of American thought and philosophy." He was equating "responsible" with centrist. Of course, adherents of the Right who rallied around Barry Goldwater argued that it was better to have a choice than an echo when entering the polling booth. During the fall campaign, Lyndon Johnson deliberately avoided the liberal label, preferring to run purely as a safe and sane centrist. On the verge of becoming vice president, Humphrey had "the commanding heights of the American political center lying open before him." In 1965, he told a visitor, "I suppose I'm left of center. I wouldn't deny that. But very moderately left of center."[47]

If Humphrey was only willing to go as far as calling himself a very moderate leftist, others were not so shy in attaching themselves to the American Left tradition. The New Left was a Jeffersonian revival in the 1960s. It recovered traditional liberalism's rejection of capitalism, statism, militarism, and imperialism. Ironically, FBI director J. Edgar Hoover was right on the mark when he declared, "The New Left is composed of radicals, anarchists, pacifists, crusaders, socialists, Communists, idealists, and malcontents"—he could also have included black power advocates and women's liberationists. The intellectuals who inspired the New Left were hostile toward the presidential ambitions of Vital Center Democrats from Roosevelt to Humphrey. For example, Dwight Macdonald respected William Jennings Bryan. He praised La Follette-Wheeler 1924 supporters Oswald Garrison Villard and Norman Thomas, saying each was "a real, old-fashioned, unreconstructed liberal who believes in freedom and justice for everybody," as opposed to the "totalitarian liberals" and "lib-labs" of the New Deal and Great Society. Macdonald opposed Humphrey's nomination and election in 1968; he supported McCarthy in the Democratic primaries and Gregory/Cleaver in the general election. In contrast to Macdonald, Zbigniew Brzezinski, chief foreign policy advisor of the 1968 Humphrey campaign, was sharply critical of the New Left. He believed it "threatened American liberalism in a manner reminiscent of the harm done to democratic American conservatism and liberal anticommunism by the McCarthy phenomenon of the 1950s."[48]

The feeling was mutual between the Humphrey wing of the Democratic Party and the New Left and Counterculture. Vice President Humphrey was hated and heckled by many students and activists as he traveled the country in the fall of 1968. Covering the 1972 presidential primaries for *Rolling Stone,* Hunter S. Thompson wrote, "There is no way to grasp what a shallow, contemptible, and hopelessly dishonest old hack Hubert Humphrey really is until you've followed him around for a while on the campaign trail." Thompson did not like George McGovern's choice of Senator Thomas Eagleton (D-MO) as a running mate, calling him a "hack" chosen to placate the "Meany/Daley/Muskie/Humphrey/Truman/LBJ axis" of Old Guard Democrats. During the 1960s and 1970s, Bob Dylan and Hubert Humphrey were. world-famous Minnesotans. Dylan, gifted artist and favorite troubadour of the New Left and Counterculture, was quite critical of American society, while Humphrey was upbeat and affirming. Early in his career, Dylan made a public break with limousine liberalism through his acerbic speech at an Emergency Civil Liberties Committee banquet in December 1963 and his subsequent move from folk to rock. It is a break Humphrey would never make. Positioned between Eugene McCarthy liberals and George Wallace conservatives, in 1968, Humphrey symbolized centrism within the Democratic Party. Two years later, he urged liberals to "scorn extremists of the left as well as extremists of the right."[49]

In 1974, two analysts wrote that Humphrey had been "moved by time and events to the deep center from the outer left wing of his party." Of course, Humphrey's former location on the Left was being exaggerated—it had been brief and more pragmatic than ideological in nature. Actually, Humphrey showed remarkable ideological consistency over the years. In the 1930s, his political hero was centrist Franklin Roosevelt, not candidates of the Left such as Thomas, Long, Borah, or Lemke. Working with ambitious Democrats and opportunistic Communists in the mid-1940s, he opposed the genuine Left within the Minnesota Farmer-Labor Party by pushing for fusion with the Democratic Party. By the late 1940s, he was publicly affiliated with the Vital Center of Americans for Democratic Action and Harry

Truman. Throughout the 1950s, he assisted Senate majority leader Lyndon Johnson, who worked with President Dwight Eisenhower in keeping the country on a centrist course.[50] Humphrey and his ADA colleagues seemed to be very liberal in 1960 only because there were no prominent voices of traditional liberalism speaking within the Democratic Party. Senator Wayne Morse (D-OR) came close to filling this role, but his presidential campaign did not take off. When a proper yardstick of the Left was available, as in 1968 and 1972, it was apparent that Humphrey was very much in the Center. Humphrey's ideological heirs in the Coalition for a Democratic Majority and the Democratic Leadership Council have often been described as "centrists." In the 1990s, left-wing Democrats sometimes described President Bill Clinton and his allies as "conservative," but they had little in common with the Right occupied by Governor George Wallace (D-AL) and other conservative populists. They were conservative only in a Hamiltonian sense. Funded by Fortune 500 companies, Clinton's New Democrats were in a tradition at least as old as August Belmont. There was nothing new about their allegiance to wealth and power. Centrist-oriented 2008 presidential possibilities like Albert Gore Jr., John Forbes Kerry, and Hillary Rodham Clinton symbolize part of Hubert Humphrey's legacy.

Radical vs. Respectable

The Power Elite and its spokespeople are suspicious of anything extreme in American politics. Politicians are expected to be responsible, mainstream, pragmatic, go along-to-get along, don't-rock-the boat centrists. Ideologues, whether of the "Radical Right" or the "Loony Left," are scorned. Members of the Establishment occupy the center of wealth and power in the nation, and they expect all proper political discourse to join them in the Center. The Center is the center not only of wealth and power but also of respectability. Pejorative adjectives are almost always attached to genuine representatives of the Left and the Right. Even populists without a clear identification with the Left or the Right are described as the radical Center, as was the case with supporters of Ross Perot and Jesse Ventura in the 1990s. Political scientist Richard Falk puts it well: "A central feature of ruling class objectives is to take the political center for granted as *the* realm of reason and responsibility. Such a position presupposes discrediting the left, and to a lesser degree, the far right. Such a centrist politics enables class privilege to persist without serious challenge."[51]

William Jennings Bryan was often called an anarchist and a socialist. He was neither of those things, but frequent use of such epithets suggests that he had a rather unrespectable political career. Congressman Bryan once said, "They call that man a statesman whose ear is attuned to the slightest pulsation of the pocket book, and they describe as a demagogue anyone who dares to listen to the heartbeat of humanity." Bryan and his allies were fiercely denounced during the 1896 presidential contest. In addition to charges of anarchism and socialism, they were attacked as agents of revolution and dishonor, as freaks and cranks, as dangerous men who posed a threat to the nation. It is remarkable that Bryan received as many popular votes as he did—47 percent—considering the unremitting hostility of virtually every metropolitan newspaper and magazine. William Randolph Hearst's *New York Journal* created a sensation when it endorsed Bryan because "the newspapers had been depicting him as a revolutionist, an anarchist, a corrupter of the young, a crack-pot, an idiot, a nihilist, a four-flusher, a confidence man and a menace to home, religion and public morals." Commenting on the results of the 1896 election, the *New York Tribune* took the opportunity to issue one more blast of invective against Bryan:

> The thing was conceived in iniquity and was brought forth in sin. It had its origin in a malicious conspiracy against the honor and integrity of the nation. It gained such monstrous growth as it enjoyed from an assiduous culture of the basest passions of the least worthy members of the community. . . . [Bryan] was only a puppet in the blood-imbued hands of Altgeld, the anarchist, and Debs, the revolutionist, and other desperadoes of that stripe. But he was a willing puppet . . . Not one of his masters was more apt than he at lies and forgeries and blasphemies and all the nameless iniquities of that campaign against the Ten Commandments. . . . He had less provocation than Benedict Arnold, less intellectual force than Aaron Burr, less manliness and courage than Jefferson Davis. He was the rival of them all in deliberate wickedness and treason to the Republic.[52]

Bryan's 1900 campaign was covered with the same hostility, if somewhat less hysteria, by the major news media. Some radical Populists, such as Henry Demarest Lloyd, liked Bryan more in 1900 than in 1896. In January 1904, Bryan told a group in New York City, "I did not have much chance to speak to some of you during the campaign. . . . You thought that we were radical; we were not; we were conservative; we were not advocating retaliation; we were simply asking that our institutions be built on justice." Bryan was willing to accept the radical label on some occasions. Following Alton Parker's nomination in 1904, Bryan announced his intention to organize

"the radical and progressive element in the Democratic party." Taking a di-
alectic approach, he told a group in Japan in 1905 that the radical and the
conservative are both "essential in a progressive state." When he ran for president again in 1908, Bryan was perceived as more conservative and the
mainstream media did not so often attack him as a radical. This was attribut-
able more to a change in the campaign climate than to a change in Bryan
himself. Two years before, Bryan told reporters that he was "more radical
than ever." Being more aware of sociopolitical ills and having grown accus-
tomed to the liberal rhetoric of President Theodore Roosevelt, voters were
demanding changes. Even Republican presidential nominee William Howard
Taft claimed to be a progressive. Some of Bryan's original issues were finally
achieving widespread acceptance, so they may have seemed less radical. On
the eve of the 1908 election, he was still a firm foe of corporate monopoly
and had taken up two new issues that represented a distinct break with the
status quo: state government ownership of railroads and publicizing of campaign contributions. In the end, almost all leading newspapers and magazines supported Taft over Bryan.[53]

Before, during, and after the 1912 election, Bryanites were viewed as radicals within the Democratic Party. When Secretary of State Bryan resigned
in 1915, the eastern press shouted "good-riddance" and denounced his "pro-
German" efforts. Ironically, although Bryan was condemned in his day for
his pacifistic stance within the pragmatic Wilson administration, he has been
pushed aside by mainstream historians who instead eulogize Woodrow Wilson as a visionary man of peace. When Bryan is remembered for anything
beyond his Cross of Gold speech, it is as a clownish figure symbolizing the
country bumpkins and religious zealots who tried to resist the coming of
the modern world. With the exception of a few scholarly instances, Bryan
did not have respectability in life or death.[54] Academia and the media are
the main bestowers of respectability in American society. Both are largely
dependent upon the Power Elite.[55] Unlike most politicians, Bryan did not
moderate his views as his career advanced. He refused to go along to get
along.

Bryan got *more* radical as the years went by. His 1896 campaign focused
on monetary policy. In the years before his 1900 campaign, he took up the
cause of anti-imperialism. In the years before his 1908 campaign, he embraced peaceful resolution of international conflicts, strict enforcement of
antitrust legislation, and local/state government ownership of natural monopolies. He went against the tide of wealth and power in opposing U.S.
entry into World War I. Far from resting on his laurels or making concessions
to the anointers of elder statesmen, Bryan was an innovative liberal in the

early 1920s. Democrats in the Bryan tradition were still being denounced as radicals during the closing years of his life. When Burton Wheeler ran for governor of Montana in 1920, the Anaconda Copper-controlled press called him "Bolshevik Burt." Senator Wheeler's attempt to expose the corruption of the Harding administration was attributed to his alleged Communism. When Bryan's brother, Governor Charles Bryan (D-NE), was running for vice president in 1924, he was attacked as a dangerous representative of socialism.[56] The 1924 Republican slogan "Coolidge or Chaos" was aimed partly at two Bryan Democrats: Progressive vice-presidential nominee Wheeler and Democratic vice-presidential nominee Bryan.

In 1939, Hubert Humphrey approvingly noted that his political hero, Franklin Roosevelt, was "no radical." An early Humphrey biography correctly points out, "No one has ever credited Humphrey with really radical opinions, except perhaps the extreme rightists, who would also class Eisenhower and Nixon and others as 'radicals.'" Rarely called a radical himself, Humphrey instead used the word against political opponents on both ends of the spectrum. He attacked reputed Communists as dangerous radicals and traitors during the Minnesota Democratic-Farmer-Labor Party power struggle of the late 1940s. In accepting the 1964 vice-presidential nomination, he condemned the radicalism of Goldwater and his supporters. The Johnson-Humphrey campaign team castigated the Goldwater effort as radical and extreme throughout the fall. Goldwater was linked to both communism and fascism. Senator William Fulbright (D-AR) compared Goldwater to Stalin and George Meany of the AFL-CIO compared him to Hitler.[57] The use of inflammatory rhetoric by President Johnson's campaign against Senator Goldwater is comparable to the rhetoric used by President Coolidge's campaign against Senator La Follette. If there is a parallel between 1964 and 1924, Hubert Humphrey was playing the role of Charles Dawes, not Burton Wheeler or Charles Bryan.

In 1965, it was reported, "Humphrey does not think of himself as ever having been radical." Humphrey said, "That's pretty conservative country I come from. . . . We don't go in for these far-out things." The question is, "far-out" by whose standards? Throughout the Gilded Age and the Progressive Era, many Minnesotans were far-out by the standards of the metropolitan press. Much to the displeasure of the eastern elite and its midwestern allies, Minnesota was a longtime hotbed of populism and progressivism. The Grange was strong in the state. People's Party cofounder Ignatius Donnelly and Non-Partisan League founder Arthur C. Townley were from Minnesota. Minnesota was a Republican state, but its Republicanism had a large liberal component. In 1912, the Progressive Party ticket of Theodore Roosevelt and Hiram Johnson carried the state. In 1920, it gave Eugene Debs of the Socialist Party his second-highest popular-vote percentage in the nation. In 1924, Minnesota was La Follette's third strongest state. La Follette delivered his controversial antiwar speech of September 1917 to an appreciative crowd of farmers in St. Paul. Minnesota was the home of Congressman Charles Lindbergh Sr., a La Follette Republican and definite radical. Farmer-Laborites Henrik Shipstead, Magnus Johnson, and Ernest Lundeen were elected to the U.S. Senate from Minnesota. The state's radically liberal tradition continued into the New Deal years. Minnesota elected Farmer-Laborites to the governor's chair in 1930, 1932, 1934, and 1936. In the early 1930s, Governor Floyd Olson (FL-MN) announced that he was a "radical," not a "liberal." The Farmer-Labor platform began by saying, "We declare that capitalism has failed." In 1936, Minnesota was the second strongest state of Union Party presidential nominee William Lemke, a La Follette Republican. Humphrey was correct in his self-assessment of nonradicalism. By 1964, he was more reminiscent of Senator Frank Kellogg than of Senator Henrik Shipstead. Humphrey may have been projecting his own ideological bent onto the people of his state. At the time he was telling an interviewer that Minnesota was a "pretty conservative" state that didn't go in for "far-out things," James Youngdale was compiling an anthology from the writings and speeches of midwestern radicals with an emphasis on Minnesota![58]

In 1968, Democratic presidential hopefuls Eugene McCarthy and Robert Kennedy were sometimes viewed as radicals. No one viewed Humphrey as a radical. During debate on the Vietnam War platform plank at the 1968 Democratic National Convention, Congressman Wayne Hays (D-OH), a Humphrey supporter, denounced the antiwar demonstrators in Chicago's Grant Park as a minority who would substitute "anarchism for ambition . . . beards for brains, license for liberty . . . pot for patriotism . . . sideburns instead of solutions . . . slogans instead of social reform . . . and . . . riots for reason."[59] New Left supporters of McCarthy were frequently attacked by Humphreyites as "radicals," "freaks," "cowards," and "pinkos" for their criticism of the status quo and opposition to the Vietnam War. In the late 1960s and early 1970s, Humphrey was most strongly opposed within the Democratic Party by campus radicals associated with the New Left and Counterculture.

Bryan was consistently attacked and ridiculed by the metropolitan press, but this was not the case with Humphrey. In Minnesota, he was received more positively by the city newspapers than by the small-town newspapers. The eastern-based media was virtually unanimous in its support of the Johnson-Humphrey ticket in 1964. Mainstream newspapers, magazines, journals, and television networks were generally respectful in their treatment of Humphrey throughout his long career.[60] Robert La Follette was the Republican counterpart to William Jennings Bryan during the 1885–1925 period. Bryan and La Follette were friends, they favored each other for the presidential nomination of their respective parties, and their commitment to liberal ideology often transcended partisanship.[61] In the context of radical vs. respectable, the contrasts between Senator La Follette and Senator Humphrey are stark. La Follette's biggest controversy in the U.S. Senate was opposing World War I; Humphrey's biggest controversy in the U.S. Senate was criticizing Harry Byrd. La Follette was a pariah in the Senate from start to finish; Humphrey was elevated to Senate majority whip and deputy president pro tem. La Follette deserted his party's presidential nominee at the end of his life; Humphrey was the presidential choice of his party's bosses at the end of his life. La Follette was widely castigated as a Bolshevik; Humphrey was widely dismissed as a bleeding heart. La Follette was most hated by Hamiltonians on Wall Street; Humphrey was most hated by Jeffersonians of the Old Right and the New Left.

William Jennings Bryan was, in comparison to Hubert Humphrey, much closer to the philosophy of Thomas Jefferson. In examining the emphases and assumptions that served as the foundation for the ideological tenets of our two exemplars of twentieth-century Democratic liberalism, we have seen that Bryan gravitated toward a clearly defined ideology, idealistic commitment, populism, social morality, the common good, agrarianism, leftism, and radicalness. In direct contrast, Humphrey gravitated toward pragmatism, political compromise, elitism, materialistic policy, special interests, urbanism, centrism, and respectability.

CHAPTER 7

Sources of Support

Liberal Interest Groups

An examination of political support must be carefully conceived if it is to yield manageable and revealing information. What types of persons and groups are most important and relevant within the context of a study of the ideological nature of Democratic Party liberalism? The question could be addressed from a positive angle or a negative angle. Support from the liberal segment of society could be examined. One problem with this approach is that many interest groups perceived as liberal today did not have eighteenth- and nineteenth-century counterparts. Feminism, ecology, abortion, animal rights, and similar causes were either nonexistent or in an incipient stage during the days of Jefferson and Bryan. Interest groups claiming to represent blocs of voters that were present during earlier periods may or may not be truly representative of their own members. According to Robert Michel's "Iron Law of Oligarchy," every organization—no matter how democratic in origin—has a tendency toward rule by the few. Thus, the aims of an interest group in 1968 may be quite different from the aims of the same group in 1896, even if the professed aims are similar. Time may well have resulted in internal oligarchization or external co-optation.

An example of this phenomenon is the American Federation of Labor. Championing the rights and aspirations of manual laborers is a component of liberalism that stretches back to the days of early American mechanics and artisans. Bryan and Humphrey each received considerable support from labor unions during their presidential campaigns. There are indications, however, that Samuel Gompers and the early twentieth-century AFL were ideologically different from George Meany and the midcentury AFL-CIO. Even during the Bryan era, many liberals felt that Gompers was too willing to compromise with the capitalistic status quo. Despite some conservative tendencies, Gompers's commitment to traditional, Jeffersonian liberalism is indicated by his support for the Populist ticket in 1892 and the Progressive ticket in 1924.[1] In contrast, it is inconceivable that Meany would have supported the Union ticket in 1936 and the Peace and Freedom ticket in 1968. The seeds of corporate liberalism present within organized labor in the 1910s had grown, taken root, and blossomed by the 1940s. The name of the organization remained the same, but its ideology had changed considerably. Far from being political radicals, according to sociologist C. Wright Mills, labor leaders "simply wanted a larger cut of the economic pie. They were rapidly becoming integrated into the main power system as a junior partner and had thus relinquished any aspirations for structural change." In addition to corporate co-optation of the unions, Mills was concerned about "growing authoritarianism and corruption in the ranks of organized labor."[2]

Monied Interests

Because of problems associated with examining support from liberal interest groups, it may be more valuable to focus on support from groups representative of Hamiltonian conservatism. Early American liberalism had a number of important tenets, but support for democracy was foundational. This support did not exist in a vacuum. *Democracy* meant something quite particular—it meant rule by the common people, and it meant opposition to aristocracy. All of the other tenets of liberalism flowed from and were linked to the democratic imperative. Thomas Jefferson believed that the purpose of a liberal political party was to curb "the excesses of the monied interests." This view of liberalism did not die with Jefferson. It was at the center of the campaigning and governing of Andrew Jackson, Martin Van Buren, and William Jennings Bryan. It did not become extinct even after the seismic 1925–1938 ideological shift within liberalism. In 1992 and 1996, liberal presidential candidates Jerry Brown and Ralph Nader invoked Jefferson's "monied interests" quote to explain their opposition to Bill Clinton.[3]

Contributions from and affiliations with the monied interests tell us something important about the nature of, if not the authenticity of, a liberal candidate for public office. If the question of liberal ideology is going to be addressed from a negative angle, it is vital that this antithesis of liberalism, that these monied interests, be clearly defined. According to Jeffersonian thought, people can be categorized as either populists or elitists, democrats or aristocrats. By personality, upbringing, and/or belief, people tend to lean toward one or the other. The most powerful elitists in the United States are known collectively as the Power Elite, the ruling class, or the Establishment.[4] Who belongs to the Establishment? In a capitalist nation, the owners of large amounts of capital are often at the top of the power pyramid. In the 1990s, presidential candidate Ross Perot referred to American citizens as "the owners of the country," but, in a strictly economic sense, his reference was inaccurate. About 1.6 percent of the American population owns 80 percent of all capital stock, 89 percent of all corporate bonds, and 100 percent of all state and municipal bonds. Five New York City-based banks hold a controlling share of stock in three-fourths of the top 324 corporations. According to political scientist Thomas Dye, about forty-three thousand Americans, or two one-thousandth of one percent of the population, control over half of the nation's industrial assets, half of all commercial and utilities assets, two-thirds of all banking assets, and over two-thirds of all insurance assets.[5]

The influence of wealthy Americans is not confined to banking, industry, and commerce: it extends to every part of society—from art to entertainment, from information to sports. Gore Vidal, a liberal populist, defines the Establishment as "a loose consortium that includes the editors of the *New York Times* and the *Washington Post,* the television magnates, the Rockefellers, Kennedys, ITT, IBM, etc." Charley Reese, a conservative populist, defines it as "that collection of investment banks, commercial banks, global corporations, and the think tanks, academics, and media outlets they own or fund or influence." Many believe that politics and government in the United States have been dominated by high finance and big business since the founding of the republic.[6] The dominant role of wealth calls into question the democratic nature of the American political system.

The historical origins of the American Establishment can be largely traced to the aristocratic Federalists of the East Coast. Centered in Boston, Philadelphia, and New York, many of these upper-class families were of English descent, and they continued to be Anglophiles in their politics and customs after the Revolution. As bankers, shippers, merchants, and lawyers, they were the driving force behind the effort to replace the Articles of Confederation with the Constitution. In the early nineteenth century, they played an important role in the rise of manufacturing and stock speculation. During that century, some immigrant families joined the English- and Dutch-descended old stock as members of the Establishment. John Jacob Astor, August Belmont, John D. Rockefeller, and Jacob Schiff were German Americans. They were not descended from *Mayflower* passengers or New

Amsterdam founders, but their acquisition of money opened the doors of high society. Originally a fur magnate, Astor increased his fortune through New York City real estate dealings. His family eventually established ties to the English aristocracy. Belmont came to America in 1837 as the U.S. agent of the House of Rothschild. While many of the Gilded Age "robber barons" and "plutocrats" were Republicans, the Belmont family were powerful Democrats. Rockefeller founded the Standard Oil Trust with the Whitney, Pratt, Harkness, Payne, Rogers, and Flagler families. He later moved into banking with National City Bank and Chase National Bank. Schiff became the head of the Kuhn, Loeb and Company banking firm. During and after the Civil War, bankers used a myriad of railroad companies to make millions through the stock market. J. P. Morgan and Company, America's most powerful banking firm for many years, originated in London as George Peabody and Company in 1838.[7] Through his bank, Morgan and his partners controlled numerous corporations, including U.S. Steel, General Electric, DuPont, Northern Pacific Railroad, AT&T, New York Life Insurance, and General Motors.

In the late nineteenth and early twentieth centuries, the nouveau riche Belmonts, Rockefellers, Schiffs, and Morgans, as well as the Vanderbilts, Mellons, Lehmans, and Harrimans, joined the Cabots, Bayards, Frelinghuysens, Wadsworths, and other more genteel, Federalist-descended families as members of the Establishment. They worked together in fashioning an economic system of monopoly capitalism and a bipartisan political system that protected and assisted the economic system.[8] It was not a conspiracy; it was a relatively small group of wealthy individuals who shared certain social and occupational traits. Considering their elite educations, eastern social networks, luxurious lifestyles, and deep-seated commitment to capitalism, it is not surprising that they often worked together on economic and political activities. Certainly some of these joint ventures were discreetly handled in private because of their impolitic nature, but most were done publicly with the metropolitan press on hand to celebrate the goings on.

Contributions

When looking at financial support for political candidates who were professed liberals, it is interesting to note how heavily they relied on large contributions from wealthy, corporate donors and the nature of the well-heeled, business-oriented donors. Were the donors tied to the center of wealth and power or were they economic and political mavericks? Were they champions of monopolistic megacorporations or leaders of midsized companies? Did the donors have a history of obtaining private gain from the public purse or were they known as liberal ideologues? Were they tied to Wall Street or were they entrepreneurs who relied on local, noneastern banks for funding?

In 1896, Democratic presidential nominee William Jennings Bryan faced Republican nominee William McKinley in the general election. McKinley was originally sponsored by John D. Rockefeller, but J. P. Morgan and the rest of Wall Street climbed on board during the fall campaign. McKinley's 1896 war chest, managed by Mark Hanna, included $50,000 from Morgan's New York Life Insurance, $174,000 from western railroads, and $250,000 from Rockefeller's Standard Oil. Every bank and trust company in New York except one and most of the insurance companies donated to the GOP candidate.

According to political scientist Louis Koenig, "While the community of financiers and industrialists provided Mark Hanna with princely sums, the substantial men in Bryan's ranks were as scarce as hen's teeth." A handful of wealthy Democrats such as shipbuilder Arthur Sewall of Maine, newspaper owner John McLean of Ohio, and banker Henry G. Davis of West Virginia made large contributions, but "neither individually nor collectively were they in the same league with Hanna's men of wealth." At the Democratic National Convention, Bryan refused to make McLean his running mate in exchange for the support of the Ohio delegation, and he later threatened to refuse the presidential nomination if McLean was given the second spot on the ticket. McLean's subsequent actions within the party confirmed Bryan's suspicions. Sewall was Bryan's Democratic running mate. The Populists refused to accept the millionaire businessman from Maine, choosing Thomas Watson of Georgia instead. Other than his rejection of McLean, Bryan did not express a preference for running mate, so the convention delegates eventually chose Sewall, a strong supporter of free silver. Davis supported the Bryan-Sewall ticket, but he was never enthusiastic about the Great Commoner's liberalism. After Bryan's 1900 defeat he expressed the hope that the party would at last be rid of Bryanism.[9] In 1904, Davis was the running mate of conservative Alton B. Parker, and Bryan campaigned only minimally for the ticket.

In an 1893 speech to the House, Bryan argued that even if mine owners favored free coinage of silver for selfish reasons, they were no more selfish than other occupational groups and were simply asking for the restoration of a right they had enjoyed from 1792 to 1873. In the 1930s, Ferdinand Lundberg reported that Marcus Daly, head of Anaconda Copper Mining Company, raised $289,000 for the Democrats in 1896. Anaconda, a Montana-based company dominated by Rockefeller's National City Bank, had silver holdings as well as copper. More recently, Louis Koenig has written that owners of silver mines in the West actually contributed relatively little to the Bryan campaign. Regardless of the truth concerning Daly's reputed involvement, one wealthy Democrat with mining ties did play an important role in the Bryan campaign. William Randolph Hearst, the son of Senator George Hearst (D-CA), was an heir to gold, copper, and silver mines. But the younger Hearst was known more as a publishing magnate than as a mining magnate. Owner of the *San Francisco Examiner* and *New York Journal,* he created a sensation when his Gotham publication endorsed Bryan for president, while all of the other major newspapers in the East were boosting McKinley and castigating Bryan. According to historian Paul Glad, Hearst was the largest contributor to Bryan's campaign. He collected $41,000, which included $20,000 of his own money.[10] Even this was small in comparison with many Republican donations.

Some have maintained that Hearst's support for Bryan in 1896 was motivated by his silver holdings in the West, by a desire for increased newspaper circulation, and by hopes of climbing to the top of the Democratic Party. Obviously, Hearst was a man of wealth and ambition, but these explanations do not explain his support for Bryan in 1900 and his record thereafter of supporting liberal candidates and causes. Hearst actually opposed free silver in 1896 and was not enthusiastic about Bryan's anti-imperialism stance in 1900. He did, however, share with Bryan a genuine opposition to monopoly. Hearst's support for the Democratic nominee did boost the circulation of the *Journal,* but he did not profit from his endorsement of Bryan because of the loss of progold advertisers. The usually reliable Ferdinand Lundberg presents a picture of Hearst that is too one-dimensional and too cynical. In the mid-1930s, liberal Oswald Garrison Villard presented a similarly negative assessment of Hearst.[11] Perhaps these unbalanced treatments can best be understood in the light of who Hearst was by the 1930s: he had become an admirer of such illiberal figures as Calvin Coolidge, Benito Mussolini, and Alfred Landon.

Regardless of what he was during his twilight years, at the turn of the century, William Randolph Hearst was widely seen as a left-wing enfant terrible. Like automobile manufacturer Henry Ford, Hearst was independent of Wall Street banks for most of his life. Hearst's bank account and publishing outlets afforded him the opportunity to personally plunge into politics. In the mid-1900s, he served two terms as a congressman from New York. He was an active candidate for the 1904 Democratic presidential nomination. In 1903, conservatives began pushing Alton B. Parker as a counterweight to the rising candidacy of Hearst. During this period, Bryan praised Hearst for his "immense service to the party" and for demonstrating that "wealth need not lead a man away from the people." Hearst supported an eight-hour work day, government ownership of railroads and telegraphs, a graduated income tax, and popular election of U.S. senators. Although Tom Watson, Bryan's 1896 Populist running mate, was an admirer of Hearst, the publisher was relatively weak in the South, which was a bastion of support for Bryan. Hearst was strong among laborers in the northern cities. Clarence Darrow, a law partner of Governor John Peter Altgeld (D-IL) and supporter of Bryan in 1896 and 1900, seconded Hearst's nomination at the 1904 convention. On the other hand, many liberal Democrats were suspicious of, if not hostile toward, Hearst. Some were scandalized by his private life. Some viewed him as an ambitious opportunist. Some disapproved of his great wealth. Senator John Kern (D-IN), who would become Bryan's running mate four years later, accused Hearst of trying to buy the presidential nomination. Bryan himself had warm words for Hearst, but he declined to endorse his candidacy.[12]

Hearst was a leader of the radical wing of the Democratic Party from 1904 to 1908. In 1906, Bryan suggested that Hearst should be considered for the 1908 nomination; in contrast, Hearst was hated by conservatives such as Thomas Fortune Ryan and Perry Belmont. When Bryan decided to run for the nomination, Hearst opposed his election. In the fall of 1908, Clarence Darrow supported Thomas Hisgen, nominee of Hearst's Independence Party. Hearst had wanted Robert La Follette to be the new party's standard-bearer, but he remained a Republican. Hearst supported Champ Clark for the 1912 Democratic nomination. Like many liberals, Hearst opposed U.S. entry into World War I and the League of Nations, and he continued to oppose involvement with the League and the World Court during the Harding years. Hearst was friendly toward liberal presidential contenders Senator Hiram Johnson (R-CA) and Senator James Reed (D-MO) during the 1920s. At the 1924 Democratic convention, he joined Bryan in proposing Senator Thomas Walsh (D-MT) for the presidential nomination. The Hearst newspaper chain supported Coolidge in the fall of 1924, but Hearst allowed his *International Magazine* to endorse La Follette.[13] Whatever his inconsistencies during and after this period, from 1896 to 1928, his financial contribution to Bryan's first campaign was not out of ideological character for either the donor or the recipient.

Despite the backing of Hearst and a few other wealthy Democrats, Bryan's campaign was largely a grassroots effort. In August 1896, Democratic Party chairman James Jones wrote an open letter to the American people pleading for money, saying, "No matter in how small sums, no matter by what humble contributions, let the friends of liberty and national honor contribute all they can to the good cause." While Democrats were strapped

for cash, money rolled into the Republican coffers. One estimate of McKinley's spending is $3.5 million, and this seems to be a rather conservative fig-
ure. The clerk of the House of Representatives later estimated that the
Republican fund was $16.5 million while the Democratic fund was
$425,000. Referring to Bryan's campaign, Governor Altgeld said, "It was
confronted by all the trusts, all the syndicates, all the corporations, all the
great papers. It was confronted by everything that money could buy, that
boodle could debauch, or that fear of starvation could coerce." Realizing
that the party could not turn to "classes that enjoy special privileges" for
money, Bryan endorsed a plan for every Democratic voter to send one dollar to the Democratic National Committee. Looking toward the 1900 election, Altgeld declared, "If the sugar trust or the Standard Oil trust would give
us $10,000,000 to make a campaign with, our cause would be lost. It would
be Clevelandism over again. Even if we won the election, our moral force
would be gone and we would accomplish nothing." Bryan minced no words
when it came to former President Grover Cleveland, contending, "He secured his nomination in 1892 by a secret bargain with the financiers; his
committee collected from the corporations and spent the largest campaign
fund the party ever had . . . Having debauched his party he was offended by
its effort to reform and gave comfort to the enemy."[14] Industrialist Andrew
Carnegie supported McKinley and vehemently warned against the election
of Bryan in 1896. In 1900, Bryan refused to downplay socioeconomic issues
to gain the backing of Carnegie, and despite sharing anti-imperialist views
with Bryan, Carnegie ended up endorsing McKinley once again.

As noted above, Bryan's rematch with McKinley in 1900 had the strong
support of publisher William Randolph Hearst. Wall Street speculator
Thomas Fortune Ryan reportedly gave a secret $500,000 contribution to
the Democrats in 1900. If Ryan did give such a gift, it did not purchase any
goodwill from Bryan. In 1904, Bryan accused Ryan and the other eastern
plutocrats who were supporting Alton Parker of contributing to the party's
defeat in 1896 and 1900. In 1906, Bryan told one of Ryan's friends, who was
trying to arrange a private meeting between the two, that the businessman
would have to "rid himself of all personal pecuniary interests, at least, all corporations having to do with public utilities, railroad stocks and bonds, and all
such properties, and invest his money in Government bonds" if he wanted
to join the fight for democracy. A resolution offered by Bryan at the 1912
Democratic National Convention specifically condemned Ryan as a member
of "the privilege-hunting and favor-seeking class." In 1900, the Republicans
reportedly spent $9.5 million on their ticket, and the Democrats, $425,000.[15]
The paucity of Democratic money was a Bryanesque phenomenon. When
conservative Grover Cleveland was the Democratic nominee in 1884 and

1892, he outspent the Republican nominee (in the latter contest, he spent $2,350,000). When conservative Alton Parker was the nominee in 1904, he was outspent by the GOP but was able to raise $1,250,000. Bryan's constant financial handicap was a result of ideology, not party.

Despite the controversy it engendered, Bryan was always willing to identify and publicize the financiers behind conservative Democrats. He was more than willing to alienate the party's biggest contributors, both privately and publicly. This was certainly true in the case of Perry Belmont and August P. Belmont, sons of the House of Rothschild banker who had led conservative Democrats during the second half of the nineteenth century. In 1899, Perry Belmont tried to organize a dinner in New York City to reconcile the Bryan and Cleveland wings of the Democratic Party. Bryan wrote to Belmont, "No party advantage is to be derived from political communion between Jeffersonian Democrats who stand upon the Chicago [1896] platform and the Republican allies who masquerade as democrats between campaigns in order to give more potency to their betrayal of democratic principles on election day." In 1902, Bryan expressed public satisfaction that Perry Belmont had been defeated in a race for Congress. Bryan's famous antiplutocracy resolution introduced at the 1912 Democratic National Convention condemned J. P. Morgan, Thomas Fortune Ryan, and August P. Belmont by name. Bryan was, however, politically close to a third Belmont brother—O. H. P. Belmont, a supporter of the Chicago platform and committed liberal despite his personal wealth.[16]

Between his 1900 and 1908 campaigns, Bryan repeatedly warned against what he believed were the dangerous effects of corporate wealth on the American political system. In his view, influences that began thriving during the Gilded Age had resulted in corruption: "Voters were bought; city councils were bribed; state legislatures became the tools of railroads and monopolies, and the instrumentalities of the federal government were turned to private gain." Recalling his 1896 campaign, he wrote,

> The plutocratic element of the party deserted and ever since that time has been plotting against the party. . . . It is planning now [1903] to give the democratic nomination to a representative of corporate wealth whose campaign would be made on money furnished by the trusts and whose administration, if won, would be controlled by Wall Street, as Mr. Cleveland's last administration was.

From 1906 to 1908, he warned against the size and secrecy of campaign contributions and took steps to limit and publicize contributions made to himself.[17]

In 1908, Bryan told Democrats that he would reject the nomination if the party platform did not contain a plank calling for campaign contribution publicity. Recognizing popular anger over the flood of corrupt money in politics, President Theodore Roosevelt and Republican nominee William Howard Taft tried to link Bryan to Standard Oil money. It was an ironic charge, since Taft himself was a political creation of the Standard Oil machine in Ohio and since John D. Rockefeller was a public supporter of Taft. Steel magnate Henry Clay Frick gave over $50,000 to the Republicans. Andrew Carnegie and J. P. Morgan and Company each gave $20,000. Unlike Taft, Bryan voluntarily publicized his own contributions. While one source says Bryan relied on small contributors during the 1908 campaign, another source points out that he did receive some large donations—the biggest being from newspaper owner Herman Ridder, who gave him $37,000. Tammany Hall gave $10,000, mining magnate William A. Clark gave $4,000, and Standard Oil gave $5,000 to the Democratic Party after the election to help defray its campaign debts. These interests may have given money because they believed Bryan's grip on the party was over after his third defeat. In 1908, the Republicans reportedly spent $1.7 million on their ticket while the Democrats spent $750,000.[18]

Bryan's magazine, *The Commoner,* refused to accept advertising revenue from trusts. Bryan joined clergyman Washington Gladden in condemning the acceptance of "tainted money" by religious groups and educational institutions. During the 1905–1909 period, Bryan waged his own battles over gifts from plutocratic philanthropists. He refused an invitation to join the board of trustees of his alma mater, Illinois College, until it severed ties to the Rockefeller-funded University of Chicago, and he resigned from the board when the college decided to apply for Rockefeller and Carnegie grants. He also opposed the acceptance of Rockefeller and Carnegie grants by the University of Nebraska.[19] In 1912, Bryan actively opposed the presidential campaigns of Governor Judson Harmon (D-OH) and Congressman Oscar Underwood (D-AL) because they were backed by Wall Street. He turned against House Speaker Champ Clark (D-MO) during the Democratic National Convention, embracing Governor Woodrow Wilson (D-NJ), because he believed—mistakenly, perhaps—that Clark had become Wall Street's choice for the nomination. In 1916, Bryan declared, "In campaigns, extending over twelve years, I polled almost the same number of votes three times; it was practically six millions and a half of votes three times; and in all that time, I never had the support of a predatory corporation or of a newspaper that was under obligation to them." As he had done in 1904 and 1912, in 1924, Bryan publicly opposed candidates for the Democratic presidential nomination whom he believed were beholden to Wall Street.[20]

Hubert Humphrey's political career began in Minneapolis, Minnesota, in the mid-1940s. His 1945 mayoral bid received a favorable response from John Cowles of the *Minneapolis Star-Journal and Tribune,* John Pillsbury of Pillsbury Mills, grain merchant Peavey Heffelfinger, and Lucian Sprague of the Minneapolis and St. Louis Railroad. His reelection campaign in 1947 was supported by the president of the chamber of commerce, vice presidents of General Mills, Pillsbury, and Honeywell, and all of the city newspapers. Humphrey had strong ties to large agribusiness companies throughout his career. In the early 1950s, the Mine, Mill, and Smelter Workers union portrayed Senator Humphrey as a tool of big business: "The men who sell Wheaties comprise the board of directors of General Mills, the grain monopoly of the Morgan empire. Wheaties is just one of their products. Gold Medal flour is another. Humphrey another." Humphrey supporters responded to such criticism by accusing the union of being controlled by Communists. Cargill, a Rockefeller-linked international grain distribution company, had a close relationship with Humphrey.[21]

For decades, Dwayne Andreas and William Benton were Humphrey's leading financial patrons. Close friends as well as campaign funders, they assisted him both personally and politically. Andreas, who served as chairman of Archer Daniels Midland (ADM), an agricultural commodities processing company, from 1970 to 1998, first contributed to Humphrey in 1948. Despite his midwestern origins, Andreas is eastern and global in orientation, and he has belonged to several elite, New York-based foreign policy groups, including the Council on Foreign Relations and Trilateral Commission. He personally introduced Humphrey to the leaders of Wall Street. Andreas's attorneys have included Thomas Dewey and Robert Strauss.[22] Dewey, a close Andreas friend, was a three-term governor of New York and two-time Republican presidential nominee. Dewey was a Wall Street favorite when he sought the White House in 1940, 1944, and 1948. Strauss is a former ADM board member and Democratic National Committee chairman. He served as U.S. trade representative and as an ambassador to the Soviet Union. Strauss has been described as "perhaps the best connected of all the leading Democrats to Wall Street and the multinationals," and he has been called the "Ultimate Capitalist." He became chairman of the Democratic Party following the 1972 election as the choice of the Humphrey-Jackson wing of the party.[23]

Senator William Benton (D-CT) contributed money to Humphrey's 1960, 1968, and 1972 presidential campaigns. Benton was a Yale graduate, advertising executive, University of Chicago vice president, encyclopedia company owner, State Department official, and U.S. senator. By the time he befriended Humphrey, Benton was a "multimillionaire liberal with access to corporate boardrooms and Eastern salons." Marvin Rosenberg of New York was head of the eastern division of the 1960 Humphrey for President Committee. Two years earlier, as treasurer of the Harriman Businessmen's Committee, Rosenberg worked for the reelection of Governor W. Averell Harriman (D-NY), a Union Pacific Railroad heir and Wall Street banker. Originally married to Marie Norton Whitney, the former wife of Cornelius Vanderbilt Whitney, Harriman contributed to the Republican Party that fielded Harding-Coolidge in 1920, sat on the board of J. P. Morgan's Guaranty Trust Company, and rubbed shoulders with the likes of Perry Belmont and Herbert L. Pratt Jr. as a member of the exclusive Jockey Club. Harriman was a pillar of the Establishment by the 1940s, and he supported Humphrey for president in 1968.[24]

Despite his ties to wealthy donors, Humphrey frequently echoed his populist father in condemning the dangerous influence of big money in politics. In 1952, he called upon a Senate committee to investigate preconvention contributions to and spending by presidential candidates. When he announced his candidacy for the 1960 presidential nomination, he told the press that he was the candidate of "the plain people of the country." Humphrey had some wealthy backers during that campaign, but he certainly lacked the personal resources of rivals John Kennedy, Stuart Symington, Lyndon Johnson, and Adlai Stevenson. Campaigning as the vice-presidential nominee in 1964, Humphrey charged that Barry Goldwater represented a "money grubbing" force. Actually, unlike Johnson-Humphrey, Goldwater ran a grassroots campaign. According to George Thayer, most contributors to Goldwater's campaign gave small amounts: "Approximately 650,000 individuals gave $100 or less, an extraordinary number considering the fact that Goldwater's chances of becoming President were never considered very good." Analysts of mid-1960s American politics compare Goldwater, not Humphrey, to William Jennings Bryan. Not only did Bryan and Goldwater both take a moralistic and nostalgic approach to politics, but both relied on relatively small donors, attacked the eastern Establishment, and ran strongest in the South and West. With big businessmen of both parties "falling over themselves to contribute to the Johnson-Humphrey treasury," the financiers of the Democratic ticket were not "grubbing" after the nation's money because they already possessed most of it. Humphrey's vice-presidential candidacy was supported by John L. Loeb Jr. of Carl M. Loeb, Rhoades; Donald Cook of American Electric Power; Henry Ford II of Ford Motor; Thomas S. Lamont of Morgan Guaranty Trust; Sidney Weinberg of Goldman, Sachs; Lewis Douglas of Western Bankcorp; Sol Linowitz of Xerox; Kenneth

Adams of Phillips Petroleum; and at least two Cabots of Boston. Dean Rusk of
the Rockefeller Foundation; C. Douglas Dillon of Dillon, Read; and Robert
McNamara of Ford Motor were already serving in the Johnson cabinet.[25]

During the period in 1964 when Lyndon Johnson was considering
whether or not to choose Humphrey as his running mate, Humphrey tried
to gain the support of Wall Street: "I had already begun an intensive effort to
woo . . . leaders of the business community . . . I had no natural ties to big
business and turned to my longtime, wealthy friend Dwayne Andreas . . . I
needed his help badly." Humphrey's need to court big business was an ac-
knowledgement of its power within the party and of its influence with the
president. He usually made it sound as if big business controlled the Republican Party and was held in check only through the valiant efforts of the Democratic Party. His justification for wooing big business is interesting:

> Each of us approaches public life with a vision limited by his experi-
> ence and training, restricted by his prejudices and background. Unless a
> person is willing to reach out to people who are not just like himself, he
> remains forever limited, explicating a narrow text, repeating old ideas.
> For liberals, this particularly means reaching into the business or finan-
> cial community; and inevitably those associations become suspect in
> many peoples' eyes. When the association brings not only ideas and in-
> formation but financial support for a campaign, both parties become
> targets for journalists and political ideologues.

He then defends Dwayne Andreas: "When I was looking for broad support
for my vice presidential nomination, he brought me into contact with corporate leaders most of whom harbored more serious reservations about me
than I did about them."[26] What a telling description! Humphrey equates traditional liberal hostility toward big business with "prejudice." Support for
democracy rather than plutocracy is "narrow," whereas backing from the tiny
group of corporate owners and managers is necessary for "broad" support.

One of Humphrey's duties as vice president was raising money for the
President's Club, an organization composed of large campaign contributors.
In 1965, he told *Fortune,* "I've changed. . . . When you come up the hard
way, as I did, you become a bit brittle. Then, when life has been good to you,
you become more tolerant." It is interesting that Humphrey equated tolerance with friendliness toward big business—as if megacorporations were
misunderstood, persecuted minorities! That same year, Humphrey told the
National Association of Manufacturers that the administration had faith in
them, told the U.S. Chamber of Commerce that the administration had a

partnership with them, and told a Fifth Avenue Club gathering that included U.S. Steel chairman Roger Blough that he was concerned about "outdated anti-trust laws."[27] As a result of Humphrey's verbal labor, big money continued to pour into the President's Club.

Setting aside Humphrey's positions on public policy issues, the funding sources for his 1968 presidential campaign would have been enough to render him "unavailable" for the Democratic nomination in the eyes of a liberal like Bryan. High finance and big business were major components of his successful campaign for the nomination. In April 1968, following President Johnson's withdrawal from the race, while considering a candidacy of his own, Humphrey flew to New York City for a private meeting at the Waldorf Astoria Hotel with Gardner Cowles of Cowles Communications and a number of his wealthy friends, including his brother and business partner John Cowles, Henry Ford II, Sidney Weinberg, John Loeb, and Dwayne Andreas. Everyone present encouraged him to run for president. A Citizens for Humphrey Committee was conceived with Loeb and John T. Connor of Allied Chemical as chairmen and Weinberg as vice chairman. Connor had served as commerce secretary under Johnson and later became a director of General Motors, General Foods, and Chase Manhattan Bank. Weinberg, known as "Mr. Wall Street," was in charge of fundraising for Humphrey during the 1968 primary season. According to political scientist Herbert Alexander, "Almost all of Humphrey's [preconvention] campaign funds came from large contributors." For the Humphrey of 1968, $2,000 was considered a "small donation."[28]

Edith Altschul Lehman served as honorary chair of United Democrats for Humphrey in New York. She was the widow of New York banker and U.S. senator Herbert H. Lehman and the sister of New York banker Frank Altschul of Lazard Frères. Herbert Lehman spent over a million dollars on the various campaigns of Governor Al Smith. Lehman Brothers was an important Wall Street investment firm in the 1930s, and it steadily grew in importance during the postwar era. Like Lehman Brothers, Brown Brothers, Harriman and Company has been one of the most powerful New York-based international banking firms. Founding partner and Union Pacific Railroad heir Averell Harriman was a Humphrey supporter in 1968. A close friend of slain candidate Robert Kennedy, Harriman quietly assisted the Humphrey campaign before the convention and throughout the fall campaign. In the spring of 1968, *Dun's Review* conducted a presidential poll among the nation's top three hundred business executives. When asked which Democrat they wanted to see nominated, 95 percent of the corporate leaders said Humphrey. In May, when a committee of leading banking and

industrial executives was formed to raise money for the Humphrey campaign, the candidate "brushed past the seeming incongruity of Hubert
Humphrey, the liberal, dining in splendor with the wealthy by declaring that
he did not intend to try to change his image for their benefit."[29] His campaign was more reminiscent of the eastern elitism of Cleveland than of the
prairie populism of Bryan.

After Humphrey gained the nomination, his aides reportedly refused to
cut a deal with some Texas oil men whereby he would champion depletion
allowances in exchange for campaign money. The oil producers were told
that Humphrey "would not be a political prostitute." The vice president's
aides may have rejected crass quid pro quo donations, but the bulk of the
money used for the Humphrey general election effort "came from very large
contributors and from loans." International banker Andre Meyer of Lazard
Frères supported the Humphrey-Muskie ticket. The powerful Lazard firm is
closely tied to the House of Rothschild and the House of Morgan. After the
election, an emissary of billionaire Howard Hughes swore that he gave
$50,000 in cash to Humphrey—a story denied by the candidate. Humphrey
sparked a flurry of grassroots funding only when he began emphasizing
peace in Vietnam during the last six weeks of the campaign. Nearly $300,000
in small contributions were received after he mentioned a conditional
bombing halt of North Vietnam in his Salt Lake City speech.

This was, however, an aberration for a campaign mostly engineered within
corporate boardrooms, luxury suites, and White House offices. Economically speaking, the types of people pushing the candidacy of Humphrey
stood in marked contrast to those pushing the candidacy of former Governor George Wallace (D-AL), a third-party nominee. According to George
Thayer, "Of all the candidates in 1968, only George Wallace could say that
most of his money came from the 'little people.'" Contributions of $500 or
less amounted to 85 percent of the campaign money taken in by the American Independent Party. In contrast, small contributions to the Republican
Party amounted to about 50 percent and small contributions to the Democratic Party amounted to about 30 percent. The Democrats finished the fall
campaign $6 million in debt, with the money being owed to "fewer than
thirty wealthy supporters." Two individuals made $240,000 loans and at least
nineteen made $100,000 loans to the party in an effort to elect Humphrey.[30]

William Benton gave Humphrey a lucrative seat on the Encyclopædia
Britannica board of directors following his 1968 loss, but in 1970 he was
once again elected to the Senate. Early front-runner Senator Edmund Muskie
(D-ME), a close Humphrey ally, garnered much of the big business money
in the race for the 1972 presidential nomination, but Humphrey received a

substantial portion of it. In March 1972, the Humphrey campaign released a list of 121 contributors of $1,000 or more. A reporter observed, "Senator Humphrey has relied heavily on wealthy donors, who contributed about 90 per cent of his $838,715 total to date." The list of Humphrey's 1972 contributors included some familiar names: John Connor, Edith Altschul Lehman, John Loeb, and Dwayne Andreas. These were some of the same people who had contributed to his 1968 campaign. Some of his new contributors were Leonard Davis of Colonial Penn Life Insurance, C. Douglas Dillon of Dillon, Read, and Delos Rentzel of Martin-Marietta.

Humphrey's 1972 campaign manager and press secretary engaged in criminal activities while working for the campaign. During the Watergate era, numerous questions of legality and ethics were raised about Humphrey's association with "big money." As one biographer noted, "When various corporations began owning up to unlawful contributions, Humphrey's name was usually on the list—Gulf Oil, Ashland Oil, American Airlines, and so on." When the dairy industry gave more than $300,000 to Richard Nixon's reelection campaign and the president then increased the level of milk price supports, consumer advocate Ralph Nader and other liberal populists saw it as a clear case of bribery. American Milk Producers, Inc. (AMPI) made illegal contributions to the Humphrey campaigns of 1968, 1970, and 1972. Illegal contributions were also made to the Humphrey 1972 campaign by John Loeb and Minnesota Mining and Manufacturing (3M).[31]

In 1975, Humphrey settled $900,000 worth of 1972 presidential campaign debts with eighteen individuals, "most of them wealthy businessmen," by paying back about four cents on the dollar. A magazine at the time noted, "By settling with his wealthy contributors for pennies on the dollar Humphrey is effectively raking in huge campaign donations, some as high as $100,000 apiece." Humphrey was an undeclared candidate for the 1976 presidential nomination. He hoped to be drafted by the party and considered jumping into the late primaries, but, in the end, he watched as Jimmy Carter gained the nomination. Friends of the senator launched some draft-Humphrey committees, but Humphrey himself did not solicit funds in 1976. In 1977, it was announced that a Hubert Humphrey Institute would be created at the University of Minnesota and that the multimillion-dollar fundraising drive would be led by Vice President Walter Mondale and Irving Shapiro. Shapiro was chairman of DuPont, cochairman of the Business Roundtable, a trustee of the Ford Foundation, and a director of Bechtel, IBM, and Boeing.[32]

Biographer Carl Solberg argues that Humphrey had the misfortune to have run for president "in the years when campaign spending reached such levels that it exploded in scandal and crime." In Solberg's eyes, although Humphrey did not break the law as Nixon had done, he was nonetheless corrupted by his association with large contributors: "The prairie Progressive who had once excoriated bankers for their grasping foreclosures stopped making speeches exposing the loopholes through which the rich avoided their taxes and grew not only tolerant of but comfortable with great wealth." Political analyst Roger Morris points out that while Minnesota Farmer-Laborites and other early twentieth-century populists and progressives condemned monopolistic corporations and international banks, Humphrey and other midcentury Democratic liberals were dependent upon these entities for the bulk of their campaign financing. These politicians eloquently spoke of standing up for the poor and oppressed, for workers, and for the middle class, yet, in many cases, their campaign bank accounts were largely a result of their friendship with high finance and big business. If it is true that "Where your treasure is, there will your heart be also," then the professed loyalty of such liberals is questionable. Hubert Humphrey's reliance on Wall Street was not a result of personality traits or political circumstances unique to him. The same reliance is found among his congressional supporters and among party leaders associated with groups such as the Coalition for a Democratic Majority and the Democratic Leadership Council.[33] It is ideological in nature.

Affiliations

When a politician chooses to affiliate with a Wall Street-controlled organization, it can be assumed that he or she shares most of that organization's values, beliefs, and priorities. There have been a number of such organizations during the twentieth century that have exerted significant influence on American economic and political life. The Council on Foreign Relations (CFR) has been selected as the affiliation case study because its existence has stretched from the Bryan era to the Humphrey era and beyond, because its membership size provides data neither too meager nor too multitudinous, and because it is an invitation-only group. Being an exclusive group only increases the significance of affiliation, because it cannot be argued that a politician joined the group primarily for the purpose of trying to change it or that the group's leadership disagreed with the politician but could not prevent him or her from joining. In the case of CFR affiliation, both organization and politician have decided that they are a good match. The CFR has also been selected because despite its virtual anonymity with the general public, sophisticated political observers see it as the leading private influence on U.S. foreign policy and as the embodiment of the Establishment.[34]

The Council on Foreign Relations was founded in 1921 by a group of international investment bankers and others friendly to big business. The organization had its roots in the Round Table (Milner) Group, a secret society founded by Cecil Rhodes for the purpose of extending a federated version of British imperialism throughout the world. The CFR was designed to be an American counterpart of the Royal Institute of International Affairs. J. P. Morgan and Company, which originated in England and maintained close ties to Great Britain, was the driving force behind the creation of the CFR. The American Institute of International Affairs was founded at the Paris Peace Conference, which drafted the Treaty of Versailles and created the League of Nations under the leadership of men such as J. P. Morgan partner Thomas W. Lamont, historian George Beer, geographer Isaiah Bowman, former Rhodes scholar Whitney Shepardson, journalist Walter Lippmann, future president Herbert Hoover, and future secretary of state John Foster Dulles.[35] Former secretary of state Elihu Root had started his own group, called the Council on Foreign Relations, in 1918. The Paris group and the Root group merged in 1921, creating the modern CFR.

Leading bankers, businesspeople, foundation executives, attorneys, educators, journalists, politicians, and government administrators are members of the group. In 2005, it had forty-two hundred life members. On public policy questions, the CFR is not monolithic in terms of means but is virtually monolithic in terms of ends. There is a consensus on matters such as elitism, statism, and imperialism. Although the organization claims to exist for the purpose of hosting discussion and fostering research, not for influencing governmental action, the CFR—through its membership—is more than influential. Council members have played vital roles in creating and implementing public policy. Of the twelve CFR vice chairmen between 1971 and 2005, one was a president of Columbia University, two were secretaries of state, two were secretaries of the Treasury, one was secretary of defense, one was secretary of Housing and Urban Development, one was ambassador to the United Nations, one was general manager of the Atomic Energy Commission, one was chairman of the Federal Reserve Bank of New York, one was president of the same bank, and one was nominated to be director of the Central Intelligence Agency. During the past eighty-five years, the membership rolls of the CFR have included seven presidents, seven vice presidents, seventeen secretaries of state, seventeen secretaries of war/defense, eighteen secretaries of the Treasury, eight chairmen of the Federal Reserve Board, nine chairmen of the Joint Chiefs of Staff, fifteen directors of the Central Intelligence Agency, and eighteen ambassadors to the United Nations. Since 1952, there have been eight presidential elections in which both major party nominees have been past, present, or future CFR members.[36]

The economic orientation of the group has not changed since 1921: it remains committed to monopolistic finance capitalism. Scholar G. William Domhoff identifies the CFR as the key link between the large corporations and the federal government. He calls it "an institution controlled by members of the upper class." Wall Street control of the council becomes apparent when looking at the seven men who led the group from 1921 to 2006: J. P. Morgan attorney John W. Davis; Wall Street attorney George Wickersham; Kuhn, Loeb partner Norman H. Davis; J. P. Morgan partner Russell Leffingwell; Chase Manhattan Bank chairmen John McCloy and David Rockefeller; and Lehman Brothers, Kuhn, Loeb chairman Peter G. Peterson. Peterson, who was commerce secretary under Nixon, has also been president of Bell and Howell and a director of American Express, General Foods, 3M, Illinois Bell, Black and Decker, RCA, and First National Bank of Chicago.

Over the years, a handful of CFR members have not subscribed to the organization's prevailing philosophy. Examples include publisher Oswald Garrison Villard, historian Harry Elmer Barnes, diplomat Spruille Braden, military officer Chester Ward, and political scientists Richard Falk and Richard Barnet.[37] It should be stressed, however, that these are exceptions to the rule. Since Hubert Humphrey was a man of the Center rather than of the Left or Right, it is not surprising that he and his allies have been comfortable within the centrist-anchored organization. Of the many prominent Humphrey supporters who have belonged to the CFR, there is no evidence that any have had fundamental disagreements with mainstream Council thought.

The elitism of the Council on Foreign Relations is probably a product of its Wall Street–saturated history, leadership, and funding. The titles of two studies of the CFR and its leaders by friendly authors are indicative of this elitist slant: one is entitled "The Wise Men of Foreign Affairs: The History of the Council on Foreign Relations"; and the other, "The Wise Men: Six Friends and the World They Made." The phrase *Wise Men* came into usage in elite media and academic circles in the 1960s. It was a reference to the "relatively small number of Wall Street lawyers and bankers" who governed the country by working hand in hand with Harry Truman and creating the presidency of Dwight Eisenhower.[38] Noting that a relatively small number of individuals held all of the first- and second-level positions in "a huge national security bureaucracy" between 1940 and 1967, Richard Barnet adds, "Most of their biographies in *Who's Who* read like minor variations on a single theme—wealthy parents, Ivy-League education, leading law firm or bank (or entrepreneur in a war industry), introduction to government in World War II." The Wise Men were listened to by the Johnson-Humphrey administration. Another indicator of the Council's elitism is the hereditary, aristocratic nature of its leadership. Examples of family ties over the course of generations include the John Foster-Robert Lansing-John Foster Dulles-John D. Rockefeller Jr.-Allen Dulles family, the Dean Acheson-William Bundy-McGeorge Bundy-Eleanor Dean Acheson family, and the John W. Davis-Cyrus Vance family.[39]

The Council on Foreign Relations is an organization founded by men who were opposed to everything for which William Jennings Bryan stood. Bryan fought monopolistic finance capitalism throughout his career; the CFR founders were investment bankers, big businessmen, and corporate attorneys. Bryan detested militarism; the CFR founders were at the core of the preparedness movement and the successful effort to involve the U.S. in World War I. Bryan was staunchly anti-imperialistic; the CFR founders were imperialistic to a man. Bryan stood for resistance to policies coming out of the Gilded Age and Spanish-American War that he viewed as destructive to equality, peace, and freedom; the CFR founders were the designers and implementers of those very policies. Former senator Elihu Root (R-NY), a Wall Street attorney-turned-White House insider, was honorary president of the Council on Foreign Relations from 1921 to 1937. Root denounced Bryan as an "anarchist" and "blasphemer" in 1896, upheld imperialism in 1900 while attacking Bryan, and despised Bryan when he served as Wilson's secretary of state. Hiram Johnson, a liberal Republican contemporary, identified Root as a leader of the antiliberal forces within both the party and the nation.[40]

The Democrats in CFR leadership positions were not Bryan Democrats. The group's founding president, John W. Davis, served as ambassador to Great Britain during the Wilson administration. At the 1904 Democratic convention, Davis voted for conservative Alton B. Parker despite Bryan's opposition to Parker and the presence of liberal alternatives. In 1922, Chief Justice William Howard Taft—the Republican who defeated Bryan in 1908—urged President Harding to appoint Davis to the Supreme Court. Harding, a conservative Republican, offered the seat to Davis, but he declined because he was making too much money as a corporate attorney. Davis's legal work on behalf of Wall Street included service as chief counsel for J. P. Morgan and Company. Bryan strongly opposed Davis's campaign for the 1924 Democratic presidential nomination and was disappointed when his brother, Charles, agreed to be Davis's running mate. One of Davis's close friends was fellow CFR member Robert Lansing. Although a nominal Democrat, Lansing was linked to prominent Republicans. He was a son-in-law of former secretary of state John Foster and an uncle of future secretary of state John Foster Dulles. Another Lansing nephew was Allen Dulles, future Central Intelligence Agency director. Elihu Root was instrumental in the selection of Lansing as counselor of the State Department in 1914. President Wilson and Senator Root used Lansing as a means to bypass Secretary of State Bryan in their pursuit of a pro-British, imperialistic foreign policy.[41] When Bryan resigned over policy differences with Wilson, Lansing succeeded him as secretary of state.

Members of the Council on Foreign Relations agreed that the organization should facilitate global economic and political leadership by the New York–Boston–Washington axis, but they disagreed on tactics. The investment bankers favored a "blunt commitment to internationalism," but the scholars and staffers favored more subtle tactics in an effort to "appear strictly impartial." There were differences over strategy, but there was no disagreement over objectives. There was also unanimity in attitude toward congressional liberals: utter disdain. For example, in the 1920s, leaders of the CFR had contempt for liberal Republican senators such as Smith Brookhart, Arthur Capper, Hiram Johnson, Robert La Follette, and William Borah. In his "passion for the appearance of impartiality," Hamilton Fish Armstrong invited Senator Brookhart to participate in a CFR-sponsored debate at the Harvard Club in 1923. Armstrong asked Russell Leffingwell to "educate him [Brookhart] and refute some of his views," but the banker declined to debate, chiding Armstrong "for offering a respectable forum to a Senate primitive like Brookhart." Paul Warburg told Armstrong that he and his friends were outraged that an "uneducable demagogue" such as Brookhart had been offered council hospitality. Other members defended Armstrong's decision to extend an invitation, but all agreed with the assessment of Brookhart offered by Leffingwell and Warburg—he was, of course, a foolish enemy. The July 1923 issue of *Foreign Affairs* carried an article entitled "The American Farmer and Foreign Policy" by Senator Capper. Armstrong and journal editor Archibald Cary Coolidge were "horrified" when they received Capper's "terrible stuff," but they decided to print it "as an exposition of the reasoning powers and literary style of a powerful body of American voters." Believing that Capper had made a fool of himself, Armstrong gleefully wrote, "I didn't change a word, but left it in all its native simplicity!" Despite providing occasional outlets for the views of ideological enemies whom they considered to be buffoons and crackpots, the CFR restricted its membership to individuals with "sound" views.[42]

In a 1923 letter to Robert Lansing, CFR president John Davis expressed scorn for the "progressive vs. reactionary" campaign rhetoric of presidential candidates William McAdoo and Hiram Johnson. In 1924, *Foreign Affairs* allowed La Follette's Progressive Party to have a spot alongside the Republicans and Democrats to explain its foreign policy views. The antidollar diplomacy, anti-imperialism article was written by Robert Morss Lovett, a University of Chicago professor of English. When Davis campaigned as the 1924 Democratic presidential nominee, he spent much of his time attacking La Follette, whom he portrayed as "a dangerous radical." Republican vice-presidential nominee Charles Dawes, a Chicago banker who later joined the CFR, heaped attacks on both Senator La Follette and Governor Charles Bryan, who had become Davis's running mate. There was no reason for Dawes to attack Davis or for Davis to attack Coolidge-Dawes because the three men essentially agreed with one another. Within a decade, Dawes and Davis were serving together on the *Foreign Affairs* Editorial Advisory Board. Walter Lippmann is another example of CFR hostility toward congressional liberals. In a 1926 *Foreign Affairs* article, Lippmann painted Senator Borah as an insecure and resentful person who "would be labeled a chronic kicker and dismissed from the society of the righteous and efficient" were he not in the unfortunate position of being chairman of the Senate Foreign Relations Committee.[43]

William Jennings Bryan was not a member of the Council on Foreign Relations. The CFR had many prominent Democrats within its ranks during the 1920s, but they were Cleveland-Wilson Democrats, not Bryan Democrats. From its inception, however, the organization would have been hospitable toward and appealing for Hubert Humphrey had he been old enough to join in the 1920s. The CFR has always been an example of corporate liberalism and represents a type of progressivism or liberalism quite distinct from the Bryan variety. Political scientist Richard Falk points out that the CFR's "liberal internationalism" is Hamiltonian, not Jeffersonian, in nature. Noting that John Davis cofounded the reactionary American Liberty League and defended segregation on behalf of South Carolina before the U.S. Supreme Court, Laurence Shoup and William Minter comment, "The Council perspective, popularly identified as 'liberal internationalism,' is, it should be clear, perfectly compatible with conservative views on the proper way to organize domestic society." It should be noted that Davis was known to be a conservative Democrat not only in the 1930s and beyond but also in the 1920s, when Bryan and his fellow liberals were horrified at the thought

of his nomination. Two of the most influential individuals behind the creation of the CFR were Thomas W. Lamont and Elihu Root. Lamont and his
banking firm were considered to be conservative in 1919. Both Root's biographer and the CFR's approved historian call Root conservative.[44] All of
this raises a recurring question, What is liberal about "liberal internationalism?"

The Council on Foreign Relations has provided underpinning for the
Vital Center, with many of its members holding high-ranking positions in
the Roosevelt, Truman, Kennedy, and Johnson administrations.[45] Democratic
governor Adlai Stevenson, a three-time Humphrey presidential favorite, was
a director of the CFR from 1958 to 1962. In the mid-1960s, Edith Altschul
Lehman gave $50,000 to a CFR capital fund in memory of her husband,
Herbert Lehman. Mrs. Lehman supported Humphrey's 1968 and 1972 presidential campaigns. CFR vice chairman C. Douglas Dillon supported his
1972 campaign. Dwayne Andreas, another wealthy Humphrey supporter and
CFR member, gave at least $10,000 to the organization in 1997. Humphrey
Democrats who have served on the CFR board of directors include Averell
Harriman, Zbigniew Brzezinski, Lane Kirkland, Jeane Kirkpatrick, and
Thomas Foley. Hubert Humphrey himself was a member of the Council on
Foreign Relations by 1960.[46]

About half of the council's four thousand members could be classified as
either "Humphrey Democrats" or "Kennedy Democrats." In either case, the
ideology is the same: post-New Deal liberalism. Before 1981, the other half
of the CFR would have been classified as "Rockefeller Republicans." Since
the liberal or even moderate labels have become unfashionable in GOP circles, many Republican members of the CFR today would describe themselves as "Reagan Republicans." Or you could call them "neoconservatives"
as adherents of a Reaganism stripped of all its original anti-Establishment
qualities. When it comes to foreign policy, almost all Republican members
of the organization possess the exact same ideology as the Democratic
members: post-New Deal liberalism. This is what puts the "liberal" in "liberal internationalism." The CFR contains few, if any, Democrats who were
George Wallace supporters in the 1960s and 1970s, or Republicans who are
in the Robert Taft-Barry Goldwater-Patrick Buchanan tradition. The council is bipartisan because its members are among the leaders of both major
parties, but its variety is one of party, not ideology. Richard Falk points out
that the Establishment "is non-partisan in the sense of party politics, but is
extremely partisan when it comes to economic affiliations and ruling class
politics." According to historian Carroll Quigley, the Establishment is "really
above parties" and is "much more concerned with policies than with party

victories." Although apparently not mentioning the CFR by name, Humphrey's home-state ideological rival, Governor Elmer Benson (FL-MN), was clearing talking about CFR-inspired foreign policy when he said in March 1948:

> Whose policy is this? Mr. Truman is the spokesman, but as he has told us so often, his policy is bi-partisan. It is the policy of the two old parties, now in all essentials, one. It is the Hoover-Vandenberg-Dulles-Stassen-Marshall-Eisenhower-Truman Doctrine. But these political figures themselves speak for another group who stand in the shadows. In the shadows, policy is made. The investment bankers whom Mr. Truman placed in political power now make foreign policy in cooperation with the military.[47]

Benson was a La Follette-Wheeler supporter in 1924 and a Wallace-Taylor supporter in 1948 because he opposed the bipartisan status quo. In his opinion, the status quo included militarism and imperialism. Senators Burton Wheeler and Glen Taylor were Bryan Democrats who did not feel at home in a party they viewed as under the control of Wall Street.

The utility of using Council on Foreign Relations affiliation as an ideological measure would be greatly diminished if the organization's philosophy underwent a major change between the Bryan era and the Humphrey era. But there was no such change. In fact, the CFR's institutional thought in 2006 seems to be essentially what it was eighty years ago. Far from repudiating its plutocratic origins, the CFR honors Elihu Root and Russell Leffingwell by sponsoring lectureships in their names. Its roster of corporate members reads like a listing of the Fortune 500. The organization remains as committed as ever to a foreign policy of internationalism née imperialism. Following the 1996 Republican National Convention, Fareed Zakaria, the managing editor of *Foreign Affairs,* urged GOP presidential nominee Robert Dole to explicitly recommit the party to internationalism lest isolationists such as Pat Buchanan become its voice on foreign policy. Zakaria condemned William Borah, Gerald Nye, and Robert Taft as historical examples of "paranoid nativism."[48] He praised Theodore Roosevelt, Henry Cabot Lodge, Elihu Root, Henry Stimson, Dwight Eisenhower, and Henry Kissinger for their passionate support for America's preeminent place in the world and vehement opposition to isolationism and neutrality.

Foreshadowing the anti-limousine-liberal campaigns of George Wallace and the blue-collar populism of "Reagan Democrats," in the early 1960s, conservative activist Mary Davison wrote,

> Insofar as a "liberal" is presumed to represent the best interests of the worker-producer (as he can be differentiated from the investor-producer), by what phantasy is his vote cast for the most notorious exploiters in history—those billionaires who acquired their wealth primarily from the control of the money. . . . It is for us to reason with the sincere liberal and make him understand that he has nothing in common with the phoney liberals of the Council on Foreign Relations.

In the early 1970s, conservative analyst Gary Allen called Hubert Humphrey "a fiery radical for the downtrodden international bankers behind the CFR."[49] It could be argued that international bankers and big businessmen changed so much between 1921 and 1941 that there was nothing illiberal about professed liberals joining an organization founded and maintained by the corporate elite. If those segments of society that were formerly scorned as robber barons and plutocrats have embraced a new-and-improved—but authentic—version of liberalism, then their contributions and affiliations would in no way taint or discredit liberal recipients. There is remarkable genealogical continuity between the corporate wealth-connected financiers, publishers, and organizers of the early twentieth century and those of the mid to late twentieth century. But, whereas these forces were enemies of liberalism during the Bryan era, they were friends of liberalism during the Humphrey era. Are we to understand that the wolves of the Gilded Age and Progressive Era fathered the sheep of the New Deal and Great Society years? Did the latter-day liberals repudiate—on a political, not personal, level—their conservative fathers, grandfathers, and great-grandfathers? There is no indication that this occurred except in rare, isolated instances. If we are to believe that a generation of wolves gave birth to a generation of sheep, we will need some assistance in understanding the process. How did the younger generation overcome its family pride and political socialization? Where did they learn to be liberals? Among their father's friends at the yacht club? As interns at Morgan Guaranty Trust? These questions must be addressed if we are to believe that Averell Harriman possessed a different ideology from that of E. H. Harriman.

What has this examination of support shown us about twentieth-century Democratic liberalism? In conducting campaigns, Bryan relied more on small donations, volunteer workers, his own speaking ability, and the force of his ideas than he did on wealthy financiers. Of the handful of large contributors to Bryan, most were not intimately linked to Wall Street. They were independent businessmen or liberal ideologues. This was not the case with Humphrey. Certainly Humphrey had some friends in Minnesota and elsewhere who contributed money because they liked the "Happy Warrior" as a person. He received money and assistance from special interest groups that approved of his positions in specific issue areas. But the bulk of his support came from bankers, businessmen, corporate attorneys, real estate investors, and others belonging to the nation's capitalist elite. He received little money directly from the grassroots.

Membership in the Council on Foreign Relations has been treated as a case study of affiliation because the organization was created by Wall Street in 1921 and has operated under its control ever since. Bryan did not join the CFR. In the 1920s, leaders of the council viewed supporters of Bryan, and his Republican counterpart La Follette, as foolish and dangerous. Humphrey joined the CFR. Two of Humphrey's wealthiest supporters have given large sums of money to support the work of the CFR. Mid-twentieth-century Democratic liberalism was very different from early twentieth-century Democratic liberalism when it came to sources of support.

CHAPTER 8

Positions on Democracy

Crux of Jeffersonianism

A useful way to measure the Jeffersonianism of a political movement is to examine an exemplar's positions on public policies. This can be done for liberalism during both the Bryan era (1885–1925) and the Humphrey era (1938–1978). Democracy will be treated in this chapter as a case study of the ways in which Bryan liberalism and Humphrey liberalism related to the Jeffersonian tenets. Democracy merits full examination for two reasons. First, it is the crux of Jeffersonianism. Of the tenets, it is first among equals because it is foundational to the liberalism of Thomas Jefferson. If you remove it or diminish it, every other tenet is affected. Above all else, Jefferson was committed to the well-being of the common people. He was a populist and a democrat. Populism is the ideology that supports the rights, aspirations, and power of the people. Democracy is the form of government in which the people control society. The very name of the political party largely founded by Jefferson serves as a testament to his belief in democracy. Second, the word *democracy* has become so debased over the course of the twentieth century that today it means everything and nothing. In America, everyone is for democracy, but few can define it. Even when individuals can provide a definition, there is no common conception to provide a frame of reference or to set the terms of debate. Yet the word *democracy* does have a meaning—an etymological, historical, and ideological meaning. We cannot prevent people from misusing the word, but we can identify its actual meaning and apply it to sociopolitical situations across time and space.

Definition and History

Democracy literally means rule by the common people. For thousands of years, since the days of ancient Greece, educated persons meant not only rule by the common people but also direct rule by the common people when they spoke of democracy. For both supporters and opponents of democracy, "indirect democracy" would have been a contradiction in terms. Democracy was wonderful or dangerous precisely because it was direct. Laws would be made by the common people en masse. Genuine public servants were to execute decisions, but the common people themselves were to be the rulers.

With only a few exceptions, the intellectual and political leaders of colonial America were monarchists and aristocrats, not democrats. The Church of England had legal dominance in Virginia. Its episcopal form of church government included a hierarchy patterned after the Roman Catholic Church, where the papacy was patterned after a monarchy. Anglicans swore both political and ecclesiastical allegiance to the king of England because he was head of the state church as well as a political leader.

The Pilgrims who sailed on the *Mayflower* and landed at Plymouth Rock were Separatists, but the Puritans soon outnumbered Separatists in New England. Despite a shared commitment to Reformed (Calvinist) theology, there were important distinctions between the two groups of English emigrants. Some Puritans believed in the presbyterian form of church government, and others, in the congregational form, but few took congregationalism to its logical conclusion—freedom to make decisions not only without the consent of other local churches but also without the consent of one man or a few men within the congregation itself. The decision to reject the episcopal form of church government was a step toward liberalization, but the Puritans wished to stay within the Church of England. Their reluctance to break with the ecclesiastical power structure was mirrored in their relatively conservative view of the state. Separatists, on the other hand, were more radical. Sometimes called "Independents," they were not only professed congregationalists but actual democrats when it came to church polity. This attitude often extended to the secular realm. While most Puritans believed in the necessity and utility of an established religion within a geographic area, Separatists rejected the Constantinian tradition.[2] Instead, they favored local churches free from government control and populated only by true believers and seekers. John Wise of Massachusetts, Roger Williams and Anne Hutchinson of Rhode Island, William Penn of Pennsylvania, John

Woolman of New Jersey, James Oglethorpe of Georgia, and members of the Iroquois confederacy of New York served, to varying degrees, as democratic influences in colonial America.

The form of government created by the United States in 1789 was not a democracy. Most of the Founding Fathers were elitists with an affinity for monarchy or aristocracy. Economic self-interest probably played some role—consciously or unconsciously—in the decisions made at the Constitutional Convention at Philadelphia in 1787. This is not, however, the whole story. Most of the framers of the Constitution were educated men interested in the ideas of statecraft. There were a variety of Old World intellectual sources from which they could have drawn in constructing a government for the new nation. They could have turned to French thinker Claude Adrien Helvétius. During the eighteenth century, Voltaire acquired a radical reputation because of his attacks on Catholicism, but Helvétius was a much more liberal philosophe on political and economic questions. They also could have consulted another contemporary of Voltaire: Jean-Jacques Rousseau. Rousseau was a Swiss-French philosopher who advocated democracy in the direct, classical sense of the word.[3] Believing that government should have merely an executive function, he viewed it as a body commissioned to carry out the will of the popular sovereign. Rather than turning to political philosophers in the democratic tradition, the Founding Fathers tied the fortunes of the United States to the nondemocratic tradition of Plato, Aristotle, Machiavelli, and their successors. The absolute monarchy urged by Hobbes and Voltaire was rejected as a suitable form of government for the new nation, but Hobbes's thought influenced Federalist leaders Alexander Hamilton and James Madison.[4]

The ideas of English philosopher John Locke and French philosopher Charles de Montesquieu were especially influential in the drafting of the Constitution. Locke was a forerunner of the Founding Fathers with his emphasis on revolution, natural rights, private property, consent of the governed, and constitutionalism. Montesquieu did not think the common people were capable of making wise policies, favored a mixed constitution, and admired the ethics and polity of the Roman Republic. Montesquieu believed that the best form of government was an aristocratic republic. He did not like absolute monarchy, but he also did not like democracy. He considered constitutional monarchy preferable to classical democracy. Montesquieu's most famous book, *The Spirit of Laws,* was criticized as too conservative by Helvétius. Montesquieu's argument in favor of the separation of powers was incorporated into the U.S. Constitution. Anti-Federalists were wary of "mixed," "complex," or "balanced" government, preferring instead "simple and responsible" government. The Founding Fathers disregarded a relatively liberal component of Montesquieu's thought: the idea that a republic was most appropriate for a small territory, and that a large territory would likely move the state from republic to monarchy. Following the English philosopher David Hume, Madison rejected the small-republic theory. Eric Black comments, "A large republic was viewed as less democratic and more elitist, which from Madison's point of view was a great selling point." Conversely, this was one of the reasons the democratic- and decentralist-minded Anti-Federalists opposed adoption of the Constitution.[5] A democratic government could not function over a large expanse of territory because its citizens would be too spread apart from one another to make decisions and too far removed from supposed public servants.

Like the Roman Republic, the American Republic was designed to be a mixed constitution. Just as the consuls, senate, and tribunes of Rome corresponded to monarchy, aristocracy, and democracy, respectively, America had corresponding branches of government: the president, Senate and Supreme Court, and House of Representatives. The Constitution's embrace of partial democracy through consent of the governed and design of one-half of Congress was a concession to, or co-optation of, popular sovereignty, but it was not the same thing as rule by the common people. Republicanism was a clear alternative to, or rejection of, democracy. Not only was democracy symbolized by only half a branch of the federal government, but the franchise was restricted and indirect. As in Athens, only certain types of people could vote. In 1796, only white, propertied men could cast ballots in most states; women, blacks, and poor people were excluded from the process. In contrast to Athenian government, the American electoral system was designed to be as indirect as possible to curtail democratic impulses. Only the House of Representatives was chosen by direct, albeit restricted, popular vote. The president was chosen by the electoral college, the Senate by the state legislatures, and the Supreme Court by the president and the Senate.

Although Thomas Jefferson was not a pure democrat, he was one of a handful of Founding Fathers who appreciated many aspects of democracy. Jefferson's democratic tendencies can be seen in his advocacy of popular sovereignty and legislative preeminence. Some view him as standing squarely in the Athenian tradition. According to Charles Wiltse, "Jefferson's whole point of view, and many of his ideas, are also to be found clearly expressed in Thucydides, notably in the funeral speech put by the historian into the mouth of Pericles." Some scholars have seen Rousseau as an influence on Jefferson. Jefferson was apparently not familiar with the writings of Rousseau, but he shared some of his beliefs, and he respected at least some of Helvétius' work. Perhaps most indebted to Locke, Jefferson leavened that thinker's republicanism with democracy, his individualism with communitarianism, and his emphasis on property with less tangible values such as equality and the pursuit of happiness.[6]

Since the 1910s, most American politicians have proclaimed allegiance to democracy. But have they supported it in the pure, classical sense of the word? This question goes beyond flag-mom-and-apple pie feelings evoked by the Fourth of July. It has important public policy implications. Democracy was a convenient rallying cry, if not propaganda tool, in the U.S. government's fight against totalitarian enemies during World War II and the Cold War, and it continues to be used in the post-Cold War era. The Persian Gulf War, for example, was widely assumed to be partly a crusade for democracy, but this seems impossible since Kuwait and Saudi Arabia have long been governed by authoritarian monarchs. Democracy has been touted as being synonymous with the "Free World" and the "New World Order," but the term seems broadly defined to the point of meaninglessness when Iran under the Shah is part of the former and China under Deng is part of the latter.

Confusion has been created in the minds of many as democracy has become a euphemism for capitalism. Many allies of the U.S. government have been capitalists without being democrats. Individual freedom and human rights may be vital elements of a democratic nation, but they do not ensure the presence of democracy. Liberty and toleration may flourish in a republic as well as in a democracy. Citizens' right to vote in competitive elections is not the same as democracy. When it comes to politics, there is an important difference between participation and rule. Regardless of electoral systems, constitutional protections, or cultural traditions, if the common people are not genuinely ruling the country, you do not have a democracy. You may actually have an aristocracy, oligarchy, or plutocracy masquerading as a democracy.

The elite approach to political science is understandably skeptical of democracy imposed from the top down. It asks, Is elite-sponsored democracy genuine democracy? Contemporary scholars of comparative politics have examined the nature of democracy with a clarity and openness rarely applied by mainstream intellectuals to the American context. Samuel Huntington is not an elite theorist, but he contends that democracy

> is as likely to be the product of oligarchy as of protest against oligarchy.
> . . . With respect to the processes necessary to bring about democratic
> development, a central requirement would appear to be that either the

established elites within an authoritarian system or the successor elites after an authoritarian system collapses see their interests served by the introduction of democratic institutions.[7]

Referring to Latin America, Terry Lynn Karl points out that

> no stable political democracy has resulted from regime transitions in which mass actors have gained control, even momentarily over traditional ruling classes. . . . Thus far, the most frequently encountered types of transition and the ones which have most often resulted in implantation of a political democracy are "transitions from above," or elite-ascendant transitions. Here traditional rulers remain in control, even if pressured from below.

Georg Sørensen makes a crucial distinction between "elite-dominated democracy" and mass-dominated democracy.[8]

With the exception of a relatively small number of media-dubbed "nuts" on the Left and the Right, few Americans understand that a republic is not a democracy, and this confusion has led to a number of other misapprehensions. In reality, the right to vote is not synonymous with popular sovereignty, interest groups do not equal the common people, big government does not offset big business, a welfare state is not the same as an egalitarian state, and special privileges do not engender equal rights. Etymologically and ideologically speaking, democracy is about rule, not about participation or noblesse oblige. The most important criteria for determining the attitude of twentieth-century American liberals toward democracy are commitment to popular sovereignty, support for democratization, encouragement of representativeness, and opposition to plutocratization.

Bryan and Popular Sovereignty

William Jennings Bryan was a leading advocate of popular sovereignty. Believing in the delegate concept of representation, he "thought that representatives of the people ought always to obey their constituents' wills rather than their own judgments, even committing themselves absolutely to keep campaign promises and fulfill party platforms." Bryan was a majoritarian: "The only escape from the rule of the majority is the rule of the minority, and if a majority make mistakes, would not a minority also? . . . The people have a right to have what they want in legislation." Such an expression of belief in popular sovereignty sounds almost trite today, but this belief was not and is not universal in American society, especially among the wealthy and powerful. Among the economic and political elite, lip service has usually been paid to the concept of the people as rulers, but it has been repeatedly denied in practice. Charles Dawes, the plainspoken 1924 Republican vice-presidential nominee who attacked Robert La Follette and Charles Bryan as radicals, publicly expressed a view privately held by many of his conservative associates. In a 1923 speech, soon-to-be vice president Dawes said, "That form of government which history has proved most futile and disastrous is the democratic. Steps taken in recent years toward the principles of democracy are leading in the direction of tyrannical mob rule under evil leaders."[9] As a lifelong small-d democrat, William Jennings Bryan agreed with Senator La Follette's optimistic campaign slogan of the 1920s: "The will of the people shall be the law of the land."

Bryan and Democratization

In the late nineteenth and early twentieth centuries, agrarian-oriented liberals agitated for democratization of American society. The initiative, referendum, and recall were the most important reforms advocated on behalf of direct democracy: the initiative empowered citizens to propose and enact laws; the referendum empowered citizens to ratify laws proposed by the legislature; and the recall empowered citizens to oust elected officials before their terms expired. Liberals who supported one reform tended to support the other two because all three were tools of democratization. Efforts to implement these reforms at the state level were most successful in the Midwest and West.[10] By the turn of the century, many liberals wanted to introduce them at the federal level.

Bryan was an influential member of the "movement toward more popular government." In 1901, he wrote, "Among those who believe in a Democratic-Republic, there is a wide difference between those who emphasize the democratic part of the name and want the government as near as possible to the people, and those who emphasize the representative part of the name and want the government as far removed from the people as possible." Bryan clearly put himself in the former category. Referring to the republic of Switzerland, he said, "It is the most democratic government on the face of the earth . . . In some of the small cantons the people meet at stated times and act upon political matters in public meeting . . . In all the cantons and in the federal government they have the initiative and referendum." Later in the decade, there was an example of democracy even closer to home. As historian Norbert Mahnken notes, "Perhaps no other territory or state was as close to Bryan as was Oklahoma. In few other areas did political leaders and the general public so enthusiastically follow the footsteps of the Peerless Leader. In no other state were so many of Bryan's theories put into practice as in Oklahoma." State political leaders Robert Owen, Thomas Gore, Elmer Thomas, and William Murray were all Bryanites. Filled with suggestions by Bryan, the Oklahoma constitution of 1907 was "progressive to the point where it appeared dangerously radical to many people."[11] It contained provisions for the initiative, referendum, and primary. In a preview of the 1908 presidential contest, William Howard Taft campaigned against the constitution, while Bryan campaigned for it. In this instance, Bryan was on the winning side.

Using words reminiscent of direct democracy à la Rousseau, Herbert Croly noted that Bryan favored "converting representative assemblies into a machinery, like that of the old French Parliaments, for merely registering the Sovereign will. Faith in the people and confidence in popular government means to Mr. Bryan an utter lack of faith in those personal instruments [who act as representatives]." The 1896 People's Party platform called for the initiative and referendum. Bryan, both the Populist and Democratic presidential nominee in that year, supported the initiative and referendum, but he was either unable or unwilling to mention these reforms in any of his Democratic Party platforms. In 1907, he warned southern Democrats that he would "drive every man out of the Democratic party" who did not support the initiative and referendum. In the end, however, in what has been described as "an act of the crudest expediency," Bryan kept the initiative and referendum out of the 1908 platform. He first suggested a national referendum on war in July 1915 and continued to be a forceful advocate for the idea until his death in 1925.[12]

Bryan and Representativeness

While most Jeffersonians during the Progressive Era wished to democratize the United States, they realized that they were operating under the constraints of a republican form of government created by the Constitution. Thus, while they worked for direct democracy reforms, they also sought to redeem the promises of a supposedly representative republic. Measures designed to open up the existing political system and to make it more truly representative included full suffrage, direct primaries, popular voting, roll call votes, term limits, and good government.

Enlarging the franchise to make the body of voters more representative of the body of citizens included allowing women and blacks to cast ballots throughout the United States. The campaign for woman suffrage began in earnest at the state level in the progressive western states. By 1900, four states—Wyoming, Colorado, Utah, and Idaho—had given women the right to vote. The Greenback-Labor Party, headed by Congressman James Weaver (D/G-IA), advocated woman suffrage in 1880. But the Populists, led by Weaver in 1892 and Bryan in 1896, did not endorse woman suffrage as a national organization because there was a split in their ranks, with opposition centered among southern and ethnic voters. Although he was sympathetic to women's rights, William Jennings Bryan did not become a proponent of woman suffrage until relatively late in his career. Once he joined the fight, however, he worked hard to allow women to vote. In 1914, he campaigned for it in Nebraska and did the same the following year in other states. Bryan's influential role in championing national equal suffrage through the Nineteenth Amendment put him at odds with the leader of his party, President Woodrow Wilson. Bryan's attitude toward equal suffrage in respect to African Americans was far less liberal. He was an apologist for the poll tax, literacy test, and other devices designed to keep southern blacks from voting.[13]

Governor Robert La Follette's pioneering efforts on behalf of the direct primary in Wisconsin were noticed throughout the nation. The primary election, through which voters would choose nominees of political parties, was designed to replace conventions and caucuses deemed more easily controlled by party bosses and special interests. Bryan made a positive public reference to the direct primary as early as 1901. He urged his fellow Democrats to adopt the system and had an endorsement of it written into the 1912 Democratic Party platform.

Bryan was also a proponent of direct voting for U.S. senators. In 1894, he recommended that the system whereby state legislatures chose members of the Senate be replaced by a system whereby voters of each state would choose their respective senators. The 1896 Populist, 1900 Democratic, and 1908 Democratic platforms called for popular election of senators. In 1901, Bryan asserted, "The people are nearly unanimous in their support of the proposition that the United States Senators should be elected by a direct vote of the people." He played an influential role in bringing about adoption of the Seventeenth Amendment, which changed the manner of senatorial selection.

The 1896 Populist platform also endorsed popular election of the president, but Bryan was not prepared to go that far because he feared a direct system would be too open to the possibility of fraud. As an alternative, in

1916, he proposed reform of the electoral college so that congressional districts as well as states would have electors. He believed that this would make it more likely that the popular majority and the electoral majority would be for the same candidate. Despite such suggestions, the electoral college was neither eliminated nor reformed. In 1900, the nonfusionist, middle-of-the-road faction of the People's Party called for popular election of federal judges. By 1908, Bryan had endorsed this idea.[14]

In the mid-1890s, Congressman Bryan joined the Populists in calling for a constitutional amendment limiting presidents to one term. Dominated by Bryan and other silverites, the 1896 Democratic National Convention adopted a plank opposing a third term for presidents. In 1896 and 1900, Bryan announced that, if elected, he would not seek reelection because of his belief in a one-term presidency. Addressing the argument that a crisis might make it inadvisable for the nation to change administrations after one term, he wrote, "The same argument could be made at the close of the second term, and . . . when the nation reaches a condition where only one man out of the whole population is able to assume and properly discharge the duties of the executive it will scarcely be worth saving." Bryan was able to get a plank put into the 1912 Democratic platform calling for a constitutional amendment to limit presidents to one term.[15]

Bryan and Plutocratization

A republic is a hybrid form of government. A "mixed constitution" contains something drawn from each of the classical forms of government: monarchy, aristocracy, and democracy. The American Republic was designed so that the monarchic and aristocratic elements were stronger than the democratic. Although the House of Representatives theoretically controlled the initiation of spending, it lacked many of the powers possessed by the aristocratic Senate. The monarchic president and aristocratic Supreme Court wielded even more power than the Senate. The Senate was democratized to some degree when it became popularly elected through ratification of the Seventeenth Amendment in 1913, but with plutocracy being dominant in both major political parties and in control of the major news media, the overall character of the upper legislative chamber did not change.

Plutocracy, a modern type of aristocracy, is rule by the wealthy few. With roots in the aristocratic Federalist and Whig periods, plutocracy solidified its grasp on America during the Gilded Age. Owners and managers of large banks and corporations insinuated themselves into the political system by personally taking positions of power, sending trusted deputies to act on their behalf, and enticing public servants to do their bidding. In this manner, corporate wealth (the monied interests) plutocratized each branch of the federal government, regardless of its nominal position in the classical scheme of polity.

Corporate wealth held tremendous sway over the major political parties in Bryan's day. With a few notable exceptions, it dominated both interparty contests and intraparty contests. Bryan drew a clear distinction between the Democratic Party under his leadership and the Republican Party of Harrison, McKinley, Roosevelt, Taft, Harding, and Coolidge. In 1890, he charged that the GOP was married to monopoly and that it served "the interests of Wall Street as against the rights of the people."

The hostility between Bryan and corporate wealth can be seen in the record of contributions and endorsements associated with his three presidential campaigns. In 1900, Bryan declared that the contest was between democracy and plutocracy, and that the opposing party was dominated by influences that tended to worship mammon. Inviting laborers to join "the Democracy," he hoped they would abandon the "party controlled by banks, corporations, syndicates and monopolies." Bryan's 1908 platform asserted, "The Democratic party stands for Democracy; the Republican party has drawn to itself all that is aristocratic and plutocratic."[16]

Bryan's denunciation of the Republican Party for being dominated by corporate wealth could be dismissed as partisan demagoguery except for the fact that he was equally plainspoken about his own party's plutocratization. While obviously intertwined with his own position as three-time presidential nominee during the 1896–1908 period, his opposition to the Democratic Party's connections to corporate wealth was apparently not motivated by personal ambition. He was not a schemer calling political rivals "plutocrats" to boost his electoral chances. His own nominations were barely challenged by conservatives. His fight against plutocratic Democrats started before and ended after he was a presidential contender. It stretched from the 1890s with his denunciation of Grover Cleveland to the 1920s with his condemnation of John W. Davis. In his famous speech at the 1896 Democratic National Convention, Bryan highlighted the chasm between plutocratic goldbugs and democratic silverites. Declaring that the nation needed a new Andrew Jackson to stand "against the encroachments of organized wealth," he asked, "Upon which side will the Democratic party fight; upon the side of 'the idle holders of idle capital' or upon the side of 'the struggling masses'?" At the 1912 convention, he introduced a resolution designed to put the party on record as opposing the nomination of any presidential candidate who was "the representative of or under obligation to J. Pierpont Morgan, Thomas F. Ryan, August [P.] Belmont, or any other member of the privilege-hunting and favor-seeking class" and demanding withdrawal from the convention of any delegates "constituting or representing the above-named interests."[17]

Bryan understood the important role of campaign contributions in the plutocratization process. The 1900 Democratic platform accused the Republican Party of protecting monopolistic corporations in return for campaign donations. Such corporations were known as "trusts." In 1905, Bryan began speaking out against "charitable" contributions to educational and religious organizations by plutocratic "philanthropists." He attempted to make the regulation of campaign contributions a central issue of the 1908 campaign. The Democratic platform called for a law prohibiting corporate contributions, limiting individual contributions, and providing for preelection publicity of all contributions. Attempting to practice what he preached, Bryan followed these reforms in his own campaign. In 1912, he noted with satisfaction an effort to extend contribution publicity to presidential nomination campaigns by the Democratic-controlled House of Representatives. In 1924, Bryan was still urging mandated disclosure of campaign contributions and expenditures and saying that public financing of campaigns was the only permanent way to free candidates from "obliging themselves to the predatory interests."[18]

Bryan attempted to curb the power of wealth within government through vigorous corporate regulation. An uncompromising enemy of private monopoly, he supported strict enforcement of the Sherman Antitrust Act. Recognizing a fundamental difference between "the being made by the Almighty and the corporation created by man," Bryan declared, "What the government creates it can control, and I insist that both the state government and the federal government must protect the God-made man from the man-made man." In the mid-1900s, he endorsed government ownership of railroads. The idea did not make it into the 1908 platform because of widespread resistance from other Democrats, but Bryan continued to hold to it.

Bryan also supported the 1914 Federal Trade Commission Act. Although creation of the FTC was sponsored by Senator Francis Newlands (D-NV) and favored by most liberal Democrats, historian Gabriel Kolko views it as a sly "triumph of political capitalism" engineered by Woodrow Wilson and his plutocratic patrons. The president filled the commission with procorporate members, thus establishing an early example of co-optative regulation.

Author of the 1912 antimonopoly plank in the Democratic Platform and supporter of the 1914 Clayton Antitrust Act, Bryan eventually realized that Wilson was not interested in breaking up monopolies. Bryan supported the

1916 Child Labor Act, shepherded through the House by Edward Keating (D-CO), a Bryanite. Bryan said, "I rejoice that the Democratic Party has put itself at the head of the movement for social justice in this country. This law says to the money-mad employer, 'You shall not dwarf the body of a child; you shall not stunt the mind of a child; you shall not coin the blood of a child into illegitimate dividends.'" He also supported the 1916 Railway Labor Act, which provided for an eight-hour work day.[19]

A second element in the relationship between corporate wealth and the federal government is subsidization. Subsidies can take the form of tariff protection, tax breaks, loan guarantees, war profits, or other governmental favors that, in effect, involve the transfer of money from the public treasury to private bank accounts. Thomas Jefferson was generally skeptical of tariffs because he did not believe government should nurture commerce. John Taylor, another early advocate of laissez-faire economics, used his pen to argue against protective tariffs, which he saw as encouraging aristocracy and creating monopoly. Political scientist G. David Garson argues,

> Though the tariff issue today seems obscure, it was the key issue of the last half of the nineteenth century. Tariffs were raised prices. The difference between the tariff price and the free-market price represented a sort of private tax taken from the consumer to subsidize business prosperity. It also brought revenue to the government and helped avoid an income tax on the new corporate elite. Thus tariffs were the single greatest subsidy to business during the Republican period, and at the same time allowed accumulation of personal wealth free from direct taxation.

A proponent of the free enterprise system, Bryan opposed monopoly capitalism and corporate welfare. His first major speech in Congress was in March 1892 on the subject of the protective tariff. Explaining the position of the Democratic Party, he told his colleagues, "We welcome to this country every industry that can stand upon its feet; but we do not welcome the industries that come to ride upon our backs. . . . We do not desire to discourage industries; we desire to restore to them the 'lost art' of self-support." Congressman Bryan sponsored a bill providing that goods produced by trusts would be duty-free, which meant that these goods would be placed on the tariff's free list, and manufacturers would receive no extra income from their sale. Bryan and other liberals believed that tariffs for revenue were acceptable, but tariffs for protection were unacceptable because they were a means of transferring wealth to the corporate elite.[20] They rejected the ar-

gument that protective tariffs were primarily intended to help factory workers, not factory owners.

Bryan opposed efforts to design the tax code for the benefit of wealthy
individuals and large corporations. He disliked the protective tariff partly
because of its regressivity as a consumption tax. Beginning in 1894 and continuing for the next two decades, Bryan criticized the regressivity of internal
revenue taxes and advocated an income tax as a fairer method of raising revenue. He criticized state governments for giving tax breaks to corporations.
During World War I, Bryan urged higher income taxes and an excess profits
tax to fund the war effort. In the mid-1920s, he opposed the Mellon Tax
Plan, calling it "tax relief for millionaires and big business" because it shifted
the tax burden from the upper class to the middle class.[21]

Bryan upheld the Jeffersonian maxim "Equal rights for all; special privileges for none" throughout his career. While he was sometimes willing to
use the "positive state" to correct social injustices it had fostered, he was
generally a believer in a "negative state" because he observed that the positive state was routinely used on behalf of the monied interests. In other
words, big, active, intrusive government usually operated at the behest of its
corporate masters. During his first congressional race, in 1890, Bryan said,
"The safety of our farmers and our laborers is not in special legislation, but
in equal and just laws that bear alike on every man. The great masses of our
people are interested, not in getting their hands into other people's pockets,
but in keeping the hands of other people out of their pockets." Bryan objected to open immigration laws partly because the forces of corporate
wealth would use cheap Asian labor to undercut American labor unions
while exploiting the immigrants themselves.[22]

The Panama Tolls Act of 1912 was passed during the Taft presidency with
strong Democratic support. It exempted Panama Canal toll payments by
American ships engaged in bicoastal trade. Liberals of both parties wanted to
encourage use of the canal in part because it provided a public alternative to
the privately-owned transcontinental railroads. Bryan, "always eager to strike
a blow against the railroads," put an endorsement of toll exemption in the
"Bryan-made" 1912 Democratic platform. Despite his Democratic affiliation, newly elected President Wilson sought repeal of the exemption. Many
liberals saw the move as a favor to monopolistic railroad companies and to
the imperialistic British government. They noted that Elihu Root, the
Carnegie Endowment for International Peace, and other plutocratic forces
were pushing for repeal. Secretary of State Bryan belatedly announced his
support for repeal in April 1914. According to Kendrick Clements, "it was
obvious that he was never very happy with repeal." Conveniently ignoring

his role in building the 1912 platform and uncharacteristically hiding his private misgivings, Bryan published a strongly worded defense of the toll exemption repeal in *The Commoner.* Turning one of the arguments used by repeal critics on its head, Bryan argued that toll exemptions for monopolistic ship companies represented a serious departure from the Democratic Party's traditional opposition to subsidies.[23]

Bryan explicitly tied plutocratization to a classical form of government: aristocracy. In 1899, he warned against the rise of "an industrial aristocracy besides which a landed aristocracy would be an innocent thing." In 1908, he charged that many Republican leaders looked at questions "from the aristocratic standpoint, the standpoint of the few." Within the Democratic Party, he identified with the wing populated by the "unnumbered throng" against the wing populated by the "corporate interests of the nation, its moneyed institutions, its aggregations of wealth and capital." Throughout his career, he depicted the contest between Bryan Democrats and McKinley Republicans as a battle between democracy and plutocracy.[24]

His supporters similarly attempted to expose and resist plutocratization. In 1922, former Senator Richard Pettigrew (R–SD) flatly declared, "The United States is a country run by and for the rich. Therefore, it is a plutocracy." Democratic governor Charles Bryan objected to the New Deal partly because it was pro-big business in orientation. Attorney Clarence Darrow and Senator Huey Long (D–LA) were critical of FDR's first term for the same reason. Even though former Senator James Reed (D–MO) was in the company of some reactionaries while opposing Roosevelt's reelection in 1944, his anti-FDR speeches "did not spare the international bankers, or the trusts and combinations."[25]

Humphrey and Popular Sovereignty

Hubert Humphrey was a majoritarian in only the most formal sense of the word. Rather than being an exponent of popular sovereignty, he was an exponent of paternalistic statism. Rather than championing rule by the common people, he worked on behalf of a strong government—advised by academic experts and staffed by bureaucratic experts—that could take care of the common people. When Bryan used the word *democracy,* he meant popular sovereignty or rule by the common people. When Humphrey used the word, he meant something quite different. In 1964, he defined *democracy* as "man's eternal struggle to govern himself." The broad, almost mythical, language used is ahistorical and not very useful. Later in the same speech, Humphrey asserted that "the heart of the democratic faith" is "a profound sense of obligation to assist the less fortunate in this country and around the world."[26] Again, the broadness of the language cripples the utility of the definition, but he seems to be identifying the essence of democracy as benevolence via government. Helping the needy says nothing about who rules. A benevolent dictatorship—rule by one who dispenses social welfare programs—could fulfill Humphrey's definition. In addition to his emphasis on paternalistic government, there are two other indications that Humphrey lacked a commitment to traditional majoritarianism: he courted voters as members of special interest groups and belonged to the power elite.

The disappearance of democratic control as an issue in American politics can be traced largely to four ideological forebears of Humphrey: Woodrow Wilson, Theodore Roosevelt, Franklin Roosevelt, and Wendell Willkie. Their domestic agendas, political strategies, and foreign policies contributed to the demise of this issue. The socioeconomic effects of the world wars into which America was pulled under the leadership of these men led to an immediate weakening and eventual disappearance of majoritarian democracy as a political topic. The public policy of elitist-oriented, urban-based, eastern-centered progressives and U.S. involvement in World War I unleashed "modernizing" influences that were deemed enlightened and inevitable by leaders of virtually every sector of society.[27]

In the 1920s and 1930s there were a few counterrevolutionary acts—the founding of the Progressive Party, the *Scopes* trial, the Bonus March, the Share the Wealth program, and the Nye Committee—that were waged on behalf of traditions, values, and beliefs presumably still held by a majority of the common people. The liberals associated with such efforts were dismissed as pitiable anachronisms and attacked as dangerous radicals. "Modernization" gained speed under the New Deal and became institutionalized during World War II.[28] What were the political results of modernization? Pluralism, individualism, and paternalism replaced majoritarianism. Fragmentation, atomization, and governmentation replaced the common people. Interest groups, corporate liberalism, and the welfare state replaced democracy. Humphrey explicitly identified with the modernization movement.[29]

Humphrey and Democratization

Hubert Humphrey was not known for advocating "power to the people." Instead, use of such slogans and possession of such sentiments characterized political enemies of Humphrey—namely, members of the New Left and, to some extent, conservative populists associated with Barry Goldwater and George Wallace. If William Jennings Bryan and Robert La Follette symbolized

populist liberalism during the Progressive Era, Woodrow Wilson and Theodore Roosevelt symbolized elitist liberalism. Following in the footsteps of
the latter pair, Hubert Humphrey and Nelson Rockefeller were elitists.[30]
According to La Follette, "the real cure for the ills of democracy is more
democracy." This view can be contrasted with that of Samuel Huntington
and Seymour Martin Lipset, political scientists who supported and advised
Humphrey. Believing that the sociopolitical ills that arose in the 1960s were
caused by an "excess of democracy," these scholars sometimes seemed to
long for a time when U.S. presidents were "able to govern the country with
the cooperation of a relatively small number of Wall Street lawyers and
bankers."[31]

There is no indication in the historical record that Humphrey had any interest in direct democracy, and his ideological ancestry partly explains his
perspective. In 1911, Woodrow Wilson opposed the recall of judges. At the
same time, he refused to say whether he favored the initiative at the state
level, and, after entering the White House, he did nothing to bring about the
initiative at the federal level. The Wilson administration blocked the war referendum proposal of Bryan, La Follette, and other populists. Wanting to appeal to western progressives, Theodore Roosevelt endorsed judicial recall
during his 1912 campaign, but he immediately backpedaled when the
speech caused a controversy. Occasional campaign rhetoric notwithstanding, eastern progressives generally disapproved of direct democracy reforms.
In the late 1930s, Establishmentarians of both parties vigorously opposed efforts by Congressman Louis Ludlow (D-IN) and Senator Robert La Follette
Jr. (Pr-WI) to provide for a national referendum on war. The Cowles publishing empire supported Humphrey over the course of four decades. In
1996, the *Minneapolis Star Tribune,* under chairman John Cowles III, opposed
an amendment to the state constitution giving Minnesota citizens the ability to recall elected officials.[32] Despite the newspaper's opposition, Minnesotans adopted the recall through the initiative process. Reflecting a
preference for republic over democracy, the newspaper's stance was illustrative of the type of liberalism embraced by Humphrey.

Humphrey and Representativeness

Humphrey's most important contribution to representativeness was in the
area of full suffrage. Women, of course, had the right to vote throughout the
nation by the time Humphrey began his political career. Although he was
not known for his feminist views, he supported the equal rights amendment

during the 1970s.[33] He favored the Twenty-Sixth Amendment, which low-ered the voting age from twenty-one to eighteen years.

A belief in equality and compassion for the downtrodden was perhaps best exemplified in the consistent and influential support Humphrey gave to the cause of black civil rights. One manifestation was his opposition to poll taxes and literacy tests during his Senate tenure. His efforts to enlarge suf-frage by protecting the right to vote of southern blacks culminated in pas-sage of the Voting Rights Act in 1965.

Humphrey's attitude toward the direct primary can be discerned in the realm of presidential politics. In 1950, he voted for an amendment that not only abolished the electoral college but also established a national primary to choose presidential nominees. Humphrey participated in primaries in two of his bids for the White House, but he also had an affinity for less re-publican methods of nomination. Many have traced Humphrey's primary-shy attitude to his surprise defeats by John Kennedy in the 1960 Wisconsin and West Virginia primaries. Humphrey's reluctance to enter presidential primaries after 1960 cannot be attributed solely to a fear of losing or linger-ing resentment. In his Senate career he pursued an insider's strategy, and this approach was characteristic of his political mentors and supporters, such as Harry Truman and Lyndon Johnson. According to Humphrey's own ac-count, he was rather dictatorial toward the Minnesota delegation at the 1952 Democratic National Convention in the face of liberal resistance to the vice-presidential nomination of Senator John Sparkman (D-AL), a segrega-tionist. To prevent any local trouble for Humphrey's 1960 campaign, Gover-nor Orville Freeman, one of his oldest and closest friends, successfully worked to abolish the Minnesota presidential primary.[34] Biographer Allan Ryskind believes that Humphrey gained the 1964 vice-presidential nomina-tion "not because he was genuinely popular, but because he was a friend of Lyndon Johnson." Certainly Humphrey had a significant degree of popular-ity among civil rights advocates, labor union leaders, and social welfare sup-porters, but convention delegates were not given a chance to vote for anyone else after Johnson made the decision. Although Humphrey missed the filing deadlines for most of the 1968 primaries because of his late entry into the race, he chose not to enter a number of others for tactical reasons. Instead, he relied on previously chosen uncommitted and Johnson delegates and on delegates chosen in subsequent caucuses. In seeking the nomination, Humphrey "campaigned in safety, taking trips down memory lane with au-diences of middle-aged Democratic supporters and dealing in smoke-filled rooms with the agents of the machine he had once challenged so brashly." While he did not run a grassroots campaign or a campaign subject to popular ratification, Humphrey did lead Robert Kennedy and Eugene McCarthy in national public opinion polls of Democrats taken in the spring of 1968.[35]

As late as September 1971, Humphrey was planning to bypass the 1972 primaries with the single exception of the last big one in California. Reluctantly, he decided he had "no choice but to bow to the spreading democratization of the party ordained by the McGovern reforms and battle the other eleven aspirants for a popular mandate." To highlight this new approach, Humphrey's slogan when announcing his 1972 candidacy was "We the People." Ironically, Humphrey ended up being the most popular primary contender, edging George McGovern and George Wallace when the votes were added up for a national total. In 1976, Humphrey again wanted the nomination, but he wanted to be drafted. He hoped the officeholders, managers, and financiers of the party would give it to him as they had done in 1968. Liberals such as former senator Harold Hughes (D-IA) and columnist Tom Wicker criticized Humphrey for desiring the nomination while sitting out the primaries.[36]

During his first year in the Senate, Humphrey introduced a bill to abolish the electoral college. In 1950, he sponsored legislation establishing direct popular election of the president. Sounding like a latter-day Bryan, he argued for the change on majoritarian and democratization grounds. Roll call voting in the Senate was curtailed during the 1940s. One reason was the departure of a number of outspoken liberal leaders. Another reason was the effect of World War II in strengthening the executive branch of government and silencing legislative critics. With the advent of the Cold War, this mentality continued in Washington, with foreign policy disputes kept to a minimum in the interest of national security and bipartisanship. Most major presidential appointments were confirmed without a roll call vote. This was especially true under the autocratic leadership of Senate majority leader Lyndon Johnson. He preferred applying pressure off the floor and then displaying unity on the floor. Humphrey was a loyal supporter of Johnson's leadership methods.[37]

Humphrey was no reformer when it came to presidential term limits. His early political hero, Woodrow Wilson, ignored the one-term pledge of the 1912 Democratic platform after he entered the White House. His later political hero, Franklin Roosevelt, completely disregarded the American officeholding tradition.[38] While Bryan would have limited presidents to one term, FDR sought four. Humphrey voted for Willkie in 1940 but evidently not on third-term grounds. While Bryan would have limited presidents to four years, Lyndon Johnson wanted to hold the office for nine. Humphrey supported Johnson's plans for reelection and Humphrey himself served five terms in the Senate.

The Humphrey version of the Democratic Party was, with two notable exceptions—full suffrage and popular voting—not very interested in encouraging representativeness. Its net effect was to make elections and government less representative. Humphrey allies such as Lyndon Johnson and William Benton were early practitioners of "new politics," which included scientific polling and the use of public relations specialists, advertising firms, and electronic media. Such political techniques relied far less on grassroots campaigning and genuine popularity, and far more on image building and a large campaign treasury. Humphrey himself relied on backroom, interest group, cocktail party methods that were more traditional but just as unrepresentative. Far from trying to open up the political system, Humphrey was an insider. He quoted with approval Johnson's advice for enacting legislation:

> You have to take it slow and easy, working your colleagues over like gentlemen—not on the floor, but in the cloakroom—explaining and trading, but always letting them see what's in it for them. Then when you're sure [you've got the votes to win] . . . you come out statesmanlike on the Senate floor and, in the spirit of democracy, have a little debate for the people.[39]

Such cynical manipulation of the process and demagogic contempt for the people were completely foreign to liberals such as Bryan and La Follette.

Humphrey and Plutocratization

The Vital Center Democracy to which Hubert Humphrey belonged rarely raised the issue of plutocracy in partisan elections. Under the leadership of Roosevelt and Willkie, Truman and Dewey, a bipartisan consensus, at the leadership level, had been reached in favor of corporate wealth and business monopoly. When reference was made to plutocracy during an election campaign, it was in a merely rhetorical, obviously partisan, almost kidding sense. On rare occasions Humphrey made allusions to Republican plutocracy, but they were weak and simplistic. He criticized the Eisenhower administration because "businessman types wandered into and out of powerful positions in Washington." He criticized the Nixon administration because the president's "belief in corporations and corporate managers" kept him from understanding that successful businessmen "do not necessarily fit well into government posts." There was an element of hypocrisy in this kind of quasi-populist rhetoric. Humphrey never uttered words of criticism about the multitudes of businessmen who filled high posts in the Roosevelt, Truman, Kennedy, Johnson, and Carter administrations. The power of corporate wealth was not used as an issue against Nixon when Humphrey was the 1968 Democratic presidential nominee. The most accurate interparty criticism of plutocracy was aimed at—not by—Humphrey and his allies. In the early 1940s, many members of the Minnesota Farmer-Labor Party did not want to merge with the Minnesota Democratic Party because they believed Democrats were "opportunists who had compromised with southern bourbons and the moneyed interests." In 1948, the Progressive Party argued that government was not battling "the money power, the railroads, the trusts, the economic royalists" because Truman-Humphrey Democrats had turned it over to "Wall Street bankers" and "spokesmen of Big Business."[40]

If Humphrey rarely criticized plutocracy in the opposing party, he never did so in relation to his own. This was a key difference between Bryan and Humphrey. Far from attacking "plutocrats masquerading as Democrats," Humphrey belonged to the plutocratic wing of his party. Despite muted attempts on a quadrennial basis to uphold their image as "the party of the people," leaders of Vital Center Democracy have assisted the growth of plutocracy throughout the twentieth century. Woodrow Wilson ran as a democrat in 1912, was elected on an antimonopoly platform, and made some notably liberal appointments. Upon closer inspection, however, it is clear that Wilson was contemptuous of Bryan, financed his campaigns with Wall Street money, and regulated on behalf of the regulatees.[41] Al Smith is known for his controversial Catholicism, wet position on Prohibition, and sidewalks-of-New York style. Less known, but more important, was his role as a political star in the Morgan-DuPont financial-industrial constellation.[42] Franklin Roosevelt is hailed as a champion of the "forgotten man" and an enemy of "economic royalists," but he filled his administration with big businessmen, relaxed with the likes of Vincent Astor, retained the friendship of multinational corporations, pushed traditional liberals out of the way, and left socioeconomic inequality pretty much the way he found it.[43]

According to conventional wisdom, if ever there was a friend of the common man in the White House, it was Harry Truman, the plainspoken man from Independence who railed against big business in 1948. Actually, Truman governed the nation hand in hand with "a relatively small number of Wall Street lawyers and bankers" and used populist campaign rhetoric to undercut the appeal of Progressive nominee Henry Wallace.[44] Adlai Stevenson, a three-time "great white hope" of liberal Democrats, was also a corporate attorney and director of the elite Council on Foreign Relations.[45] Despite initial skepticism, liberals associated with Americans for Democratic Action eventually aided the presidential ambitions of John Kennedy. Son of a Wall Street speculator and linked to the British aristocracy, Kennedy was a loyal Establishmentarian who brought representatives of the big foundations, corporations, and banks into his cabinet.[46] Lyndon Johnson was greeted with even more skepticism when he ran for the 1960 nomination, but ADA liberals were singing his praises by 1964 and his Great Society was viewed as the best thing to happen to America since the New Deal. A favorite of corporate America, Johnson has been compared to William McKinley and contrasted with William Jennings Bryan.[47] Jimmy Carter had not been the first choice of most movement liberals during the 1976 primary season, but after choosing Senator Walter Mondale (DFL-MN) as his running mate and agreeing to a centrist platform, they rallied around him. The southern born, Bible-quoting, love spreading, truth-telling, ever-smiling peanut farmer from Plains was also a founding member of the elite Trilateral Commission and a friend of Wall Street.[48] Humphrey was politically close to each of these Vital Center leaders. It was not a matter of Humphrey working with these men despite their plutocratic ties: he worked with them partly because of such ties. He sincerely agreed with their Vital Center ideology, a key component of which is friendship with the monied interests.

Throughout his career, Humphrey was criticized by more traditional liberals for being a member of the plutocratic wing of the Democratic Party.[49] When entering the Senate in 1949, he came upon a long-standing East-South alliance between eastern Wall Street Republicans and southern Bourbon Democrats. The alliance was held together during the postwar years by northern-based corporations anxious to move manufacturing plants away from union strongholds and local southern elites eager to receive them. Bryan and his allies favored a West-South alliance based on populism, not an East-South alliance based on elitism. Humphrey initially opposed the East-South alliance, but he soon fell in with the group through his friendship with Lyndon Johnson.[50] Immediately after the 1964 Democratic National Convention, Johnson told his running mate,

> Hubert, you and I are going to put an end once and for all to the reputation the Democratic party has of being anti-business. I want you to go to every businessmen's luncheon and meeting that you can possibly go to. Tell them, You don't need to be afraid of us just because we're looking after the old people and the kids. We're going to be mighty liberal on things like Medicare, Social Security and free milk for the babies, but we gotta have profitable companies in this country to make it work.

This is a clear description of the essence of corporate liberalism. The Johnson-Humphrey ticket espoused trickle-down economics. Neither Humphrey nor most of his allies were seriously interested in campaign finance reform. Like his political heroes, Humphrey relied heavily on "big money" for his senatorial and presidential campaigns.[51] In 1974, he voted to table a conflict of interest amendment prohibiting the receipt of honoraria and other payments to members of Congress for writing or speaking and receipt of income from any enterprise regulated or financed by the U.S. government.

The wing of the Democratic Party to which Humphrey belonged had never been very strong on the issue of regulating corporate wealth. Despite paying lip service to it during the 1912 campaign, Woodrow Wilson rejected the antimonopoly, trust extirpation position of Bryan. Even though it was fairly mild in language, President Wilson relied less on the 1914 Clayton Antitrust Act than he did on the Federal Trade Commission in his official relations with big business. His reliance on the FTC did not pose a serious problem for monopolistic companies because he filled the FTC and other regulatory agencies with procorporate members. Partly as a result of Wilson's statements and policies, by the 1920s, "big business" was widely viewed as an inevitable and beneficial element in society instead of something that should be curbed if not eradicated.

FDR followed Wilson's lead in abandoning the trust-busting position of the Democratic Party under Bryan's leadership. For example, in the early 1930s, many traditional liberals objected to the promonopoly nature of the National Recovery Act (NRA).[52] Hubert Humphrey Sr. admired Wilson and Roosevelt, but he did not share their view of economic concentration and price fixing. By the early 1940s, the younger Humphrey had rejected his father's populist stance on trusts. Mayor Humphrey had what can only be called a cozy relationship with the monopolistic business leaders of Minneapolis, and in Washington he worked on behalf of Minnesota bankers and grain merchants. Nonetheless, he sometimes used antiplutocratic language during his first few years in the Senate. In 1949–1950, he denounced "monopolistic corporate business interests" and called "growing monopoly" the "greatest threat to free enterprise in America."[53]

With the exception of generalities occasionally used for partisan purposes and his remarkable speech of September 17, 1963, after the Birmingham church bombing, Humphrey's anticorporate blasts disappeared after the early 1950s. During the Johnson administration, the major oil companies were protected from antitrust action and corporate-friendly persons were appointed to regulatory commissions. Humphrey approved of these policies. In 1964, he declared, "I do not think that we have many real grievances to be urged against bigness in business today. To the contrary. For the most part, big corporations are a source of strength and economic vitality. And certainly, big business is here to stay." On the campaign trail, Humphrey told the leading businessmen of Texas, "Talk about being liberal, there is no more humanitarian and progressive force in American life than the American business community." In 1965, Attorney General Nicholas Katzenbach promised the Business Council that the antitrust division of the Justice Department would give them a "breathing spell," and Vice President Humphrey told a gathering of the nation's economic elite that he was concerned about "outdated anti-trust laws."[54]

Given his basic orientation from the 1940s to the 1970s, it is not surprising that Humphrey was a consistent advocate of government, or taxpayer, subsidization of corporations. During the Humphrey-Rockefeller era, the tariff issue became confusing as many Bryan-La Follette liberals found themselves identified as opponents of free trade. They had not become friends of corporate-favoring protective tariffs, but they refused to go along with the new trade program. In the early 1930s, traditional liberals welcomed Franklin Roosevelt's pledge to lower tariffs, but, by the end of the decade, many believed they had been victims of a bait and switch. Instead of getting at the heart of the tariff problem, which was the subsidization of monopolistic corporations, the Roosevelt administration had transplanted the heart into a new body with reciprocal trade agreements. Extension of the Reciprocal Trade Agreements Act (RTAA) in 1940 was opposed by many liberals not only because it abrogated legislative authority and tended to encourage entangling alliances, but because the opening of foreign markets was being pushed by big business. It was seen as a manifestation of the old Wall Street-Bourbon alliance, whereby northeastern banking and industrial companies and southern cotton growers benefited at the expense of midwestern and western farmers, mining companies, and small, domestic-oriented manufacturers. In 1940, Humphrey had not yet entered the Senate, but he praised Secretary of State Cordell Hull's trade agreements at the time of the debate and supported extension of the RTAA in 1955. By the early 1960s, tariff policy was no longer an important political issue as a result of the bipartisan consensus in favor of the globalization of finance and commerce.[55]

During the 1938–1978 period, tax policy continued to be a battleground between supporters and opponents of the subsidization of business. In 1950, Humphrey made a Senate speech exposing tax loopholes for big business and wealthy individuals contained in that year's tax bill. All of the loophole closing amendments offered by Humphrey and his friend Paul Douglas (D-IL) were defeated, but the speech brought the issue of tax fairness into the open. The oil depletion allowance was a provision in the federal tax code that exempted oil and gas companies from paying any taxes on a certain percentage of their total income. Beneficial to petroleum and natural gas producers in Oklahoma, Texas, and Louisiana, the loophole was protected by Lyndon Johnson and his Bourbon friends. Humphrey supported efforts to reduce the allowance in 1951 and 1958, and it was abolished in 1975 through a Tax Reduction Act amendment supported by Humphrey. In 1960, he charged, "The federal tax laws are rigged against the middle- and low-income families—and for the big corporations." After moving into legislative and executive leadership positions, Humphrey urged toleration of corporate tax loopholes, including a huge tax break for the DuPont family in 1962. The Tax Reduction Act of 1964, originally pushed by President Kennedy and eventually signed by President Johnson, was in the tradition of the Mellon Tax Plan. Kennedy's tax cut was regressive, with upper-income Americans being disproportionately helped. With tax rates being dramatically decreased for wealthy individuals and with corporate taxes also being cut, the bill earned the support of the U.S. Chamber of Commerce and American Bankers Association. Running for vice president, Humphrey criticized Republican presidential nominee Barry Goldwater for voting against the "$11.5-billion tax cut for the American citizens and American business."[56]

In addition to tariff schedules and tax laws, there were many ways corporations could receive favors from government during the Humphrey-Rockefeller era. Perhaps the most lucrative subsidies were those derived from systemic policies. By 1912, the most "advanced," "enlightened," and "progressive" leaders of big business had come to understand the necessity and utility of taking steps to ameliorate the social injustice and political discontent produced by modern capitalism. The nation's biggest industrialists and bankers, many of whom where affiliated with the National Civic Federation, began giving approval to a variety of reform measures. Apparently acting more out of shrewd self-interest than humanitarianism, they backed some laws that were designed to produce the opposite of the measure's purported goal. They backed some laws that genuinely did something to lessen human suffering. They backed no laws that threatened the power and privilege of corporate wealth. Corporate Liberalism fostered superficial and minor changes, but it did not alter the basic structure of American economics and politics.[57]

Humphrey was a proponent of the welfare state. The welfare state is usually seen as government trying to help the poor, but it actually has a three-pronged approach—one for each economic class. Welfare can be defined as assistance, handouts, or subsidies that go beyond the traditional, minimalistic, negative-state duties of government included in the social contract. Welfare for the middle class consists of entitlements such as Social Security, Medicare, student loans, farm loans and crop subsidies, small business loans, and natural disaster relief. When citizens and politicians complain about welfare, they are almost always referring to handouts for the lower class. Since most members of the middle class take their handouts for granted, politicians do not usually get much credit among middle-class voters for boosting their level of subsidization. In contrast, most members of the lower class are acutely aware of who is helping them, and if they decide to vote in an election, they are likely to remember their benefactors.

With the poor not making enough to pay much in federal taxes and with the rich relying on attorneys and accountants, tax shelters and tax loopholes, Middle America bore the brunt of paying for the benevolence of the Great Society. Thus, while the strength of the Goldwater-Miller ticket lay with the middle class, the Johnson-Humphrey ticket was embraced most enthusiastically by the upper class and lower class. In addition to the electoral "vote-buying" component of welfare programs, a system of subsidization serves to pacify and neutralize the common people; it co-opts the masses and creates a climate of dependency. It could be thought of as one-half of the bread-and-circuses strategy used by the Roman Empire to keep its domestic population content and docile. There is also an economic element to the upper class-lower class relationship. In 1965, sociologist Richard Hamilton pointed out that clearheaded businessmen realize that "there's money in poverty." There is one more explanation for the existence of the welfare state: the undeserving wealthy and powerful soothe their consciences when they help the poor and downtrodden. Well-publicized charity—consisting of either a tiny fraction of their own money funneled through a private foundation or middle-class money funneled through a public agency—serves to make them feel better while simultaneously cultivating good public relations and maintaining their own privileged lifestyles.[58]

If welfare for the poor is thought of as bread, it amounts to crumbs in comparison to welfare for the rich. Corporate welfare accounts for tens of billions of budgetary dollars each year, from economic development corporations at the local level to the Commerce Department at the federal level.[59] Ever the consensus builder, Humphrey favored a partnership between government and business. He did not see this as a compromise or betrayal of his liberalism. On the contrary, he viewed it as a cornerstone of his ideology. In a 1950 speech on the welfare state, for a second, Humphrey sounds like Bryan, noting that big business used the protective tariff to benefit itself, but then he turns the issue on its head—he is using it as an argument *for* the

welfare state, not *against* the welfare state. Instead of saying that class legislation for the rich is bad, so, in fairness, there should not be class legislation for
the poor, he said that class legislation for the rich is good, so, in fairness,
there should also be class legislation for the poor. Humphrey himself put it
this way: "Many of these Government subsidies to business are desirable. But
if they are desirable to help profits, they are desirable to help people." He was
a friend of both the underprivileged and the overprivileged, largely at the
expense of the middle class. The liberalism of Humphrey included encouragement for big business because, in his view, as the gross national product
rose, the lives of all Americans—from rich to poor—would get better. He
compared this to a pie growing larger and larger, thereby enabling everyone
to have a larger piece. This "enlarged-pie economics" is simply another
name for trickle-down economics, and it does not address the basic issue of
just distribution. Specifically, it ignores the unfair methods used by some to
acquire and maintain a larger piece of the pie. In fact, it actually *helps* them
in their using of unfair methods. Harry Truman criticized the trickle-down
economics of the Republican Party during the 1948 campaign and similar
attacks were made on Reaganomics during the 1980s, but the Democratic
Party has been committed to a similar economic philosophy since at least
the 1930s.[60]

In looking at specific examples of corporate subsidization, it is important
to note that this policy has been institutionalized. The Departments of
Commerce, Defense, and State are little more than conduits whereby tax
dollars are transferred to monied interests. While not overlooking its humanitarian veneer or geopolitical intent, it must be conceded that foreign
aid is an example of corporate welfare. When it comes to foreign aid, privately made goods are purchased by the government to be sent abroad, private loans are arranged by a government agency, or public money is given to
allow for the purchase of private goods. In any case, the largest American
banks and industries benefit from the transaction. It was no accident that the
architects and administrators of foreign aid in the 1940s and 1950s were 'intimately tied to big business.[61] The revolving door of the military-industrial
complex and the lucrative realm of military contracts are well-known phe-
nomena.[62] "Dollar diplomacy" and "gunboat diplomacy" on behalf of corporations with overseas investments did not die out in 1913 or 1933. In the opinion
of many analysts, foreign policy throughout the Humphrey-Rockefeller era
was driven to a large extent by the desire to secure foreign markets, overseas
investments, and cheap international labor.[63]

Through the 1953 Tidelands Act, the federal government renounced its
rights to submerged lands of coastal states, thus giving offshore oil deposits

to the states. Denouncing it as a "giveaway," opponents believed that the ultimate goal of the bill was to ensure the leasing of oil rights to private companies. Humphrey voted against the bill. Debate over the 1954 Atomic Energy Act followed similar lines. Senator Wayne Morse (D-OR) called it a "give-away to Big Business." Humphrey joined Morse in voting against the bill.

Nine years later, Senator Humphrey was taking a different position on a similar issue. In 1963, he was a driving force behind the Communications Satellite Act. It was viewed as "one of the greatest giveaways in American history" by the liberal senators who fought it because it essentially "turned the taxpayers' enormous investment in space research over to private industry for exploitation."[64] The shift in Humphrey's actions from the 1950s to the 1960s can be attributed to partisanship or to maturity, but either way it reflects poorly on his reputation as a foe of powerful special interests. Significantly, Paul Douglas—a man with La Follette roots—was the only Humphreyite in the Senate to vote against the satellite bill.

Corporate subsidization as one element of plutocratization occurred throughout the twentieth century, under both Democratic and Republican presidents and Congresses. But it reached new heights during the presidency of Richard Nixon. There was considerable irony in this, since Nixon the campaigner cast himself as a champion of the hardworking, play-by-the-rules, elite-hating, free enterprise-believing "Silent Majority." The early 1970s saw two sizeable loan guarantees given to major corporations on the verge of shutdown or bankruptcy. The Emergency Rail Services Act bailed out Penn Central Transportation. Humphrey was not in the Senate at the time, but most of his supporters voted for the bill. In 1971, Humphrey himself voted for the Emergency Loan Guarantee Act, which bailed out Lockheed Aircraft. Campaigning for president in 1972, Humphrey declared that he was proud to have cast the deciding vote for the Lockheed bailout.

There was an underlying democracy/plutocracy element to the battle over the Panama Canal treaties in 1977–1978. On the face of it, it would seem that the decision by the U.S. government to return the canal to Panama was simply a repudiation of an imperialistic past. There was, however, more to it than that. The imperialistic wings of the two major parties were enthusiastic about the treaties. The economics of the situation apparently played a role in their enthusiasm. Figures associated with multinational corporations and international banks negotiated the treaties and then pushed hard for their ratification. A revised relationship with Panama was sought by advocates of a type of imperialism more sophisticated than territorial imperialism. They had learned from history that dollar diplomacy is often more effective than gunboat diplomacy in obtaining desired ends. Public opinion polls showed that Americans opposed the canal transfer by a two-to-one margin. Hubert Humphrey was the Carter administration's point man on the Panama Canal treaties until his death in January 1978.[65] A few months later, almost all of his allies in the Senate, including his widow, Muriel Humphrey (DFL-MN), voted for ratification.

In terms of democracy vs. plutocracy, Humphrey started out as less liberal than his father. He sometimes used populist language during his first few years in the Senate, but by the mid-1950s he had entered into an alliance with Lyndon Johnson and the overtly procorporate wing of the Democratic Party. Humphrey became a blatant booster of big business in 1964. By 1972, when Democratic presidential hopefuls George Wallace and George Mc-Govern were calling attention to tax injustice, corporate foundations, illegal campaign contributions, and limousine liberal hypocrisy, Humphrey was comfortably residing in the center of these things. When it came to corporate wealth, Humphrey did not measure up to the liberal standards set by Bryan and other early twentieth-century Jeffersonians. For example, after blasting plutocracy in his maiden speech, Senator Jeff Davis (D-AR) was ridiculed or ignored by the press and most of his colleagues for the remainder of his years in the Senate. In contrast, despite his early anti-Harry Byrd faux pas, Hubert Humphrey soon joined the Senate establishment. As he grew older, Senator Richard Pettigrew (R-SD) began to see Bryan as weak and ignorant, but he was still willing to say, "Bryan never knowingly served the vested interests. He fought them to the extent of his ability."[66] This could never be said of Humphrey.

Referring to liberal news media in the early 1990s, Roger Morris wrote, "They might deplore the primitive social prejudices of groups like the Christian Coalition or pay homage to token feminism, gay rights, artistic freedom, or civil liberties, but they could not confront the inequity of income and power that was the crux of their own status." The same could be said about modern-day liberals in general.[67] Economic growth has supplanted economic justice. The idealized role of the common people in the political process has changed from ruling to voting. Post-New Deal liberalism lacked a commitment to authentic representativeness, let alone genuine democracy. Cut off from their ideological taproot, most liberals have gone from one trendy and narrow social cause to another, lacking a historical context and possessing a superficial understanding.

CHAPTER 9

Positions on Domestic Policy

Decentralization

Some historians have depicted the populism of William Jennings Bryan as being supportive of efforts to offset an "increasingly centralized economy" with "increasingly centralized political control." Bryan has been seen as an opponent of laissez-faire economics, as a pioneer of the welfare state, and as a forerunner of the New Deal. There is an element of truth in this description, but it leaves the wrong impression. Amidst great socioeconomic change, Bryan was willing to move closer to the positive state than Martin Van Buren had been willing to endorse, but he did not reject laissez-faire, was not a welfare statist, and would have objected to at least some of the key provisions of the New Deal.[1]

Decentralization involves more than states' rights: it also means minimalistic government at every level. This is the negative state or bare-bones approach to government. The ultimate decentralization is individual self-governance or anarchy. William Jennings Bryan was not an anarchist, but he was influenced by Leo Tolstoy, a proponent of nonviolent, Christian anarchism. Unlike Tolstoy, Bryan believed government could be a force for good, but he worked for a just government—not a compassionate government. Firmly committed to the Jeffersonian principle "Equal rights to all; special privileges to none," Bryan believed in equality of opportunity, not equality of result. He was not opposed to the free enterprise system.[2] On the contrary, he wanted to free the American economy from the control of monopoly capitalists. Laissez-faire had given way to special interest economics. This is why he strongly favored the use of antitrust legislation. Breaking up private monopolies was a negative act designed to restore the nation's economic freedom, competition, and balance. Neither a state socialist nor a state capitalist, Bryan viewed monopoly, whether economic or political, as antithetical to both equality and diversity because it concentrated power into the hands of a small group of like-minded individuals.

Under the leadership of Bryan and other liberals, the 1896, 1908, and 1912 Democratic platforms strongly endorsed states' rights. Many Bryan Democrats lived in the South and were segregationists, but it would be a mistake to view their support for states' rights as mere cover for institutionalized racism. Although in some instances this may have been the case, prejudice was not restricted to one region and decentralization predated the Missouri Compromise, Civil War, and Jim Crow. Bryan Democrats based their states' rights stance not only on the words of Jefferson but also on the Constitution. Bryan advocated decentralization at home and praised its existence abroad. Recognizing that the U.S. had a dual form of government, he was willing to use federal power to break up trusts and control corporations, but only as an addition to, not as a substitution for, efforts at the state level. He believed that natural monopolies associated with power, communication, and transportation could be operated by government because competition in private hands was not possible, but he wanted control at the lowest possible level of government.[3]

Like his hero Franklin Roosevelt, Hubert Humphrey was a proponent of political maximization and centralization. When challenged, he sometimes justified increases in the power and responsibility of the federal government on the basis of the *general welfare* phrase found in the Preamble and Article I, Section 8 of the Constitution. Humphrey's interpretation of the clause was in direct opposition to Madison's in *The Federalist* No. 41 and Hamilton's in *The Federalist* No. 83. According to the framers of the Constitution, the national legislature would not possess unlimited powers because providing for the general welfare was limited and defined by the enumeration of particular powers. Jefferson had the same interpretation.[4]

Despite his Democratic heritage, Humphrey had little respect for the principle of political decentralization even from his earliest adult years. In his famous speech at the 1948 Democratic National Convention, Humphrey said, "There are those who say, this issue of civil rights is an infringement on states' rights. The time has arrived for the Democratic party to get out of the shadow of states' rights and walk forthrightly into the bright sunshine of human rights." His implication was that states' rights are incompatible with human rights. In his 1976 autobiography, he praised President Lyndon Johnson's accomplishments in the areas of education, health, and conservation, adding, "None of those laws paid much homage to states' rights but, rather, called on the states to be partners in the achievement of national goals and national commitments." This was Humphrey's basic attitude toward traditional areas of state and local control. He believed that the federal government should mandate ethnic inclusiveness. He glibly brushed aside states' rights objections to the Civil Rights Act of 1964.[5]

The "urban, industrial, corporate nation" that Humphrey argued necessitated political centralization did not come about by accident: it was a result of planning by the captains of industry and finance and developed with the assistance of their allies in government. Having replaced trust-busting with regulating, it is questionable how effective big government has been as a countervailing force to big business, that is assuming this has actually been the goal. What in theory was regulation *of* business has usually been in practice regulation *for* business. Humphrey was an open advocate of the welfare state. This included federal largesse for every socioeconomic group—including the upper class and its corporations. He was best known, however, for being a bleeding-heart liberal who wanted the federal government to help needy Americans. Referring to the U.S. citizen, in 1958, Humphrey said, "Today, the federal government's influence is everywhere, in the states, in the cities, in the towns, on the highways, in the airways, in the Main Street bank, in the country store, affecting his life in a hundred different ways every hour of the day, every day of the year." He viewed this as a positive development. It may or may not have been, but it was certainly an utter repudiation of Madison's promise in *The Federalist* No. 45 and the guarantee written into the Tenth Amendment.[6]

In 1964, conservative Republicans criticized Humphrey's ties to Americans for Democratic Action, saying, "It should frighten every citizen who does not want to see Socialism and centralized government installed in the United States of America." It was Humphrey's glorification of pervasive federal involvement in citizens' lives that gave rise to charges of socialism, but there was nothing subversive about Humphrey or his ADA colleagues in a radical or anti-Establishment sense of the word. If they were socialists, they were devotees of the "Harvard socialism" of the power elite and were more influenced by London than by Moscow. In March 1976, Humphrey argued that the Democratic presidential nominee "should not run as an opponent of 'big government' but as the champion of all that it can accomplish." Humphrey predicted that the party would capture the White House in November "because most Americans want a strong central government." The Humphrey-Hawkins Full Employment and Balanced Growth Act of 1978 symbolized the culmination of his lifelong dedication to paternalistic government.[7]

By the late 1960s, many if not most Americans had soured on the welfare state. They were disgusted by the inherent contradiction of limousine liberalism and objected to the heavy burden placed on middle-class taxpayers. They were skeptical of a bureaucratic, trickle-down system of payments to the poor. Fundamental assumptions of the welfare state were called into question. Some argued that there can be no such thing as "compassionate government" because only individual human beings can have compassion. The motives of bleeding-heart public officials were viewed with suspicion. Despite the rising tide of discontent with big government and social welfare, Humphrey remained an unapologetic defender of both throughout the 1970s.[8] This may have been one of his finest demonstrations of principle. He would have had a better chance of obtaining the 1976 presidential nomination had he trimmed his sails to better fit the mood of the country, but he boldly stuck with his old message and watched as a younger, more demagogic Democrat gained the nomination and the presidency. Humphrey's interest in government on a grand scale was not confined to American borders. Just as he was willing to sweep aside claims of state sovereignty in domestic affairs for the good of humanity, he was willing to do the same on a global scale when it came to national sovereignty.[9]

Construction of the Constitution

In keeping with his thesis that Bryan, La Follette, Wilson, and the two Roosevelts all shared the same ideology, historian Henry Steele Commager declared that what populism and progressivism "meant in terms of constitutional theory was the unqualified triumph of the doctrine of broad construction." Herbert Croly, a contemporary of William Jennings Bryan, probably gives a more accurate account. He believed that the dedication of Bryan and other Jeffersonians "to such things as strict construction of the constitution and states' rights had so hamstrung the government that little could be done to thwart the tyranny of allied business and political interests." In 1901, Bryan called "adherence to the Constitution" one of the "fundamental principles" of the Democratic Party. In 1908, he said, "I am a strict constructionist, if that means to believe that the Federal Government is one of delegated powers and that constitutional limitations should be carefully observed." Today, some conservative heirs of Robert Taft go beyond strict construction of the Constitution to constitutional idolatry: they deify the framers and have an irrational reluctance to amend it. A believer in popular sovereignty, Bryan was not of this school. In 1921, Bryan advocated changing the Constitution to make it easier to amend.[10] Loose constructionists do not have to bother with the arduous amendment process; they simply look past the literal constraints of the Constitution.

When Hubert Humphrey called himself a "constitutionalist," he was stretching the traditional meaning of the word—as befits a loose constructionist. In 1939, he wrote, "The Constitution is a declaration of fundamental political and social principles. It is subject to interpretation. As time goes on, it expands here and contracts there. If it were incapable of growth it would long ago have become a dead and lifeless thing." This is a succinct summary of the broad interpretation position. Strict constructionists argue that although the Declaration of Independence is partly a declaration of principles, the Constitution is a rule book or social contract: it has specific provisions meant to be adhered to and makes an allowance for growth—the amendment process. Humphrey approved of Franklin Roosevelt's loose interpretation of the interstate commerce, due process, and general welfare clauses. In addition to referring to the Constitution as a holdover from "horse and buggy" days, during his first term, FDR advised Congress to set aside doubts about constitutionality, "however reasonable," when considering important pieces of legislation. When Harry Truman tried to seize control of the steel mills in 1952 and the Supreme Court struck down his executive order as unconstitutional, he complained, "That's what is the trouble with the Senate and the High Court! Those two bodies are controlled by the past." Humphrey agreed that "the forces of progressive democracy" should be released from "the restraints and shackles of rigid constitutional limitations." Humphrey's loose constructionism came not only from the example of Vital Center chief executives, but also from his own warmhearted personality and pragmatic philosophy.[11]

Banking

The essence of capitalism is the lending of money at a rate of interest. Usury is most often handled by banks. Capitalism is not synonymous with free enterprise. A society can have private exchange of goods and services without using money or interest. Most forms of capitalism are not laissez-faire. In the United States, private business is heavily regulated and subsidized. Under a system of finance capitalism, banking (high finance) controls industry (big business). American finance capitalism is geographically and ideologically centered on Wall Street. From Wall Street, it reaches into every corner of the world through international investment banking and multinational or transnational corporations. Capitalism also includes national corporate stock exchanges, national agricultural commodity markets, and world currency markets. The American financial establishment is comprised of commercial and investment banks, insurance companies, brokerage houses, and law firms.

Early American liberals were especially opposed to centralized banking, but they also objected to banking itself.[12] They were opponents of capitalism, viewing it as a linchpin of aristocracy and considering bankers, stockjobbers, and speculators to be members of the pernicious idle class. The People's Party and the Democratic Party under Bryan's leadership extended this antibanking, anticapitalism legacy into the twentieth century. In the mid-1890s, "free silver" meant a policy of bimetallism, with silver being coined at a sixteen-to-one ratio with gold. The demonetization of silver in 1873, resumption of gold specie payments in 1879, and repeal of the purchasing clause of the Sherman Silver Purchase Act in 1893 were opposed by agrarian liberals not only because the new financial policy depreciated the value of farm products, but because it symbolized domination of the U.S. government by an Anglo-American banking syndicate headed by J. P. Morgan, August Belmont, and the House of Rothschild.[13] Bryanites believed that the provision of the 1900 Gold Standard Act turning the U.S. currency supply over to the national banks was a violation of the constitutional clause empowering Congress to coin money and regulate its value, and a repudiation of the Jefferson-Jackson tradition of opposing private control of the nation's finances.[14]

By the end of the nineteenth century, Jefferson's warnings had gone unheeded, and banking was firmly established throughout the nation. When latter-day Jeffersonians objected to banking they were not primarily referring to relatively small, community-based, locally owned banks but rather to large commercial banks and international investment banks. These institutions were centered in large cities and controlled by families such as the Morgans, Rockefellers, Harrimans, and Warburgs. As early as 1900, Bryan condemned the idea of a central bank for the United States because he believed the major New York bankers would monopolize the system. In 1908, a National Monetary Commission was created to devise a plan for a central bank. Bryan was a leading opponent of the Aldrich-Vreeland Act, which created the Commission. The currency reform recommended by the commission was the Aldrich Plan, a centralized banking system that could easily be controlled by Wall Street. In 1912, Bryan strongly opposed the Aldrich Plan and presidential hopeful Woodrow Wilson came out against it as part of his strategy to gain Bryan's support for the Democratic nomination. Once in office, Wilson began working with conservative Democrats to create a central bank.[15] Supported by Wilson, the Glass Bill was a decentralized version of the Aldrich Plan. Favoring an alternative bill sponsored by Senator Robert Owen (D-OK) that provided for public control of the Federal Reserve Board and its issuance of money, Secretary of State Bryan threatened an all-out fight and considered resignation when Wilson was on the verge of pushing for adoption of the Glass Bill. Wilson agreed to incorporate the substance of the Owen Bill into his proposal, and Bryan supported the resulting Glass-Owen Bill. Fearing the measure was still a capitulation to Wall Street, Bryan Democrats in Congress worked to improve the bill with amendments. The amendments were opposed by Wilson, and the most significant ones were defeated.[16]

Bryan's strong support was probably the single most important factor in passage of the Federal Reserve Act in 1913. Liberals such as Bryan believed it was a good bill partly because it was opposed by the American Bankers Association and former senator Nelson Aldrich (R-RI). Despite some specific complaints, most big bankers favored the bill because it retained the essence of the Aldrich Plan. Since the Federal Reserve Banks would be privately owned, notes issued by the Federal Reserve would technically be private, not public, currency. A majority of the men appointed to the Federal Reserve Board by President Wilson were friends of Wall Street. Despite being a system of twelve regional banks, it soon became apparent that the New York Bank would dominate the ostensibly decentralized Federal Reserve. Within a few years, many Bryan Democrats were having second thoughts about the reform measure they had helped to pass. In 1921, Bryan privately condemned Wilson for "turning over the Reserve Bank to the control of Wall Street" and publicly accused the Federal Reserve of being "the tool of Wall Street."[17]

Throughout his career, Bryan fought the influence of international bankers such as August P. Belmont and J. P. Morgan within the Democratic Party. One reason he opposed a national debt was because it was largely owed to private bankers. The 1892 and 1896 Populist platforms called for the creation of postal savings banks as an alternative to private, commercial banks. The 1908 Democratic platform also endorsed such banks, provided they had decentralized deposit and investment. Bryan condemned as foolish and immoral gambling done "on the board of trade or the stock exchange" as much if not more than the gambling done "at the card table, the wheel of fortune, and other games," saying such "speculation upon the market injures the producers, consumers and legitimate dealers who try to conduct their business honestly and who themselves do not deal in futures or options." He refused to invest in corporations, choosing instead to invest in government bonds and real estate.[18]

Raised in South Dakota by a populist-minded father, Hubert Humphrey grew up viewing the Federal Reserve System and Wall Street as "manipulators of money" who exploited the farmers and small businessmen of the Midwest. At the same time, his father inculcated an admiration for Woodrow Wilson and Franklin Roosevelt—thus setting the stage for banking ambivalence. As late as 1960, Humphrey was still, on occasion, denouncing Wall Street bankers. In 1970, he told a biographer that he remained suspicious and fearful of the nation's financial establishment. But this is only part of the story. In the mid-1940s, Mayor Humphrey was close to Minneapolis business interests, including bankers. As a freshman member of the Senate, he did favors for leading Minnesota bankers. By 1964, his disparaging public references to eastern money changers had disappeared, and he was actively courting the favor of Wall Street. By the late 1960s, Humphrey's closest political friends included Sidney "Mr. Wall Street" Weinberg and Robert "The Ultimate Capitalist" Strauss.[19]

The Roosevelt-Truman-Johnson-Humphrey wing of the Democratic Party was thoroughly committed to economic, military, and foreign policy management by the Wise Men of Wall Street.[20] Humphrey had a "fear of private debt," but he did not have a fear of public debt. Unlike populist congressman Jerry Voorhis (D-CA), he was not concerned about government borrowing from private bankers. Humphrey's 1968 and 1972 presidential campaigns received substantial support from top financiers. Neither Humphrey nor any of his congressional supporters ever seriously attempted to investigate, reform, or abolish the Federal Reserve System. In the 1960s, Humphrey supported the pro-Wall Street/Federal Reserve policies of the Kennedy and Johnson administrations when they were challenged by populist House Banking and Currency Committee chairman Wright Patman (D-TX).[21]

Legislature and Executive

William Jennings Bryan supported legislative preeminence over the executive branch. He did not hesitate to publicly disagree with presidents from his own party, namely, Cleveland and Wilson. In 1901, he criticized as unconstitutional President McKinley's going to war against the Filipinos "in the absence of congressional authority." He opposed the Spooner Amendment relating to governance of the Philippines, arguing that it gave the president "arbitrary and imperial power." He supported the right of the Senate to amend President Theodore Roosevelt's arbitration treaties. Bryan favored "diminishing the authority of the President by allowing him only a suspensive veto on legislation." In 1916, he approvingly noted that when the Constitution was framed, the power to declare war had been given to the most popular branch of government. During World War I, Bryan believed that Congress had a right and obligation to fully debate public policy lest despotism be substituted for democracy. Referring to President Wilson in the context of the League of Nations debate, in 1920, he wrote, "No large party in a democracy can hope to appeal to the conscience and judgment of a nation unless it has a higher purpose than sycophantic service to one autocratic individual."[22]

A wholesale abdication of congressional authority occurred during the post-New Deal era. The Vital Center to which Hubert Humphrey belonged played an integral role in the transfer of power. According to Arthur Schlesinger Jr., "The imperial Presidency was essentially the creation of foreign policy." Adulators of forceful presidents, proponents of internationalism, and field marshals of the Cold War, Schlesinger and his fellow Vital Center Democrats assisted in the building of the Imperial Presidency brick by brick. Referring to Humphrey's years as mayor of Minneapolis, a biographer comments, "As mayor he was never a Richard Daley (he hadn't a dictatorial bone in his body), and he never was much of an organizer."[23] Despite his own managerial style, Humphrey admired such autocratic administrators as Woodrow Wilson, Franklin Roosevelt, Harry Truman, and Lyndon Johnson. Unlike Bryan, there was no major issue over which Humphrey felt compelled to publicly disagree with any Democratic president.

In 1937, Humphrey approved of Franklin Roosevelt's plan to enlarge the Supreme Court. Opposing extension of the Reciprocal Trade Agreements Act in 1940, Congressman Hamilton Fish (R-NY) called reciprocal trade "the worst delegation of power in our history." A supporter of RTAA extension, Humphrey "did not object to executive control of both the negotiation and ratification stages" of trade agreements. In his autobiography, Humphrey charged that Senator Robert Taft and other Republican critics of Harry Truman were serving to encourage the growth of fascism in America by their strong attacks on the duly elected president. Ideological heirs of Taft see the situation quite differently. Historian Samuel Francis comments, "The cute little sign that Harry Truman kept on his desk that read 'The buck stops here' was in fact little more than a not-very-subtle pretense that the Chief Executive is really the monarch of the United States." Francis concludes that Truman was "perhaps about as close an imitation of *Il Duce* [Mussolini] as this country has ever produced."[24] Senator Humphrey was a loyal supporter of President Truman, and he worked for his renomination in 1952.

The Bricker Amendment of 1954 attempted to prevent executive agreements with international organizations from overriding domestic laws. The constitutional amendment sponsored by Senator John Bricker (R–OH) was designed to protect both national sovereignty and the separation of powers. Executive agreements are de facto treaties negotiated by presidents without the advice or consent of Congress. A watered-down version of the Bricker Amendment was defeated by one vote. Humphrey voted against it partly because he did not want to "curb the powers of the presidency at a sensitive time." Arguing against a foreign aid amendment opposed by President Kennedy, in 1962, Senator Humphrey said, "A parliamentary body is incapable of conducting a nation's foreign policy because it is composed of equal voices and could not act as promptly as conditions require."[25] Humphrey compiled a small record of support for legislative power in the early 1970s in conflicts with President Nixon. It is, however, difficult to tell whether this was based more on principle or partisanship since it was at variance with his long-standing record. Regardless of motivation, Humphrey opposed giving the line-item veto to the president because he believed it was an unconstitutional abdication of congressional authority. He was a leading opponent of Nixon's practice of impounding appropriated funds, asserting that it was unconstitutional. In 1973, he voted to override the Office of Management and Budget confirmation bill veto. Humphrey also favored overriding the veto of the War Powers Act of 1973. He did not, however, use the occasion to condemn a decades-old pattern of presidential usurpation of the legislative war-making power. His tone was conciliatory and vague. In 1976, Humphrey referred to the Nixon presidency as verging on "autocracy," but he concluded that the answer "lies not in weakening the presidency, but in choosing individuals for that office who can be trusted with its vast powers."[26]

Judiciary

Committed as he was to popular sovereignty, it is not surprising that William Jennings Bryan was critical of the Supreme Court, the most undemocratic branch of the federal government. The justices are appointed for life and are not subject to recall. Five individuals, making a completely arbitrary decision, can strike down a law made by the people's elected representatives. Such a decision can be overturned only by constitutional amendment or by waiting until a new version of the Court reverses the ruling. The People's Party was at the forefront of opposition to judicial tyranny. As a presidential candidate in 1896, Bryan condemned the Supreme Court for striking down the income tax law and denounced federal judges for settling labor disputes by injunction. In his Cross of Gold speech at the Democratic National Convention, he said, "They criticise us for our criticism of the Supreme Court . . . If you want criticisms, read the dissenting opinions of the court. . . . The income tax . . . did not become unconstitutional until one of the judges changed his mind." By 1908, Bryan had called for popular election of federal judges. Upset by Supreme Court decisions in the 1911 Standard Oil and American Tobacco cases, he wrote, "Whatever may be said in favor of the appointment for life of men engaged in *interpreting* the law, no good reason can be given for the appointment, especially for life, of a *legislative* body." Early Bryan supporters Governor John Peter Altgeld (D-IL) and Senator Richard Pettigrew (R-SD) were also staunch enemies of usurpation of power and judicial tyranny by the Supreme Court and lower federal courts.[27]

Hubert Humphrey was aware of Bryan-era attempts to curb the power of the federal judiciary, but he never advocated curbing its power himself. The issue of judicial restraint vs. judicial activism was of concern to many American citizens by the mid-1960s. Controversial cases involving racial desegregation, school prayer, and criminal rights sparked grassroots discontent with a seemingly arbitrary and undemocratic judicial process. Focusing its criticism on the chief justice, the John Birch Society conducted an "Impeach Earl Warren" campaign. Alabama's Democratic governor George Wallace cited Jefferson's warnings about judicial tyranny in calling for a constitutional amendment to limit the power of the Supreme Court.[28] While they spoke for millions, if not a majority, the Birch Society was tainted by extremism, and Wallace, by racism. Among mainstream politicians, the Supreme Court, like the Federal Reserve System, is a sacrosanct institution. For this reason, no judicial reform bills made it onto the floor of either house of Congress during the Humphrey era.

The matter of an unelected judiciary involves tension between majority rule expressed through legislative actions and popular initiatives and minority rights protected by judicial decisions. Humphrey Democrats were champions of the Supreme Court and lower federal courts, in part because they were seen as guarantors of the rights of minority groups. There is, however, some question concerning the nature of the minority most often protected by the judiciary. While often rendered in the name of downtrodden minorities, judicial decisions are made by a privileged minority—namely, the wealthy and powerful. The Supreme Court was dominated by Ivy League graduates and corporate attorneys during the 1938–1978 period. James Madison, the father of the Constitution, was interested in protecting the rights of the nation's wealthy minority. The Supreme Court has generally operated exactly as it was intended to operate: it has kept democracy in check. Since the 1930s, it has exemplified the dual nature of the welfare state (discreet, large subsidies for the wealthy and powerful; well-publicized, small subsidies for the poor and unpowerful). Members of the Court have often handed down decisions that benefit lowly members of society, but the Court's rulings have rarely disturbed the infrastructure of state capitalism. They seem to emanate more from a sense of noblesse oblige or upper-class mores than from principled, constitutional interpretation. For minority groups to place their destiny in such an arrangement seems disempowering if not dangerous, depending as it does on the magnanimity of five remote individuals rather than on creating solidarity among themselves or good relations with their neighbors.[29] Neither Humphrey nor his congressional allies were interested in deeper questions concerning majority rule, minority rights, and federal judges.

Civil Liberties

William Jennings Bryan had a mixed record on civil liberties. During the antianarchist clamor that followed the assassination of President McKinley in 1901, Bryan suggested that immigrants should be required to swear their allegiance to the Declaration of Independence. This was as far as he was willing to go, though. Considering himself "the victim of as much malice and vituperation as have ever been employed against an American," he was still "opposed to placing any additional restriction upon the freedom of speech or the freedom of the press." In 1902, he was critical of antianarchy bills that curtailed constitutionally recognized freedoms, and he defended socialist newspapers discriminated against by the post office. Bryan was a strong Christian, but he did not want to create a sacral state. In 1906, he wrote, "The attempt to unite church and state has never been helpful to either government or religion." During World War I, Bryan was more of a patriotic American than a civil libertarian.[30] Despite his pacifistic stance from 1915 to 1917, after war was declared, he had little sympathy for those who continued to oppose militarism. According to Bryan, after the nation has entered a war,

No one should be permitted to cloak attacks upon his government or to [give] aid to the enemy under the claim that he is exercising freedom of speech. No sympathy, therefore, will be wasted upon those who have been arrested for unpatriotic utterances. They abuse free speech. And this applies to attacks on the Allies as well as attacks on the United States. We can no more allow our allies to be crushed than we can afford to be crushed ourselves. . . . There are only two sides to a war—every American must be on the side of the United States.

This is Bryan at his simplistic worst. It seems absurd to claim that governments or entire nations can be "crushed" by words. He asserted that conscientious objectors should receive toleration, provided they did not try to influence others. During times of war, he believed that "the government's interests" should be put above "the interest of the individual."[31] Bryan neither actively supported nor actively opposed the Red Scare perpetrated by the Wilson administration after the war.

Vital Center Democracy is often given credit for withstanding the irresponsible attacks of red-baiting Republican senator Joseph McCarthy of Wisconsin and ultimately helping to bring him down. The story is actually more complex than this. The Roosevelt-Truman-Humphrey wing of the Democratic Party had a dismal record on civil liberties. When condemning McCarthy in 1954, it was truly a case of the pot calling the kettle black. Armed with the Selective Service Act, Espionage Act, and the Sedition Act, Woodrow Wilson used "manipulative and authoritarian" techniques to stifle criticism and curb freedom during World War I. After the war, the administration unleashed a national reign of intimidation and deportation against socialists, anarchists, pacifists, populists, progressives, and other enemies of the president through the Red Scare and Palmer Raids.

The civil liberties record of Franklin Roosevelt was even worse than that of Wilson.[32] In 1940, he pushed through the Alien Registration Act (Smith Act) and the Selective Service Act (Burke-Wadsworth Act). The former included a sedition section; the latter created the nation's first peacetime draft.[33] The Brown Scare of 1939–1941 was a period of Nazi-baiting and fifth column-smearing by the president and his supporters. New Dealers, Stalinists, and gunboat liberals called into question the patriotism of populists, isolationists, anticommunists, and other domestic enemies of FDR and the Communist Party USA (CPUSA). In the early 1940s, Roosevelt put tens of thousands of Japanese Americans into internment camps. He retained J. Edgar Hoover as director of the Federal Bureau of Investigation and granted him greater powers to conduct "internal security surveillance." Many traditional liberals believed that pro-FDR "totalitarian liberals" were largely responsible for fostering an atmosphere of intolerance and for developing the witch-hunting techniques they later so loudly condemned during the McCarthy Era. According to historian Harry Elmer Barnes, Bryan-La Follette liberals, who "supported freedom of speech and expression for their opponents as well as their friends," stood in marked contrast to New Deal liberals, who were concerned about civil liberties only on a selective basis.[34]

After Republicans successfully used red-baiting against Democrats in the 1946 congressional election, President Truman began his own campaign against "communist subversion." A full three years before McCarthy's speech in Wheeling, West Virginia, the Truman administration launched "the most extensive drive against civil liberties since the enactment of the Alien and Sedition Laws at the close of the eighteenth century." Under Truman's leadership, Vital Center Democracy unveiled the attorney general's list of subversive organizations, created the federal employee loyalty program, and prosecuted "seditious" individuals under the Alien Registration Act. Traditional liberals and Taftian conservatives who opposed or questioned what they viewed as the militaristic and imperialistic nature of the Cold War were denounced as either full-fledged Communists or unwitting dispensers of Kremlin propaganda. Concerns about civil liberties were rarely raised by mainstream Democrats until after 1950, when the anticommunist credentials of the Truman administration were called into question by the Red Army victory in China and the accusations of Senator McCarthy. Truman's foreign policy fearmongering played a role in fanning domestic fears of Communists. As a Humphrey biographer puts it, "The anti-Communism crusade abroad inevitably led to McCarthyism at home."[35]

Considering that Democratic presidents initiated the Red Scares of the late 1910s and late 1940s, the party leadership's later condemnation of McCarthy seems hypocritical and opportunistic. There may well have been some elitism involved as well. Regardless of the validity of McCarthy's accusations and methods, there was a populist element to the efforts of the senator, his allies, and his admirers. McCarthy's attacks on elite figures such as Dean Acheson, Alger Hiss, Charles Bohlen, John McCloy, Paul Nitze, William Bundy, Robert Stevens, and Paul Hoffman reveal an underlying, perhaps unconscious, resentment against Wall Street domination of the U.S. government and its foreign policy.[36] McCarthy may have been a bully in other instances, but in dealing with these men it was a case of someone relatively small taking on well-connected giants. They were more than capable of defending themselves and, eventually, bringing down McCarthy. At the beginning of the Cold War, the Truman administration attempted to institute compulsory, universal military training, but it settled for a peacetime draft through the 1948 Selective Service Act. Conscription continued under the Kennedy and Johnson administrations, which were marked by a host of other civil liberties violations.[37]

In the late 1940s, Hubert Humphrey and his associates engaged in widespread red-baiting as they attempted to drive communists, socialists, traditional agrarian populists, and anyone else who refused to enlist for the Cold War out of the Minnesota Democratic-Farmer-Labor (DFL) Party. During his first two years in the Senate, Humphrey made some efforts on behalf of civil liberties. In 1949, he warned, "The real danger we face is that a spirit of fear will produce an atmosphere of timidity and suspicion that will discourage independence of thought, original investigation and association. The real danger we face is that a program of suppression will seriously endanger effective operation of our democracy." He voted to reconfirm Leland Olds as a member of the Federal Power Commission despite accusations of pro-communism against Olds. In 1950, he was angered over red-baiting associated with Fair Employment Practices Commission legislation he favored. Nevertheless, Humphrey was not a leading opponent of McCarthyism. According to Hays Gorey, Humphrey's aversion to communism "made him clearly more tolerant of excesses against its adherents or suspected adherents than he ever was concerning similar actions against any other segment of American society." In 1950, he verbally opposed the Internal Security Act (McCarran Act) yet ended up voting for it. Two weeks later, he voted to sustain Truman's veto of the bill, saying "I want to be on the side of the angels on this one." The veto was overridden and the bill became law. Four years later, Humphrey boasted on the floor of the Senate that the Democratic Party had passed the Internal Security Act, calling it "an effective law against communism." In 1951, he criticized McCarthy for breeding "fear and suspicion." Three years later, he sponsored an amendment to the Communist Control Act that would have outlawed the CPUSA. Party members would have been subject to five years in prison and a fine of $10,000 under his proposal. Humphrey's amendment was approved by the Senate in an 84–0 vote. The final bill did not, however, outlaw the party; instead, it declared that the party "should" be outlawed. In this instance, Humphrey "carried his anti-Communism to a length never proposed by Joe McCarthy," who actually "helped to pull the teeth from some of the harshest Humphrey provisions."[38] Later in the year, Humphrey voted to condemn McCarthy.

A decade later, renewed opposition to the Cold War led to renewed red-baiting on Humphrey's part. In 1965, the vice president was criticized by some liberals for calling antiwar hecklers "Communists." Two years later, he accused antiwar protesters of giving "aid and comfort to the Communist enemy." Ironically, Humphrey himself played a role in strengthening communist dictatorships through his support for détente, even as he criticized relatively powerless American citizens for exercising freedom of speech. Humphrey supported the 1968 Omnibus Crime Control and Safe Streets Act. This act was described by civil libertarians as a "wire-tapping bill," and they called it "frightening" and "a genuinely oppressive piece of legislation." Shortly before the opening of the 1968 Democratic National Convention, he was asked by the press if he would retain J. Edgar Hoover as FBI director if he were elected president. Despite Hoover's complicity in the Palmer Raids and the long history of civil liberties violations under his leadership, Humphrey expressed high regard for Hoover. Humphrey did nothing to prevent or apologize for the conduct of the Chicago police force during the convention. At its close, he said, "I think the blame ought to be put where it belongs. I think we ought to quit pretending that Mayor Daley did anything wrong. He didn't."[39]

Ethnic Groups

While William Jennings Bryan received substantial support from the Indian Territory delegation at the 1896 Democratic National Convention, he had little to say about American Indians and, in true missionary fashion, he advanced a proposal in 1923 that amounted to a suppression of Native American religion. Partly of Irish descent himself and helped by his opposition to English imperialism, Bryan sought and received substantial Irish American support throughout his career. He courted German Americans but was less successful in winning their votes. Bryan was "friendly, courteous and sympathetic" toward Asians on a personal level—Yamashita, a boy from Japan, even lived with the Bryans for five years—but he favored immigration restrictions on Chinese and other Asians. He was concerned about cheap foreign labor undercutting American organized labor and about exploitation of the immigrants themselves by wealthy individuals and large corporations. His desire for exclusionary laws also included a concern for social homogeneity. Bryan's contrast between a "homogeneous republic" and a "heterogeneous empire" had roots in early American liberalism, but there had always been some tension between this idea and belief in ethnic inclusiveness. The language Bryan and his supporters used to express their belief in homogeneity makes it seem like a veiled, perhaps unconscious, manifestation of racism.[40]

Bryan was not anti-Catholic. He sought the support of Roman Catholics when running for president. In 1920 he proposed David Walsh for the Democratic presidential nomination and supported Thomas Walsh's nomination four years later. He opposed Al Smith's nomination not because of his religion but because of his ties to the liquor industry and Wall Street.[41] While some historians have emphasized the supposedly anti-Semitic nature of the People's Party and other Gilded Age manifestations of agrarian discontent, "Populists did not employ anti-Semitic language nearly as often as they used the language of an English conspiracy, and the central focus of Populist conspiracy-theorizing was on bankers as a class rather than as Jews."[42] Bryan was not anti-Semitic. He praised the "Hebrew race" during his 1896 presidential campaign, supported Louis Brandeis for the Supreme Court, and condemned Henry Ford's attacks on the Jews. He proposed Isidor Rayner for the Democratic presidential nomination in 1912, and Samuel Untermyer and Brandeis, in 1920. According to one biographer, Bryan "often meliorated the extreme nativist views of his supporters."[43]

Bryan had a poor record when it came to social and political inclusiveness for African Americans. He was not a race-baiter or hate-monger, but he believed in white supremacy and accepted segregation of the races. Some of Bryan's prominent supporters—notably Josephus Daniels, Thomas Watson, Benjamin Tillman, Jeff Davis, and James Vardaman—were masters of playing the race card in the South.[44] While it does not excuse, from a liberal perspective, the sorry record of Bryan Democracy, it should be understood that the conservative, anti-Bryan Democrats of the South were also racist. Bourbons were just more refined in their expressions of white supremacy.[45] The fact that southern whites were his base of electoral support probably did not have a great effect on Bryan's actions in relation to race since he usually acted on the basis of principle, not expedience. Bryan was an apologist for the poll tax, literacy test, and other Jim Crow devices used to keep southern blacks from voting. In 1903, he recommended that blacks concentrate on building up personal character rather than worrying about voting, officeholding, and lynching. Justifying restrictions on voting in the South, Bryan blamed the victim and engaged in astonishing mental gymnastics in attempting to show that his beliefs did not contradict the principles of the Declaration. He held these views on suffrage qualifications and black inferiority for the remainder of his life. After the Brownsville episode of 1906, a few prominent blacks—most notably A.M.E. Zion bishop Alexander Walters and soon-to-be NAACP cofounder W. E. B. Du Bois—endorsed Bryan for president in 1908. Most blacks stayed with the Republican Party in the light of the Democratic Party's hostile heritage. Secretary of State Bryan supported the segregation policies of the Wilson administration. He condemned the lynching of blacks but "had a tendency to try to 'explain' southern white action on this point." He opposed the Dyer Anti-Lynching Bill in 1922. Bryan

told Democrats that it was "superlatively unfortunate" that a prejudiced organization like the Ku Klux Klan existed in America, but he did not believe
a frontal assault was the best way to stop it. He spoke against an anti-KKK
platform plank at the 1924 Democratic National Convention.[46]

Hubert Humphrey played the lead role in creating a DFL Party strong-
hold out of the Red Lake Reservation of the Chippewas (Ojibwes) through
his support for the restructuring of tribal government in the late 1950s. This
led to the installation of Red Lake chairman Roger Jourdain, a Humphrey
ally who remained in power for the next thirty years. Although he did advocate helping them through federal government programs, Humphrey was
not generally known as a champion of American Indians. He *was* known as
a champion of open immigration. In his 1954 booklet *The Stranger at Our
Gate,* Humphrey attempted to expose "myths of immigration." He condemned Asian exclusion laws; mandatory literacy tests; the Burnett Immigration Act of 1917; the National Origins Act (Johnson Immigration Act) of
1924; and the Immigration, Naturalization, and Nationality Act (McCarran-
Walter Act) of 1952. He was critical of McCarran-Walter for discriminating
against eastern and southern Europeans, Asians, and blacks. In 1964,
Humphrey favored legislation designed to end the national origins quota
system. Throughout his career, he attempted to fight discrimination on the
basis of race, religion, and nationality. In the mid-1940s, he denounced anti-
Semitism in Minneapolis, and he remained a friend of Jewish Americans for
the rest of his life. In 1968, presidential nominee Humphrey—running with
Edmund Muskie, a Roman Catholic Polish American—received 81 percent
of the Jewish vote and 85 percent of the African American vote.[47]

Possessing humanitarian instincts, Humphrey was most Jeffersonian in the
area of ethnic inclusiveness. His record on black civil rights put Bryan's record to shame. In sincerity and consistency, he far surpassed the opportunism-
tainted Roosevelt, Truman, Kennedy, and Johnson. In a 1947 letter, he argued
that the national Democratic Party needed to be realigned through an exo-
dus of racist southern Democrats so it could more fully act as a liberal force.
At the 1948 Democratic National Convention, Mayor Humphrey and Americans for Democratic Action successfully sponsored a strong civil rights platform plank over the objection of many party leaders. After the fact,
Humphrey freely admitted that his desire for a strong plank was motivated
by his belief in equality under law and a tactical hope of undercutting the
appeal of Henry Wallace and Thomas Dewey. During his first month in
Washington, he appointed the first black to a Senate staff position. According to political scientist Nelson Polsby, during the 1949–1965 period, Humphrey, "more than any other single Senator," kept the pressure on the Senate

to pass civil rights legislation. In 1953, he sponsored bills to protect against lynching in the United States and to outlaw the poll tax for federal elections. Jackie Robinson, the man who made headlines by integrating professional baseball, supported Humphrey for president in 1960 because of his stellar record on civil rights. Senate floor manager of the Civil Rights Act of 1964, Humphrey viewed its passage as his "greatest achievement."[48]

In his book *The Cause Is Mankind,* Humphrey took a sympathetic approach toward the "new militancy" of blacks who demanded "Freedom now." When faced with the reality of his words, however, he was uncomfortable. He reacted with hurt and anger when leaders of grassroots black organizations refused to show proper respect for President Johnson and appreciation for everything the Democratic Party had tried to do for their race. There was a paternalistic element to Humphrey liberalism that was incompatible with the growing black power movement. Humphrey received considerable support from older blacks when he ran for president in 1968 and 1972, but many younger blacks supported more "radical" candidates.[49]

By 1976, Humphrey's presidential luster had diminished in the eyes of many white Democrats. This had happened in part because of popular disgust over the role played by limousine liberals in mandating ethnic inclusiveness for others while excusing themselves from such inclusiveness. The most glaring example of the perceived hypocrisy was forced busing. As was the case with many leading liberals, Humphrey supported court-ordered racial integration of public schools but sent his own children to a private high school in rural Minnesota. Humphrey's obvious belief in and record of support for racial equality were compromised on occasion by his political alliance with pro-segregation Senate Bourbons.[50] It must be emphasized that even with such compromises, Humphrey's overall civil rights record surpassed that of most of his political contemporaries in terms of Jeffersonian liberalism.

Spending

Liberals throughout the nineteenth and early twentieth centuries tried to emulate Jefferson's frugal attitude toward government spending. In theory, if not practice, members of the Jackson–Van Buren wing of the Democratic Party were "plain republicans" who advocated "republican simplicity." The 1892 Populist platform promised that "all State and national revenues shall be limited to the necessary expenses of the government, economically and honestly administered." Possessing an "extreme simplicity of taste," William

Jennings Bryan's personal habits were in keeping with his public policies. The liberal Democratic platform of 1896 denounced "the lavish appropriations of recent Republican Congresses" and demanded "a return to that simplicity and economy which befits a Democratic Government, and a reduction in the number of useless offices, the salaries of which drain the substance of the people." Under Bryan's leadership, the 1900, 1908, and 1912 platforms also condemned "frightful extravagance" and advocated "strict economy." Throughout the McKinley and Roosevelt administrations, Bryan and his allies criticized the Republicans for their high levels of spending. Imperialism was opposed partly because of the large expenditures needed to maintain an overseas empire. In 1905, Bryan criticized plans to raise the salaries of cabinet officers, arguing that the federal government should be run according to "the simplicity that befits a republic," not in imitation of extravagant European monarchies. Belonging to the Jefferson–Jackson tradition, Bryanites opposed deficit spending and the existence of a national debt.[51]

Largely constructed by Woodrow Wilson and Franklin Roosevelt, the "warfare-welfare state" involves massive expenditures. World War I, World War II, and the Cold War (including Korea and Vietnam) were responsible for large hikes in federal spending and debt.[52] The subsidization of every economic class in America, including huge outlays for corporate welfare, has been a costly endeavor. Hubert Humphrey looked to Wilson and Roosevelt as role models, supported U.S. entry into World War II and the Cold War, and defended the welfare state. He developed a reputation as a big spender from his first days in the Senate. In 1949, he opposed an amendment by Senator Kenneth Wherry (R–NE) to cut federal spending by a flat 10 percent in every department. He told his colleagues, "To those who have been calling me the greatest spender, I want to say you haven't seen anything yet." According to one biographer, in a compilation of Humphrey's voting record on key issues from 1949 through 1964, of the 156 votes recorded, you "cannot find any—not one—in which Humphrey voted to cut spending in domestic affairs." In a 1957 speech, he declared, "I have always said that between the platforms of Santa Claus and Scrooge, I will stick with jolly Santa. Any time anyone wants to run on that platform, they can count me in." Humphrey's record on spending was virtually the opposite of Senator Harry Byrd (D–VA), who had a Jeffersonian stance on government spending. If Humphrey objected to the conservative reputation of Byrd, he still could have joined liberals such as Wayne Morse (D–OR) and William Proxmire (D–WI) in championing frugal government during the 1950s and 1960s.[53] Instead, he supported profligate spending and borrowing.

Beginning in the early 1950s, Middle Way Republicanism and Vital Center Democracy jointly fostered an American obsession with economic growth, as measured by the gross national product. The "growth liberalism" of Eisenhower, Rockefeller, Kennedy, Johnson, and Humphrey rejected traditional values such as thrift and frugality. The prosperity of the new American economy was built on consumer spending fueled by artificial needs, manipulative mass advertising, shameless materialism, personal indebtedness, planned obsolescence, and corporate welfare disguised as defense spending. The federal government encouraged and helped coordinate the underpinnings of economic growth. If the economy was not growing fast enough to suit Keynesian economists, the government "primed the pump" through deficit spending. Humphrey believed that government debt was an automatic result of recession and that deficit spending was an appropriate response. In the 1950s, he called a balanced federal budget a "futile dream," and Americans for Democratic Action endorsed an unbalanced budget in the interest of increasing the purchasing power of industries and consumers. Humphrey supported the 1964 Tax Reduction Act, which was opposed by some as a "budget buster." In 1972, he opposed legislation establishing a federal spending ceiling.[54]

Although Humphrey on many occasions boasted of his big spending ways, by the mid-1970s, he sometimes sounded a fiscally responsible note more in keeping with the tenor of the times. Yet, he was unable to consistently repress his feelings and views about spending. Responding to criticism of big government, in 1974, Humphrey said, "Not to spend, that's not the answer. That's just political bunkum." Referring to spending for social programs, he wrote, "I've listened day after day, decade after decade, to political and theoretical arguments about cost per person, waste in government programs, and all the other clichés that come so easily to those who have. None of the arguments makes much sense to me when measured against the human gain." In 1976, Humphrey declared that it was "pap" to argue "that existing social programs would have to be scaled down in order to make room for new ones, or to contend that the nation cannot afford to launch a major initiative such as national health insurance." He dismissed fears of a $70 billion budget deficit: "Seventy billion compared to what? Seventy billion compared to a trillion five hundred billion dollar economy!"[55]

Taxation

During the nineteenth century, high taxation was a legacy passed on from Hamilton and the Federalists to Whigs and conservative Republicans. Most liberal Democrats, liberal Republicans, and Populists stood for the Jeffersonian tradition of low taxation resulting from government simplicity and frugality. The 1892 Populist platform called for economy in government because the agrarian-labor coalition believed "that the money of the country should be kept as much as possible in the hands of the people." In 1893, Congressman William Jennings Bryan urged the Democratic Party to honor its promise to lighten the burden of taxation on the people. He was an early advocate of an income tax—not because he wanted to add to the tax burden of the common people, but because he wanted to lighten that burden by shifting revenue-raising from the tariff and other regressive consumption taxes to a progressive tax on incomes that would fall only on the wealthiest citizens. Bryan's original 1894 proposal was a graduated tax that began with incomes of $2,500 and would have been paid by less than 100,000 people out of a national population of 70 million. On the House floor, he championed a bill providing for a flat 2 percent tax on personal and corporate incomes of over $4,000. The 1896 Democratic platform denounced the Republicans for draining "the substance of the people" through high taxes. The 1900 platform condemned them for keeping "taxes high" and threatening "the perpetuation of the oppressive war levies." The 1908 platform argued that lavish appropriations were "a crime against the millions of working men and women, from whose earnings the great proportion of these colossal sums must be extorted through excessive tariff extractions and other indirect methods." The 1912 platform criticized "oppressive taxation."[56]

Following the Spanish-American War, Bryan Democrats opposed a large military establishment in part because it placed a heavy tax burden upon the people. In the early 1900s, Bryan wrote, "The tax eaters control the republican organization and their appetite grows with the feeding." In the 1910s, he was pleased that a federal income tax had been created after ratification of the Sixteenth Amendment, thereby transferring "a considerable percentage of the burden that was formerly borne by the over-taxed masses to the backs of those who have large incomes, but who had escaped their just share until the income tax law was passed." Most citizens paid no income tax during the Bryan era. The opposition of Bryan Democrats to burdensome taxation was quite different from complaints about high taxes by conservatives during the 1910s, 1920s, and 1930s. Conservatives were concerned about income taxes and inheritance taxes paid by the wealthy people, not about excise taxes and tariffs paid by the common people. The Mellon Tax Plan of the 1920s and the American Liberty League of the 1930s were examples of self-interested corporate wealth, not of a principled commitment to low taxation, frugal government, or Jeffersonian ideology.[57]

The record of Hubert Humphrey and his allies on taxation is virtually the history of the United States during the twentieth century. As was the case with spending, the warfare-welfare state gave rise to record levels of taxation. World War I, World War II, and the Cold War were responsible for large hikes in federal taxation. More than any other president, Franklin Roosevelt was responsible for dramatically increasing the tax burden on lower-class and middle-class Americans. The Revenue Acts of 1942 and 1943 "created the modern federal income tax system" by expanding the tax brackets and instituting a paycheck withholding tax. Before this time, most Americans had never filed an income tax return because the tax applied to wealthy individuals and large corporations. The 1942 tax bill passed unanimously. Liberal opponents of the 1943 bill included Senators Robert Wagner (D-NY), Theodore Bilbo (D-MS), and Robert La Follette Jr. (R-WI). While the new income tax system was presented to the American people "as a temporary wartime necessity, it remained a permanent feature of national life in the postwar era." An unfair distribution of the federal tax burden existed under President Truman.[58] High federal taxes during the postwar era were the result not only of increased military spending and foreign aid but also higher domestic expenditures. Animated by a combination of noblesse oblige, a desire to purchase political support from various blocs of voters, and a hope of enshrining their names as benefactors of humanity, members of the upper class instituted expensive social welfare programs for which they received credit while the common people paid the bills. Humphrey and his senatorial supporters endorsed virtually every aspect of the warfare-welfare state from the 1930s through the 1970s.

As a candidate for president in 1960, Senator Humphrey argued that higher taxes were necessary to fight the Cold War and expand the welfare state. In 1965, Vice President Humphrey boasted that he had been "an early advocate of a reduction in both corporate and personal income taxes." It is important to understand, however, that President Kennedy's push to cut taxes was apparently motivated more by concern for economic growth and corporate welfare than it was by concern for the well-being of the common people. The 1964 Tax Reduction Act supported by Humphrey and his allies was a descendant of the 1924 Mellon Tax Plan opposed by Bryan and his allies. It is true that income taxes were cut for all Americans, but the wealthy were disproportionately helped. Later in the decade, the Johnson-Humphrey administration raised taxes to pay for the Vietnam War.[59] During the 1968–1976 period, when Governor George Wallace argued that the nation's super-rich and influential foundations were not paying their fair share of taxes, Humphrey was silent on the issue.

CHAPTER 10

Positions on Foreign Policy

Military

William Jennings Bryan was not a pure, doctrinaire pacifist, but his Jeffersonian suspicion of standing armies and Christian preference for nonviolence were such that he was often called one. When used broadly to mean peacemaker or resisting militarism, the term *pacifist* can be appropriately applied to Bryan. Opposed to a large military establishment, he urged a substantial cut in appropriations for the army following the Spanish-American War. The 1900 Democratic platform condemned militarism, warning, "It means conquest abroad and intimidation and oppression at home." In the early 1920s, Bryan was a proponent of disarmament—even unilateral disarmament. He believed that substituting a military draft for volunteer soldiering was "un-American" and "a subversion of the ancient and fixed principles of a free people." After the U.S. entered World War I, however, he supported the Selective Service Act. Bryan Democrats Thomas Gore, William Kirby, and Charles Thomas were among the eight senators who opposed President Wilson's call for conscription. Bryan opposed compulsory, universal military training before and after World War I.[1]

Bryan supported Cuban independence from Spain but hoped that a war between the U.S. and Spain over the issue could be avoided. In April 1898, he supported a declaration of war against Spain. Bryan served as a colonel in command of a regiment of Nebraska volunteers during the Spanish-American War. When American imperialism reared its head during the war, Colonel Bryan told the commander-in-chief that the Nebraskans had "volunteered to attempt to break the yoke of Spain in Cuba," and that they "did not volunteer to attempt to subjugate other peoples, or establish United States sovereignty elsewhere." After the war with Spain ended, he opposed the McKinley administration's decision to make war against the Filipinos who wanted to be free of American rule. Conversations in 1903 with Leo Tolstoy, the famed Russian novelist and Christian philosopher, strengthened Bryan's pacifistic inclinations. Tolstoy was an advocate of nonviolence who shared Bryan's allegiance to God and his concern for the common people.[2] Bryan wanted the Democratic Party to campaign against the militarism of President Theodore Roosevelt in the 1904 election. In 1914–1915, Secretary of State Bryan supported military action against Haiti and Mexico; later, as a private citizen, he opposed Pershing's Mexican expedition. Despite some glaring exceptions, Bryan was a pacifistic influence within the Wilson administration. He negotiated thirty bilateral arbitration treaties providing for an investigatory "cooling off" period before armed hostilities could commence. In 1915, he left the cabinet because he opposed the warlike actions of the president in regard to the European conflict. After resigning his position, he opposed the preparedness campaign in America and worked to prevent U.S. entry into World War I. Bryan argued against the creation of a League to Enforce Peace because he believed that an international organization based on military force would lead to less peace, not more.[3] If he had been a member of Congress in April 1917, Bryan would have voted against a declaration of war against Germany. Three days before the vote, he wrote to a congressman, "If I were a representative and convinced that my constituents desired war, I would resign and leave them to speak through someone in harmony with their views. I would not share responsibility for this Nation entering the War." Bryan Democrats William Stone and James Vardaman were among the six senators who voted against the war resolution. Despite Tolstoy's influence on Bryan, rejection of patriotism was one Tolstoyan element that was never embraced by the Commoner. He loyally supported the Wilson administration throughout the war, but he criticized the British and French governments for deciding to drop explosives on German cities, asserting, "Future generations will blush to read that BOTH sides resorted to the deliberate murder of innocent women and children."[4]

Preferring Christ to Napoléon, Bryan called the latter a "grand master of the art of slaughter." This was indicative of his rejection of the martial spirit in American society. He proposed that toys for children should be of a nonmilitary nature, saying that it was "strange that the birthday of the Prince of Peace should be celebrated by the presentation of toys illustrating mimic warfare." Bryan opposed the organizing of rifle clubs by the federal government, believing they were part of a campaign "to thoroughly inoculate the

American people with the virus of war." During the last twenty-five years of his life, he tried to de-glamorize war and exalt peace.[5]

Distinguishing liberalism from pacifism, Hubert Humphrey placed himself "in the ranks of those who believe that the [military] forces of totalitarianism must be met with the [military] forces of free men." His reputation as a man of peace was largely derived from his work throughout the 1950s on behalf of multilateral nuclear limitation and disarmament. These efforts culminated in 1963 with the ratification of the Limited Nuclear Test Ban Treaty. Humphrey was still advocating nuclear arms control in the 1970s by opposing the deployment of anti-ballistic missiles. He was not, however, opposed in principle to the development or deployment of nuclear weapons. Humphrey praised DuPont for responding "magnificently" when the U.S. government asked the corporation to "take on mass production of plutonium." He viewed the successful production of the world's first atom bomb as an example of how big business can be a good thing. Humphrey approved of Truman's decision to drop atomic bombs on the Japanese people, and he did not criticize Truman's decision to create the hydrogen bomb.[6] Unlike Bryan, Humphrey did not warn of perceived dangers associated with a large standing army or military establishment. A consistent supporter of presidential-requested appropriations for the Pentagon, he "prided himself that he never voted for a cut in a military budget." In this area, he stood in direct contrast with an earlier Democratic senator with presidential ambitions: Burton Wheeler of Montana, a Bryanite who "opposed every major arms appropriation on principle." In the early 1950s, Humphrey condemned isolationists in the Senate who opposed efforts to increase military spending for research and development, contending that failure to boost spending amounted to national suicide. He supported increased military spending throughout the 1960s. Running for vice president in 1964, he boasted of large military increases under President Johnson, including a 150 percent increase in the number of nuclear warheads. During a debate on the eve of the 1972 California presidential primary, Humphrey denounced as dangerous George McGovern's plan to cut the defense budget by $20 billion.[7] Humphrey and his senatorial supporters voted to extend conscription throughout the 1950s and 1960s.

Humphrey "believed strongly in peace and the brotherhood of man," yet he strongly supported World War II, the Korean War, and the Vietnam War. Living in the Orwellian world of the mid-twentieth century, he could easily support such endeavors because they were portrayed as "wars for peace" and "bloodshed for the brotherhood of man." Unlike Bryan during World War I, there is no record that Humphrey objected to the wholesale killing of civilians by the U.S. government and its allies during World War II. Since he approved of the Hiroshima and Nagasaki atomic bombings, it is unlikely that he disapproved of the conventional bombings of Dresden and Tokyo. From his first day in Washington to his last, Humphrey was a champion of the Cold War with its attendant hot wars. In addition to supporting Truman's decision to enter the Korean War in 1950, he favored the 1954 resolution supporting Eisenhower's military intervention in Guatemala. He praised Kennedy for his "firmness and skill" during the Cuban missile crisis. When Johnson sent U.S. troops to the Dominican Republic to prevent a "communist takeover" in 1965, Vice President Humphrey was reportedly "not really pleased" with the course of events. Regardless of possible private reservations, he publicly supported the invasion.[8]

During his years as vice president, Humphrey was criticized by some liberals for "changing his views and compromising his principles to get in line with Johnson's policies," but, in fact, his basic position on Vietnam remained relatively constant during his first twenty years in Washington. In the early 1950s, he did not want to send U.S. troops to Indochina, but he supported the French military effort, saying victory over communism there was essential. In 1955, it was Humphrey who made the motion to ratify the Southeast Asia Collective Defense Treaty (SEATO Pact), which obligated the U.S. to defend South Vietnam. This pact would later be used as a legal justification for the Vietnam War. In 1962, he supported Kennedy's decision to quietly enter the civil war in South Vietnam. In 1964, he voted for the Gulf of Tonkin Resolution and praised Johnson's military response to the supposed incident. By 1966, Humphrey had become the leading spokesman for the administration's war policy.[9] During that year, he wrote to a friend,

> There is a suggestion in your article that I may well have a different viewpoint from the President, but that I cannot express differences with the President . . . I must tell you privately that I am thoroughly in agreement with the President. If somehow I should become President tomorrow, I would follow essentially the same pattern, I believe, on the basis of the evidence I now have.

Visiting Saigon in 1967, he said, "I believe that Vietnam will be marked as the place where the family of man has gained the time it needed to finally break through to a new era of hope and human development and justice. This is the chance we have. This is our great adventure—and a wonderful one it is!"[10] Humphrey viewed and portrayed Lyndon Johnson as a wounded leader who was suffering as much as the troops in Vietnam and who wanted peace as much as the protesters in America did.[11]

Humphrey supported Johnson for renomination in 1968 and implored him to stay in the race after his weak showing in the New Hampshire primary. He supported Johnson's Vietnam plank at the 1968 Democratic National Convention. In a bid for the support of antiwar voters, Humphrey made a much-publicized but relatively minor "break" with Johnson during a nationally televised speech in Salt Lake City in September 1968. According to both Humphrey and his friend Edgar Berman, the vice president was privately opposed to expansion of the war in 1965 and secretly wanted to get out as soon as possible throughout 1968. It seems that Humphrey was either a wholehearted supporter of the war who later rewrote history to rehabilitate his reputation or he was an unprincipled, weak, and dishonest presidential candidate. Regardless of the truth concerning the 1965–1968 period, Humphrey always believed in the legality and morality of U.S. military intervention in Vietnam. In 1970, he endorsed a resolution calling for a "firm and unequivocal commitment to withdrawal" of all U.S. troops from Vietnam within eighteen months.[12] Running for president in 1972, he was a "peace candidate," as were most other contenders for the Democratic nomination.

Humphrey had a mixed record on the militarization of American society. His attitude toward universal military training (UMT) during the 1940s is unclear, but it is likely that he favored the idea since its sponsors included Franklin Roosevelt and Harry Truman. He supported President Truman when he "insisted on civilian control over the military" by firing General Douglas MacArthur from his Korean command in 1951. He was not, however, averse to having retired military officers make public policy. In 1948, Humphrey and many of his ideological allies favored General Dwight Eisenhower for the Democratic presidential nomination. In 1950, he voted to change a military-officer prohibition in the National Security Act to allow General George Marshall to become secretary of defense. In contrast to Bryan's reliance on pacifist Leo Tolstoy, Humphrey's thinking on foreign affairs was most influenced by Reinhold Niebuhr, Paul Douglas, and Max Kampelman—former pacifists who influenced Humphrey after they had become militarists. During the 1930s, the Minnesota Farmer-Labor Party was "pacifistic, and certainly neutralist, forever passing resolutions condemning du Pont and other munitions makers as the fomenters of America's wars." In the late 1940s, Humphrey helped to push pacifism and neutralism out of the Minnesota Democratic-Farmer-Labor Party. Under the new version of liberalism, Irving Shapiro of DuPont helped lead fundraising for the Hubert Humphrey Institute in 1977 and helped finance the 1984 presidential campaign of Humphrey protégé Walter Mondale.[13]

Foreign Policy

Two schools of thought have dominated the debate on U.S. foreign policy during the past century. One school of thought has been called imperialism, internationalism, interventionism, globalism, alliances, interdependence, Free World, and New World Order. The other school of thought has been designated isolationism, nationalism, noninterventionism, continentalism, neutrality, independence, Fortress America, and America First. For the sake of this study, the first school will be called imperialism, and the second, isolationism. These terms are, in a sense, epithets. Despite their controversial nature, these labels concisely express two divergent types of foreign policy.

As with all labels, these are oversimplifications. Isolationists do not advocate ignoring the rest of the world or cutting all ties to people of other countries. They do, however, believe that the U.S. should "mind its own business." The U.S. should be a republic rather than an empire and thereby remain somewhat isolated from the troubles of the rest of the world. Imperialists do not advocate the creation of a monarchical form of government headed by an emperor. They do not use the word *colonies* to describe U.S.-controlled territories and U.S.-dominated client states. They do, however, believe that under strong presidential leadership the U.S. government should protect its vital interests throughout the world. The U.S. should promote the spread of capitalism and democracy abroad and thereby instigate de facto economic, political, and cultural imperialism. The bias of mainstream scholarship is revealed by its use of the epithet *isolationism* to describe the first school of thought and the euphemism *internationalism* to describe the second.[14] Consistency and fairness require that we use balanced language. *Isolationism* and *Imperialism* are fairly accurate and understandable terms.

Scholars might argue that referring to a distinguished American politician as an imperialist is to lower oneself to the language of propagandists and pamphleteers. This is not, however, only the language of propaganda and pamphlets. It is a valid term associated with history and political theory. The word *imperialism* has fallen out of favor as a self-designation among U.S. politicians, but this was not the case in Bryan's day. At that time, there were leading political figures who were proud to call themselves imperialists because they wished to bring international power and glory to their country in the tradition of the British Empire. In our own day, especially since 2003, it has become commonplace for mainstream scholars and analysts to use words such as *empire* and *imperialism* in connection with the foreign policy of the world's only remaining superpower. Academic journals and publishers' catalogs are teeming with this language. Democratic Party criticism of the Bush administration's unilateralism does not dispute the underlying imperial assumptions; it merely recommends multilateralism as a more effective means of reaching the same goal.

William Jennings Bryan viewed isolationism as a liberal policy. He made anti-imperialism the cornerstone of his 1900 presidential campaign: "We assert that no nation can long endure half republic and half empire, and we warn the American people that imperialism abroad will lead quickly and inevitably to despotism at home." Bryan supporters Richard Pettigrew (R-SD) and William Allen (Pop-NE) were the most outspoken senatorial critics of the annexation of Hawaii in 1898. Bryan urged independence for Cuba and the Philippines, criticized British colonial rule in India, condemned Western atrocities during the Boxer Rebellion in China, supported the Boers in their war for independence, opposed the Hay-Bunau-Varilla Treaty, favored home rule for Ireland, and rejected the idea of global Manifest Destiny for America.

Bryan was, however, paternalistic toward the weaker nations of the Western Hemisphere: he embraced the Monroe Doctrine and supported military intervention in Latin America. This was a type of "benevolent" imperialism. Although Jefferson himself supported the Monroe Doctrine, Secretary of State Bryan's application of it in relation to Mexico, the Caribbean, and South America in the 1910s represented his most glaring departure from the fundamental principles of Jeffersonian foreign policy.[15]

Bryan and his supporters resented conservative attempts to make American economic and foreign policy subservient to that of England.[16] In 1916–1917, Bryan argued against the proposed League to Enforce Peace, opposing this early version of the League of Nations partly on isolationistic grounds: "America first! . . . Beware of Entangling Alliances." He rejected the idea that the U.S. government should be the world's policeman. In 1919–1920, he supported ratification of the Treaty of Versailles and U.S. membership in the League of Nations in the hope that more cooperation would lead to more peace. Bryan and his ally Senator Thomas Walsh (D-MT) proposed sovereignty protecting amendments to the treaty. Most Bryanites either joined Bryan in supporting ratification of the treaty with or without reservations or joined Wilson in supporting it without reservations, but some were "irreconcilables" who opposed it completely. Senator James Reed (D-MO) was a leading member of the third camp. At the 1924 Democratic National Convention, Bryan proposed a plank calling for a national referendum on joining the League of Nations and opposed internationalist Newton D. Baker's plank calling for U.S. entry into the league.[17]

In 1916, Bryan was willing to call for an international court whose rulings would be advisory, but he remained committed to the concept of national sovereignty. When he endorsed U.S. adherence to the Permanent Court of International Justice (World Court) in 1923, he added that participation in the court "should always be on the condition that we shall not be bound by the action of other nations except insofar as our government [especially Congress] affirmatively endorses the action taken." In 1922, Bryan supported the Four-Power Treaty only after a reservation was added to make clear that the treaty would not commit the U.S. to an armed alliance.

Bryan's occasional, conspicuous departures from isolationism stemmed from a conflict between his Jeffersonian desire to avoid foreign entanglements and his Christian desire to make the world a better place. Highlighting the resulting ambivalence, Kendrick Clements calls Bryan a "missionary isolationist." Indebted to Thomas Jefferson and Leo Tolstoy above all other political thinkers, Bryan's views on foreign policy were usually based on idealism and morality. He flatly rejected "power politics" (i.e., balance of power, national glory, military might, and other concepts of the realist school of international relations).[18]

Although born and raised in a haven of isolationism, Hubert Humphrey was a committed imperialist. He would never have described himself in such terms, but he was a lifelong advocate of a paternalistic, humanitarian version of empire.[19] Eastern progressives associated with Middle Way Republicanism were overt imperialists at the beginning of the twentieth century and became covert imperialists after the word fell out of popular favor. Humphrey's career followed this Theodore Roosevelt–Henry Stimson–Walter Lippmann tradition, as well as the example set by Woodrow Wilson, Robert Lansing, and John W. Davis. It was this bipartisan group of internationalists who formed the Council on Foreign Relations as a think tank to assist in the enlarging and safeguarding of the American empire. Largely funded by international banks and multinational corporations with a vested interest in U.S. foreign policy, the council's ranks eventually included Hubert Humphrey.

From the very beginning of his public career, Humphrey was a leader in efforts to eradicate isolationism from the Minnesota Democratic-Farmer-Labor Party and the national Democratic Party.[20] In January 1953, the outgoing Democratic administration decided that Humphrey should be placed on the Senate Foreign Relations Committee to help offset the isolationistic influence of La Follette heirs Robert Taft (R-OH) and William Langer (R-ND). There was a big difference between the bilateral peace treaties negotiated by Bryan and the multilateral military treaties supported by Humphrey. Humphrey and other Democratic enthusiasts of the Cold War were referred to as "gunboat liberals" or "NATO liberals" by traditional liberals. Foreign aid was an integral component of postwar imperialism. It was a discreet way of dominating other nations, as well as being a modern form of dollar diplomacy.[21] Humphrey was a champion of foreign aid throughout his career. On occasion, he explicitly rejected American imperialism and eloquently acknowledged the right to national self-determination, but this was a minority position in terms of words. More typical was his 1962 endorsement of the Monroe Doctrine during tensions between the U.S. and Cuban governments. Significantly, Humphrey endorsed only half of the Monroe Doctrine—the part about keeping Europe out of the United States' geographic neighborhood. He said, "What goes on in Europe today is vital to our security—what goes on any place in the world is vital to our security—although the Monroe Doctrine specifically denied that we wished to involve ourselves in Europe's affairs." He noted approvingly that the U.S. government had formal alliances with forty-two nations. Combined with his support for armed peacemaking, his support for U.S. involvement in every corner of the world amounted to a wholehearted endorsement of a Pax Americana.[22]

Humphrey's commitment to benevolent imperialism can be seen in his support for the United Nations, Marshall Plan, and North Atlantic Treaty Organization, and in his opposition to the Bricker Amendment.[23] He believed that the Senate made a terrible mistake in rejecting the League of Nations in 1919–1920. Largely the creation of men associated with Cecil Rhodes's secret society, the league was intended to be a stepping-stone toward an eventual federated world government led by Anglo-American neo-imperialists.[24] Throughout World War II, one plan after another was proposed to unite the English-speaking nations of the world into a new federal state or even all of the democracies of the world into a free world government.[25] The United Nations was founded by individuals similar in background and outlook to those who had founded the League of Nations—namely, elite-minded politicians, diplomats, scholars, and international bankers and businessmen. In the late 1940s, the Atlantic Union Committee and United World Federalists were formed to promote regional and world government. NATO and the UN were viewed by AUC and UWF members as vehicles through which they might attain their goals. Atlanticists favored political union of the United States, Great Britain, the Dominions, and other western European democracies, with a long-term goal of world union. The idea may sound far-fetched today, but it had ultrarespectable backing during the two decades after World War II. New York governor Nelson Rockefeller, a leading Republican presidential contender, endorsed the concept in his 1962 book *The Future of Federalism.* Calling for a Declara-

tion of Interdependence, on July 4, 1962, President Kennedy endorsed immediate regional government ("concrete Atlantic partnership") and eventual world government ("union of all free men"). The Atlantic Council has
quietly worked for these goals since the early 1960s, when it was founded by
former secretary of state Christian Herter. Herter was a Middle Way Republican with close ties to the nation's economic elite through his wife,
Standard Oil heiress Mary Caroline Pratt. Economic centralization efforts
have gone hand in hand with political centralization efforts.[26] Individuals
associated with international banks and transnational corporations have
been at the forefront of creating a unified political, economic, and cultural
system for the New World Order, or the less ominous sounding "Global Village".[27] A member of the Council on Foreign Relations, supporter of the
Atlantic Union Committee, and honorary director of the Atlantic Council,
Humphrey joined many other Vital Center Democrats in supporting "any
honest program of world cooperation and world government." Humphrey
wanted to strengthen the modern International Court of Justice. In 1960, he
sponsored legislation to repeal the Connally Reservation, which reserved
for the U.S. the power to decide what cases were of a domestic nature and
thus beyond World Court jurisdiction.[28]

An aura of amorality and the practice of "dishonesty in the service of
democracy" have accompanied Vital Center Democracy's embrace of imperialism. Humphrey was a great admirer of Reinhold Niebuhr, a father of the
"realism" school of international relations. A champion of the Cold War for
three decades, Humphrey was generally supportive of the Central Intelligence Agency, with its inherent dishonesty and illegality.[29] He supported a
multitude of repressive, neofascist regimes in the Third World from the
1940s to the 1970s.[30] Despite initial resistance to the idea of friendly relations with communist dictators, Humphrey supported increased trade with
the Soviet Union and its Eastern European satellites in the early 1960s, and
supported the détente policies of Henry Kissinger in relation to the Soviet
Union and Communist China in the early 1970s.[31] Humphrey's thinking
on East-West trade and aid was primarily influenced by powerful businessmen, such as Dwayne Andreas, not by morality or ideology. Echoing the
conclusion of *Animal Farm* three decades earlier, labor leader Charles Levinson believed that détente was a convenient arrangement whereby materialistic, power-driven American and Soviet elites mutually derived personal
benefits. Despite shared mindsets and personal friendships at the highest levels of politics and economics, the populace of both nations continued to
shoulder the burdens of imperial competition: militarism, high taxation,
heightened fear, loss of soldiers' lives. Most criticism of détente during the

1960s and 1970s came from conservative populists. For example, running against the Ford-Rockefeller ticket from within the Republican Party, in 1975, former California governor Ronald Reagan criticized grain sales to the USSR: "Are we not helping the godless tyranny maintain its hold on millions of helpless people? Wouldn't those helpless victims have a better chance of becoming free if their slave masters collapsed economically? Maybe there is an answer—we simply do what's morally right. Stop doing business with them."[32] American liberals could easily dismiss détente criticism coming from "reactionaries" such as Reagan or even-less-respectable sources such as the John Birch Society because of basic disagreements on domestic policy. Libertarian socialists Orwell and Levinson, however, were criticizing what they saw as an international elite charade from a perspective to the left of Humphrey. Condemnation from neither Right nor Left changed the course pursued by Ford, Humphrey, and other centrist politicians.

CHAPTER 11

The Post-Humphrey Era and Jeffersonian Transcendence

Evidence of Declining Influence

The historical facts suggest that Thomas Jefferson's political thought was a declining influence on American liberalism within the Democratic Party as the twentieth century unfolded. There was a shift in descent, philosophy, support, and positions between early and mid-twentieth-century Democratic liberalism. Compared to Bryan liberals, Humphrey liberals were less indebted to figures such as Jefferson, John Taylor, Andrew Jackson, Martin Van Buren, Lyman Trumbull, and James Weaver. They were more closely tied to Wall Street and the nation's other monied interests, in terms of contributions and affiliations. They were less Jeffersonian in their positions on public policies and federal appointments. Looking at the twelve tenets of Jefferson's political thought, Bryan liberalism was clearly more Jeffersonian than Humphrey liberalism in every area except ethnic inclusiveness. Criticism of Humphrey in this book should not be misunderstood. He "fell short of the mark" in many ways when using Jeffersonianism as the measure. If Hamiltonianism is preferred, Humphrey was superior to Bryan in almost every way. Regardless of perspective, it can be said that neither man was perfect, but that each was a cut above most of his political contemporaries, in terms of honesty and idealism.

The Respectable Rulers: Heirs of Humphrey

Since the death of Hubert Humphrey in 1978, the two Democrats who have served as president of the United States—Jimmy Carter and Bill

Clinton—have both been members of the Humphrey "fraternity" of the party. Carter proposed a Humphrey-Wallace ticket in 1972, placed the name of Humphrey ally Henry Jackson into nomination for president at the national convention later that year, and selected Humphrey protégé Senator Walter Mondale (DFL-MN) as his running mate in 1976 and 1980. President Carter filled his administration with Humphrey Democrats, including Zbigniew Brzezinski, Robert Bergland, and Edmund Muskie. Although he was denied the presidential nomination by the relatively young Georgian in 1976, Senator Humphrey loyally supported President Carter during his first year in office.

Bill Clinton began public life as a protégé of Senator J. William Fulbright (D-AR), a Bourbon politician who seconded Humphrey's nomination for vice president at the 1956 convention. Despite his antiwar and countercultural reputation, which were often discussed during the 1992 presidential campaign, Clinton was no radical during his student days at Oxford University. He was a Rhodes scholar and was committed above all else to maintaining his "political viability within the system." According to political scientist and former National Security Council staffer Roger Morris, Clinton may have also been a Central Intelligence Agency informant. His future wife, Hillary Rodham, worked for the Humphrey campaign in the fall of 1968, when many of her college peers favored Eugene McCarthy, Dick Gregory, or Eldridge Cleaver for president—or boycotted the election—because they hated the Johnson-Humphrey administration. Her close friend at elite Wellesley College, Eleanor Dean Acheson, joined her in working for Humphrey. From the 1940s to the 1960s, Eleanor's grandfather, Secretary of State Dean Acheson, was a personification of the American Establishment.[1]

In many ways, the Clintons represent the antithesis of Bryan Democracy. Despite being named William Jefferson Clinton and taking a much-publicized journey from Monticello to Washington on the eve of his 1993 inauguration, Clinton stands in the conservative Democratic tradition of August Belmont, Grover Cleveland, and John W. Davis. He was elected governor of Arkansas in 1978. In 1980 he lost his bid for reelection but regained the position in 1982. For the next ten years, Clinton continued in power as a partner of the state's largest corporations, utilities, and banks.[2] Far from being a serious advocate for children or for people lacking the money to buy health insurance, Hillary Rodham Clinton was a corporate attorney who represented the powerful, prosperous, and privileged during her years in Little Rock. The Clintons' ideological orientation is illustrated by Bill's reliance on Tyson Foods and Hillary's directorship of Wal-Mart. Such corporations have played important roles in the destruction of family farms and disintegration of small towns.[3]

Within the national Democratic Party, Governor Clinton identified him-self with the Humphrey-Jackson wing, not the McCarthy-McGovern wing. Before seeking the 1992 presidential nomination, he served as chairman of the Democratic Leadership Council (DLC), a successor of the Coalition for a Democratic Majority (CDM). Other DLC founders included Lyndon John-son's son-in-law Senator Charles Robb of Virginia, and Clinton running mate Senator Albert Gore Jr. of Tennessee. Centrism, defined as Hamiltonian conservatism toward economic, military, and foreign policy issues, played a significant role within the Democratic leadership of Congress and the White House during the 1980s and 1990s. House Speakers James Wright and Thomas Foley were former officers of the CDM, and House majority leader Rich-ard Gephardt was a founder of the DLC. Senate majority leader George Mitchell was a director of the Council on Foreign Relations (CFR). Presi-dent Clinton was a CFR member, and council board members included his secretaries of state, Warren Christopher and Madeleine Albright, and secre-tary of the Treasury, Robert Rubin. Three other Clinton cabinet members, Donna Shalala, Les Aspin, and William Cohen, were also directors of the CFR. Even Clinton's two appointees to the Supreme Court—Ruth Bader Ginsburg and Stephen Breyer—were CFR members.[4]

Pamela Harriman was instrumental in the national rise of both Bill Clin-ton and Al Gore. She epitomized the Anglo-American Establishment as a daughter of Lord Digby, daughter-in-law of Winston Churchill, lover of Baron Elie de Rothschild, and wife of Averell Harriman. From 1980 to 1987, she raised $10 million for the Democratic Party, more than any other single person. House Speaker Wright and Senate majority leader Robert Byrd courted her favor and sang her praises. Harriman gave money to Humphreyites Gore, Gephardt, and Senator Paul Simon when they sought the 1988 Democratic presidential nomination. She was on hand to greet Gore after the 1992 vice presidential debate and was appointed ambassador to France after Clinton entered the White House. Referring to an event held at her Georgetown mansion, Senator John Forbes Kerry crowed, "We eat like Republicans and think like Democrats." Of course, their ideology was not that of Jefferson, Jackson, or Bryan.

Clinton's successful campaign for the 1992 presidential nomination was largely fueled by contributions from investment banks, corporate law firms, and transnational corporations.[5] Running against Clinton, former California governor Jerry Brown contended that the presidential nominating process was "debased by endless fund raising from Wall Street." By inference, he linked Bill Clinton to John Davis: "It is very much like it was in the '20s, where the Democrats were, in some cases, more conservative than the Republicans." After entering the White House, Clinton's appointments, policies, and

fundraising made clear his preference for plutocracy. In 1994, Governor
Brown asserted that President Clinton had "gone as far toward business interests as any Democrat since Grover Cleveland."[6] The only thing new
about Clinton's "New Democrat" self-designation was the overt nature of
his embrace of traditional conservatism. The Clinton administration was
Hamiltonian in almost every policy area, with a mixed record on ethnic inclusiveness and spending.

The 1968–1976 struggle within the Democratic Party between elitist politics à la Hubert Humphrey-Edmund Muskie-Henry Jackson and populist
politics à la Eugene McCarthy-George McGovern-Fred Harris ended in a
clear triumph for the former during the decade following Humphrey's
death. The nomination and election of Bill Clinton publicized and solidified
this triumph. Humphrey's old friend and benefactor, Dwayne Andreas, was
an important financier of Clinton and the Clinton-controlled Democratic
Party. The Clinton administration's senior economic and foreign policy advisers were respectable Humphreyites, not radical McGovernites. There
were few, if any, New Left Democrats holding high-ranking posts within the
administration. Clinton's first-term actions surprised and disappointed many
of his less pragmatic colleagues in the baby boom generation—individuals
who voted for him in 1992 under the mistaken assumption that he was a
leftist at heart. A number of his decisions symbolized utter repudiations of
the Jeffersonian revolt of the 1960s. In the 1960s, Secretary of Defense Robert
McNamara epitomized the military-industrial complex and was viewed by
many as a war criminal for his role as an architect of the Vietnam policies of
the Kennedy and Johnson administrations. During his first vacation as president, Clinton stayed at McNamara's house on Martha's Vineyard, a seemingly small but symbolically significant act, which was a slap in the face of
every 1960s radical and every Democratic war opponent from Wayne Morse
and Ernest Gruening on down.

In 1968, Chicago's corrupt and autocratic mayor, Richard J. Daley, pre-
sided over the violent and contentious Democratic National Convention
that nominated Humphrey for president. His son, Mayor Richard M. Daley,
gave crucial assistance to Clinton during the 1992 Illinois primary. Clinton's
1992 campaign manager and 1993 Democratic National Committee chairman was David Wilhelm, manager of the younger Daley's mayoral bids.
Richard M. Daley's brother, attorney William Daley, was Clinton's chief
North American Free Trade Agreement promoter during his first term and
became secretary of commerce in his second term. Seeking to erase the
stigma of 1968, Clinton selected Chicago as the site of the 1996 Democratic
National Convention.[7]

Hubert Humphrey never became president of the United States, but Humphreyites sat for twelve years in the Oval Office. In a more personal way, his legacy lives on through his son and grandson. Minnesota attorney general Hubert "Skip" Humphrey III ran for governor in 1998, but he was one of two major-party losers to Jesse Ventura of the Reform Party. In 2002, Hubert "Buck" Humphrey IV was the unsuccessful Democratic nominee for Minnesota secretary of state.

Bill and Hillary Clinton's liberal reputation is largely derived from the fiery rhetoric of individuals such as Newt Gingrich and Rush Limbaugh. It is worth pointing out that neither Gingrich nor Limbaugh had long-standing ties to the conservative movement: the former was a Rockefeller Republican until conservatism was seen as the GOP wave of the future, and the latter did not even vote for Reagan in the 1980s. Setting aside language used in the *Punch and Judy Show* of electoral politics and personal ambition, it should be asked, Just how liberal are the Clintons? The personnel and policies of the Clinton administration were distinctly illiberal when liberalism is defined in traditional Jeffersonian terms. The Clintons themselves do not want to be identified with the word *liberalism* even in its Humphreyite form. That is the whole point of the "New Democrat" self-designation. According to Clinton insider Paul Begala, Hillary Rodham Clinton has "contempt for fuzzy-headed traditional liberal thinking."[8] In September 1996, Bill Clinton flatly denied Robert Dole's accusation that he was a liberal. In his victory speech on the night of November 5, the president proclaimed that the "Vital American Center" is alive and well.

It was during the Republican presidency of Clinton's successor that an important legacy of Hubert Humphrey unexpectedly popped up. For twenty years, members of the Old Right, the paleoconservatives, had been engaged in a power struggle with Cold War liberals, the neoconservatives, who had left the Democratic Party and joined the Republican Party. The "paleocons" were individuals in the Robert Taft-Barry Goldwater tradition, including presidential candidates Patrick Buchanan and Howard Phillips, intellectual Russell Kirk, writer Joseph Sobran, thinkers associated with the Rockford Institute, and members of the John Birch Society. In the 1960s and 1970s, the "neocons" were supporters of and advisers to Humphrey and his ally Democratic senator Henry "Scoop" Jackson of Washington. As mentioned in chapter 5, the Coalition for a Democratic Majority was created in December 1972 by Humphrey-Jackson Democrats wishing to purge the party of populist and radical impulses associated with the McGovern campaign. The Democratic activists they detested were part of a grassroots "New Politics" that was to the left of McGovern himself and that emphasized egalitarianism, pacifism, and isolationism, stances repugnant to the Vital Center tradition of Humphrey, Jackson, and the CDM.[9] There is a direct line of descent from Humphrey and the Coalition for a Democratic Majority to Clinton and the Democratic Leadership Council.

By the 1980s, the CDM types who did not remain in their party became a new variety of Reagan Republicans. By 2001, many of these—Richard Perle, Michael Ledeen, Paul Wolfowitz, Douglas Feith, and Elliott Abrams— had found a power base in the George W. Bush administration, with special access to the Defense Department and the vice president's office. When the Iraq War began, the general public became aware of the existence of neo- conservatives for the first time as the media began revealing their influential role within the Bush administration and their pre-9/11 plan for attacking Iraq.[10] These ex-Democrats, half-converted Trotskyites, and latter-day Ja- cobins opposed Robert Taft and supported Johnson-Humphrey over Gold- water in 1964; they were not part of Reagan's insurgent campaign in 1976. This history, coupled with their ongoing New Deal-Great Society views on domestic policy, makes their claims of conservatism suspect before even get- ting to the matter of foreign policy.

Longtime supporters of the Israeli government, the neocons have a grander vision beyond the Middle East: they favor aggressively exporting U.S.-style democracy and capitalism to the rest of the world by force if nec- essary. Part of this hawkish vision is an open belief in "benevolent imperial- ism," or American hegemony. It is the opposite of the paleoconservatives' isolationistic emphasis on the American republic and its unique traditions. The neoconservatives in Washington have worked hand in hand with Rockefeller-Ford Republicans such as Rumsfeld, Cheney, Powell, and Rice. Conspicuously missing in the Bush administration are any notable Goldwater- Reagan Republicans. This is especially interesting for a self-described "con- servative" presidency since room was even found in the cabinet for a Clinton Democrat: Norman Mineta. President Bush himself is the son of a man who opposed Reagan's first three campaigns for the White House.

Ironically, in terms of foreign policy, the ideological ancestry of the George W. Bush administration, like Bill Clinton's, can be traced back to Humphrey. The global aims and messianic rhetoric of Bush have been rou- tinely described as Wilsonian.[11] Bush resembles Humphrey on domestic policy as well. From a ballooning budget deficit to encroachment on states' rights in Supreme Court cases, from the Patriot Act to No Child Left Be- hind, from his idea that taxpayers should finance premarital counseling to his proposal to fund the use of veterans to teach kids how to read after school, there is no area of American life that is seen by Bush as being beyond the proper reach of federal power. "We have a responsibility that when somebody hurts, government has got to move." Humphrey in 1963? No, it is Bush in 2003. According to the White House Web site, he was speaking in Richfield, Ohio, on Labor Day.

By the 1990s, Hubert Humphrey's ideology had triumphed in the United States and, by extension, throughout most of the world, even if its crop of practitioners preferred to call it something other than liberalism. More surprising than the triumph of Humphrey's thought has been the emulation of his personality in American politics. American politics have become emotionalized. The philosophy of Hamiltonianism includes an aversion to clearly stated principle. While not negating the underlying ideology of the centrists, this type of pragmatism tries to direct citizens' attention to emotion or volition rather than to thought. In Humphrey's case, terms such as *heart, feeling, joy,* and *compassion* permeated his speeches. Humphrey's approach to politics has been adopted by mainstream politicians and the media. In politics, the current trend is toward maudlin, emotionally manipulative, and intellectually empty campaign speeches. In the 1990s, populists accused Bill Clinton and Al Gore of hiding their elitist actions behind sentimentality. Despite possessing a hot temper and a personal history that suggests selfishness if not exploitation, Clinton has a widespread reputation for being a caring person: the catchphrase *I feel your pain* has come to symbolize his public persona. In Gore's case, the emphasis has been on his wooden personality and on his carefully scripted self-depreciating jokes. Gore's invocations of his nearly killed son and deceased sister at the 1992 and 1996 Democratic conventions may have set a new low for the mawkish genre of campaign oratory. According to friends of the Clintons, the American people should be impressed by Hillary Rodham Clinton's great intelligence, political savvy, child advocacy, and cookie baking skills. Her ideology is never discussed. Although many of her critics denounce her as a liberal, they are unwilling or unable to define what that means in specific terms.

Leading Republicans have also depicted themselves and been depicted on an emotional canvas. President George H. W. Bush promised a "kinder, gentler government" when he took office in 1989. The GOP's 1994 congressional victory was widely attributed to the votes of "angry white men." Democrats denounced Republicans as "mean-spirited." Democrats repeatedly referred to Speaker of the House Newt Gingrich as the "Grinch," and the media devoted lots of attention to the Gingrich/Grinch connection. They mentioned in passing Gingrich's former fondness for Nelson Rockefeller and present admiration for Franklin Roosevelt but did not delve into the intriguing question of how such a man could be viewed as the nation's leading conservative. One of Bob Dole's major obstacles to gaining the presidency was his reputation for being "mean." In contrast, the media emphasized Jack Kemp's "optimism." When Kemp campaigned in Harlem, New York Democratic congressman Charles Rangel called him "a very nice guy in a mean-spirited party."[12] This was the level of serious political discourse in America in 1996! Governor Bush campaigned in 2000 calling himself a "compassionate conservative," as if he were applying to work in a soup kitchen rather than seeking the most powerful office in the world. Throughout the 2004 campaign, Republican spokespeople criticized Democrats for being "mean-spirited" and "pessimistic." John Kerry responded that he too was a card-carrying "optimist," and he built his campaign around fuzzy phrases such as *A Stronger America* and *Hope Is on the Way*. Compare these vacuous slogans with Bryan's 1908 slogan that addressed the central issue of politics, *Shall the People Rule?*

The midterm election of 2002 brought several reminders of Hubert Humphrey's career to national attention through the U.S. Senate race in his home state of Minnesota. The reelection of Senator Paul Wellstone was in doubt partly because he had lost much of his populist appeal. Wellstone had always been indebted to the Humphrey ideological tradition, but as an organizer for Jesse Jackson in 1988 and having run such a refreshingly grassroots campaign in 1990, he was less elitist than most in the Humphrey tradition. Although Wellstone retained the love and respect of most liberal Democrats throughout the nation, by 2002, some of his former supporters believed that his two terms in Washington had turned him into just another professional politician.[13] When Wellstone tragically died during the closing days of the campaign, old Humphrey protégé Walter Mondale filled the DFL slot. Possessing all of Wellstone's vices and none of his virtues, Mondale failed to energize the late senator's peace-and-justice base and was unable to convincingly play the part of a populist. Mondale lost, but the Humphrey legacy was still perpetuated by the winner: Norm Coleman. Mayor Coleman of St. Paul was a Hubert Humphrey III protégé, self-proclaimed "Clinton Democrat," and supporter of Wellstone's reelection in 1996 before suddenly switching parties.[14] Coleman is a modern example of Vital Center/Middle Way bipartisanship (or opportunism). The mayor's party switch was an echo of a switch fifty years earlier by the soon-to-be mayor of Minneapolis.

In 1944, Senator William Langer (R-ND) asserted that small groups of "millionaire monopolists, international bankers, or crooks" were selecting the presidential nominees of both the Democratic and Republican parties. In 1951, Congressman Usher Burdick (R-ND) said, "Both old parties want war and profits and the plain people like you and me have no means of bringing our vote to account. We will have to support one or the other of the great party candidates and when both are against us you can see how powerless we are." Throughout the twentieth century, statism and imperialism were two other guiding principles of the U.S. government under both Democrats and Republicans. Today, regardless of party affiliation or ideological label, virtually all leading politicians favor "central government control over diverse states, provinces, or regions" and "a permanent policy of massive global intervention by the United States."[15] It is obvious that Alexander Hamilton's vision for America has triumphed over Thomas Jefferson's vision:

> The bureaucracy has become immense; there has been a spectacular rise in centralized fiscal and industrial power; the governing bodies have added incrementally to their own governing power; American behavior in the world has been largely based on standard geopolitical calculations involving wealth, power, and prestige.[16]

Many, if not most, Americans remain Jeffersonian in orientation, but their views are underrepresented in Washington.[17] Political scientist Richard Falk does not exaggerate when he asserts, "Disputes between leading Democrats and Republicans are generally restricted to tactics and nuances. Underlying assumptions are rarely questioned, and genuine alternatives of policy are almost never advocated." Even Ronald Reagan, who was optimistically described by a populist aide as "probably the most Jeffersonian President since Martin Van Buren," was not much different from his predecessors and successors. Reagan has been more accurately labeled "the man who spoke like Jefferson and acted like Hamilton." When Congressman Ron Paul (R-TX), a longtime Reaganite, resigned from the GOP in 1987, he pointed to the less flattering side of the Reagan legacy: "unprecedented deficits, massive monetary inflation, indiscriminate military spending, an irrational and unconstitutional foreign policy, zooming foreign aid, the exaltation of international banking, and the attack on our personal liberties and privacy."[18]

With the end of the Cold War, announcement of a New World Order, and waging of the Persian Gulf War, President George Bush Sr. had gone so far in the direction of internationalism—an unrivaled American empire managing the entire world—that a popular reaction set in among Americans who believed that foreign burdens were multiplying and domestic concerns were being ignored. When conservative Patrick Buchanan challenged Bush for renomination on an America First platform, he was attacked by Vice President Dan Quayle as being a "closet liberal" à la George McGovern with his 1972 slogan "Come Home, America." Democratic leaders temporarily cloaked their Wilson-Humphrey aura and sounded a quasi-isolationist note in attempting to appeal to voters.[19] Bill Clinton unseated Bush by stressing unaddressed domestic issues. During his first term Clinton had more of a domestic focus than did his predecessor, but his Rhodes scholarship and CFR membership were signs of a dormant commitment to an aggressive internationalist foreign policy. He pursued this agenda during his second term by intervening in Haiti, attacking Iraq, and waging wars in Bosnia and Kosovo. Clinton set aside the controversial *New World Order* phrase but continued to pursue the goal in a more discreet fashion. Republicans, who had supported the first war against Iraq and who would later support the second, criticized Clinton for imperial overreaching and nation building in places having no direct bearing on national security. Madeleine Albright, a protégé of Humphrey's 1968 adviser Zbigniew Brzezinski, was the first woman to head the State Department, and she did not exemplify the stereotype of women being more peaceful and less jingoistic than men. Justifying the 1998 bombing of Iraq, she remarked, "If we have to use force, it is because we are America. We are the indispensable nation. We stand tall and we see further into the future."[20] The inbred nature of the U.S. foreign policy establishment is illustrated by the fact that Secretary of State Albright is the daughter of Josef Korbel, a former diplomat and professor. Secretary of State Condoleezza Rice is also a protégé of Korbel.

"Liberal internationalism"—the bipartisan, seemingly unchangeable foreign policy of the United States—is a twentieth-century manifestation of Hamilton's ideas of governance and international relations. Writing on the eve of the 1988 election, former secretaries of state Henry Kissinger and Cyrus Vance presented the Republican and Democratic views of foreign policy in *Foreign Affairs.* For the sake of convenience, the two party's views were combined into one article. Kissinger and Vance start out by saying, "We disagree on some policy choices. But we are convinced that the American national purpose must at some point be fixed. If it is redefined—or even subject to redefinition—with every change of administration in Washington, the United States risks becoming a factor of inconstancy in the world." The American people must not be allowed to tamper with the Hamiltonian status quo.[21]

In 1989, a neoconservative primer entitled *The Democratic Imperative: Exporting the American Revolution* was published. According to Richard Nixon's blurb on the book jacket, "Isolationists of both the left and the right will not like Fossedal's conclusions: that if the Democratic trend is to continue, it will be because the United States ensures that it does by pursuing an activist, even interventionist, foreign policy." Who else praised the book? Republican Jack Kemp and Democrat Al Gore also commended this work. Both Kemp and Gore had run for their party's presidential nomination the previous year. Seven years later, these men would compete against one another as vice-presidential nominees. By the 1990s, Kemp, a neoconservative, and Gore, a New Democrat, represented the bipartisan legacy of Humphrey-Jackson Cold War liberalism. Gore's words of praise for the Fossedal book—"a forceful analysis of what American foreign policy should stand for, and how it can prevail"—cast doubt on the widely held assumption that the Iraq War and broader war on terror would not have occurred after 9/11 had Gore been in the White House. Given Gore's own neoconservative philosophy, his support for the first Gulf War, his anti-Iraq stance during eight years as vice president, and his choosing of hawk Joseph Lieberman as a running mate, we cannot assume that Gore would not have initiated an attack on Iraq during his presidency. Or he may have chosen instead to launch full-blown military intervention into Colombia, a country that has been linked to both the war on drugs and the Gore family's extensive ties to Occidental Petroleum.[22] It is inaccurate to see Gore as a principled opponent of interventionism or war.

In the mid-1990s, a Democratic sage, Arthur Schlesinger Jr., warned that if we are not prepared to pay for a New World Order "in blood as well as in words and money," we will be left with the "anarchy of nation-states," while a Republican sage, William Kristol, told us that the "appropriate goal" of U.S. foreign policy is the preservation of "American hegemony" so we can continue to fulfill our "responsibility to lead the world."[23] The résumé of Kristol's coauthor, Robert Kagan, could be considered quintessential for a servant of the Power Elite. All of the usual suspects are found: Yale, Harvard, *Public Interest, Washington Post, The New Republic, The Weekly Standard,* U.S. Information Agency, State Department, George Pratt Shultz, Carnegie Endowment for International Peace, Council on Foreign Relations, Henry Jackson Society, Project for the New American Century, New World Order, and—appropriately enough—an Alexander Hamilton fellowship at American University.

A recent jointly authored article by two Establishment heavyweights continues this theme. James Schlesinger was the director of the Central Intelligence Agency and secretary of defense under Nixon before becoming secretary of energy under Carter. Thomas Pickering was a career diplomat, with ambassadorial stints in key places such as El Salvador, Israel, India, and Russia before becoming UN ambassador under Bush Sr. and undersecretary of state in the Clinton administration. The ease with which they moved from Republican to Democratic administrations is indicative of the bipartisan nature of the U.S. foreign policy establishment. In 2004, they were serving as cochairs of a task force on postwar Iraq convened by the Council on Foreign Relations. The full title of their newspaper editorial sums up their advice to presidential rivals Bush and Kerry: "Keep Iraq above Politics: Washington Needs to Remain Deeply Engaged in the Postwar Mission despite Shifts in American Public Opinion." In other words, politicians should not allow the people to interfere with policy. Schlesinger and Pickering argue, "Election-year politics must not be allowed to jeopardize the U.S. commitment to security and reconstruction . . . it is critical that the shift in the perceptions of the American public not create a momentum for withdrawal during this election year. The presidential candidates need to rise above partisanship and lead on this issue." There was no need to worry. Bush and Kerry did rise above democracy and they did keep the Iraq issue high on a shelf (safely tucked away from the childish masses who might have been tempted to tamper with vital national security interests). That is the elite perspective.[24]

The Radical Remnant: Heirs of Bryan

The fact goes largely unrecognized, but the liberalism of 2006 and the conservatism of 2006 are ideological cousins. They are both descendents of Jeffersonianism; the Left and the Right are built upon a common foundation of populism and both oppose the elitism of the Center. Franklin Delano Roosevelt's most important contribution to American politics may be the transformation of many conservatives into liberals. This seeming ideological alchemy created semantic confusion and provided cover for reactionaries who had previously been easy targets for criticism. Before the late 1930s, there was overall unity among the common people and their political representatives. They were Jeffersonians as opposed to Hamiltonians. Jeffersonians were liberals, progressives, insurgents, populists, and democrats; Hamiltonians were conservatives, reactionaries, standpatters, elitists, aristocrats, and plutocrats. By 1940, FDR had become the measure of all things liberal, and liberalism was being interpreted to mean support for political centralization, exorbitant spending by the federal government, a managed economy through an overt government alliance with big business, and imperialism operating under the euphemism *internationalism*. Those who focused on the New Deal's pro-common people, pro-labor, pro-civil rights rhetoric remained liberals. Liberals who accepted these aspects of the New

Deal but could not swallow its concentration of power, fiscal irresponsibility, and interest in foreign wars became conservatives.

During the Roosevelt years, many plutocratic conservatives, such as Averell Harriman, became liberals, and many liberals, such as Amos Pinchot, became value conservatives. Lifelong liberals were being called conservatives because they repeatedly disagreed with the Roosevelt administration. Pinchot, Hiram Johnson, Gerald Nye, Thomas Gore, Burton Wheeler, Oswald Garrison Villard, and many other prominent populists and progressives were surprised to hear that they were no longer liberals simply because they refused to follow Roosevelt in his embrace of Hamiltonian domestic and foreign policies. Wall Street Republicans such as Wendell Willkie, Harold Stassen, and Thomas Dewey—members of the wing of the party that had always been known as conservative—suddenly became "liberal Republicans" or "progressive Republicans." Because he was the central figure within the GOP opposing this new type of liberalism, Senator Robert Taft (R-OH) was dubbed a conservative, despite the fact that he was far closer in spirit to liberal champions Thomas Jefferson and Robert La Follette than the Wall Street Republicans were. Another striking example is Congressman Hamilton Fish (R-NY), who was openly known as a Republican liberal in 1936 but was dismissed by the Roosevelt administration and the mainstream media as a terrible reactionary by 1940.[25]

In the 1970s, Richard Falk aptly distinguished Hamiltonian conservatism from Jeffersonian-Taftian conservatism within the Republican Party:

> The dominant sector of the ruling classes should not be confused with the reactionary outlook of the political right. No, indeed, the ruling class is itself attacked from the right as a tool of the Communists and the like. The right proposes a set of policies that promote the interests and values of national capitalism, favoring protectionism, low taxes, the elimination of welfare programs, balanced federal budgets, and old-style nationalism. These policies are not compatible with the dynamic, internationalist sector of corporate and banking leadership.[26]

From the 1930s through the 1970s, many Jeffersonian conservatives were affiliated with the Democratic Party because they liked its tradition of limited government and grassroots democracy, as opposed to the Republican Party's association with country clubs and big business. Many conservatives supported the presidential campaigns of Governor George Wallace in the 1960s and 1970s not because they were racists, but because they were populists.[27] Wallace took on the Establishment. He favored states' rights, criticized the nation's unfair tax structure, condemned assistance to communist dictators, ridiculed the haughty intelligentsia, advocated traditional moral values, was a representative of the working class, and pointed out that there was not a dime's worth of difference between the two major parties. By the late 1970s, many "Wallace Democrats" had become "Reagan Republicans." The New Right and Religious Right were grassroots movements populated by Jeffersonian conservatives who tried to build upon the legacies of Governor Wallace and Senator Barry Goldwater by supporting the presidential candidacies of Governor Ronald Reagan. The wing of the GOP that opposed "Country Club Republicans" at the local level and Wall Street Republicans at the national level, and that championed traditional religion, social morality, smaller government, and national sovereignty, was eventually led by presidential candidates Pat Robertson in 1988 and Pat Buchanan in 1992, 1996, and 2000. The most famous politicians in the United States since the New Deal have been FDR/Dewey-style Hamiltonians, but a minority have been conservative Jeffersonians. Denounced and ridiculed by the mainstream media and given little opportunity for national advancement, they have been part of a "radical remnant" that has resisted the triumph of Hamiltonianism within both major parties and within government at every level of society.

The actual power of the Religious Right within the Republican Party has often been exaggerated. Conservative Christians represent a large bloc of voters, but they lack the economic clout to challenge the dominant Wall Street wing of the party when it comes to public policy. During the Reagan years of the 1980s, Jerry Falwell and Jesse Helms were high-profile Republicans, but they were not running the country. If any single person at the time could have been identified as doing so—and we know that power is more complex than this—David Rockefeller would be a more plausible possibility. Consider Ronald Reagan's choices for secretary of state, the most powerful position in his cabinet. He did not choose a person who had been paying dues for years within the conservative movement: Helms, Barry Goldwater, Strom Thurmond, John Ashbrook, or Phyllis Schlafly. Instead, he went with two non-Reaganite, pro-Establishment choices: Kissinger protégé Alexander Haig and Nixon official George Pratt Shultz. Haig was a director of Chase Manhattan Bank, and Shultz, an heir to Standard Oil. Both of these companies belong to the Rockefeller financial empire. The same sort of thing is true today. George W. Bush selected self-described "Rockefeller Republican" Colin Powell to be his first secretary of state and Shultz protégé Condoleezza Rice to be his second. Before being chosen, neither of them had any connection to the grassroots conservative movement or Religious Right (unless we count suspicion because they are both pro-choice on abortion). Incidentally, Rice was a director of Chevron, an oil company with Rockefeller roots. Someone like James Dobson serves as a lightning rod for conservative inspiration and liberal criticism, but he isn't pulling the strings in the White House or on Capitol Hill. The relationship between Republican power brokers and Christian voters tends to be a one-way street. Evangelicals elect politicians but receive only crumbs from the resulting table. The crumbs are well publicized for the benefit of the GOP faithful in the hinterland. Democratic Party leaders and their allied interest groups also magnify the importance of the crumbs as a means of stirring up fear and raising money among nonevangelicals. Conservative Christians serve the interests of one party for the purpose of electoral exploitation and the other for the purpose of "bogeyman" exploitation. While this is true at the national level, evangelicals at the local and state levels tend to have more political power.

Although some tenets of traditional liberalism were openly abandoned in the wake of FDR—including decentralization, frugality, pacifism, and isolationism—liberal politicians of the post-New Deal era continued to profess allegiance to democracy, ethnic inclusiveness, protection of civil liberties, and concern for the poor and downtrodden. Grassroots liberals, indebted to the New Left and Counterculture movements of the 1960s, have made a partial return to the early American liberalism of Jefferson by adding hostility toward capitalism, rejection of militarism, and opposition to imperialism. The Jeffersonian tradition of liberalism still exists despite the confusing conversion of the La Follette wing into the Taft wing of the GOP and creation of an illiberal form of liberalism within the two major parties. Most liberal Jeffersonians have not emphasized decentralization and frugality, and most conservative Jeffersonians have not stressed ethnic inclusiveness and pacifism. Senator Robert Taft, Senator William Proxmire, and Governor Jerry Brown may have been the most balanced, most fully realized Jeffersonian politicians of the post-New Deal era. While generally acknowledged as a father of modern conservatism, Senator Taft's policy positions in the 1940s and 1950s were later echoed by the New Left of the 1960s and the McGovern campaign of 1972. Taft, for example, was an outspoken critic of Wall Street domination of his party and an early opponent of imperialism in French Indochina (Vietnam).[28] In 1963, Senator Proxmire described himself as "dedicated to economy in government and human rights and vehemently opposed to special privilege." Proxmire was known as a maverick because Jeffersonian liberalism was an exotic creature in American politics by the 1950s. In his 1980 presidential campaign, Governor Brown attempted to put together an unusual Jeffersonian coalition based on environmental protection, fiscal responsibility, future focus, equality, peace, and isolationism.[29] His 1992 effort was more successful in attracting a wide range of populist support as he placed greater emphasis on economic justice and political reform.[30]

Speaking of economic justice, it should be noted that most Jeffersonians seek fairness when it comes to economics—not government mandated equality. Opponents of monopoly and special privilege, their emphasis is on equal opportunity. They do not want governments dispensing unfair advantage to wealthy individuals and corporations seeking to purchase political influence. Free enterprise is an enemy of monopoly capitalism because the latter relies on government favor, eliminates competition, and reduces consumer choice. Historically, Jeffersonians do not support class legislation or redistribution of wealth. These are big government ideas (state socialism and state capitalism). Instead of statism and artificial economic leveling through coercion, Jeffersonians tend to support equal opportunity through government neutrality in the marketplace, with occasional use of antitrust, pro-competition action to prevent monopoly. They do not worship a golden calf of economic theory, hold corporate "persons" above real people, or serve mammon instead of God. At the same time, they are not welfare statists, social engineers, or devotees of paternalistic governance. Neither materialists who coldly follow economic abstractions and embrace consumerism run amok, nor sentimentalists who naively look to government for benevolence from cradle to grave, most Jeffersonians try to practice spirituality and humanism in the best sense of the words.

A line of ideological descent can be traced from Jefferson through Bryan and his Republican counterpart La Follette to the radical remnant of the past few decades. This is true for both liberal populists on the Left and conservative populists on the Right. The New Left of the 1960s was largely Jeffersonian in nature. Barry Goldwater grew up as a Jeffersonian Democrat and retained these tendencies throughout his career. The New Right and Green movements that arose in the late 1970s and early 1980s were both Jeffersonian efforts. Repeatedly invoking the name of Thomas Jefferson while running for president in 1992, Jerry Brown claimed to be fighting "latter-day Federalists" on behalf of the common people. Ross Perot considers himself a Jeffersonian, citing his views on morality, democracy, decentralization, and frugality. In 1992, Walter Berns, a political scientist and representative of the American Enterprise Institute, attacked Perot for proposing direct democracy, for promising to do "precisely what Hamilton warned against and worked so assiduously to prevent, namely, to bridge the distance between the people and their government."[31] Possessing similar strengths and weaknesses, Ross Perot could be thought of as an Andrew Jackson of the electronic age.

Populist is a modern word for democrat and a synonym for Jeffersonian. The transcendent nature of populism is an important component of American politics. The surprising fact that traditional liberals and modern conservatives often share anti-Establishment sentiment has been recognized, usually in passing, by a number of political writers.[32] The "defining principle" of populist coalitions is "'a consensus among heterogeneous mass social groups' in the struggle against forces monopolistically dominating society." Populism accounts for Left-Right confluence against the Power Elite, or Center. In the 1890s, members of the People's Party in Kansas and in many other states used the "agrarian myth" to build a powerful political coalition. Populists "appealed to values implicit within the myth in order to transcend diverse political ideologies." The Kansas Populist coalition broke apart over the divisive issues of woman suffrage and alcohol prohibition. Early Populist success in the South was thwarted by the divisive issue of white supremacy. The rise of "corporatism" (government-business-labor partnership) and "pluralism" (special interest groups) during the 1910s furthered the fragmentation of the common people on a national scale. After the 1924 election, Senator Hiram Johnson (Pr/R-CA) told Harold Ickes that the "heterogeneous elements which ostensibly came together for La Follette could never be brought together under any one banner again."[33] Johnson was right. Since that time, populists have come together on an ad hoc basis to work on a handful of controversial public policy issues, but they have been unable to unite on a presidential candidate or political party.[34]

Popular cohesiveness was further eroded in the late 1930s and early 1940s through ideological alchemy at the highest levels of politics. Distrustful of FDR and opposed to many aspects of his program, millions of Jeffersonians were alienated from the liberal label. In the 1960s and 1970s, conservative Jeffersonians were further estranged from liberal Jeffersonians by the addition to liberalism of elements that were quite different from traditional Jeffersonianism. Hot-button social and moral issues grafted onto modern liberalism include hostility toward the nation's predominantly Christian cultural heritage, criminal rights over victim rights, illegal drug use, sexual promiscuity, homosexuality, legalized abortion, and racial quotas. In the 1980s, mandated selective hypersensitivity, known as political correctness, became a hallmark of many self-professed liberals. Despite such unsettling factors, the Left and the Right have sometimes been able to work together because they share many underlying values as a result of their common descent from Thomas Jefferson's political thought. Opposition to U.S. entry into World War II was a joint venture of liberals and conservatives. In 1946, Oswald Garrison Villard wrote to Richard Koch, "Undoubtedly there is something in what you say about a basic kinship between my liberal ideas and those upheld by certain honest and fearless conservatives."[35] In the 1960s, former senator Gerald Nye (R-ND), a La Follette liberal since the 1920s, was affiliated with the Goldwater movement. Libertarian Murray Rothbard was an important Left-Right bridge builder during this period. Karl Hess and G. William Domhoff were among those who urged their New Left colleagues to reach out to grassroots conservatives. Barry Goldwater told Hess, "When the histories are written, I'll bet that the old right and the New Left are put down as having a lot in common and that the people in the middle will be the enemy." George Wallace's 1968 campaign produced leftist-sounding language on capitalism and militarism. Underlying shared values and uneasy cooperation efforts produced some seemingly strange results in the realm of presidential politics. Some 1964 Goldwater voters supported Eugene McCarthy in 1968. In 1972, George McGovern was the second choice of some Wallace supporters. Some 1972 Wallace voters supported Jesse Jackson in 1988.[36]

The past twenty years have seen a rebirth of transcendent populism in American politics. The majority of Americans have always embraced both liberty and justice for all. During the 1930s, the common people became artificially divided between conservatives, who put a premium on liberty, and liberals, who put a premium on justice. Certainly there are sometimes tensions between the two values, but they are not mutually exclusive. By the late 1980s, many Americans realized that while they may disagree with fellow populists on specific hot-button issues, they tend to share a deep-rooted hostility toward plutocracy and imperialism, toward a domineering state and a materialistic world view. They decided they could set aside differences to work together, at least on a temporary basis, because they shared a third core value: democracy. There has been a growing awareness that a coalition of the populist Left and populist Right can thwart the divide-and-conquer strategy of the elitist Center.[37]

The first notable instance was in 1989 and 1991 when liberal Ralph Nader and conservative Pat Buchanan led the public outcry against attempts to enact a congressional pay raise. In 1990–1991, many liberals and conservatives united in opposition to the Persian Gulf War. Liberals are suspicious of involvement by the U.S. government overseas because they see it as an agent of exploitation and domination. With the end of the Cold War, many conservatives returned to their foreign policy roots of isolationism. Opposition to the Gulf War did not form an organized coalition, but many critics of the war shared a fellowship of mind and heart with unlikely colleagues (e.g., conservative columnist Joseph Sobran was recommending the writings of liberal scholar Noam Chomsky). In their coverage of the antiwar movement, the mainstream media focused on the predictable sight of protests by radicals in tie-dyed shirts, but members of the John Birch Society were also active in opposing military involvement. Richard Falk anticipated such a convergence when he wrote, "Ironically, perhaps, the Jeffersonian heritage may be more active both on the conservative right, with its dislike for political centralization, and on the progressive left, with its receptivity to change and deep concern with values."[38] In 1992, there was widespread disgust with Republican presidential nominee George Bush and Democratic presidential nominee Bill Clinton. Citizen anger toward politics as usual and yearning for something different were expressed through votes for Pat Buchanan and Jerry Brown during the primary season. Surprisingly, conservative Republican Buchanan was the second choice of some who supported liberal Democrat Brown and vice versa.[39] Citizen discontent culminated in the general election when independent Ross Perot received nearly twenty million votes for president. Perot received support from both Buchanan Republicans and Brown Democrats.[40] Perot, Buchanan, and Brown all opposed the Gulf War and each stressed democratization in their campaigns for the White House.

In 1992–1993 populists united in opposing the North American Free Trade Agreement (NAFTA). In 1994, they worked against the General Agreement on Tariffs and Trade (GATT) with its World Trade Organization (WTO). A Jeffersonian coalition of labor union members, environmentalists, human rights supporters, Brown Democrats, Buchanan Republicans, and Perot Independents opposed NAFTA and GATT. The anti-NAFTA and anti-GATT efforts approached the level of genuine coalitions, with prominent liberals and prominent conservatives holding joint press conferences to denounce the agreements. In the case of GATT, they did not agree on everything or oppose it for all of the same reasons, but they did agree that the compact was undemocratic because it would take power out of the hands of elected representatives in America and turn it over to unelected bureaucrats in Geneva. With both NAFTA and GATT, they also agreed that the compacts were undemocratic because they were designed for the benefit of wealthy individuals and large corporations, not for the benefit of the common people. Most surprising of all, they agreed that the compacts were bad because they represented a dangerous level of political centralization and threatened the national sovereignty of the United States. These threats were not coming from a foreign government; they were coming from American-based transnational corporations and global banks. Going one step further—for the first time in history—liberal Jeffersonians charged that the monied interests were attempting not only to diminish U.S. sovereignty but also to create a de facto world government.[41] This had long been the seemingly paranoid cry of conservative Jeffersonians, including John Birchers, Goldwater Republicans, and Wallace Democrats.

The populist reunion in opposition to NAFTA-GATT was especially appropriate considering the long history of Jeffersonian involvement in disputes over imperialism, trade policy, and labor protection. Liberals traditionally opposed tariffs not because of a commitment to free trade but because of a commitment to democracy. Their opposition to tariffs was a component of their opposition to plutocracy. Jeffersonians opposed tariffs in 1800 and 1900 for the same reason they opposed NAFTA and GATT in 1993: they saw them as devices designed to benefit special interests, namely, big businessmen and bankers. The NAFTA debate was foreshadowed by discussions about annexation of Hawaii and the Philippines in the 1890s. Bryanites warned against economic imperialism, uncontrolled immigration, and labor exploitation. The global economy is more integrated today than at any time in world history, but it is not completely new. The U.S.-dominated New World Order is doing on a grander scale what the British Empire attempted to do a century ago. The current free trade strategy of exploiting cheap labor around the world was used by the British government in China and India. Many of the same elements were involved in debates over the Reciprocal Trade Agreements Act during the 1934-1940 period. Bryan Democrats and La Follette Republicans argued that Cordell Hull's free trade program would cede congressional authority to the president, that the nation would be flooded with products made by cheap overseas labor, that it would hurt urban workers and small farmers, and that it would benefit the wealthy segment of society. Hubert Humphrey and Nelson Rockefeller— exemplars of the new FDR/Dewey type of liberalism—supported RTAA. The phenomenon of the U.S. government encouraging and helping transnational corporations to move their production plants from America to nations with cheap labor forces was noticed as early as 1974 in connection with the Rockefeller-supported Overseas Private Investment Corporation.[42] In the eyes of today's Bryan-La Follette heirs, exploitation of workers abroad and destruction of community at home are inherent parts of the global economy and the New World Order created by the Vital Center of Humphrey, Rockefeller, and their ideological allies.

The loose-knit "Halloween Coalition" forged through the NAFTA and

GATT battles continued to operate on issues of mutual concern in the mid-1990s.[43] Examples include support for term limits, campaign finance reform, and civil liberties; opposition to military interventions in the Balkans, bailout of Wall Street and the Mexican government, and continuation of most-favored-nation (MFN) status for China; and interest in the presidential campaigns of Buchanan, Perot, and Nader. In 1998, the nation was shocked when Jesse Ventura—a former professional wrestler with a modest political background—was elected governor of Minnesota. He was elected on the Reform ticket but belonged to a minority within the national party that was hostile to party founder Ross Perot. Ventura and his friends had backed former governor Richard Lamm (D-CO) for president in 1996, but he lost the nomination to Perot. Most people who voted for Ventura did so despite, not because of, his flamboyant entertainment career. He was supported by a populist coalition of Perot, Buchanan, and Nader supporters, young first-time voters, and disaffected former voters because he was not a career politician and because he advocated political reform. He was also plainspoken and seemed honest.[44]

The 1998 Minnesota gubernatorial election illustrates the Establishmentarian legacy of Hubert Humphrey in his home state. The Democratic nominee was Humphrey's son Attorney General "Skip" Humphrey. The Republican nominee was St. Paul mayor Norm Coleman, a protégé of the younger Humphrey who eventually switched parties. In debates with the drab Humphrey and Clintonesque Coleman, both of whom offered the same old clichés and generalities to voters, Ventura was a refreshing and genuine alternative. Spending a fraction of the money, Ventura defeated Coleman and Humphrey, boosted voter turnout, and became the first third-party statewide officeholder since the heyday of the Minnesota Farmer-Labor Party. The mainstream media, major parties, and special interest groups were scandalized, but a plurality of Minnesotans were excited and encouraged by this exercise in grassroots democracy. While his election remains a landmark event, Governor Ventura proved to be somewhat of a disappointment to many of his supporters. His populism was mixed with a libertarianism that bordered on libertinism. His populist instincts were often smothered by his mainstream political advisers drawn from the "sensible Center," hindered by a lack of personal political knowledge, and sacrificed in favor of petty, ego-centered squabbles with legislators and reporters.

At the height of his popularity, some wanted Jesse Ventura to run for president. He chose to not do so, but he did play an interesting role in the 2000 presidential election. In 1999, conservative populist Pat Buchanan ended his third attempt at the Republican presidential nomination by jumping to the

Reform Party of Perot and Ventura. Partly out of real policy differences about social morality and trade policy, and partly out of personal pride and ambition, a Reform Party civil war broke out involving Perot, Ventura, and Buchanan. Perot formed an alliance with Buchanan to push the Ventura/Lamm wing out of the party. During this early period, Ventura proposed wealthy businessman Donald Trump for president as an alternative to Buchanan. Eventually thwarted at the national level, Ventura quit the party in a huff and renamed his home state vehicle the Independence Party. With Ventura no longer a threat to his control of the party, Perot double-crossed Buchanan and tried to derail his campaign for the Reform presidential nomination. Perot's camp formed a bizarre alliance with Hindu transcendental meditation spokesman John Hagelin. Leader and perennial presidential candidate of the Natural Law Party, Hagelin hoped to be the 2000 nominee of a joint Reform–Natural Law ticket.

Meanwhile, Buchanan formed an equally surprising alliance with Lenora Fulani, an African American woman from New York who had twice been the presidential nominee of the left-wing New Alliance Party.[45] Fulani signed on as cochair of Buchanan's campaign for the Reform nomination. Although Buchanan himself seemed genuinely eager to go into the fall campaign as head of a populist, beyond-Left-and-Right coalition, his long-time base of conservative Christian ex-Republicans was not willing to embrace Fulani and her group of pro-choice, pro-gay socialists. The tenuous coalition was splintered on the rocks of ideology and ambition as the Buchanan campaign approached the Reform national convention. Feeling disrespected by the Buchanan forces, Fulani withdrew her endorsement, proposed Ralph Nader of the Green Party for the Reform Party nomination, and, eventually, joined the Perot camp in support of Hagelin. After months of careful organizing, Buchanan had a majority of duly elected convention delegates. When this became apparent, the Hagelin-Perot-Fulani group held its own rump convention and the national Reform Party split into two parts with two nominees. Lawsuit and countersuit followed. Reform Party intrigue and self-destruction, coupled with conservative Republicans' thirst for a GOP victory after eight years of Clinton-Gore, led to a very weak fourth-place finish for Buchanan in November. Green Party nominee Nader failed to meet the 5 percent threshold needed to turn the Greens into a nationally recognized party, but he still managed to net almost three million votes in the face of intense pressure on liberal Democrats by the Gore campaign during the closing weeks. Despite high hopes at the beginning of 2000, in the end, neither Buchanan nor Nader were able to construct a broad-based populist coalition to challenge the Establishment in the voting booths of November.

In the early 2000s, George W. Bush's administration reignited the nation's populist coalition. Presidential threats to domestic civil liberties, perceived imperial overreaching abroad, and executive disdain for congressional authority were among the factors causing a shift from post-9/11 unity to considerable populist suspicion and anger. Liberal senator Russ Feingold (D-WI) and conservative congressman Ron Paul (R-TX) were among the relatively small number of legislators who opposed the USA Patriot Act in 2001 and the Homeland Security Act in 2002. A similar Left-Right coalition opposed the 2003 Iraq War, with strong criticism of the invasion coming from both Ralph Nader and Pat Buchanan, the Green Party and the America First Party, *The Nation* and *Chronicles*.[46] Mid-decade examples of joint populist efforts include opposition to ratification of the Central American Free Trade Agreement (CAFTA) and extension of the Patriot Act, as well as criticism of two important U.S. Supreme Court rulings: *Kelo v. New London* (governments can use eminent domain authority to take homes and land for private economic development) and *Gonzales v. Raich* (the federal government can strike down state medicinal marijuana laws under the commerce clause).

In recent years instances of Jeffersonian transcendence temporarily uniting the Left and Right have taken place outside the confines of the two major parties. There have been a few presidential campaigns of a populist nature by insurgent Democrats and Republicans but most strands of Jefferson's legacy have been found among third parties. Breaking away from the ideological constraints and off-putting image of the Green Party, in 2004 Ralph Nader mounted an independent run for the White House. He attempted to create a sizeable populist coalition of alienated liberals, moderates, conservatives, and nonvoters. Nader was supported by writer-activists such as Alexander Cockburn on the Left, Pat Choate in the middle, and Justin Raimondo on the Right. Economist Choate was a supporter of protectionist Democrats in the 1980s, Perot's running mate in 1996, and a Buchanan campaign chair in 2000. Predicting cross-label appeal by Nader because of his stances on the budget deficit, trade, and Iraq, Choate told the press, "A good number of independent voters are going to be for him, and I think a lot of the old white-shoe conservative Republicans are going to be interested, along with the more traditional liberals of the Democratic Party."[47] Nader received the nomination of the Reform Party, thereby following in the footsteps of Perot and Buchanan.

Despite a promising start, in the end Nader had very little success. He made tactical mistakes in his relations with the Green Party and his choice of a running mate did not broaden his base. The Democrats used a large amount of money and string-pulling to keep him off state ballots and tied up in court. He was excluded from the debates, and both major parties cast the 2004 election in apocalyptic terms, which successfully frightened their core voters from straying to Nader or other alternatives. Although Nader received far fewer votes than he had four years earlier, more of his support probably came from disaffected conservative Jeffersonians than it had in his previous two campaigns.[48] There was another twist associated with the Nader 2004 effort. Exit polls showed that 3 percent of the voters who said that "moral values" was the most important issue in the campaign voted for Nader. Among the main issue blocs, he received by far the most support from this group, and it was disproportionately high compared to his total vote percentage. The common assumption is that moral-values voters were members of the Christian Right, but Nader stood in the stream of Jeffersonian moralism, and he received a significant amount of support from moralists of every variety.

CHAPTER 12

Democratic Politics Today and Tomorrow

Religion and Politics

The political role played by evangelical Christianity during the post-Humphrey era is worth examining in some detail because of its importance in contemporary America. Politics is not just about elections and politicians; it is also about culture and people. In the mid-1970s, during a national period of charismatic and neoevangelical revival, born-again Christians began to be active as an organized group in electoral politics as they sought to "return America to God." This politicization included the election of Jimmy Carter, the subsequent shift of many evangelicals from the Democratic Party to the Republican Party after being disappointed by the Carter presidency, and the founding of the Moral Majority. Today the political role played by conservative Christians of the Religious Right has become a topic of not just national but international attention. It is manifested in talk about a "culture war," in analysis of the red state/blue state divide, and in disparaging comparisons of Christian fundamentalists to Islamic fundamentalists. Competing visions of the world have led to significant political polarization as religion is found at the center of many important issues.

In some ways, George W. Bush can be compared to William J. Bryan. Both have been notable evangelical Christian politicians and have been scorned by social elitists for being champions of the "ignorant bumpkins" of America's heartland. Almost every modern U.S. president has played the role of God-fearing leader as he publicly prays, closes speeches with the obligatory "God Bless America," and is photographed with Billy Graham. Bush, however, has brought the subject of presidential religion into a new realm of controversy, and his conspicuous piety has inspired both appreciation from most white evangelicals and criticism from almost everyone else. In this, he is unlike Hubert Humphrey, who had a thoroughly secular reputation. Cynics note that Bush's conversion to' the born-again subculture roughly coincided with his role as outreach coordinator to the evangelical community during his father's campaign for the 1988 Republican nomination (running against conservative-populist-evangelical favorites Jack Kemp and Pat Robertson, among others).[1] However, it is equally plausible that his campaign role naturally resulted from a real conversion experience.

At first glance, Bush the Christian resembles Bryan the Christian, but there are significant differences between the two. It is easy to contemptuously criticize the religion of George W. Bush if one does not share it, but it is fairer and less elitist to take his faith seriously and to use it as the standard by which to judge his actions. When it comes to religion, the problem with Bush—from the Bryan perspective—is not that he is too Christian, but that he is not Christian enough. Assuming his profession of faith in Jesus Christ is sincere, it could be argued that Bush is an immature and worldly Christian. Having accepted a shallow form of Christianity—one that views salvation as a sort of personal ticket to heaven and accompanying self-improvement plan—he has not moved on toward a clearer understanding of discipleship and the Kingdom of God.[2] As a politician, Bush operates on the basis of American civil religion rather than by the spirit of genuine Christianity as depicted in scripture. This is not to criticize Bush for being too politically conservative but rather for continuing to approach life on the basis of traditional worldly principles, not the transcendent principles of the New Testament. From the Christian perspective, the present world system is organized on the basis of the "cosmic principles of force, greed, selfishness, ambition, and pleasure." Surrounded by practical secularists such as Karl Rove, Richard Cheney, and Donald Rumsfeld, Bush seems to be very much at home with the world's business-as-usual, might-makes-right principles.[3]

Dispensationalism is a school of Christian theology created in the nineteenth century by Irish minister J. N. Darby and popularized in the United States by evangelist D. L. Moody and Bible annotator C. I. Scofield. Its thought includes literal interpretation of scripture, a clear differentiation between ancient Israel and the church, and belief in a Rapture followed by the Antichrist, Great Tribulation, Battle of Armageddon, and premillennial Second Coming of Christ. The extent of this theology's direct influence on Bush is unknown, but he does have some key backers who subscribe to its general tenets, and most Christians who support him take modern, simplified versions of dispensationalism for granted.[4]

In Bryan's day, dispensationalists understood the difference between "the church" and "the world" and did not want to mix the two because the latter would invariably corrupt the former. Back then dispensationalists were largely apolitical because they believed spiritual ills needed spiritual cures. They may have voted as part of their civic duty, but they had no faith in politicians who were propping up an evil system that needed to be replaced, not reformed. Although a minority position among evangelical Christians, there has always been a strain of theology that advocates a line of demarcation or wall of separation between church and state on religious, not irreligious, grounds. Donatists of the fourth century, Anabaptists of the sixteenth century, Baptists and Quakers of the seventeenth century, and dispensationalists of the nineteenth century all objected to the marriage of Christianity to worldly power. In their eyes, the Roman Catholic and mainstream Protestant traditions erred by setting aside the principles of the New Testament in favor of an Old Testament model and by perpetuating pagan traditions in which politics and religion were bound together in what scholars call the *sacral state* or *Constantinianism*. Patriotism became synonymous with spirituality. They believed that this milieu fostered European religious wars, persecution, clerical arrogance and corruption, pervasive defensiveness and intolerance, and widespread hypocrisy as people pretended to be something they were not to avoid punishment.[5]

On a micro level, George W. Bush's faith may have helped him with his substance abuse problem, but on a macro level it does not seem to have changed his view of the world or his acceptance of its basic principles. It has also had the unfortunate effect of infusing Bush's preexisting arrogance with an almost messianic sense of self-righteousness because he sees himself as speaking for God. During the opening weeks of the Iraq War, *USA Today* published a behind-the-scenes look at the commander-in-chief as revealed by friends and advisers. The words used to describe how he is holding up under the pressure have a Christlike ring. Bush is "burdened," frustrated when others "express doubts," and views himself as an "aggrieved victim" who is "being tested." He "rebukes," "prays," and "encourages others not to lose faith in the war plan." The rebuking is of aides who "question the tactics, pace or human costs of the war." Bush's interpersonal relations under wartime stress fall somewhat short of Christian ideals: he is "irritated," "infuriated," "impatient," and "imperious." According to close friend Commerce Secretary Don Evans, Bush "believes he was called by God to lead the nation at this time" (reporter's paraphrase). Later in the article, we learn from Evans that Bush's faith is sustaining him: "He knows that we're all here to serve a calling greater than self. . . . He understands that he is the one person in the country, in this case really the one person in the world, who has a responsibility to protect and defend freedom."[6] Some might interpret such words as indicative not of selflessness but rather megalomania with a Christian veneer.

In a private meeting with Palestinian leaders in June 2003, Bush said, "I'm driven with a mission from God. God would tell me, 'George, go and fight those terrorists in Afghanistan.' And I did, and then God would tell me, 'George, go and end the tyranny in Iraq . . .' And I did. And now, again, I feel God's words coming to me, 'Go get the Palestinians their state and get the Israelis their security.'" Rebutting the BBC documentary that revealed the conversation, a Bush spokesman issued a denial, but the words ring true and several witnesses confirmed the accuracy of the account. According to the White House Web site, in March 2004, Bush told a faith-based and community initiatives conference audience, "We're really talking about miracles here. . . . God loves you, and I love you. And you can count on both of us as a powerful message that people who wonder about their future can hear." The garbled syntax suggests that the president may have been talking off-the-cuff, but Bush's symmetrical pairing of himself with God is clear. In a July 2004 private meeting with an Amish group in Pennsylvania, Bush reportedly said, "I trust God speaks through me. Without that, I couldn't do my job."[7] When the world's most influential evangelical Christian leads a life characterized by love of power, preference for wealth, glorification of war, and practice of deceit, something has gone terribly awry. It is a situation of which Bryan would certainly not approve, and it says more about the state of American evangelicalism than it does about this one man.

As for Bush, his pride and self-satisfaction probably preclude his considering for even a moment the disturbing implications of the words of Jesus Christ, when Jesus spoke of those who wrongly presume to act in his name.[8] Later, Jesus speaks of his second coming and the subsequent judgment, using care for the hungry, thirsty, estranged, naked, sick, and imprisoned as at least one set of criteria for judgment. Those who have failed to care for the weak will be sentenced to eternal punishment. Ironically, the president who routinely calls enemies of the U.S. government "evil" could—by his own standards—be labeled an evildoer. Just as Jesus strongly condemned the ostentatiously religious Pharisees for their ungodly actions, the actual nature of Bush's religiosity is open to debate. To even suggest such a possibility would enrage many Americans because Bush has successfully co-opted a religious "brand" to the extent that he stands as the definer of Christianity rather than the other way around. Referring to the true nature of religious individuals, Jesus tells us that we "will know them by their fruits." In the case of Bush, there is an evangelical tradition that finds his powerful efforts on behalf of wealth and war to be in obvious conflict with the principles of Jesus Christ.[9] Traditions of men and justifications of court chaplains notwithstanding, evidence can be found through a literal reading of Matthew, Mark, or Luke.

In truth, from his upbringing to his present position, Bush's life more closely resembles Caesar's than it does Christ's. Acting as a frontman for those seeking political and economic power through the unequal yoking of the church and the world, he presides over an empire reminiscent of Babylon or Rome. Bush has been widely compared to William McKinley, not to William Jennings Bryan.[10] Like Bush, McKinley was a professed Christian who was surrounded by pragmatic secularists primarily interested in domestic power, corporate wealth, and overseas empire. President McKinley's faith should not be dismissed as unauthentic, but nothing about it interfered with traditional worldly politics. Similarly, Bush may have genuine Christian convictions, but his religious base of support receives encouraging but empty talk about moral and social issues while the Wall Street wing of the party receives the vast majority of administrative action. When push comes to shove, Bush invariably sides with the party's economic conservatives, not with the social conservatives. A perfect example of this betrayal was his crucial support for Rockefeller-liberal, pro-choice senator Arlen Specter over conservative, pro-life congressman Pat Toomey in the 2004 Pennsylvania GOP primary.[11] Meanwhile, tens of millions of sincere Christians have put their faith—they call it "trust"—in this man, and he does not deflect this adulation. For them, Bush has become the measure of all things American, conservative, Republican, and Christian.

A portion of a 1900 speech delivered by Bryan in Baltimore must be quoted at length on the grounds of importance and timeliness:

> A Republican Senator said the other day that God opened the door of the Philippine Islands, pushed us in and shut the door. The question that arose in my mind was, who told him so? When a man tells me that it is God's will, I demand to know when God told him so. . . . I believe in God; I believe that He influences the thoughts and the purposes of men; but I am not willing to blame God for every thought and every purpose that a man may have. . . . The Bible tells us that nineteen hundred years ago, the devil took the Saviour up on a high mountain and pointed out all the kingdoms of the earth and their glory and offered them to him if he would fall down and worship him . . . When the Republican leaders were taken up on a high mountain and shown the Philippine Islands, instead of saying, 'Get thee behind me, Satan,' they

hunted up the Spanish monarch, and said, 'We will give you $2.50 apiece for the Filipinos.' I want to denounce this doctrine that God has selected the Republican party to wage in His name a war of conquest. . . . I will not deny that there may be prophets to-day. But the trouble is to tell the true prophets from the false ones. . . . There may be prophets, but you will pardon me if I express it as my deliberate opinion that when God gets ready to speak to the American people he will choose somebody besides Mark Hanna as his mouth-piece.[12]

Bryan finished this portion of his campaign speech by saying, "Against the infernal doctrine of conquest, I want to place the words of the Master himself, that He came not to destroy but to save." It would be easy enough to substitute Iraq for the Philippine Islands and Karl Rove, Dick Cheney, or Don Rumsfeld for Mark Hanna. Is there any Democratic leader who would dare, or even think, to utter such words in a public forum today?

Bryan made appropriate use of scriptural language in the public arena. When biblical phrases were used, they were in the service of ideals and practices compatible with Christianity: justice, honesty, freedom, and peace. Bryan believed that all people should strive to be on "God's side." He was not a politician who routinely flattered his supporters or tickled their ears with boasts of having God on "our side." When thinking of Bryan's sermon-like speeches such as "Naboth's Vineyard" from 1898 or "Prince of Peace" from 1904, it is difficult to imagine that Bush could deliver them with conviction, let alone actually write them. Bush's words are provided by speechwriters who presumably think they are clever because they are evoking Christian language to push the right buttons of listeners, and apparently Bush himself does not recognize inappropriate wording when he sees it. When he declared war against terrorism in November 2001, Bush paraphrased the words of Christ: "You're either with us or against us." On the first anniversary of 9/11, Bush said, "This ideal of America is the hope of all mankind. . . . That hope still lights our way. And the light shines in the darkness. And the darkness has not overcome it." In the Bible, Jesus Christ is the hope of creation and the light of the world. Bush has cited his favorite hymn and autobiography title, "A Charge to Keep," in saying our charge is to "do everything we can to protect the American homeland." In the actual Charles Wesley song, the charge refers to "a God to glorify" and "a never-dying soul to save." During his 2003 State of the Union address, Bush borrowed language from an old revival song in declaring, "The need is great. Yet there's power, wonder-working power, in the goodness and idealism and faith of the American people." According to the song, there is "power,

power, wonder-working power in the blood of the Lamb." Such misuse of scripture and Christian imagery is not only inappropriate but also blasphemous. Civil religion is a type of idolatry as faith is transferred from God to man and loyalty is taken from heaven and given to one portion of the world.[13]

Even with all of his enthusiasm for politics and social reform, Bryan never made the mistake of confusing the American Republic with the Kingdom of God. Certainly his faith informed his political views, but he was not trying to build a Constantinian state or man-created theocracy. Bryan advocated for sociopolitical policies not only because he believed in them as a Christian but because the majority of Americans shared his views.[14] He was not trying to impose something on the people that they themselves did not want. Bryan was personally committed above all else to God and to Christianity as he understood it, but in the temporal realm he believed in democracy more than anything else. To him, popular sovereignty was a logical extension of Christianity since humans share a common creator, God disregards worldly rank, man has been given free will, and the dispersal of power is the safest approach in a fallen world. Bryan's philosophy can be summed up in the idealistic words of the South Dakota state motto: "Under God, the People Rule." It is not just the wise, wealthy, or well-connected who rule but the people as a whole.

Today, it is difficult to think of many nationally known Democratic politicians who are evangelical Christians. Millions of rank-and-file Democrats are evangelicals. Many if not most are blacks who have their own rich tradition in American religious history, but the number of white evangelical Democrats continues to dwindle.[15] To find a white liberal Democrat in a local evangelical church is unusual today. This is why Bryan seems like such an exotic creature when we consider his religious views in relation to his political views. In recent decades, Senators Mark Hatfield (R-OR) and Harold Hughes (D-IA) probably come closest among prominent white politicians in resembling Bryan. Hatfield and Hughes were both liberal populists and evangelical Christians during the 1960s and 1970s. Examples of evangelicals known as conservative populists include Senator Jesse Helms (R-NC), Congressman John Kasich (R-OH), and Senator Tom Coburn (R-OK). These two sets of populist politicians certainly possess some differing emphases because of the Left/Right split of Jeffersonianism, but both have been characterized by a deeper, more consistent embrace of theologically orthodox, biblically based Christianity than anyone found within the George W. Bush administration.

There are many African Americans who have combined liberal populist ideology with traditional Christian theology (albeit with less emphasis on doctrinal purity than many evangelicals). Examples from the civil rights generation of the 1960s include Martin Luther King Jr., Ralph Abernathy, Hosea Williams, and Fannie Lou Hamer. Congresswoman Barbara Lee (D-CA) is a more recent example of an elected official with this perspective. In September 2001, the Senate voted 98–0 and the House voted 420–1 to authorize President Bush to use military force as he saw fit in retaliation for the 9/11 terrorist attack. As a result, he began a war with Afghanistan. Lee cited her Christian convictions as one reason for being the lone dissenter: "I take my faith seriously. I'm not going to wave the Bible. . . . But let me tell you: I am a person of deep faith. I think my vote was based in my religion and my faith. Where else do you go to at a time like this?"[16] Turning from evangelicalism with its roots in the Protestant Reformation, we could mention Roman Catholics such as labor leader Cesar Chavez, Governor Robert Casey (D-PA), Congressman David Bonior (D-MI), and Congresswoman Marcy Kaptur (D-OH) on the populist Left. Examples on the populist Right include activist Phyllis Schlafly, presidential candidate Alan Keyes, Congressman Chris Smith (R-NJ), and Congressman Steve Chabot (R-OH). Strong religious belief is an important counterweight to corporate power in the American political context. Attachment to something higher than money and material possessions can negate much of the appeal of business-bestowed favor. That is why sincere religion often goes hand in hand with populism.

Although he has a well-publicized Christian reputation, George W. Bush acts as if he has never read the Hebrew prophetic scriptures, the Magnificat, the Sermon on the Mount, most of the rest of the four Gospels, the book of James, or Revelation chapters 13–18. His is a stunted, if not twisted, type of Christianity. The modern Democratic Party is not able to take advantage of this weakness and inconsistency because it has ceded the ground of religion and morality to the Republican Party. One exception to this ceding might be Sundays on the campaign trail when white candidates show up at A.M.E. and black Baptist churches. As a result of the national Democratic Party's wholesale abandonment of serious Christianity, the Republican Party has inherited millions of voters despite its exploitative approach and questionable theology. A century ago, under Bryan's leadership, the Democratic Party knew how to talk to those who took the Bible and their relationship with God seriously. Many important Democrats could credibly speak the language and capture the hearts and minds of Christians. They could condemn the Republicans on moral and spiritual grounds without provoking eye rolls or laughter. As an institution, today's Democratic Party has virtually abandoned all claims to knowing anything about the Bible. Even if we assume that such ignorance is a principled stance reflecting a progressive, enlightened philosophy, it is still problematic on other levels, including cultural literacy and political expediency. When Vermont's former governor Howard Dean was the front-runner for the 2004 presidential nomination there were concerns that he was a secular-minded candidate unlikely to appeal to religious voters. Asked to identify his favorite book of the New Testament, Dean answered, "Job," and went on at some length with an arid explanation. Unfortunately, he was talking about an Old Testament book—a mistake someone familiar with the Bible likely would not make. Even a Democratic candidate who tries to reach out to religious voters botches the attempt because it is not coming from a place of reality. It comes off as a transparent political ploy.

Condemning slavery in 1781, Thomas Jefferson wrote, "I tremble for my country when I reflect that God is just, that his justice cannot sleep forever." Condemning corporate power in 1899, William Jennings Bryan said,

> When God made man as the climax of creation he looked upon his work and said that it was good . . . We looked upon his work and said that it was not quite as good as it might be, and so we made a fictitious person called a corporation . . . When God made man he breathed into him a soul and warned him that in the next world he would be held accountable for the deeds done in the flesh, but when we made our man-made man we did not give him a soul, and if he can avoid punishment in this world he need not worry about the hereafter. . . . We are not dealing with the natural man; we are not dealing with natural rights. We are dealing with the man-made man and artificial privileges. . . . Government must protect the God-made man from the man-made man.[17]

Even though Democrats presumably want to marshal their strongest arguments against Republicans, one cannot imagine John Kerry condemning the war in Iraq by saying it is an evil enterprise contrary to the teachings of the Prince of Peace. Hillary Clinton is unlikely to condemn globalization by saying that the corporations behind it are like the ambitious men who built the Tower of Babel as a challenge to God. You will not hear such things coming from Kerry or Clinton partly because they do not hold these positions and partly because they do not think in these terms.

The point is not that Christians have a monopoly on populism or social morality. Obviously there have been and continue to be people of other religions and those with no religion who possess Jeffersonian-style values and virtues. But political parties want to win elections, and the vast majority of

Americans are professing Christians. When a party is successfully depicted as being anti-Christian, it becomes increasingly difficult to attract the votes of Christians who take their religion seriously. The modern Democratic Party certainly does not need to embrace theocracy to solve the problem; what is needed is tolerance in terms of candidates nominated and issues stressed. Exchanging dogmatic secularism for pluralism and majoritarianism would be a significant step toward a more electorally viable position.

Democratic Standard Bearers

With his economic populism and pacifistic foreign policy, if William Jennings Bryan had been the 2004 Democratic presidential nominee, he might have been able to defeat George W. Bush since the election was held during a time of corporate scandals and an unpopular war. Bryan was an evangelical Christian whose personal lifestyle, ecclesiastical involvement, and prominence in moralistic political endeavors would have put Bush's brand of religious politics to shame. In addition to his clear voice in favor of popular sovereignty and international peace, Bryan's traditional values in regard to religion and culture and natural ability to relate to average Americans might well have made him a winning candidate in 2004. At the very least, the Great Commoner would not have been saddled with the liabilities—privileged background, haughty demeanor, oratory deficiencies, policy inconsistencies, corporate indebtedness, and war complicity—possessed by John Forbes Kerry. The fact that the Democratic Party nominated Kerry, and therefore could not present a clear contrast to the Republican nominee on the most pressing issues of the day, is a direct result and clear example of its earlier abandonment of Jeffersonianism.

In 1904, when the Democratic Party nominated Alton B. Parker as its standard bearer, two-time nominee Bryan gave only minimal support to Parker because he had no real differences with the Republican nominee on the central question of plutocracy. One hundred years later, the plutocratic Kerry was hailed by every faction of the party, from Kucinich to Lieberman. Prominent anticorporate and antiwar activists far to the Left of the Democratic establishment almost universally rejected Nader and other Jeffersonian-minded third-party candidates while strongly pushing Kerry's candidacy. That path of expedience was not the path taken by Bryan in 1892 or 1920 when faced with Democratic nominees who were incompatible with his own beliefs. In the case of 1904, Bryan opposed Parker's nomination strenuously before and during the convention, but he ultimately supported him because Parker's forthright condemnation of imperialism reflected the views of most Democrats and clearly set Parker apart from the Republican nominee. None of that was true a century later. Kerry was given a blank check even though he was out of step with grassroots Democrats on the Iraq War and supported the goal of American global hegemony.

If Bush had run against someone like Bryan, he probably would have emphasized different issues and projected a different persona. He might have dropped some of his down-home Texas affectations and boasted of his blue-blooded, Ivy League background, and Bush might have been the one stirring up fears about ignorant, religious fanaticism while trying to appeal to yuppies and secularists. With such a contest, it is likely the red state/blue state map would have looked quite different. Bush probably would have carried more East Coast and West Coast states, and Bryan would have done much better than Kerry in the Midwest and South. The Democratic Party's turning away from Jeffersonianism between Bryan's last presidential campaign in 1908 and Humphrey's first in 1960 has endangered its electoral viability in many parts of the nation, including traditional Democratic strongholds. Despite this history, if the Democrats had deigned to adopt something like the Kansas City platform of 1900 instead of the tepid, status quo-affirming Boston platform of 2004, and if they had chosen a nominee in harmony with the party's pledges, they would likely be in the White House today.

Although criticized by Republicans for being so liberal, powerful Democrats such as Senators John Kerry and Hillary Clinton do not even come close to being as liberal as Senator Russ Feingold or Congresswoman Cynthia McKinney. In the 2004 election, Feingold ran five percentage points ahead of Kerry in Wisconsin. He beat his Republican opponent by a margin of 11 percent while Kerry's margin of victory in the state was 0.4 percent. Feingold's popularity stems not so much from being a leftist as from being a populist. He supports the entire range of Jeffersonian tenets, including fiscal responsibility. He earns the respect of those who disagree with him on particular issues because he is a man of integrity who speaks with a clear voice; this is even true for some who disagree with his pro-choice views on abortion. Feingold openly condemns the influence of the Democratic Leadership Council, a group which has become almost synonymous with party leadership since 1992. McKinney ruffled so many feathers in Washington that the party establishment recruited a primary opponent in Georgia to defeat her in 2002. She made a comeback two years later with principles intact. Many antiwar conservatives disagree with McKinney's stands on social issues, but they can respect her opposition to the Iraq War, her questions concerning Middle East policy, and her skepticism toward U.S. government attempts to control the world.

Politicians such as Feingold and McKinney are able to serve in Washington at the pleasure of their local constituents, but it is unlikely they will ever achieve real power within the national party. Today's Democratic Party does not have a Jefferson, Jackson, or Bryan to nurture and protect such populists. Swimming upstream against both party and media elites, they are ignored, mocked, or attacked when they attempt to gain access to a national forum. Meanwhile, such supposed leftists as Kerry and Clinton are given great deference because they have the right friends, the correct positions, and large treasuries. The disingenuous nature of their careers and campaigns is politely ignored while the flaws, real and imagined, of party mavericks are trumpeted by the smug talking heads and the frothy news magazines. If Senator Feingold were to somehow gain the Democratic presidential nomination, he would likely be given the same treatment that Bryan was in 1896 or that Goldwater was given in 1964 by leaders of the national party. That is, he would be abandoned if not attacked. The leaders of both major parties would rather see their party lose an election if losing is the only way to retain control of the organization and to stay faithful to their true, usually unstated principles. This partly explains why the exceedingly rare non-Establishment presidential nominees tend to lose the general election. Genuine rabble-rouser candidates may excite the grassroots, but they do not generally appeal to those characterized by green of a different sort. As those who pay the piper, party financiers are used to calling the tune, and they resent musical interlopers sincerely playing populist songs.

Democrats and National Security

After the 2004 election, the Democratic Leadership Council argued that Republicans won because Democrats were seen as weak on national security. DLC founder Al From advised Democrats, "Come to terms with the main reason we lost the red states: Too many Americans doubt whether Democrats will be tough enough in the war on terror. . . . Democrats owe the country a muscular strategy of our own. We need to be the party of Harry Truman and John Kennedy, not Michael Moore." This is an odd argument. Democrats nominated two Vietnam veterans—Gore and Kerry—both of whom were on the hawkish side as senators, in two successive presidential elections. As the 2004 campaign got under way, Gore's 2000 campaign manager Donna Brazile publicly anticipated From's words by calling for a "muscular internationalism" as opposed to traditional Republican isolationism and the ideas of the "peace wing" of the Democratic Party. Brazile placed herself squarely in the tradition of bellicose twentieth-century presidents and Senator "Scoop" Jackson, who is accurately described as "the Democratic mentor of some of today's most prominent Republican hawks." Brazile's commentary was published in the *Wall Street Journal,* a publication presumably read by few rank-and-file Democrats but conducive to corporate-friendly party leaders. It is entitled "What Would Scoop Do?" which invites the response, Probably the opposite of what Jesus would do. Democrats almost unanimously supported the launching of the open-ended war on terror, including the war against Afghanistan. Party leaders of both houses of Congress supported Bush's war with Iraq. Ex-president Bill Clinton stood with his friend Tony Blair in backing Bush's hard-line, ultimately violent approach.[18] Of the presidential contenders who sat in Congress, all of the first-tier candidates for the 2004 nomination (Kerry, Edwards, Lieberman, and Gephardt) and the 2008 nomination (Clinton, Kerry, Edwards, and Bayh) voted for the war resolution in October 2002. During the 2004 campaign, John "Reporting for Duty" Kerry milked his brief stint in Vietnam for all it was worth (he was in the war zone for five months, which was still five months more than draft dodgers Clinton, Bush, and Cheney).

Kerry promised to send *more* troops to Iraq, not less, and he certainly did not propose withdrawing the ones who are there. Americans want a government that defends our country, but by November 2004 it had become clear to most that the war in Iraq had nothing to do with defending America. It was an offensive war from the beginning and for Democratic leaders in Washington to later express surprise about this fact reveals them as either dishonest or dense. A legitimate rationale for the war was that the despotic and murderous record of Saddam Hussein warranted an American invasion to liberate the Iraqi people. This case can be made and debated, but it has nothing to do with national defense. Instead of calling Bush to account for lies told and lives lost, Kerry supported the war every step of the way and hinted that Iran might be next on his list of targets. During the fall campaign, Kerry declared that even if he had known that Saddam Hussein had had no weapons of mass destruction (WMDs), he *still* would have voted to give Bush a blank check to wage war. By the end of the campaign, Kerry was actually more hawkish than Bush.[19] It is wrong to think that Kerry lost because he was insufficiently militaristic.

Muscular American imperialism is not a winning issue for any political party. Politicians usually cloak their imperial designs while campaigning because the idea of expending American blood and money in obscure places halfway around the world does not appeal to average Americans. They care far more about practical domestic issues. The U.S. government acting as policeman of the world has never been a popular idea among Americans. In the mid-1970s, even Hubert Humphrey assured the country that he did not believe in this role. It is costly and implies that our own society has reached such a state of perfection that we can easily afford to look elsewhere for problems to solve. Meddling in other people's affairs creates enemies and can actually make our own people less safe. There is a difference between being a helpful big brother and being an arrogant empire. Even if we concede the existence of good intentions on our part, perception becomes reality for people in the rest of the world. The Iraq War was never really popular. A vast majority of Americans rallied around the president when the invasion began in 2003, but there was widespread resistance throughout 2002 when the idea was first raised because many Americans did not see Saddam Hussein as a genuine threat to our country. After the much-touted WMDs failed to materialize and the American death count continued to rise after Bush's declaration of "Mission Accomplished," opposition to the war grew. During the 2004 fall campaign, half of Americans believed the war was a mistake. A year later, a majority felt that way. According to a Harris poll published in the *Wall Street Journal,* 53 percent said taking military action against Iraq was the "wrong thing to do," and only 34 percent thought it was right. The shift in opinion, depending on circumstances, indicates that support for the war had always been soft and conditional.[20]

If a Democratic presidential candidate had taken a strong and principled stand against the war from the beginning in 2002—not a double-talker such as Wesley Clark or a multilateral imperialist such as Howard Dean—he or she might well have motivated antiwar Americans and educated the many who were on the fence. Second-tier candidates—Al Sharpton, Carol Moseley Braun, and Dennis Kucinich—tried to do this, but they lacked the blessing of the mainstream media and party high rollers, plus each carried too much negative baggage to be viable options for most Americans (e.g., Kucinich's flip-flop on abortion called into question his integrity and his New Age spirituality would not have endeared him to Middle America had it become widely known). Ironically, it was the "unelectable" Democrats who had the right message to win the election, while the "electable" ones could not embrace the message because the bestowers of respectability were united in support of an unpopular war. If ever there was an election season that cried out for a clear, credible, and culturally mainstream voice with Bryan-like views on foreign policy, it was 2004. Before World War II and at the beginning of the Cold War, the Republican Party had Senator Robert

Taft even though it refused to nominate him for president. A half-century later, Senator Russell Feingold is as close as can be found in the Democratic Party but he has little chance of being nominated given the current cast of party managers and financiers, not to mention the national leadership's embrace of Hamiltonianism since the 1930s.

Americans are not pacifists. The vast majority are not even close to the quasi pacifism of Bryan. We live in a country that glorifies the military. Still, it must be said that most Americans are also not as callous and martial as those who rule in Washington; after all, it is their loved ones who are personally experiencing the brutality and bloodletting. Presidents may fret about wars while photographers snap pictures and reporters note their burdened souls, but they do not send their children into combat. Like the Bush administration, most Americans are unilateralists. In fact, they are unilateralists of an isolationist, not internationalist, sort, so it is a unilateralism that exceeds that of Republican leaders. Unlike many Democrats, they do not think we need the permission of Kofi Annan, Jacques Chirac, or any other foreigner to wage war in defense of ourselves. The question is, Was this truly the case with Iraq or were there other motives behind the attack and occupation? Many patriotic citizens either opposed the war from the start or soured on it when they realized that the Iraqi government had been no threat to us. Americans who support more of an interventionist foreign policy tend to view our government as a good Samaritan on the global stage. In most cases, they wrongly attribute their own well-meaning attitudes and Judeo-Christian values to their leaders. They assume that these leaders operate on the basis of moral idealism. This is a largely mistaken impression. Regardless of the rhetoric used as policy justification, our leaders are usually guided by the principles of political realism and their less than altruistic policies have led to the widespread perception of the U.S. not so much as a good Samaritan as a schoolyard bully. Most people are not grateful for U.S. intervention because it is often accompanied by military violence and political domination.

Opposition to an ongoing war is a complicated thing, emotionally and intellectually. Americans find it difficult to believe that friends and family members are wounding and being wounded, killing and being killed for ignoble reasons. Even if it might be true, the cognitive dissonance is far too great for most to embrace such a thought. Cindy Sheehan, mother of Army Specialist Casey Sheehan who was killed in Iraq, is an exception. She has become a grassroots antiwar leader by publicly blaming Bush for her son's death and calling for the withdrawal of all U.S. troops. Referring to Senator Hillary Clinton, Sheehan has stated, "After she met with me, she said she has to make sure our sons didn't die in vain. That is a totally Republican talking point. . . . I would love to support Hillary for president if she would come out against the travesty in Iraq. But I don't think she can speak out against the occupation because she supports it." While Sheehan describes Clinton as "a brilliant woman," she adds, "But to characterize her as one of the leading liberals in Congress is absolutely false. With her position as a senator she's become more 'let's see which way the wind blows, and what's going to get me re-elected or elected, or how am I going to benefit from this.'"[21] While opportunism does seem to be a factor, Clinton's ideology as a Humphrey Democrat is probably the main reason she supports the war. This ideology has always been supportive of imperial military endeavors. In November 2005, when hawkish congressman John Murtha (D-PA) called for withdrawal of all U.S. troops from Iraq as soon as possible, party leaders gave him no support. Republican leaders then crafted an immediate-withdrawal resolution as a political trap for Democrats, forcing them to go on record about this contentious issue. Almost all Democrats took the path of evasion and convenience by voting against the resolution. While an obvious ploy, it was also a clear antiwar resolution that those with the courage of their convictions should have been able to support. The resulting 303–3 vote is reminiscent of the Senate's 88–2 vote for the Gulf of Tonkin Resolution in 1964.

Average Americans may be turned off by the self-promoting, clownish aspects of filmmaker Michael Moore. Still, Moore's generally commonsense, populist views are based on majoritarian values. These values are perhaps better exemplified by the enduring popularity of heartland musicians such as Johnny Cash, Bob Dylan, Bruce Springsteen, and John Mellencamp. They symbolize American roots music, a successful blending of most of the cultures that constitute the USA—not in an artificial, forced way, but in a natural way. All have been generally antiwar. Unlike Moore, they are not tainted by shrill delivery, adoption by the Hollywood crowd, and excessive partisanship. Like Moore, they are closer in spirit to the majority of American people than are Al From and his Democratic Leadership Council associates. The DLC is not an honest surveyor of the political landscape. Its primary objective is to retain control of the party. To consolidate their dominant position, DLC leaders have formed a social-issue alliance with gun control advocates, gay rights supporters, and mainstream feminists. In doing so, they have played a part in redefining the word *progressive* in ways contrary to its traditional economic and foreign policy sense (thus the name of a subsidiary: the Progressive Policy Institute). The DLC wishes to attract red-state support by talking about personal responsibility and traditional values. The words ring a bit hollow when the group that gave us Bill Clinton talks about rewarding those who "play by the rules" and helping "parents protect their children from a coarsening culture."[22] The DLC continues to be allied with the Clintons so it is unlikely to be accepted by many as a credible champion of ethics and morality.

The prowar position of Senate minority leader Thomas Daschle (D-SD) did not help him to win reelection in 2004, and it may have contributed to his defeat by dispiriting liberal populists. Having courted liberals of the Hollywood/Manhattan variety through "choice" and "orientation" issues and having gone along with the Wall Street/DLC agenda of corporate subservience, big government, economic globalization, and armed international dominance, he found it difficult to stir up loyalty and enthusiasm back home. His wife's job as a high-powered lobbyist and their two million dollar house in Washington made Daschle even more vulnerable to Republican attacks. It did not matter that many of these attacks were coming from a place of hypocrisy. Leaving behind the farmers, ranchers, teachers, clerks, and small business owners of the prairie, the senator had bought into the sophisticated culture of power and wealth, and in 2004 the bill came due. As a result, he became the first Senate party leader to lose his seat since 1952. What did Tom Daschle do after losing? Did he return to Aberdeen to rejoin the South Dakotans he had served for so long? No, he stayed in Washington and continued to serve other masters by joining a K Street corporate law firm. Daschle's life from Catholic altar boy to Capitol Hill populist to NARAL fundraiser and DLC cheerleader serves as a parable of the modern Democratic Party. His career could be seen as one of principle and growth, but in the eyes of most Americans the principles are bad and the growth is in the wrong direction. This is not to say that Democrats should necessarily change their positions on controversial issues. But they might at least face up to the problem by reexamining their philosophical roots and by going beyond knee-jerk responses, reliance on dollars, and glib use of put-downs aimed at those with whom they disagree. While Daschle was losing in South Dakota, his populist neighbor to the north, Byron Dorgan (D-ND), was winning by a 2-to-1 margin.[23]

Democrats and Cultural Controversies

After the 2004 election, DLC leaders argued that there was no need to change the party's stance on issues such as "guns, gay rights, and abortion"; Bill Clinton had, after all, carried red states in two elections while holding the same positions. But Clinton won despite his views on these issues, not because of them. He faced weak, diffident Republican opponents who had alienated their party's base of conservative populists. Support for same-sex marriage and unlimited abortion were unpopular positions in the 1990s and they remain so today. On Election Day 2004, twenty million Americans voted in eleven states on the issue of whether or not to protect traditional marriage and exclude same-sex marriage by state constitutional amendment. The amendments passed in all eleven states by an aggregate 2-to-1 margin. The closest contest was in Oregon, where it won with a mere 57 percent of the vote. The most lopsided result was in Mississippi, where it passed with 86 percent of the vote. This is the state in the union with the largest percentage of African Americans. Most black Christians see homosexuality as unnatural and ungodly. They do not oppose respect and tolerance, but they balk at endorsement and glorification. Traditional marriage outpolled Bush by 26 percent in Mississippi, and many of the Democrats who voted for the amendment were presumably African American. The amendment was popular in the Rust Belt states of Michigan and Ohio, where, again, it outpolled Bush. Kansas, a traditional hotbed of populism, approved a measure 2-to-1 in 2005. The only region of the country that has resisted the popular trend is the old stomping grounds of the Federalist Party: New England.[24]

Public opinion polls that suggest majority support for *Roe v. Wade* are misleading. There is a core minority that wants abortion legal under all circumstances and a similar group that wants it illegal under all circumstances. In the middle is a majority that supports it under certain circumstances. In a poll, you can net either a pro-choice or pro-life majority, depending on how you word the question around those certain circumstances. If you ask, Do you support keeping abortion legal in cases of rape, incest, and life of the woman? a majority will say yes. If you ask, Do you support making abortion illegal except in cases of rape, incest, and life of the mother? a majority will say yes. In fact, the hardcase exceptions are rare. Most abortions are not related to these circumstances. A majority of Americans oppose abortion as a form of birth control or for sex selection. The majority also object to their tax dollars being used to pay for abortions and to abortions performed in the second and third trimesters or without parental consent in the case of minors. The unpopularity of a position does not make it wrong, and a principled politician may need to go against the popular grain on occasion, but the Democratic Party should not delude itself into thinking that its "abortion at-any-time for-any-reason" stance is widely popular.[25] The Liberty Party of the 1840s held an unpopular position on an important issue of its day: abolition of slavery. It sacrificed electoral success in favor of doing what it considered to be the right thing. The Democratic Party may wish to do the same, but it should do so proudly, instead of hiding behind the euphemism *choice*. It should do so with an understanding that abortion historically has nothing to do with women's rights or Democratic liberalism: its roots were in the eugenics movement and the *Playboy* philosophy before it was adopted by feminists in the late 1960s. The party should also do so with the knowledge that it is going to pay a price on election day for being so far "out ahead" of the American people.[26] When it comes to elective termination of pregnancy and state-mandated recognition of homosexuality being viewed as positive goods, four of the Democratic Party's largest constituencies—blue-collar workers, Roman Catholics, Hispanic Americans, and African Americans—tend to disagree with the party's stance; these groups largely hold what has become known as conservative views on such moral and social issues. This does not even count the many Catholics and Southern Baptists who left the party long ago as a result of these issues. An added dose of militarism does not counteract the effects of the divisive cultural issues, and dismissing them as "phony" or "unimportant" is not a sufficient answer.

Pro-choicers often quip that pro-lifers only care about children before they are born. This presupposes a Humphreyite view that concern for human beings is primarily expressed through government programs. A genuine prochild stance does not necessitate support for the welfare state. A more valid critique of the pro-life movement concerns the warfare state. The term *pro-life* is a misnomer: most activists are only antiabortion. There is rarely a consistent support-for-life ethic present. Ironically, many of the most ardent proponents for the protection of innocent unborn human life are the loudest advocates for war, with its attendant destruction of innocent human life. These deaths are usually deliberate and inevitable. This is true for both civilians and soldiers.

If Bryan were still on the political stage today, he would most likely be pro-life in every way. He opposed capital punishment on moral grounds in his day, and he was close to pacifism during the last twenty years of his life. Incidentally, opposition to war is far more linked in philosophical consistency to antiabortionism than is opposition to the death penalty, since the latter assumes the person is not innocent but rather guilty of a heinous crime. Bryan's pro-life ethic was so strong that he opposed this ultimate human punishment despite Old Testament sanction. Humphrey supported *Roe v. Wade* as the abortion issue heated up in the mid-1970s.[27] In 1972, the U.S. Supreme Court struck down most death penalty statutes as unconstitutional because they were not being evenhandedly applied to defendants. In

1974, the U.S. Senate considered a bill (S. 1401) establishing new standards to pave the way for reimposition of capital punishment for various federal crimes. The bill easily passed, but Humphrey and many of his allies voted against it. This was probably motivated by the perceived link between the death penalty and racial discrimination. During the past decade, national Democrats have taken the issue of capital punishment off the electoral table as a partisan issue. Bill Clinton, Al Gore, and John Kerry joined Republicans in supporting the death penalty for at least some crimes. This was one of the many issues that separated Ralph Nader from his three Democratic opponents.

While promoting his new book in 2005, former president Jimmy Carter, in the words of a reporter, "condemned all abortions and chastised his party for its intolerance of candidates and nominees who oppose abortion." Carter himself said, "I've never been convinced, if you let me inject my Christianity into it, that Jesus Christ would approve abortion." He told reporters that he thought some Democratic leaders were outside of the American mainstream and hindering the party's electoral chances by "overemphasizing the abortion issue." During the same press conference, Carter disagreed with Bush's Iraqi war policy: "I have a commitment to worship the Prince of Peace, not the Prince of Preemptive War."[28] With his evangelical Christianity, humble family origins, meteoric rise, self-described populism, and interest in world peace, James Earl Carter could be considered the figure closest to William Jennings Bryan in the Democratic Party of the past thirty years. There are, however, also important differences between the two. Carter's Bryan-like rhetoric about abortion and war is rather late in coming. When he was in a position to influence his party and nation on abortion, he championed its legal status. As a candidate in 1976, Carter opposed both a constitutional amendment to outlaw abortion and one that would have returned legislative choice to the states by reversing *Roe v. Wade.* His opposition to federal funding led to criticism from some pro-choicers, but he never wavered in his support for the Court's 1973 decision. Sarah Weddington, the winning attorney in *Roe v. Wade,* was chosen by Carter to be a presidential assistant. It is unlikely that someone genuinely opposed to abortion would have made such an appointment.

The "Reagan build-up" of the U.S. military began under Carter. The bloody Soviet war in Afghanistan was privately welcomed as a Vietnam-style "trap" by the Carter administration, which publicly feigned outrage. Carter's support for the oppressive shah of Iran triggered the hostage crisis. Professed concern for human rights was also nowhere to be found in his support for the Indonesian dictatorship that brutalized East Timor. The president was personally friendly with the Soviet and Chinese dictators, Leonid Brezhnev and Deng Xiaoping, respectively, as human rights were trumped by geopolitical and economic considerations. Carter's links to big business certainly distinguish him from Bryan. Alex Garnish, a Wallace delegate from Massachusetts at the 1976 national convention, noted during a speech that the Carter bandwagon ran on "Standard Oil, not peanut oil."[29] The close relationship between Carter and David Rockefeller, who would later decline the president-elect's offer to be secretary of the Treasury, was quite unlike the frosty relationship between Bryan and John D. Rockefeller, who was a patron of Bryan's opponents McKinley and Taft. Governor Carter accepted Rockefeller's invitation to be a founding member of the elite Trilateral Commission in 1973, and he joined the Council on Foreign Relations after leaving the White House. Being on both sides of an issue is nothing new for Carter. As liberal speechwriter Robert Shrum discovered during his brief stint on the campaign trail with Carter during the 1976 primaries, the candidate was deliberately fuzzy on the issues, coldly calculating, and disingenuous. This seems strange today because Carter has worked hard since leaving office to rehabilitate his reputation through well-publicized good deeds. Nevertheless, Carter's presidential hawkishness, imperial predilections, corporate subservience, and political straddling remain un-Bryanlike.

Jimmy Carter's belated recognition that there is strong opposition to abortion rights in the American electorate and little support for the idea in the Christian tradition is reminiscent of some of Bill Clinton's recent maneuvers. Late in the 2004 campaign, Clinton reportedly advised John Kerry that he should defuse the gay marriage issue by supporting state bans. When public opinion on the Iraq War had clearly shifted by late 2005, Clinton declared that the invasion was a "big mistake." Soft-pedaling your positions and flip-flopping on issues will take you only so far. When there is a seemingly clear, viable alternative present, you tend to be out of luck in terms of attracting support from all sides of a controversial issue. People will rightly wonder if your latest pronouncement is a change in position or just a change of strategy after realizing that the position is a net political liability. This is one of the dilemmas facing a pragmatic Democratic Party.

The DLC's New Democrats are denounced by *The Nation* and other left-wing Democrats for being conservative, but they are not conservative in a George Wallace or "Reagan Democrat" sort of way (even setting aside the racial component of Wallace's ideology). They generally affirm post-1970 liberal dogma when it comes to moral and cultural issues. They are also not conservative in the Jeffersonian sense of the word. Jefferson was decentralist and libertarian. The set of Democratic Party talking points distributed in

2005 when Samuel Alito was nominated by President Bush for the Supreme Court was entitled "Judge 'Scalito' Has Long History of States Rights, Anti-Civil Rights, and Anti-Immigrant Rulings." Regardless of the accuracy of the characterization, it is ironic for Democrats to lead with the supposedly scandalous accusation of support for states' rights. The Democratic Party itself had a long history of supporting states' rights until the 1930s. Another factor that has contributed to the unpopularity of modern Democrats is their tendency to support unelected judges in lieu of elected representatives. Democrats often turn to undemocratic courts for the adoption of measures lacking popular support, thus revealing a deep-seated elitism. Modern Democrats tend to get it wrong—from a Jeffersonian viewpoint—even when it comes to what has been the party's most Jeffersonian tenet since the advent of the New Deal. An offspring of 1980s political correctness, multiculturalism is a moving-away from Jeffersonian ethnic inclusiveness into condescending glorification of "The Other" and minimization of American traditions.[30] It is condescending because it comes from a group of privileged and powerful people who are well-insulated from cultural heterogeneity in their day-to-day lives, with the possible exceptions of deferential students, dependent employees, and domestic servants. Luther compared the world to a drunken man who falls off his horse first on the left side and then over-compensates thus falling off on the right. In reaction to the ethnic snobbery and racial prejudice of some, multiculturalism is forced upon all. Racism and multiculturalism both overemphasize our differences. Ethnic inclusiveness acknowledges differences and respects the right to be different—even when it is seen as incorrect—but stresses what we have in common.

In addition to multiculturalism, other issues relating to ethnicity or race have been addressed by the party in ways injurious to both its ideological integrity and electoral success. The benefits of affirmative action have been stated quite well, but its drawbacks have been either ignored or silenced with an accusation of racism. This is true when it comes to the question of group justice vs. individual justice, its patronizing tendency, its disregard of economic class, and its potential divisiveness. Many well-intentioned Americans view these programs as reverse discrimination. Such concerns about fairness have been unsuccessfully swept under the rug. Also, there are many libertarians in the Jeffersonian tradition who may agree with the inclusive goal but disagree with the coercive means. Immigration has been handled in a similarly high-handed yet ham-fisted manner. Instead of acknowledging traditional Jeffersonian concerns about labor and cultural issues associated with immigration and recognizing the obvious difference between arriving legally and illegally, the Democratic elite joins the Republican elite in supporting porous borders for the sake of cheap labor and ethnic pandering. The latter approach is aimed more at interest groups than at actual voters since legal immigrants themselves tend to oppose multiculturalism and illegal immigration.[31]

Eight decades after the *Scopes* trial, the debate between evolution and creation is in the news again with controversial public education decisions by a state board in Kansas and a local board in Pennsylvania. Today, creationism dons a new label: intelligent design. The details of Darwinian evolution are debated in academic circles, and there is evidence in scientific fields beyond macrobiology that could call into question some of its assumptions, but the vast majority of contemporary scientists accept it as well-established truth.[32] In this sense, it is misleading to pretend that a theologically grounded theory, such as intelligent design, is as scientifically valid as a biologically grounded theory, such as evolution. The changes in name and tactics by opponents of evolution seem somewhat dishonest. On the other hand, the modern practice of setting nature in opposition to the supernatural would have come as a surprise to eminent scientists such as Galileo Galilei, Johannes Kepler, Blaise Pascal, Isaac Newton, Michael Faraday, and Louis Pasteur (all of whom believed in God and embraced Christianity). They may have been wrong, but they did not see any inherent contradiction. It is not clear why physics should trump, or even conflict with, metaphysics. As the nineteenth century unfolded, agnosticism, atheism, and, to a lesser extent, pantheism became the philosophical orthodoxies of academic science, so it is not surprising that the most well-known scientists since that time—Darwin, T. H. Huxley, Albert Einstein, Carl Sagan, Stephen Jay Gould, and Stephen Hawking—have not shared the theology of their predecessors. As brilliant as these more recent men have been, they have stood on the shoulders of giants who were almost uniformly theistic. The question is, Have the religious assumptions of earlier scientists been rendered obsolete or shown to be incorrect by new data obtained by later scientists?

Regardless of the origin of the universe and of species found on our planet, human beings in twenty-first-century America continue to debate an issue that was prominent at the very end of Bryan's life. Bryan's participation in the *Scopes* trial would do a great disservice to his legacy. He is remembered more for that event than for anything else, which is an absurd reductionism of his career. If Bryan were alive today, he would probably support the option of teaching divine creation in public schools. He would do so on biblical, democratic, and socioethical grounds. With his secular mindset and reliance of expertise, Humphrey would probably have little interest in the controversy beyond an endorsement of the scientific consensus.

Thomas Jefferson, a progenitor of the idea of separation of church and state and a father of public education, would undoubtedly have an opinion concerning these latest developments. Jefferson was opposed to established churches, priestcraft, superstition, and intellectual bondage, but he was not opposed to religion per se. Even his famous line from an 1800 letter in support of free thinking was linked to the divine: "I have sworn upon the altar of God, eternal hostility against every form of tyranny over the mind of man."[33] As an amateur scientist, he saw no conflict between rational inquiry into nature and belief in a creating God, hence the Declaration's wording "endowed by their Creator." Jefferson's belief in popular sovereignty and strict constructionism and his dislike of judicial tyranny and federal consolidation suggest that he would look with disfavor upon a federal judge striking down a local school board decision as a supposed violation of the U.S. Constitution (a social contract and legal document that mentions neither Darwinian evolution nor intelligent design).[34] At the same time, he would most likely be uncomfortable with the personal demeanor, religious practices, political allegiances, and scientific credentials of the Protestant fundamentalists most vociferously opposed to evolution.

Advocates of evolution find it difficult to accept that under a quasi-democratic system a minority—no matter how educated, intelligent, or enlightened—sometimes has to accede to the wishes of the majority. According to a 2004 CBS opinion survey, 65 percent of Americans favor teaching both creation and evolution in public schools. A 2005 CBS poll shows that 51 percent believe that God created humans in our present form, 30 percent believe that God guided the process of evolution, and 15 percent believe that evolution occurred without any divine involvement.[35] It could be argued that we should let scientists decide what is taught in science classes. This is a valid point, but there are other legitimate arguments: we should allow the public to decide what is taught in public schools and we should allow parents to decide what is taught to their children. These contesting claims represent two different orderings of values and two different perceptions of truth. Evolution is not a partisan issue, and most Americans, regardless of party, are creationists of one sort or another. Democratic leaders are, however, more free to voice support for evolution, genetic engineering, stem cell research, cloning, and other controversial elements of modern science. Secular-minded Republican leaders are forced to downplay their support because well-organized evangelical Christians serve as an important component of the party's base, and they view these trends as Frankensteinian. There are Jeffersonians on the Left who approach bioethical issues without traditional Christian scruples but are wary of what they see as tampering with nature from a place of greed and hubris. They decry the commercialization of science and commodification of life.

When considering the 2000 and 2004 presidential elections, both the popular vote and the electoral college totals are somewhat misleading. Looking at a map of U.S. counties, we find a sea of red with islands of blue mostly representing metropolitan centers. The national Democratic Party is embarrassingly weak in small cities, towns, and rural areas. This is why it has lost five of the last seven presidential elections (a 71 percent failure rate from 1980 to 2004).

The Democratic Party has largely lost Middle America voters because the party is no longer a good fit for them. It is a party of Hamiltonian elitism. Campaign rhetoric to the contrary notwithstanding, its national leadership is antimajoritarian in its conservative economic and foreign policies (subservience to corporations, unrestricted immigration, outsourcing through globalization, multilateral imperialism) and its liberal cultural and moral policies (gun control, unrestricted abortion, homosexual activism, vulgar entertainment, coldness toward Christianity). It is an unpopular mix usually fronted by nominees lacking charisma and any real connection with the vast majority of voters. These nominees are usually far more at home with New York bankers and Hollywood celebrities than with Ohio factory workers and Iowa farmers. For the most part, it is only residual party identification, self-seeking interest groups, a sea of corporate cash, and fearmongering that keep the party somewhat competitive. Some populists are willing to overlook disagreement on moral and social issues if they find a champion on economic and international issues. In other words, some pro-life voters will vote for a pro-choice candidate who is good on bread-and-butter, war-and-peace issues. It is one thing to take an unpopular position on partial-birth abortion, same-sex marriage, and restriction of the Second Amendment. It is quite another to combine those stances with unpopular positions on fundraising, term limits, corporate power, trade policies, and global management. That tips the scale. If the Democratic Party is unwilling to embrace either half of a populist agenda, then the Republican Party is happy to step in and pick up support by paying lip service to the moral and social half.

Sam Smith, a liberal Jeffersonian, concisely summarizes the problem of contemporary Democratic liberalism:

> We have liberals who seem to believe that politics begins and ends with abortion and gay rights, and in a cargo cult that delivers salvation through SUVs, Botox injections, the right wine, and *Vanity Fair*. . . . The decline of the Democratic Party has been accelerated by the growing

number of American subcultures deemed unworthy by its advocates: gun owners, church goers, pickup drivers with confederate flag stickers. Yet the gun owner could be an important ally for civil liberties, the churchgoer a voice for political integrity, the pickup driver a supporter of national healthcare.[36]

We know that such populist coalitions are possible because we have seen numerous examples since the late 1980s. Some even yield a small measure of success. *What's the Matter with Kansas?* illustrates how Republican elitists have welcomed and exploited the multitude of voters turned off by Democratic elitists. Most populists in Kansas have always belonged to the Republican Party, but in the 1890s many left the GOP to join with like-minded Democrats in the new People's Party.[37] Whereas they used to be called "ignorant, radical liberals," their ideological heirs are now derided as "ignorant, radical conservatives" because of the post-New Deal semantic confusion. Most are Republicans. Even within the modern Democratic Party of Kansas, however, there is a streak of populism. Joan Finney was elected governor in 1990 on a populist platform that included support for the creation of initiative and referendum. Although she was a traditional liberal Democrat, Finney received support from Republicans who shared her pro-life views as she successfully unseated a pro-choice, procorporate Republican governor. When Perot ran his populist campaign for president in 1992, Kansas was his fifth best state, in terms of percentage. When given a choice instead of an echo, many average voters will opt out of the divide-and-conquer game, vote for the common good, and decline to be taken for granted by the major parties. It may be that the only hope for a Jeffersonian reunification of the common people in the electoral arena is the creation of a broad-based, ideologically diverse populist party that encompasses everyone from the Green Party on the Left to the Constitution Party on the Right. The Perot 1992 campaign was perhaps the closest we have seen in decades to this range (despite obvious weaknesses stemming from its top-down, one-man nature). Such a party would have to be willing to tolerate disagreement within its ranks on secondary and tertiary issues for the greater good of coalescing around primary issues.

The various transcendent populism efforts during the past twenty years are important not because they have been successful—thus far, each has failed in the end—but because they symbolize the contemporary relevance of Thomas Jefferson's political thought. They suggest that John Taylor's vision of a united common people is slowly being restored.[38] The Federalist vision is that of selfish special interests competing against one another, with government acting as arbiter. A minimalistic government is impossible under such conditions. Ruled by passions as they are, the common people need specialists, wise men, educated individuals, those to the manor born with a proper sense of noblesse oblige to make the final decisions, to put a good foot forward when meeting foreign dignitaries, and to prevent chaos from breaking out at home. This is the perspective of Alexander Hamilton, and it was essentially embraced by Hubert Humphrey. It is the dominant perspective of American political leaders today. We live in a Hamiltonian world. The influence of Jefferson's thought has declined within American liberalism, but some liberals—and self-styled conservatives—remain committed to the ideological tenets he so eloquently expounded. Modern-day Jeffersonians are a distinct minority among politicians. They do not share in the respectability sought after by so many public figures. They rarely win political battles. Still, they are spread throughout America in large numbers, perhaps waiting for a genuine political champion.

Democrats and Electoral Success

It could be argued that national Democratic Party leaders moved from Jeffersonianism to Hamiltonianism because the latter is more successful at the polling place. Five straight Democratic presidential victories in the 1930s and 1940s would seem to support that contention. However, that unusual period was marked by economic depression, world war, and Republican nominees who were unpopular, bland, and guilty of me-tooism. Of the fourteen presidential elections from 1952 to 2004, Democrats lost nine of them. Bill Clinton was the only Democratic president to be reelected since FDR, and even in his case he was opposed by a majority of voters (57 percent in 1992 and 51 percent in 1996). Clinton was an exceptionally talented politician and his victories were largely personal in nature. Scores of gubernatorial, state legislative, and congressional seats were lost by Democrats during his presidency. This included the loss of a majority in both houses of Congress for the first time in forty years. Meanwhile, Jeffersonians within the party gained little as Clinton pursued a Republican-lite agenda ("triangulation") and squandered his political capital through personal self-indulgence.

To use a biblical analogy, one could say that the Democratic Party exchanged its birthright for a mess of pottage. It is true that William Jennings Bryan did not win his three contests as the Democratic nominee, but neither did Hubert Humphrey in 1968 or Humphrey-allied nominees Adlai

Stevenson in the 1950s, Jimmy Carter in 1980, Walter Mondale in 1984, and Al Gore in 2000. Conversely, Bryan carried states a century ago that have since become reliably Republican in presidential elections (Solid South, Rocky Mountain, and Great Plains states).[39] Bryan was also more competitive in several other Republican-dominated states: Indiana, Ohio, North Dakota.

Some might say that circumstances have changed so much since 1908 that it is not surprising—or even regrettable—that the party has lost the Solid South. Bryan was carrying the southern states during a time when Jim Crow laws disenfranchised African Americans. True, but the great expansion of southern black voting since the Voting Rights Act should have added to Democratic majorities. By the 1960s, most blacks had switched from being Republican to Democratic. But didn't Democratic support for civil rights drive many southern whites from the party, thus explaining the net loss of voters? Isn't it for the best because the party was doing the right thing? There is some truth to these assertions, but they are not the whole story. Most southern whites were not slaveholders in the Old South and, as historian Wallace Hettle points out in his enlightening book *The Peculiar Democracy,* most probably opposed secession. Loyalty to the Democratic Party predated national debates over slavery and segregation. Jefferson and Jackson built a solid base throughout the South, and their appeal was not grounded in white supremacy. For most southern Democrats, class was usually a more important issue than race. What did a humbly born southerner have in common with a prep-schooled New Englander or a moneylender of Wall Street? In other words, average whites in the South gravitated toward the party that was not led by wealthy men of the North. They were primarily repelled by the elitism of the Federalist, Whig, and Republican parties and attracted by the populism of Jefferson and Jackson. For most, any proslavery or segregation attraction was secondary.

No doubt many southern whites were racist in their thinking during the 1960s and 1970s, but the same could be said for their northern counterparts. One of the great libels of American history is the idea that bigotry was the essence of what it meant to be a white southerner and that racial prejudice was confined to or primarily found in the South. At times white supremacy may have been more overt in Dixie, but the region has never held a monopoly and was never defined solely by this trait. Most state and local governments in the South remain Democratic. It should have been possible for the national Democratic Party to have built a biracial coalition between its traditional base of support and the new, post-1965 voters. With far fewer resources and much more hostility, the Populist Party put together just such a coalition in the 1890s.[40] The 1982 gubernatorial campaign of George C. Wallace is a more recent example.[41] Instead, national Democrats flaunted their elitism and offered very little to poor, working-class, and middle-class southern whites to assuage their traditional fears of being displaced by black voters—fears that had been successfully exploited for years by wealthy party leaders in the region.

Governor George Wallace supported Governor Jimmy Carter after being bested in the 1976 primaries. Carter would not have defeated Ford without the support of Wallace Democrats in the general election (he carried every southern state except one or two—the best showing for a national Democrat since 1944). What did they get in return for their support? An administration filled with Rockefeller Establishment types in the highest posts, with lesser positions going to representatives of various party factions.[42] Noticeably absent was anyone connected with the Wallace wing of the party, despite its vital role in the victory and its ten million adherents. There was certainly no Jim Allen, Woody Jenkins, or Larry McDonald sitting in the cabinet, let alone Wallace himself. Contrast that with the successful co-optation of Bryan and his supporters in 1912–1913. President Wilson also went with elite appointees, but he gave Bryan the preeminent spot as secretary of state and installed Josephus Daniels as secretary of the navy. Similarly, FDR repaid his Democratic populist and Republican progressive supporters with appointments: Daniels was made the ambassador to Mexico; Ruth Bryan Owen was minister to Denmark; Thomas Walsh was named attorney general but died before taking office; Harold Ickes was appointed secretary of the interior; and Thomas Amlie was nominated for the Interstate Commerce Commission. These appointments may have been mostly window dressing, but they did represent an open show of respect and were an attempt to maintain party unity. In 1976–1977, the average Wallace supporter may not have been paying close attention to the personnel roster of the new administration, but it soon became apparent that Carter's much-publicized piety and folksy manner did not prevent a presidency characterized by Trilateral Commission economic and foreign policies, garnished with things like staff cocaine use, support for legalized abortion, and the usual catering to special interests. By 1980, most Wallace Democrats—and not just in the South—were ready to give Ronald Reagan a try. For the most part, they have stuck with the national Republicans ever since.

White southern Democrats left the national party not so much because of its endorsement of black civil rights but because of its open rejection of populist policy and traditional morality. They may not have liked the taste of the former, but they could not swallow the latter. That was the deal breaker.

The national party could have added the large bloc of African American voters it had gained by 1970 and retained the overwhelming support of traditional constituencies, such as southern Dixiecrats, northern hard hats, and faithful Catholics, despite some turmoil and resistance within the new coalition, if it had only paid enough attention to those longtime Democrats. Even mere rhetorical attention might have been enough. Instead, these voters were taken for granted and the numerically larger old constituencies were exchanged for the new. That is the price of preferring elitism to populism. It may or may not be the right thing to do, but it does not help to win elections. Meanwhile, during each election cycle party leaders make flowery promises and use scare tactics to gain the votes of African Americans. After the votes are counted, these faithful Democrats are ignored until the next election. This bloc of the party has desirable votes but lacks real power because it does not have sufficient dollars. It is political exploitation of the worst sort.[43]

Democratic presidential nominees who were Jeffersonian in rhetoric were successful over their Federalist rivals in five of the six elections from 1796 to 1816. They were successful over their National Republican, Whig, and Republican rivals in six of the eight elections from 1828 to 1856. Hamiltonian rhetoric has never been popular with American citizens. Hamiltonian policies evoke widespread criticism when the majority is paying attention. The most successful Democratic nominees have used Jeffersonian words on the campaign trail even if they didn't follow through on their promises. This truth was evident to the postelection commentators in 2004 who noted that the party would need to find someone like Bill Clinton who can speak in the language of the common people if it wishes to recapture the White House.[44] Such talk is mostly cynical because Democratic movers and shakers are well aware that Clinton and his DLC sponsors are, above all else, servants of corporate America, not the forgotten middle class or the general public. Thinking of stiff, unpopulist-like nominees such as Dukakis, Gore, and Kerry, party leaders are really looking for a more persuasive demagogue. Unfortunately, this is not an honest solution to the problem, and it does not address the deeper issues of philosophy and ideology.

Where did the Democratic Party go? It began leaving Thomas Jefferson and his ideological successors in the 1910s as leadership passed from William Jennings Bryan to Woodrow Wilson. The party made its final migration into the realm of Alexander Hamilton in the 1930s with Franklin Roosevelt acting as guide. It was permanently settled in that nondemocratic land by the time Hubert Humphrey joined in 1944. The Hamiltonian tendencies of today's Democratic Leadership Council are nothing new; they are merely more overt than in the past. With most conservative Jeffersonians being Republicans or ex-Democrats and facing only timid opposition from liberal Jeffersonians within the party, Democratic leaders are under little pressure to return the party to its place of origin. Party electoral self-interest could be an important incentive, but party leaders are players in a bipartisan game rigged so that they reap personal political and economic benefits regardless of the outcome of elections. Thus, the political thought of Thomas Jefferson and the transcendent populist coalitions it has sometimes sparked usually find voice and deed outside the borders of Jefferson's party. It remains to be seen if this will always be so.

NOTES

PREFACE

1. For additional information about the thoughts, careers, and senatorial allies of William Jennings Bryan and Hubert Humphrey, and their Republican counterparts Robert La Follette and Nelson Rockefeller, see Jeff Taylor, *From Radical to Respectable*.

2. Richard F. Pettigrew, *Imperial Washington: The Story of American Public Life from 1870 to 1920*, 240–47; Ferdinand Lundberg, *America's Sixty Families*, 109–48; Gabriel Kolko, *The Triumph of Conservatism: A Reinterpretation of American History, 1900–1916*, 204–82; Philip H. Burch Jr., *Elites in American History*, 2:201–44.

3. Dwight Macdonald, *Henry Wallace: The Man and the Myth*; Carroll Quigley, *Tragedy and Hope: A History of the World in Our Time*, 938–56, 1244–46; James M. Shields, *Mr. Progressive: A Biography of Elmer Austin Benson*, 309, 323–28; Charles A. Madison, *Critics and Crusaders: A Century of American Protest*, 599.

4. Thomas Frank, *What's the Matter with Kansas? How Conservatives Won the Heart of America*, 242.

5. Ibid, 244, 108.

CHAPTER 1: INTRODUCTION

1. Merrill D. Peterson, *The Jefferson Image in the American Mind*, 342.

2. Jefferson, *The Life and Selected Writings of Thomas Jefferson*, 715.

3. Plato, *Great Dialogues of Plato*, 460–521. For an analysis of how transcendent ideas and universal forms were interpreted by Plato, Augustine, medieval scholastics, Bonaventure, and Kant, see Frederick Copleston, *A History of Philosophy*, bk. 1, 1:163–206, 2:68–73, 136–55, 258–70, 284–89, bk. 2, 6:180–392.

4. Staughton Lynd, *Intellectual Origins of American Radicalism*; Blanche Wiesen Cook, Alice Kessler Harris, and Ronald Radosh, eds., *Past Imperfect: Alternative Essays in American History, Volume 2: From Reconstruction to the Present*, 330–32.

5. C. S. Lewis, *The Abolition of Man, or, Reflections on Education with Special Reference to the Teachings of English in the Upper Forms of Schools*; J. Budziszewski, *Written on the Heart: The Case for Natural Law*; J. Budziszewski, *What We Can't Not Know: A Guide*.

6. Aristotle, *The Politics*, 85–87; Exod. 22:25; Deut. 23:19–20; Neh. 5:1–13; Ps. 15:1–5; Prov. 28:6, 28:8; Ezek. 18:5–18; Luke 6:34–35, 14:12–14; Will Durant and Ariel Durant, *The Story of Civilization: The Age of Faith*, 4:630–33.

7. Jefferson, *Life and Selected Writings,* 574, 714–15; Niccolò Machiavelli, *The Prince and The Discourses,* 35–36.

CHAPTER 2: JEFFERSON AND EARLY AMERICAN LIBERALISM

1. Jefferson, *Life and Selected Writings,* 544–46; Fawn M. Brodie, *Thomas Jefferson: An Intimate History,* 407–12, 431.

2. John Taylor, *An Inquiry into the Principles and Policy of the Government of the United States,* xxx.

3. Gore Vidal, *Matters of Fact and of Fiction: Essays, 1973–1976,* 160.

4. Brodie, *Thomas Jefferson: An Intimate History,* 345–52; Eric Black, *Our Constitution: The Myth That Binds Us,* 27–29; Alexander Hamilton, *The Basic Ideas of Alexander Hamilton,* 126, 102, 105, 106.

5. Charles Maurice Wiltse, *The Jeffersonian Tradition in American Democracy,* 99; Major L. Wilson, *The Presidency of Martin Van Buren,* 28; Jefferson, *The Political Writings of Thomas Jefferson: Representative Selections,* xix.

6. Jefferson, *Life and Selected Writings,* 715.

7. Claude G. Bowers, *Jefferson and Hamilton: The Struggle for Democracy in America,* 95; Jefferson, *Life and Selected Writings,* 632–33, 389; Jefferson, *Political Writings of Thomas Jefferson,* xvii; Wiltse, *Jeffersonian Tradition in American Democracy,* 137.

8. Brodie, *Thomas Jefferson: An Intimate History,* 99–100. See also Jefferson, *Thomas Jefferson on Democracy,* 43.

9. Jefferson, *Life and Selected Writings,* 436.

10. Norine Dickson Campbell, *Patrick Henry: Patriot and Statesman,* 392; Jefferson, *Life and Selected Writings,* 545; Arthur M. Schlesinger Jr., ed., *History of American Presidential Elections,* 1:122.

11. Jefferson, *Thomas Jefferson on Democracy,* 34.

12. Merrill Jensen, *The New Nation: A History of the United States during the Confederation, 1781–1789,* 240; Jefferson, *Political Writings of Thomas Jefferson,* 86, 91; George Woodcock, *Anarchism: A History of Libertarian Ideas and Movements,* 50; Jefferson, *Life and Selected Writings,* 618; Wiltse, *Jeffersonian Tradition in American Democracy,* 148, 220.

13. Jefferson, *Life and Selected Writings,* 670–73, 729–30; Jefferson, *Political Writings of Thomas Jefferson,* 87; Jefferson, *Thomas Jefferson on Democracy,* 38; C. William Hill Jr., *The Political Theory of John Taylor of Caroline,* 289.

14. Richard Falk, *The End of World Order: Essays on Normative International Relations,* 121; Wiltse, *Jeffersonian Tradition in American Democracy,* 99.

15. Wiltse, *Jeffersonian Tradition in American Democracy,* 99; Jefferson, *Life and Selected Writings,* 436, 460, 80–85.

16. Jefferson, *Life and Selected Writings,* 531–32, 545; Taylor, *Inquiry into the Principles and Policy,* 555. See also Jefferson, *Thomas Jefferson on Democracy,* 30, 52–55; Brodie, *Thomas Jefferson: An Intimate History,* 410–11; and William J. Watkins Jr., *Reclaiming the American Revolution: The Kentucky and Virginia Resolutions and Their Legacy.*

17. Donald W. Livingston, "Republicanism, Monarchy, and the Human Scale of Politics," *Chronicles,* August 2005, 16; Jefferson, *Life and Selected Writings,* 698; Moses Clapp, "Child Labor," *Congressional Record,* August 8, 1916, 12298; Edward N. Doan, *The La Follettes and the Wisconsin Idea,* 283.

18. Jefferson, *Life and Selected Writings,* 83–85.

19. Wiltse, *Jeffersonian Tradition in American Democracy*, 127; Jefferson, *Life and Selected Writings*, 323, 88–89, 437, 442, 450–51, 460, 469–71; Herbert Croly, *The Promise of American Life*, 172.

20. Chomsky, *Radical Priorities*, 247; Louis L. Ludlow, "The Vision of Jefferson: Lessons He Taught Us," 479; Jefferson, *Life and Selected Writings*, 412, 221; Richard K. Matthews, *The Radical Politics of Thomas Jefferson: A Revisionist View*, 124; Woodcock, *Anarchism: A History*, 49–50; Henry J. Silverman, ed., *American Radical Thought: The Libertarian Tradition*, 5.

21. Dumas Malone, *Jefferson and His Time*, 1:304; Wiltse, *Jeffersonian Tradition in American Democracy*, 90, 173; Taylor, *Inquiry into the Principles and Policy*, 556–57; Jefferson, *Life and Selected Writings*, 573. See also Bowers, *Jefferson and Hamilton*, 74–79; Noble E. Cunningham Jr., *In Pursuit of Reason: The Life of Thomas Jefferson*, 265–66; Claude G. Bowers, *Jefferson in Power: The Death Struggle of the Federalists*, 208–9; and David N. Mayer, "The Misunderstood Mr. Jefferson."

22. John Taylor, *Construction Construed and Constitutions Vindicated*, ii; Jefferson, *Political Writings of Thomas Jefferson*, 125–26.

23. Matthews, *Radical Politics of Thomas Jefferson*, 116.

24. Albert Jay Nock, *Mr. Jefferson*, 163; Jefferson, *Life and Selected Writings*, 512, 514; Jefferson, *Letters and Addresses*, 161, 247. See also Jefferson, *Thomas Jefferson on Democracy*, 76–77; and Bowers, *Jefferson and Hamilton*, 74–90.

25. Jefferson, *Life and Selected Writings*, 657–58, 669, 673; Jefferson, *Thomas Jefferson on Democracy*, 79; Charles A. Lindbergh, *Why is Your Country at War, and What Happens to You after the War, and Related Subjects*, 83.

26. Jensen, *New Nation*, 424–27.

27. Wiltse, *Jeffersonian Tradition in American Democracy*, 99; Jefferson, *Political Writings of Thomas Jefferson*, xix; Arthur M. Schlesinger Jr., *The Imperial Presidency*, 453; Alexander Hamilton, James Madison, and John Jay, *The Federalist Papers*, 435–40.

28. *The American Heritage Book of the Presidents and Famous Americans*, 2:100; Malone, *Jefferson and His Time*, 1:305; Arthur A. Ekirch Jr., *The Civilian and the Military: A History of the American Antimilitarist Tradition*, 45; Jefferson, *Political Writings of Thomas Jefferson*, 4; Jefferson, *Life and Selected Writings*, 427–28, 435–36, 438, 83.

29. Jefferson, *Political Writings of Thomas Jefferson*, 464; Schlesinger, *Imperial Presidency*, 30–31; Jefferson, *Life and Selected Writings*, 545. See also John C. Miller, *Alexander Hamilton and the Growth of the New Nation*, 315.

30. David N. Mayer, "Jefferson's Legacy of Liberty," *Liberty Tree* 7 (1993): 5; Schlesinger, *Imperial Presidency*, 34; Cunningham, *In Pursuit of Reason*, 314; Wiltse, *Jeffersonian Tradition in American Democracy*, 125; Jefferson, *Life and Selected Writings*, 670–71. See also Jefferson, *Thomas Jefferson on Democracy*, 58–59.

31. Gore Vidal, *The Second American Revolution, and Other Essays (1976–1982)*, 257; Miller, *Alexander Hamilton*, 201, 484. See also Hamilton, *Basic Ideas of Alexander Hamilton*, 180–93.

32. Jefferson, *Thomas Jefferson on Democracy*, 62–65; Schlesinger, ed., *History of American Presidential Elections*, 1:171; Brodie, *Thomas Jefferson: An Intimate History*, 547; Cunningham, *In Pursuit of Reason*, 249.

33. Brodie, *Thomas Jefferson: An Intimate History*, 549; Wiltse, *Jeffersonian Tradition in American Democracy*, 121; Jefferson, *Life and Selected Writings*, 671.

34. Bowers, *Jefferson and Hamilton*, 386–411, 376. See also Miller, *Alexander Hamilton*, 483–85.

35. Jefferson, *The Portable Thomas Jefferson*, 303, 304.

36. Jefferson, *Thomas Jefferson on Democracy*, 108–16; Jefferson, *Life and Selected Writings*, 311–13, 545; Wiltse, *Jeffersonian Tradition in American Democracy*, 123; Cunningham, *In Pursuit of Reason*, 117–18; Schlesinger, ed., *History of American Presidential Elections*, 1:119–20. For contrasting evaluations of President Jefferson's record on civil liberties, see Bowers, *Jefferson in Power*, 502; and Leonard W. Levy, *Jefferson and Civil Liberties: The Darker Side*.

37. Black, *Our Constitution*, 42; Miller, *Alexander Hamilton*, 41, 122, 294, 485; Schlesinger, ed., *History of American Presidential Elections*, 1:177.

38. Jefferson, *Life and Selected Writings*, 341; Howard Zinn, *A People's History of the United States*, 125. See also Jefferson, *Life and Selected Writings*, 578–80; Jefferson, *Thomas Jefferson on Democracy*, 105–7; Matthews, *Radical Politics of Thomas Jefferson*, 53–65; Brodie, *Thomas Jefferson: An Intimate History*, 50, 105–6, 191–92, 557, 587; Bernard W. Sheehan, *Seeds of Extinction: Jeffersonian Philanthropy and the American Indian*.

39. Jefferson, *Life and Selected Writings*, 216–18; Brodie, *Thomas Jefferson: An Intimate History*, 407, 431; Bowers, *Jefferson and Hamilton*, 374.

40. Bowers, *Jefferson and Hamilton*, 417–19; Stephen Hess, *America's Political Dynasties: From Adams to Kennedy*, 157; Schlesinger, ed., *History of American Presidential Elections*, 1:122–23, 171; Jefferson, *Thomas Jefferson on Democracy*, 116–17.

41. Brodie, *Thomas Jefferson: An Intimate History*, 105, 103; Jefferson, *Life and Selected Writings*, 25, 255; William J. Cooper Jr. and Thomas E. Terrill, *The American South: A History*, 1:80. See also Zinn, *People's History of the United States*, 72–73; and Cunningham, *In Pursuit of Reason*, 61; .

42. Jefferson, *Life and Selected Writings*, 218–19, 508; Jefferson, *Letters and Addresses*, 62; Brodie, *Thomas Jefferson: An Intimate History*, 431; Schlesinger, ed., *History of American Presidential Elections*, 1:175; James W. Loewen, *Lies My Teacher Told Me: Everything Your American History Textbook Got Wrong*, 142. See also Jefferson, *Life and Selected Writings*, 278–79, 641–42; Jefferson, *Thomas Jefferson on Democracy*, 100–103; and Brodie, *Thomas Jefferson: An Intimate History*, 454–57.

43. Cooper and Terrill, *American South*, 79–80.

44. Wiltse, *Jeffersonian Tradition in American Democracy*, 105; Cunningham, *In Pursuit of Reason*, 62; Matthews, *Radical Politics of Thomas Jefferson*, 68. See also Jefferson, *Life and Selected Writings*, 641–42; and Brodie, *Thomas Jefferson: An Intimate History*, 584–85.

45. Eugene A. Foster et al., "Jefferson Fathered Slave's Last Child," *Nature* 396 (November 5, 1998): 27–28; Eric S. Lander and Joseph J. Ellis, "Founding Father," *Nature* 396 (November 5, 1998): 13–14. See also E. A. Foster et al., "The Thomas Jefferson Paternity Case," *Nature* 397 (January 7, 1999): 32; Eliot Marshall, "Which Jefferson Was the Father?" *Science* 283 (January 8, 1999): 153–54; and Egon Richard Tausch, "Tom and Sally and Joe and Fawn," *Chronicles*, March 1999, 13–16.

46. Robert F. Turner, ed., *The Jefferson-Hemings Controversy: Report of the Scholars Commission;* Willard Sterne Randall, *Thomas Jefferson: A Life*, 176–77; Brodie, *Thomas Jefferson: An Intimate History*, 584–87.

47. Loewen, *Lies My Teacher Told Me*, 142; G. David Garson, *Power and Politics in the United States: A Political Economy Approach*, 279; Robert V. Remini, *Andrew Jackson and the Course of American Democracy, 1833–1845*, 120–29; Shaw Livermore Jr., *The Twilight of Federalism: The Disintegration of the Federalist Party, 1815–1830*, 152; Schlesinger, ed., *History of American Presidential Elections*, 1:354, 2:496–98, 578–600, 650, 749–83.

48. Harry V. Jaffa, *A New Birth of Freedom: Abraham Lincoln and the Coming of the Civil War*, 212, 407–9, 206, 429, 221, 412–19.

49. For more on Calhoun's reputation for opportunism, see Gerald M. Capers, *John C. Calhoun, Opportunist: A Reappraisal*.

50. Chester M. Morgan, *Redneck Liberal: Theodore G. Bilbo and the New Deal*, 241.

51. Wallace Hettle, *The Peculiar Democracy: Southern Democrats in Peace and War*, 164, 150–62. See also William H. Skaggs, *The Southern Oligarchy: An Appeal in Behalf of the Silent Masses of Our Country against the Despotic Rule of the Few*; and *I'll Take My Stand: The South and the Agrarian Tradition, by Twelve Southerners*.

52. Leslie H. Southwick, *Presidential Also-Rans and Running Mates, 1788–1980*, 314–21, 329–37.

53. David Donald, *Charles Sumner and the Coming of the Civil War*, 166, 6, 153. See also Charles Sumner, *The Selected Letters of Charles Sumner*, 1:243–50; and David Donald, *Charles Sumner and the Rights of Man*, 208, 423, 449, 532.

54. Larry E. Tise, *Proslavery: A History of the Defense of Slavery in America, 1701–1840*, 235; Carol Moseley-Braun, "Statement on the Extension of the Patent of the Insignia of the United Daughters of the Confederacy," 24.

55. William T.S. Barry, comp., *Journal of the State Convention*, 86. See also Jaffa, *New Birth of Freedom*, 214–25.

56. Brodie, *Thomas Jefferson: An Intimate History*, 349; Thomas A. Bailey and David M. Kennedy, *The American Pageant: A History of the Republic*, 143.

57. Miller, *Alexander Hamilton*, 454; Schlesinger, ed., *History of American Presidential Elections*, 1:120, 165; Jefferson, *Life and Selected Writings*, 545; Noble E. Cunningham Jr., *The Jeffersonian Republicans: The Formation of Party Organization, 1789–1801*, 214; Jerry Voorhis, *Out of Debt, Out of Danger: Proposals for War Finance and Tomorrow's Money*, 15, 28–29, 37–38; Bowers, *Jefferson in Power*, 503.

58. Bailey and Kennedy, *American Pageant*, 143–46; Bowers, *Jefferson and Hamilton*, 419; Miller, *Alexander Hamilton*, 504–5.

59. Jefferson, *Political Writings of Thomas Jefferson*, 5, 86; Miller, *Alexander Hamilton*, 400–403; Jefferson, *Life and Selected Writings*, 548, 340; Charles A. Beard, *The Economic Basis of Politics and Related Writings*, 181; Schlesinger, ed., *History of American Presidential Elections*, 1:171, 165; Jefferson, *Thomas Jefferson on Democracy*, 75–76.

60. Richard H. Kohn, *Eagle and Sword: The Federalists and the Creation of the Military Establishment in America, 1783–1802*, 286; Brodie, *Thomas Jefferson: An Intimate History*, 349, 407, 347–49; Miller, *Alexander Hamilton*, 21, 390, 453.

61. Miller, *Alexander Hamilton*, 470–71, 474, 480–83, 494–95.

62. Wiltse, *Jeffersonian Tradition in American Democracy*, 135; Jefferson, *Thomas Jefferson on Democracy*, 123–26, 132–33; Jefferson, *Political Writings of Thomas Jefferson*, 5; Jefferson, *Life and Selected Writings*, 450–52, 545, 548; Miller, *Alexander Hamilton*, 453; Schlesinger, ed., *History of American Presidential Elections*, 1:119; Ekirch, *The Civilian and the Military*, 46–47.

63. Bailey and Kennedy, *American Pageant*, 169–70; Brodie, *Thomas Jefferson: An Intimate History*, 558, 555–67; Bowers, *Jefferson in Power*, 159–205, 224, 501; Schlesinger, ed., *History of American Presidential Elections*, 1:192.

64. Ekirch, *The Civilian and the Military*, 47–49; Kohn, *Eagle and Sword*, 303; Crackel, *Mr. Jefferson's Army: Political and Social Reform of the Military Establishment, 1801–1809*, 59; Jefferson, *Political Writings of Thomas Jefferson*, 181; Brodie, *Thomas Jefferson: An Intimate History*, 567–69.

65. Brodie, *Thomas Jefferson: An Intimate History*, 349, 407; Miller, *Alexander Hamilton*, 36, 495; Matthews, *Radical Politics of Thomas Jefferson*, 116; Falk, *End of World Order*, 121.

66. Jefferson, *Life and Selected Writings*, 507, 545; Schlesinger, ed., *History of American

Presidential Elections, 1:119; Cunningham, *Jeffersonian Republicans,* 214; Jefferson, *Political Writings of Thomas Jefferson,* 44; Jefferson, *Thomas Jefferson on Democracy,* 126–33.

67. Jefferson, *Political Writings of Thomas Jefferson,* 187; Jefferson, *Life and Selected Writings,* 620, 657; Jefferson, *Thomas Jefferson on Democracy,* 179–80.

68. Robert Morss Lovett, "American Foreign Policy: A Progressive View," 49.

69. Donald, *Charles Sumner and the Rights of Man,* 443.

CHAPTER 3: COMPETING PHILOSOPHIES

1. Jefferson, *Life and Selected Writings,* 322.

2. Nock, *Mr. Jefferson,* 167.

3. Livermore, *Twilight of Federalism,* 102–3; Jefferson, *Life and Selected Writings,* 714–15; Remini, *Andrew Jackson and the Course of American Democracy,* 336–46; Wilson, *Presidency of Martin Van Buren,* 26–29; Miller, *Alexander Hamilton,* 443; Samuel Francis, *Beautiful Losers: Essays on the Failure of American Conservatism,* 35–59.

4. Bowers, *Jefferson in Power,* 258–59, 501–3; Jefferson, *Life and Selected Writings,* 544–46.

5. Jefferson, *Life and Selected Writings,* 715, 632–33, 431; Nock, *Mr. Jefferson,* 167.

6. Herbert J. Storing, *What the Anti-Federalists Were For,* 20–23, 45–46, 72–76; William Appleman Williams, *The Contours of American History,* 98–99, 107–8; Jefferson, *Life and Selected Writings,* 280; Matthews, *Radical Politics of Thomas Jefferson,* 116; Jean M. Yarbrough, *American Virtues: Thomas Jefferson on the Character of a Free People;* Rex Burns, *Success in America: The Yeoman Dream and the Industrial Revolution.*

7. Wiltse, *Jeffersonian Tradition in American Democracy,* 220; Richard K. Matthews, *If Men Were Angels: James Madison and the Heartless Empire of Reason.*

8. Jean Jacques Rousseau, *The Social Contract;* Sydney E. Ahlstrom, *A Religious History of the American People,* 1:169–99, 264–71, 303–5; Croly, *Promise of American Life,* 172; Jefferson, *Life and Selected Writings,* 88–89, 437, 442, 450–51, 460, 469–71.

9. Jefferson, *Life and Selected Writings,* 280.

10. Ibid., 280–81.

11. Matthews, *Radical Politics of Thomas Jefferson,* 48; Jefferson, *Political Writings of Thomas Jefferson,* xvii; Wiltse, *Jeffersonian Tradition in American Democracy,* 137; Cunningham, *In Pursuit of Reason,* 55–56; Jefferson, *Life and Selected Writings,* 389–90.

12. Richard J. Hardy, *Government in America,* 229; Jefferson, *Life and Selected Writings,* 469–71, 478–80.

13. Matthews, *Radical Politics of Thomas Jefferson,* 98; Matthews, *If Men Were Angels;* Zinn, *People's History of the United States,* 125–26; Garson, *Power and Politics in the United States,* 279–80; Livermore, *Twilight of Federalism,* 14, 19.

14. Schlesinger, ed., *History of American Presidential Elections,* 1:197, 185–221; Cunningham, *In Pursuit of Reason,* 282; Garson, *Power and Politics in the United States,* 279; Burch, *Elites in American History,* 1:100; Livermore, *Twilight of Federalism,* 56–57, 102–3. For Van Buren's interaction with Jefferson and his view of the Monroe administration, see Wilson, *Presidency of Martin Van Buren,* 27–29; and John Niven, *Martin Van Buren: The Romantic Age of American Politics,* 146–48, 163–64.

15. Remini, *Andrew Jackson and the Course of American Democracy,* 336–46, 518; Beard, *Economic Basis of Politics,* 187; Wilson, *Presidency of Martin Van Buren,* 26–29, 35–37, 202–3; Niven, *Martin Van Buren,* 260; Edward M. Shepard, *Martin Van Buren,* 446.

16. Robert V. Remini, *Andrew Jackson and the Course of American Freedom, 1822–1832,* 129. See also John Ashworth, *"Agrarians" and "Aristocrats": Party Political Ideology in the*

United States, 1837–1846, 127–29; Barton J. Bernstein, ed., *Towards a New Past: Dissenting Essays in American History,* 84; and Lee Benson, *The Concept of Jacksonian Democracy: New York as a Test Case,* 33–37, 94–97, 106.

17. Roy Franklin Nichols, *Franklin Pierce: Young Hickory of the Granite Hills,* 214; Burch, *Elites in American History;* Irving Katz, *August Belmont: A Political Biography;* David Black, *The King of Fifth Avenue: The Fortunes of August Belmont.*

CHAPTER 4: BRYAN, HUMPHREY, AND THEIR IDEOLOGICAL DESCENT

1. Bryan was U.S. representative from Nebraska from 1891–1895 and a presidential nominee in 1896, 1900, and 1908. He served as secretary of state from 1913 to 1915. Humphrey was mayor of Minneapolis from 1945 to 1948 and a senator from Minnesota from 1949 to 1964 and from 1971 to 1978. Humphrey was a presidential contender in 1960, 1968, 1972, and 1976 and was vice president from 1965 to 1969. In 1968, he was the Democratic presidential nominee.

2. Bruce Palmer, *"Man over Money": The Southern Populist Critique,* 41; Louis W. Koenig, *Bryan: A Political Biography of William Jennings Bryan,* 37–38, 303; Bryan, *The First Battle: A Story of the Campaign of 1896,* 60; Bryan, *The Credo of the Commoner: William Jennings Bryan,* 44–46; Paul W. Glad, *The Trumpet Soundeth: William Jennings Bryan and His Democracy, 1896–1912,* 30, 32; Bryan and Mary Baird Bryan, *The Memoirs of William Jennings Bryan,* 245.

3. William Allen, "Speeches at a Jacksonian Banquet," 1541; Lawrence W. Levine, *Defender of the Faith: William Jennings Bryan: The Last Decade, 1915–1925,* 227; Croly, *Promise of American Life,* 156.

4. Chester McArthur Destler, *American Radicalism: 1865–1901,* 59–60, 194–97, 229; Ralph J. Roske, *His Own Counsel: The Life and Times of Lyman Trumbull,* 172–73; Koenig, *Bryan: A Political Biography,* 42–43, 134, 177, 211.

5. Aylmer Maude, *The Life of Tolstoy,* 250–53; Leo Tolstoy, *Tolstoy's Letters,* 2:587–88, 657–58; Bryan and Bryan, *Memoirs of William Jennings Bryan,* 460–61; Merle Eugene Curti, *Bryan and World Peace,* 135–36.

6. Bryan, *The Second Battle, or, the New Declaration of Independence, 1776–1900: An Account of the Struggle of 1900,* 493, 243–44, 206–7; Allen, "Speeches at a Jacksonian Banquet," 1539. See also Bryan, *The Commoner: Condensed,* 27–29, 98–100, 279–80.

7. M. R. Werner, *Bryan,* 15, 29; Koenig, *Bryan: A Political Biography,* 108–9.

8. Humphrey, *The Cause is Mankind: A Liberal Program for Modern America,* 109; Humphrey, *The Political Philosophy of the New Deal,* 106. See also Allan H. Ryskind, *Hubert: An Unauthorized Biography of the Vice President,* 25; Michael Amrine, *This is Humphrey: The Story of the Senator,* 31; and Humphrey, *Hubert Humphrey: The Man and His Dream,* 31, 61.

9. Paul H. Douglas, *In the Fullness of Time: The Memoirs of Paul H. Douglas,* 230; Ryskind, *Hubert: An Unauthorized Biography,* 195; Ferdinand Lundberg, *The Rich and the Super-Rich: A Study in the Power of Money Today,* 544; Carl Solberg, *Hubert Humphrey: A Biography,* 136, 205, 307; Schlesinger Jr., *The Vital Center: The Politics of Freedom,* 16, 177, 181, 187; Schlesinger Jr., "Ideology vs. Democracy," 247.

10. Amrine, *This is Humphrey,* 75, 32, 35, 19; Humphrey, *Political Philosophy of the New Deal,* 100, 109–14; Humphrey, *Beyond Civil Rights: A New Day of Equality,* 12; Charles Lloyd Garrettson III, *Hubert H. Humphrey: The Politics of Joy,* 9; Ryskind, *Hubert: An*

Unauthorized Biography, 25, 231; Solberg, *Humphrey: A Biography,* 457; Douglas, *In the Fullness of Time,* 20–21, 149.

11. Amrine, *This is Humphrey,* 18; Solberg, *Humphrey: A Biography,* 20, 457; Humphrey, *The Education of a Public Man: My Life and Politics,* 13; Humphrey, *Political Philosophy of the New Deal,* 115–16; Ryskind, *Hubert: An Unauthorized Biography,* 231; John E. Miller, *Governor Philip F. La Follette, the Wisconsin Progressives, and the New Deal,* 146–47.

12. W. A. Swanberg, *Norman Thomas: The Last Idealist;* Belle Case La Follette and Fola La Follette, *Robert M. La Follette: June 14, 1855–June 18, 1925,* 2:1116–17, 1127, 1224–25; Kenneth Campbell MacKay, *The Progressive Movement of 1924,* 255; Ryskind, *Hubert: An Unauthorized Biography,* 179, 289; Lionel Lokos, *Hysteria 1964: The Fear Campaign Against Barry Goldwater,* 127; Peter Kihss, "Many Socialists Backing Johnson: Thomas Will Tour Nation to Support President," *New York Times,* October 11, 1964, 73.

13. Swanberg, *Norman Thomas,* 249, 283–90, 316, 492–93; Francis, *Beautiful Losers,* 103; Garrettson, *Hubert H. Humphrey,* 247–73; Norman Thomas, "For McCarthy-McGovern Coalition," *New York Times,* August 22, 1968, 36.

14. Humphrey, *Education of a Public Man,* 98; James T. Patterson, *Mr. Republican: A Biography of Robert A. Taft,* 158, 193, 253, 255, 331, 377, 571, 583; Robert A. Taft, "The Future of the Republican Party"; Patterson, *Mr. Republican,* 377; "Taft Hits Stassen on 'Liberal' Issue," *New York Times,* April 22, 1948, 14; Michael W. Miles, *The Odyssey of the American Right,* 182–83; Roger T. Johnson, *Robert M. La Follette Jr. and the Decline of the Progressive Party in Wisconsin,* 119, 146–48; Russell Kirk and James McClellan, *The Political Principles of Robert A. Taft,* 112–13, 132; "Taft's Appraisal of '52 Loss Bared," *New York Times,* November 25, 1959, 1, 14; Quigley, *Tragedy and Hope,* 1244–45.

15. Douglas, *In the Fullness of Time,* 225; Bill Kauffman, *America First! Its History, Culture, and Politics,* 59; R. Alan Lawson, *The Failure of Independent Liberalism, 1930–1941,* 40.

16. Solberg, *Humphrey: A Biography,* 430.

17. Humphrey, *Education of a Public Man,* 55, 74; Millard L. Gieske, *Minnesota Farmer-Laborism: The Third-Party Alternative,* 276–332; Ryskind, *Hubert: An Unauthorized Biography,* 38; Solberg, *Humphrey: A Biography,* 89; Robert M. La Follette, *The Political Philosophy of Robert M. La Follette as Revealed in His Speeches and Writings,* 117–19, 287–88; Bill Kauffman, "A Mighty Long Fall: An Interview with Eugene McCarthy," 14–15.

18. Jacob K. Javits, *Javits: The Autobiography of a Public Man,* 153; Francis X. Gannon, *Biographical Dictionary of the Left,* 2:159–81; Gary Allen, *Richard Nixon: The Man Behind the Mask,* 102–6; Robert Griffith, ed., *Major Problems in American History since 1945: Documents and Essays,* 167–77.

19. Richard Hofstadter, *The American Political Tradition and the Men Who Made It,* 245. See also Pettigrew, *Imperial Washington;* Lundberg, *America's Sixty Families;* Kolko, *Triumph of Conservatism;* and Burch, *Elites in American History.*

20. Dwight Macdonald, *Memoirs of a Revolutionist: Essays in Political Criticism,* 285–87; Harry Elmer Barnes, *The Chickens of the Interventionist Liberals Have Come Home to Roost: The Bitter Fruits of Globaloney;* Charles A. Beard, *Giddy Minds and Foreign Quarrels: An Estimate of American Foreign Policy;* Griffith, ed., *Major Problems in American History,* 183–84.

21. Humphrey, *Political Philosophy of the New Deal;* Arthur M. Schlesinger Jr., *The Age of Roosevelt;* Griffith, ed., *Major Problems in American History,* 147–55, 171; Harry S. Truman, "A Year of Challenge: Liberalism or Conservatism."

22. Griffith, ed., *Major Problems in American History,* 183; Amos R. E. Pinchot, *History of the Progressive Party, 1912–1916,* 146; Charles Forcey, *The Crossroads of Liberalism: Croly, Weyl, Lippmann, and the Progressive Era, 1900–1925,* 116, 125–27, 142; Robert D.

Schulzinger, *The Wise Men of Foreign Affairs: The History of the Council on Foreign Relations*, 19; Nicol C. Rae, *The Decline and Fall of the Liberal Republicans: From 1952 to the Present*, 20, 61; Schlesinger, *Vital Center*, 23, 32.

23. R. Jeffrey Lustig, *Corporate Liberalism: The Origins of Modern American Political Theory, 1890–1920;* Christopher Lasch, *The Agony of the American Left*, 11; Walter Lippmann, "The Goldwater Movement," 13.

24. Solberg, *Humphrey: A Biography*, 41; Humphrey, *Education of a Public Man*, 376; Humphrey, *Political Philosophy of the New Deal*, 116–21; Robert Sherrill and Harry W. Ernst, *The Drugstore Liberal*, 29–30.

25. Lustig, *Corporate Liberalism*, 205–6; Kolko, *Triumph of Conservatism*, 216, 204–6, 281, 260–61, 278; E. Digby Baltzell, *Puritan Boston and Quaker Philadelphia: Two Protestant Ethics and the Spirit of Class Authority and Leadership*, 200; Peterson, *Jefferson Image in the American Mind*, 343–44; Cook, Harris, and Radosh, *Past Imperfect*, 132–33; Arthur S. Link, *Woodrow Wilson and the Progressive Era, 1910–1917*, 8–10; Lundberg, *America's Sixty Families*, 109–33; Hofstadter, *American Political Tradition*, 238–51; Koenig, *Bryan: A Political Biography*, 476–78; Bryan, *William Jennings Bryan: Selections*, 201–2.

26. Humphrey, *Education of a Public Man*, 16; Douglas B. Craig, *After Wilson: The Struggle for the Democratic Party, 1920–1934*, 3, 56, 95, 114–37, 158–67; Koenig, *Bryan: A Political Biography*, 374–98, 465, 483–87, 475–78, 491, 616–17; Levine, *Defender of the Faith*, 160, 299; Lundberg, *America's Sixty Families*, 178–80; Lundberg, *Rich and the Super-Rich*, 172, 793; Antony C. Sutton, *Wall Street and FDR*, 106–19; "Political Note: Warrior to War," *Time*, February 3, 1936, 14–15; George Wolfskill, *The Revolt of the Conservatives: A History of the American Liberty League, 1934–1940*, 142–52.

27. Edgar Berman, *Hubert: The Triumph and Tragedy of the Humphrey I Knew*, 27; Humphrey, *Political Philosophy of the New Deal;* Winthrop Griffith, *Humphrey: A Candid Biography*, 243; Bryan, *Credo of the Commoner*, 127; James MacGregor Burns, *Roosevelt: The Lion and the Fox;* Howard Zinn, *Declarations of Independence: Cross-Examining American Ideology*, 17–18.

28. Burns, *Roosevelt: The Lion and the Fox*, 22–23, 25–26, 51–52, 60–64; Willard H. Smith, *The Social and Religious Thought of William Jennings Bryan*, 90.

29. Frank Freidel, *Franklin D. Roosevelt*, 2:56–58, 226, 182; Paolo E. Coletta, *William Jennings Bryan, vol. 3: Political Puritan, 1915–1925*, 112; Levine, *Defender of the Faith*, 155–75, 299–300, 315–21; Hiram W. Johnson, *The Diary Letters of Hiram Johnson, 1917–1945*, 3:2–6–20, 4–2–20, 4:7–10–24; Koenig, *Bryan: A Political Biography*, 590–92, 622–25; Burton K. Wheeler, *Yankee from the West*, 247–51; Craig, *After Wilson*, 87–88; Larry G. Osnes, *Charles W. Bryan: Latter-Day Populist and Rural Progressive*, 341–42, 364.

30. Craig, *After Wilson*, 206; Burch, *Elites in American History*, 3:20–21; Nelson W. Aldrich Jr., *Old Money: The Mythology of America's Upper Class*, 229–39; Freidel, *Franklin D. Roosevelt*, 2:235–40, 92–93, 248–59; Quigley, *Tragedy and Hope*, 951–54; Laurence H. Shoup and William Minter, *Imperial Brain Trust: The Council on Foreign Relations and United States Foreign Policy*, 11–20, 103–7; Sutton, *Wall Street and FDR*.

31. "Roosevelt's Soft Answer to Smith's Wrath," *The Literary Digest*, April 30, 1932, 3–4; "Is Franklin Roosevelt 'the Bryan of 1932'?" *The Literary Digest*, June 4, 1932, 3–4; Johnson, *Diary Letters of Hiram Johnson*, 5:4–17–32, 4–24–32, 5–1–32; Ronald A. Mulder, *The Insurgent Progressives in the United States Senate and the New Deal, 1933–1939;* Ronald L. Feinman, *Twilight of Progressivism: The Western Republican Senators and the New Deal;* Otis L. Graham Jr., *An Encore for Reform: The Old Progressives and the New Deal;* James T. Patterson, *Congressional Conservatism and the New Deal: The Growth of the Conservative Coalition in Congress, 1933–1939;* Wayne S. Cole, *Roosevelt and the Isolationists, 1932–1945*.

32. Lundberg, *America's Sixty Families,* 259; "Willkie Boom," *Newsweek,* May 13, 1940, 31.

33. Wheeler, *Yankee from the West,* 389. See also Burton K. Wheeler, "Nominations of Henry L. Stimson and Frank Knox," 8694–96.

34. Philip La Follette, *Adventure in Politics: The Memoirs of Philip La Follette,* 247.

35. Robert E. Burke, "A Friendship in Adversity: Burton K. Wheeler, Hiram W. Johnson"; Barnes, *Chickens of the Interventionist Liberals,* 6–7; Bernard A. Weisberger, *The La Follettes of Wisconsin: Love and Politics in Progressive America,* 297–300, 310; Johnson, *Robert M. La Follette Jr.,* 77–82, 96–101; Patterson, *Congressional Conservatism,* 16, 54–55; Levine, *Defender of the Faith,* 86–87, 194–95, 213–16, 296–99; Cole, *Roosevelt and the Isolationists,* 37–38.

36. Peterson, *Jefferson Image in the American Mind,* 362, 332; Benson, *Concept of Jacksonian Democracy,* 109; Alsop, *Nixon and Rockefeller: A Double Portrait,* 169; Rothbard, "Conservative Movement R.I.P.?" 20; Sobran, "Questioning Myths of 'The Good War' Still Forbidden," 6A; Kauffman, *America First!* 11; Francis, *Beautiful Losers,* 103.

37. Humphrey, *Education of a Public Man,* 58; Solberg, *Humphrey: A Biography,* 98; Macdonald, *Henry Wallace,* 27, 20–21, 82–83, 177.

38. Griffith, ed., *Major Problems in American History,* 179–84; Sutton, *Wall Street and FDR,* 71–105; Steve Neal, *Dark Horse: A Biography of Wendell Willkie,* 10, 21, 53; Richard Norton Smith, *Thomas E. Dewey and His Times,* 294; J. T. Salter, ed., *Public Men In and Out of Office,* 68; Southwick, *Presidential Also-Rans and Running Mates,* 538.

39. "Republican Convention: Wendell Willkie Is People's Choice," *Life,* July 8, 1940, 61, 64; Robert M. La Follette, *La Follette's Autobiography: A Personal Narrative of Political Experiences,* 46, 55, 178–79, 302, 311; Johnson, *Diary Letters of Hiram Johnson,* 2:5–5–18, 3:1–6–19, 6–23–22, 11–20–23, 6:2–10–35; Allen, *Richard Nixon,* 92–93; Smith, *Thomas E. Dewey,* 295; Neal, *Dark Horse,* 50–52, 53, 66–79; Oren Root, *Persons and Persuasions,* 29–36; Phyllis Schlafly, *A Choice Not an Echo,* 33–44; "Willkie Named for Trust Board," *New York Times,* September 5, 1941, 29.

40. Salter, *Public Men,* 57; Usher Burdick, "The Republican Party and the City of Philadelphia," *Congressional Record,* June 19, 1940, 8641; Neal, *Dark Horse,* 159, 93, 117–18; Southwick, *Presidential Also-Rans and Running Mates,* 549; Johnson, *Diary Letters of Hiram Johnson,* 7:1–19–41; Wayne S. Cole, *Senator Gerald P. Nye and American Foreign Relations,* 180–81, 190, 212–14.

41. Humphrey, *Political Philosophy of the New Deal,* 116; Humphrey, *The Man and His Dream,* 61; Ryskind, *Hubert: An Unauthorized Biography,* 38–39; Amrine, *This is Humphrey,* 82–83, 87–88.

42. Macdonald, *Henry Wallace,* 36–37.

43. "William Jennings Bryan," *The Nation,* August 5, 1925, 154; Oswald Garrison Villard, *Prophets: True and False,* 202–14; Oswald Garrison Villard, "Issues and Men: Honor to William J. Bryan," *The Nation,* November 20, 1935, 583; Macdonald, *Henry Wallace,* 177–81.

CHAPTER 5: MODERN PHILOSOPHY 101

1. For the philosophical foundations and ideological manifestations of the Center, see Lustig, *Corporate Liberalism;* C. S. Lewis, *That Hideous Strength: A Modern Fairy-Tale for Grown-Ups,* 99; Rick Tilman, *C. Wright Mills: A Native Radical and His American Intellectual Roots,* 11; Laurence H. Shoup, *The Carter Presidency and Beyond: Power and Politics in*

the 1980s, 5; and Calvin F. Exoo, ed., *Democracy Upside Down: Public Opinion and Cultural Hegemony in the United States*, 80.

2. Koenig, *Bryan: A Political Biography*, 293, 367; Schlesinger, ed., *History of American Presidential Elections*, 5:1845; Bryan, *The Commoner*, 8–9; Bryan, *Under Other Flags: Travels, Lectures, Speeches*, 240; Paolo E. Coletta, *William Jennings Bryan, vol. 1: Political Evangelist, 1860–1908*, 402–3.

3. Bryan, *Under Other Flags*, 236.

4. Koenig, *Bryan: A Political Biography*, 367; Paolo E. Coletta, *William Jennings Bryan, vol. 2: Progressive Politician and Moral Statesman, 1909–1915*, 36.

5. White, "The End of an Epoch: The Passing of the Apostles of Liberalism in the United States," 569–70; Burns, *Roosevelt: The Lion and the Fox;* Zinn, *Declarations of Independence*, 17–18.

6. Ronald Schaffer, *America in the Great War: The Rise of the War Welfare State*, xiv; Burns, *Roosevelt: The Lion and the Fox*, 474–76; Gary Gerstle, "The Protean Character of American Liberalism," 1043–44; Richard Hofstadter, *The Age of Reform: From Bryan to F.D.R.*, 308–23; Humphrey, *Political Philosophy of the New Deal*, 15; Peterson, *Jefferson Image in the American Mind*, 332; "Political Notes: Roosevelt Renounced," *Time*, September 21, 1936, 19; Michael Wreszin, *Oswald Garrison Villard: Pacifist at War*, 249; Macdonald, *Henry Wallace*, 36.

7. Goldwater, *With No Apologies: The Personal and Political Memoirs of United States Senator Barry M. Goldwater*, 94–95; Mills, *The Power Elite*, 330; Tilman, *C. Wright Mills*, 11, 186–88.

8. Amrine, *This is Humphrey*, 242, 243.

9. William Bowen, "What's New About the New Hubert Humphrey?" 143; Griffith, *Humphrey: A Candid Biography*, 321; Solberg, *Humphrey: A Biography*, 458; Berman, *Hubert: The Triumph and Tragedy*, 56, 59; Ryskind, *Hubert: An Unauthorized Biography*, 39; Dan Cohen, *Undefeated: The Life of Hubert H. Humphrey*, 14.

10. Humphrey, *Political Philosophy of the New Deal*, 85–86; Humphrey, *Education of a Public Man*, 55; Cohen, *Undefeated: The Life of Hubert Humphrey*, 11; Ryskind, *Hubert: An Unauthorized Biography*, 126; Garrettson, *Hubert H. Humphrey*, 47.

11. Humphrey, *Education of a Public Man*, 159–60, 97–98.

12. Humphrey, *Cause is Mankind*, ix, 17, 51.

13. Bowen, "What's New?" 144; Amrine, *This is Humphrey*, 243; Solberg, *Humphrey: A Biography*, 341–42.

14. Humphrey, *Education of a Public Man*, 70, 97–98, 355; Hedrick Smith, "Humphrey Gone, Carter Loses Key Ally in Senate."

15. Berman, *Hubert: The Triumph and Tragedy*, 75, 39.

16. Ibid., 43; Ryskind, *Hubert: An Unauthorized Biography*, 193–96; Humphrey, "Foreign Assistance Act of 1974," 38124; David English et al., *Divided They Stand*, 217.

17. Humphrey, *Education of a Public Man*, 130; Amrine, *This is Humphrey*, 17; William P. Hoar, "Hubert Humphrey: The Dark Horse Is at the Gate," 7; Warren Weaver Jr., "Humphrey Joins Presidency Race; Calls for Unity," *New York Times*, April 28, 1968, 1, 66; Humphrey, "Humphrey Talk Transcript," *New York Times*, April 28, 1968, 66; Berman, *Hubert: The Triumph and Tragedy*, 175, 231, 232.

18. Ibid., 26, 94, 113; Humphrey, *Education of a Public Man*, 71, 90, 102, 93; Solberg, *Humphrey: A Biography*, 155; Clare Crawford, "It's Not Tough Sledding Anymore for the New Serene Hubert Humphrey," 10–11, 8.

19. Berman, *Hubert: The Triumph and Tragedy*, 241, 246.

20. Ibid., 138, 208.

21. Ibid., 190.

22. Stephen P. Depoe, *Arthur M. Schlesinger Jr. and the Ideological History of American Liberalism*, 10–11; Berman, *Hubert: The Triumph and Tragedy*, 60.

23. Humphrey, *Political Philosophy of the New Deal*, 79; Humphrey, *Education of a Public Man*, 101, 100, 110; Depoe, *Arthur M. Schlesinger Jr.*, 45–46; Thomas C. Reeves, *A Question of Character: A Life of John F. Kennedy*, 195.

24. Phillips, *Arrogant Capital: Washington, Wall Street, and the Frustration of American Politics*, 123.

25. Koenig, *Bryan: A Political Biography*, 293–94; Bryan, *Under Other Flags*, 234; Bryan and Bryan, *Memoirs of William Jennings Bryan*, 299; Bryan, *The Commoner*, 301.

26. Koenig, *Bryan: A Political Biography*, 367, 384; J. C. Long, *Bryan, the Great Commoner*, 91; Bryan, *The Commoner*, 191–94; Werner, *Bryan*, 94; Curti, *Bryan and World Peace*, 127–29; Paul W. Glad, ed., *William Jennings Bryan: A Profile*, 60, 80; Kendrick A. Clements, *William Jennings Bryan: Missionary Isolationist*, 68.

27. Koenig, *Bryan: A Political Biography*, 383–84; Bryan, *Speeches of William Jennings Bryan*, 2:50; Bryan, *Credo of the Commoner*, 93; Schlesinger, ed., *History of American Presidential Elections*, 5:2083.

28. George W. Norris, "Bryan as a Political Leader," 859–67; Bryan, *Credo of the Commoner*, 97; Levine, *Defender of the Faith*, 132–365.

29. Cohen, *Undefeated: The Life of Hubert Humphrey*, 14; Amrine, *This is Humphrey*, 97–98.

30. Amrine, *This is Humphrey*, 158; Berman, *Hubert: The Triumph and Tragedy*, 59; Humphrey, *Education of a Public Man*, 96–97.

31. Griffith, *Humphrey: A Candid Biography*, 321–22.

32. Ryskind, *Hubert: An Unauthorized Biography*, 171–72, 17; Crawford, "It's Not Tough Sledding Anymore," 11.

33. King Jr., *The Words of Martin Luther King Jr.*, 24; Ryskind, *Hubert: An Unauthorized Biography*, 172; J. Rogers Hollingsworth, *The Whirligig of Politics: The Democracy of Cleveland and Bryan*, 27; Bryan, *The Commoner*, 71–73; Koenig, *Bryan: A Political Biography*, 366–73, 385, 411–15, 434, 451; Berman, *Hubert: The Triumph and Tragedy*, 89.

34. Garrettson, *Hubert H. Humphrey*, 214–15; Berman, *Hubert: The Triumph and Tragedy*, 217; Bryan, *Bryan: Selections*, 201–2; Humphrey, *The Man and His Dream*, 340–43.

35. Humphrey, *Education of a Public Man*, 73; Amrine, *This is Humphrey*, 98; Ryskind, *Hubert: An Unauthorized Biography*, 17, 171–72; Hays Gorey, "'I'm a Born Optimist': The Era of Hubert H. Humphrey," 65.

36. Berman, *Hubert: The Triumph and Tragedy*, 26, 94, 113; Griffith, *Humphrey: A Candid Biography*, 321; Solberg, *Humphrey: A Biography*, 171.

37. Koenig, *Bryan: A Political Biography*, 350; Coletta, *Political Evangelist*, 386–89; LeRoy Ashby, *William Jennings Bryan: Champion of Democracy*, 106–10; Macdonald, *Henry Wallace*, 179–80.

38. Richard Hofstadter, *Anti-Intellectualism in American Life*, 155–56; Levine, *Defender of the Faith*, 227; Ashby, *Bryan: Champion of Democracy*, 89; Koenig, *Bryan: A Political Biography*, 240, 367.

39. Amrine, *This is Humphrey*, 19; Ryskind, *Hubert: An Unauthorized Biography*, 231; Schaffer, *America in the Great War*, xiv–xv, 212. For popular resistance to U.S. involvement in World War I, see Harry Elmer Barnes, *In Quest of Truth and Justice: De-Bunking the War-Guilt Myth*, 98–105; Charles Callan Tansill, *America Goes to War;* and Christopher C. Gibbs, *The Great Silent Majority: Missouri's Resistance to World War I.*

40. Humphrey, *Cause is Mankind*, 13; Humphrey, *Political Philosophy of the New Deal*,

30; Sutton, *Wall Street and FDR;* Gerard Colby and Charlotte Dennett, *Thy Will Be Done: The Conquest of the Amazon: Nelson Rockefeller and Evangelism in the Age of Oil,* 115; George Donelson Moss, *Moving On: The American People since 1945,* 16–18.

41. For scholarly examinations of Roosevelt's machinations on behalf of U.S. involvement in World War II, see Charles A. Beard, *American Foreign Policy in the Making, 1932–1940: A Study in Responsibilities;* Charles A. Beard, *President Roosevelt and the Coming of the War, 1941: A Study in Appearances and Realities;* Charles Callan Tansill, *Back Door to War: The Roosevelt Foreign Policy, 1933–1941;* and Harry Elmer Barnes, ed., *Perpetual War for Perpetual Peace: A Critical Examination of the Foreign Policy of Franklin Delano Roosevelt and Its Aftermath.*

42. Gore Vidal, *United States: Essays, 1952–1992,* 1269.

43. Macdonald, *Henry Wallace,* 180; Robert Sherrill, *The Accidental President,* 58; Robert A. Caro, *The Years of Lyndon Johnson: The Path to Power,* 39, 663–64; Lundberg, *Rich and the Super-Rich,* 772; John T. Flynn, *As We Go Marching.*

44. Barnes, *Chickens of the Interventionist Liberals,* 8–9; Francis, *Beautiful Losers,* 95–117, 103; Depoe, *Arthur M. Schlesinger Jr.,* 133–34.

45. Solberg, *Humphrey: A Biography,* 75; Humphrey, *Education of a Public Man,* 189, 327, 160; Berman, *Hubert: The Triumph and Tragedy,* 47.

46. Benson, *Concept of Jacksonian Democracy,* 86–109, 332; Berman, *Hubert: The Triumph and Tragedy,* 279.

47. Ryskind, *Hubert: An Unauthorized Biography,* 175; Humphrey, *Education of a Public Man,* 59; Noam Chomsky, *American Power and the New Mandarins,* 74.

48. Thomas R. Dye, *Who's Running America? The Reagan Years,* 128.

49. Solberg, *Humphrey: A Biography,* 240, 416–17; Gorey, "'I'm a Born Optimist,'" 62; Levine, *Defender of the Faith,* 132–365.

50. Humphrey, *Education of a Public Man,* 285, 327; Gregory, *No More Lies: The Myth and the Reality of American History,* 249–51; James Perry, *Us and Them: How the Press Covered the 1972 Election,* 68. See also Theodore H. White, *The Making of the President, 1972,* 120–21, 126–30; and Hunter S. Thompson, *Fear and Loathing: On the Campaign Trail '72,* 371.

51. Humphrey, *Education of a Public Man,* 27.

52. Davison, *The Secret Government of the United States,* 84–85; Allen and Larry Abraham, *None Dare Call It Conspiracy,* 31–32; Allen, *The Rockefeller File,* 63; Farah, "Hollywood Hypocrisy," *The New American,* February 12, 1990, 36; "Kennedy is Chided on Agnew Criticism," *New York Times,* February 8, 1972, 37; Wallace, *What I Believe: Governor Wallace Lays It Out Straight,* 7.

53. The saying "Live simply that others may simply live" is attributed to Elizabeth Ann Seton; Meehan, "A Housecleaning for American Liberals," 107.

54. "Come Home, Democrats," *New York Times,* December 7, 1972, 14; "Power Struggle," *The New Republic,* December 16, 1972, 8; Irving Louis Horowitz, "The Operators Make Their Play"; Jerry W. Sanders, *Peddlers of Crisis: The Committee on the Present Danger and the Politics of Containment,* 150, 213–14, 217–18.

55. Robert Kuttner, "Red-Faced White Boys," *The New Republic,* March 21, 1988, 9–10; Joshua Muravchik, "Why the Democrats Lost Again," *Commentary,* February 1989, 20–22; William Greider, *Who Will Tell the People: The Betrayal of American Democracy,* 262–63; Roger Morris, *Partners in Power: The Clintons and Their America,* 66–70, 102–6, 130–31, 153–54, 262–63; Peter Goldman et al., *Quest for the Presidency, 1992,* 26, 37, 39–40, 58; Christopher Matthews, "Jerry Brown is Right On Target"; Ken Silverstein, "D.L.C. Dollars."

56. Paul Piccone, "The Crisis of American Conservatism"; Llewellyn H. Rockwell Jr., "Paleos, Neos, and Libertarians"; E. J. Dionne Jr., *Why Americans Hate Politics,* 55–76; Paul E. Gottfried, "Conservative Crack-Up Continued"; Paul E. Gottfried, "Geneology [sic] of a Movement," *Chronicles,* December 1995, 33–34; Samuel Francis, "Neo-Con Invasion," *The New American,* August 5, 1996, 27–31; Francis, *Beautiful Losers,* 95–117; Viguerie, "A Populist, and Proud of It," *National Review,* October 19, 1984, 42; Sanders, *Peddlers of Crisis,* 218.

CHAPTER 6: MODERN PHILOSOPHY 102

1. Smith, *Social and Religious Thought of Bryan,* 17–40, 167–218; Donald W. Dayton, *Discovering an Evangelical Heritage;* Paul Bullock, *Jerry Voorhis: The Idealist as Politician,* 8; Gerstle, "Protean Character of American Liberalism," 1047; Coletta, *Political Puritan,* vol. 3; Koenig, *Bryan: A Political Biography,* 367; Bryan, *Credo of the Commoner,* 93–94; Macdonald, *Henry Wallace,* 180; Schlesinger, ed., *History of American Presidential Elections,* 5:2060.

2. Werner, *Bryan,* 87, 153; Bryan, *The Commoner,* 47; Bryan, *Under Other Flags,* 247; Ashby, *Bryan: Champion of Democracy,* 188–93.

3. Stephen Jay Gould, "William Jennings Bryan's Last Campaign"; Gabriel Kolko, *Another Century of War?* 87–88; Smith, *Social and Religious Thought of Bryan,* 182–202; Tolstoy, *Tolstoy's Letters,* 2:590, 623, 665; Bryan and Bryan, *Memoirs of William Jennings Bryan,* 526–56; Marvin N. Olasky and John Perry, *Monkey Business: The True Story of the Scopes Trial.*

4. Schaffer, *America in the Great War,* 103.

5. Garrettson, *Hubert H. Humphrey,* 19, 23–27, ix; Macdonald, *Memoirs of a Revolutionist,* 371–72; Berman, *Hubert: The Triumph and Tragedy,* 279; Daniel J. Elazar, *American Federalism: A View from the States;* Daniel J. Elazar and Joseph Zikmund II, eds., *The Ecology of American Political Culture: Readings;* Ira Sharkansky, "The Utility of Elazar's Political Culture: A Research Note."

6. Elizabeth Anne Cobbs, *The Rich Neighbor Policy: Rockefeller and Kaiser in Brazil,* 9–10; Humphrey, *Political Philosophy of the New Deal,* 79.

7. Amrine, *This is Humphrey,* 76; Humphrey, *Political Philosophy of the New Deal,* 22, 80.

8. Hofstadter, *Age of Reform,* 315; Gerstle, "Protean Character of American Liberalism," 1044.

9. Schlesinger, ed., *History of American Presidential Elections,* 8:3187–88; Lustig, *Corporate Liberalism,* 234; Depoe, *Arthur M. Schlesinger Jr.,* 33.

10. Solberg, *Humphrey: A Biography,* 460, 280; Humphrey, *Cause is Mankind,* 33–46, 52, 29; Bowen, "What's New?" 144, 238; Colby and Dennett, *Thy Will Be Done,* 400–402, 337–39, 401–2; Schlesinger, ed., *History of American Presidential Elections,* 5:1849.

11. Dionne, *Why Americans Hate Politics,* 203; Barry M. Goldwater, *The Conscience of a Conservative,* 10–11; Theodore H. White, *The Making of the President, 1964,* 231, 364; Tilman, *C. Wright Mills,* 11; Phil Kerby, "California Runs the Gamut," *The Nation,* January 29, 1968, 144.

12. Arthur M. Schlesinger Jr., "The Case for George McGovern," *The New Republic,* February 26, 1972, 15–17; White, *Making of the President, 1972,* 44–45, 119–21, 131–32; Gore Vidal, *Homage to Daniel Shays: Collected Essays, 1952–1972,* 449; Thompson, *Fear and Loathing;* Walter Dean Burnham, "Political Scientists on the Political Process," *Society,* November/December 1973, 80–81.

13. Destler, *American Radicalism*, 17; Donald Bruce Johnson and Kirk H. Porter, comps., *National Party Platforms, 1840–1972*, 91.

14. Schattschneider, *The Semisovereign People: A Realist's View of Democracy in America*, 70, 71, 77, 80.

15. Werner, *Bryan*, 27, 49; Bryan, *The Commoner*, 158–60; Bryan, *Second Battle*, 285, 163–64.

16. Bryan, *Second Battle*, 224; Bryan, *The Commoner*, 160, 42–45; Bryan and Bryan, *Memoirs of William Jennings Bryan*, 174–75.

17. David P. Thelen, *Robert M. La Follette and the Insurgent Spirit*, 116–19, 165, 192; Carl R. Burgchardt, *Robert M. La Follette Sr.: The Voice of Conscience*, 110, 115, 208–11; Eugene M. Tobin, *Organize or Perish: America's Independent Progressives, 1913–1933*, 147–48, 156.

18. Lowi, *The End of Liberalism: Ideology, Policy, and the Crisis of Public Authority*, 46; Humphrey, *Political Philosophy of the New Deal*, 7, 36.

19. Humphrey, *Political Philosophy of the New Deal*, 90–91.

20. Humphrey, *Education of a Public Man*, 105–6; Humphrey, *The Man and His Dream*, 61–62; Humphrey, *Cause is Mankind*, 15–16.

21. William H. Riker, *Liberalism against Populism: A Confrontation between the Theory of Democracy and the Theory of Social Choice*, 16; White, *Making of the President, 1972*, 130.

22. Bryan, *Credo of the Commoner*, 53; Glad, ed., *Bryan: A Profile*, 135; Bryan, *Bryan: Selections*, 75–78; Levine, *Defender of the Faith*, 227–28.

23. Schlesinger, ed., *History of American Presidential Elections*, 5:1846, 1849–50.

24. Levine, *Defender of the Faith*, 81; Donald K. Springen, *William Jennings Bryan: Orator of Small-Town America*, 158, 169.

25. Craig, *After Wilson*, 29; Osnes, *Charles W. Bryan*, 341–42, 364; Levine, *Defender of the Faith*, 322.

26. Destler, *American Radicalism*. For the People's Party response to industrialization, see Norman Pollack, *The Populist Response to Industrial America: Midwestern Populist Thought*.

27. Schlesinger, ed., *History of American Presidential Elections*, 5:1850, 1823; Gompers, *Seventy Years of Life and Labor: An Autobiography*, 143; Coletta, *Political Evangelist*, 169; Keating, *The Gentleman from Colorado: A Memoir*, 79, 136–39; Koenig, *Bryan: A Political Biography*, 225, 252, 438–40; James A. Barnes, "Myths of the Bryan Campaign," 402; Ashby, *Bryan: Champion of Democracy*, 70; Bryan, *Speeches*, 2:164–80; Coletta, *Progressive Politician*, 139–42.

28. Gibbs, *Great Silent Majority*, 109–20; Solberg, *Humphrey: A Biography*, 115; Quigley, *Tragedy and Hope*, 941.

29. Humphrey, *Education of a Public Man*, 132.

30. Amrine, *This is Humphrey*, 108; Humphrey, *Education of a Public Man*, 166; Griffith, *Humphrey: A Candid Biography*, 102–3.

31. Cole, *Senator Gerald P. Nye*, 232; Griffith, *Humphrey: A Candid Biography*, 305; Zbigniew Brzezinski, *Between Two Ages: America's Role in the Technetronic Era*, 205; Amrine, *This is Humphrey*, 108.

32. Humphrey, *Cause is Mankind*, 15; Humphrey, *Education of a Public Man*, 122–23.

33. William Langer, "Promotion of National Defense—Increase in Personnel of Armed Forces," *Congressional Record*, June 19, 1948, 8982–83; Garrettson, *Hubert H. Humphrey*, 78, 86; Humphrey, *The Man and His Dream*, 128; Charles Levinson, *Vodka-Cola*, 131–32; Cohen, *Undefeated: The Life of Hubert Humphrey*, 436; "Humphrey vs. Ford and Reagan," *Des Moines Register*, May 11, 1976, 1A.

34. Berman, *Hubert: The Triumph and Tragedy*, 29–30, 56–57, 79; Amrine, *This is*

Humphrey, 247, 93; Nelson W. Polsby, *The Citizen's Choice: Humphrey or Nixon*, 7, 10–11; Solberg, *Humphrey: A Biography*, 164, 183; Humphrey, *The Stranger at Our Gate: America's Immigration Policy*.

35. Humphrey, *Cause is Mankind*, 47, 53–60; Dan B. Fleming Jr., *Kennedy vs. Humphrey, West Virginia, 1960: The Pivotal Battle for the Democratic Presidential Nomination*, 24; Albert Eisele, *Almost to the Presidency: A Biography of Two American Politicians*, 150–51, 205, 199–200, 326–27; Ryskind, *Hubert: An Unauthorized Biography*, 17; "Committee Hails Humphrey," *New York Times*, April 12, 1968, 22; "Labor's Best-Heeled Power-house," *Time*, March 1, 1976, 10–11; "Unions' Strategy for Putting Man They Want in White House," *U.S. News and World Report*, March 1, 1976, 68.

36. Downs, *An Economic Theory of Democracy*, 135.

37. William Langer, "Proposed Investigation of Republican National Convention of 1940," *Congressional Record*, January 17, 1944, 287; William Langer, "Wartime Method of Voting by Members of the Armed Forces," *Congressional Record*, February 4, 1944, 1250; Robert Griffith, "Old Progressives and the Cold War," 347; Kauffman, *America First!* 204; Downs, *Economic Theory of Democracy*, 263.

38. Lustig, *Corporate Liberalism*; Sutton, *Wall Street and FDR*; Robert M. Collins, "Positive Business Responses to the New Deal: The Roots of the Committee for Economic Development, 1933–1942," 369–91; Mills, *Power Elite*, 122; Shoup, *Carter Presidency and Beyond*, 10; G. William Domhoff, *Who Rules America Now? A View for the '80s*, 85–92.

39. Kolko, *Triumph of Conservatism*.

40. Falk, *End of World Order*, 122, 124; Richard Falk, *The Promise of World Order: Essays in Normative International Relations*, 34.

41. Bryan, *Bryan: Selections*, 88; Levine, *Defender of the Faith*.

42. Schlesinger, *Vital Center*, 11–50, 258, 50, 144–50, 159–60, 166, 257; Depoe, *Arthur M. Schlesinger Jr.*, 11; F. Ross Peterson, *Prophet without Honor: Glen H. Taylor and the Fight for American Liberalism*.

43. Humphrey, *Education of a Public Man*, 55; Solberg, *Humphrey: A Biography*, 94, 111–12; Ryskind, *Hubert: An Unauthorized Biography*, 95, 116–17; Sherrill and Ernst, *Drugstore Liberal*, 51–55; Shields, *Mr. Progressive: A Biography of Elmer Austin Benson*, 17, 23–26.

44. Falk, *End of World Order*, 124; Levinson, *Vodka-Cola*.

45. Truman, "Year of Challenge"; Ryskind, *Hubert: An Unauthorized Biography*, 271; Humphrey, *Cause is Mankind*, 17.

46. Solberg, *Humphrey: A Biography*, 76, 70; Bernstein, *Towards a New Past*, 276; Depoe, *Arthur M. Schlesinger Jr.*, 5; Ryskind, *Hubert: An Unauthorized Biography*, 118, 179–80, 271–72; Amrine, *This is Humphrey*, 134; Griffith, *Humphrey: A Candid Biography*, 185; Humphrey, *Education of a Public Man*, 129.

47. Depoe, *Arthur M. Schlesinger Jr.*, 61; Solberg, *Humphrey: A Biography*, 244, 257; Humphrey, *The Man and His Dream*, 281; Lokos, *Hysteria 1964*, 170; Bowen, "What's New?" 143.

48. Dwight Macdonald, *Discriminations: Essays and Afterthoughts*, 388–89, 400–401, 36, 302; Tilman, *C. Wright Mills*, 184–88; Lynd, *Intellectual Origins*; Ethel Grodzins Romm, *The Open Conspiracy: What America's Angry Generation Is Saying*, 151; Macdonald, *Memoirs of a Revolutionist*, 285–301; Michael Wreszin, *A Rebel in Defense of Tradition: The Life and Politics of Dwight Macdonald*, 167, 458–66; Brzezinski, *Between Two Ages*, 236.

49. Thompson, *Fear and Loathing*, 209, 367, 371; "Dylan and Humphrey," *Des Moines Register*, November 10, 1975, 4A; Stephen J. Whitfield, *A Critical American: The Politics of*

Dwight Macdonald, 105–6; Kauffman, "Mighty Long Fall," 14–15; Tor Egil Førland, "Bringing It All Back Home or Another Side of Bob Dylan: Midwestern Isolationist"; Samuel Francis, "Principalities and Powers: First Things Last," *Chronicles,* March 1997, 33; Robert Shelton, *No Direction Home: The Life and Music of Bob Dylan,* 222–28; Richard M. Scammon and Ben J. Wattenberg, *The Real Majority,* 155–57; Solberg, *Humphrey: A Biography,* 418.

50. Rowland Evans and Robert Novak, "Expect Ford to Offer Key Post to Humphrey," *Des Moines Register,* August 9, 1974; Caro, *Johnson: Path to Power;* Thomas M. Gaskin, "Senator Lyndon B. Johnson, the Eisenhower Administration, and U.S. Foreign Policy, 1957–60," *Presidential Studies Quarterly* 24 (Spring 1994): 341–61.

51. Shoup, *Carter Presidency and Beyond,* 5.

52. Springen, *Bryan: Orator,* 151–52; Coletta, *Political Evangelist,* 319, 58; Koenig, *Bryan: A Political Biography,* 415, 218, 231–36, 250, 254; Paul W. Glad, *McKinley, Bryan, and the People,* 172; Ferdinand Lundberg, *Imperial Hearst: A Social Biography,* 83; Werner, *Bryan,* 116.

53. Koenig, *Bryan: A Political Biography,* 312–13, 385; Bryan, *Under Other Flags,* 304; Long, *Bryan, the Great Commoner,* 188; Bryan, *Speeches,* 2:208; Glad, ed., *Bryan: A Profile,* 130–32; Paxton Hibben, *The Peerless Leader: William Jennings Bryan,* 270; Coletta, *Political Evangelist,* 410–11.

54. Coletta, *Progressive Politican,* 36, 129, 134, 140–41; Weisberger, *La Follettes of Wisconsin,* 190; Loewen, *Lies My Teacher Told Me,* 12–13; Ferdinand Lundberg, *The Myth of Democracy,* 91; Tansill, *America Goes to War;* Gould, "Bryan's Last Campaign"; Kazin, *A Godly Hero.*

55. Lundberg, *America's Sixty Families,* 244–407; Arthur Goddard, ed., *Harry Elmer Barnes, Learned Crusader: The New History in Action,* 314–15; Chomsky, *American Power;* Burnham, "Political Scientists on the Political Process"; John Trumpbour, ed., *How Harvard Rules: Reason in the Service of Empire;* Larry Abraham, *Call It Conspiracy,* 263–71; Robert F. Arnove, ed., *Philanthropy and Cultural Imperialism: The Foundations at Home and Abroad;* Exoo, *Democracy Upside Down,* 80; Donald Lazere, ed., *American Media and Mass Culture: Left Perspectives,* 83–84; Edward S. Herman and Noam Chomsky, *Manufacturing Consent: The Political Economy of the Mass Media.*

56. Levine, *Defender of the Faith;* Kauffman, *America First!* 192; Harry M. Daugherty, *The Inside Story of the Harding Tragedy,* 167–68; Wheeler, *Yankee from the West,* 233; Coletta, *Political Puritan,* 193; MacKay, *Progressive Movement of 1924,* 167–69; Southwick, *Presidential Also-Rans and Running Mates,* 481.

57. Humphrey, *Political Philosophy of the New Deal,* 20; Amrine, *This is Humphrey,* 251; Ryskind, *Hubert: An Unauthorized Biography,* 116–17; Humphrey, *The Man and His Dream,* 279; Solberg, *Humphrey: A Biography,* 257–58; Lokos, *Hysteria 1964,* 165, 147, 153.

58. Bowen, "What's New?" 143; Charles A. Lindbergh, *Banking and Currency, and The Money Trust;* Bruce L. Larson, *Lindbergh of Minnesota: A Political Biography;* Solberg, *Humphrey: A Biography,* 59; La Follette and La Follette, *Robert M. La Follette,* 2:1062–64; Johnson, *Diary Letters of Hiram Johnson,* 4:1–13–25, 1–21–25; James M. Youngdale, ed., *Third Party Footprints: An Anthology from Writings and Speeches of Midwest Radicals.*

59. Massimo Teodori, ed., *The New Left: A Documentary History,* 445–50; Eisele, *Almost to the Presidency,* 256–364; "'Weak' Nixon Lead Found among Top Businessmen," *New York Times,* May 20, 1968, 38; Burch, *Elites in American History,* 3:235–37; Scammon and Wattenberg, *Real Majority,* 154.

60. Humphrey, *Education of a Public Man,* 123; White, *Making of the President, 1964,*

351–52; Lokos, *Hysteria 1964;* "Forgive Us Our Debts," *Review of the News,* November 1, 1975; "A Majority Leader," *New York Times,* December 15, 1976, A24; Berman, *Hubert: The Triumph and Tragedy,* 150.

61. La Follette, *La Follette's Autobiography,* 146–49, 160, 318; Coletta, *Political Evangelist,* 391; Koenig, *Bryan: A Political Biography,* 420; La Follette and La Follette, *Robert M. La Follette,* 1:426, 444–45; Fred Greenbaum, *Robert Marion La Follette,* 79–80; "Bryan May Bolt National Ticket: Harmon or Underwood Will Drive Him to Alliance with Republican Radicals, Is the Report," *New York Times,* April 1, 1912, 1.

CHAPTER 7: SOURCES OF SUPPORT

1. Bernard J. Brommel, *Eugene V. Debs: Spokesman for Labor and Socialism;* Nick Salvatore, *Eugene V. Debs: Citizen and Socialist;* Pettigrew, *Imperial Washington,* 109–17; Lustig, *Corporate Liberalism,* 144–46; Gompers, *Seventy Years of Life and Labor,* 143.

2. Tilman, *C. Wright Mills,* 21, 23. See also Shoup, *Carter Presidency and Beyond,* 178–79; "Lane's Friends," *The Nation,* January 19, 1980, 37–40; Holly Sklar, ed., *Trilateralism: The Trilateral Commission and Elite Planning for World Management,* 41–42.

3. Terry Hitchins Nicolosi and Jose L. Ceballos, eds., *Official Proceedings of the 1992 Democratic National Convention,* 237; Ralph Nader, "The Greens and the Presidency: A Voice, Not an Echo," *The Nation,* July 8, 1996, 19.

4. Jefferson, *Life and Selected Writings,* 715; Mills, *Power Elite;* Richard H. Rovere, *The American Establishment and Other Reports, Opinions, and Speculations,* 3–21; Domhoff, *Who Rules America?;* Thomas R. Dye, *Who's Running America? Institutional Leadership in the United States;* Michael Parenti, *Democracy for the Few;* Gary Allen, "They Run America," *American Opinion,* May 1978 and June 1978, 1–4, 71–88 and 33–56, 105–10; Michael Schwartz, ed., *The Structure of Power in America: The Corporate Elite as a Ruling Class.*

5. Parenti, *Democracy for the Few,* 11–12; Richard J. Hardy, American Government lecture, University of Missouri–Columbia, September 5, 1990; John Rensenbrink, *The Greens and the Politics of Transformation,* 54–56; Schwartz, *Structure of Power,* 3.

6. Vidal, *Matters of Fact and of Fiction,* 263; Reese, "Buchanan Won't Score Points with American Establishment," 4A; Charles A. Beard, *An Economic Interpretation of the Constitution of the United States;* Burch, *Elites in American History;* Lundberg, *America's Sixty Families;* Greider, *Who Will Tell the People;* Phillips, *Arrogant Capital.*

7. Katz, *August Belmont;* Black, *King of Fifth Avenue;* Quigley, *Tragedy and Hope,* 50–53, 60–62, 327, 945, 950–54.

8. Hess, *America's Political Dynasties;* Burch, *Elites in American History,* vol. 1; Tise, *Proslavery: A History of the Defense of Slavery;* E. Digby Baltzell, *The Protestant Establishment: Aristocracy and Caste in America;* Baltzell, *Puritan Boston and Quaker Philadelphia;* Shoup, *Carter Presidency and Beyond,* 9; Quigley, *Tragedy and Hope,* 70–76, 934–56, 1244–45.

9. Lundberg, *America's Sixty Families,* 57–60; Glad, *McKinley, Bryan and the People,* 168–69; Koenig, *Bryan: A Political Biography,* 238, 201–7, 307, 315, 369; Southwick, *Presidential Also-Rans and Running Mates,* 407–9, 423.

10. Bryan, *Bryan: Selections,* 12–13; Lundberg, *America's Sixty Families,* 65, 113, 272–73; Koenig, *Bryan: A Political Biography,* 238; Lundberg, *Imperial Hearst,* 19, 83; Glad, *McKinley, Bryan, and the People,* 171–72.

11. W. A. Swanberg, *Citizen Hearst: A Biography of William Randolph Hearst,* 99–104, 218–21; Lundberg, *Imperial Hearst;* Villard, "Issues and Men," *The Nation,* July 11, 1936, 46.

12. Koenig, *Bryan: A Political Biography,* 375; Hollingsworth, *Whirligig of Politics,* 212;

Swanberg, *Citizen Hearst*, 251–52, 255; Clarence Darrow, *The Story of My Life*, 88–95, 100–111; Kevin Tierney, *Darrow: A Biography*, 42–45, 53–55, 124–26, 172–75; Long, *Bryan, the Great Commoner*, 79, 154, 184; Bryan, *Under Other Flags*, 350.

13. Coletta, *Political Evangelist*, 373–74; Coletta, *Political Puritan*, 187, 188; Croly, *Promise of American Life*, 164; Schlesinger, ed., *History of American Presidential Elections*, 5:2067–69, 6:2352; Lundberg, *Imperial Hearst*, 124, 245, 256–57, 233, 260–64, 374–75; Johnson and Porter, comps., *National Party Platforms*, 151–52; Thelen, *La Follette and the Insurgent Spirit*, 66; Swanberg, *Citizen Hearst*, 394–97; Oswald Garrison Villard, "Hiram W. Johnson," *The Nation*, June 5, 1920, 748; Johnson, *Diary Letters of Hiram Johnson*, 4:5–19–22; Lee Meriwether, *Jim Reed, "Senatorial Immortal": A Biography*, 166–68; Richard W. Leopold, *Elihu Root and the Conservative Tradition*, 72.

14. Glad, *McKinley, Bryan, and the People*, 171, 169; Lundberg, *America's Sixty Families*, 60, 55; Werner, *Bryan*, 100, 111; Koenig, *Bryan: A Political Biography*, 312; Allen, "Speeches at a Jacksonian Banquet," 1540–41; Bryan, *Credo of the Commoner*, 105.

15. Koenig, *Bryan: A Political Biography*, 232, 335–36, 394, 410–11; Curti, *Bryan and World Peace*, 127–29; Pettigrew, *Imperial Washington*, 320–25; Bryan, *Under Other Flags*, 309; Werner, *Bryan*, 85, 126–29; Lundberg, *America's Sixty Families*, 500, 55; Coletta, *Political Evangelist*, 321; Bryan and Bryan, *Memoirs of William Jennings Bryan*, 174–75.

16. Koenig, *Bryan: A Political Biography*, 385, 303–6; Coletta, *Political Evangelist*, 321; Katz, *August Belmont*; Black, *King of Fifth Avenue*; Bryan, *The Commoner*, 377; Bryan and Bryan, *Memoirs of William Jennings Bryan*, 174–75; Bryan, *Bryan: Selections*, 131–32; Pinchot, *History of the Progressive Party*, 65.

17. Bryan, *Credo of the Commoner*, 56, 104; Bryan, *Under Other Flags*, 300; Hibben, *Peerless Leader*, 270–71, 279, 285.

18. Schlesinger, ed., *History of American Presidential Elections*, 5:2076, 2080–83; Lundberg, *America's Sixty Families*, 98–103, 158–59, 55.

19. Werner, *Bryan*, 137; Smith, *Social and Religious Thought of Bryan*, 34–35.

20. Coletta, *Progressive Politician*, 38; Koenig, *Bryan: A Political Biography*, 473–79, 616–17, 622–23; Lundberg, *America's Sixty Families*, 109; Springen, *Bryan: Orator*, 158; Levine, *Defender of the Faith*, 298–300, 315; Robert K. Murray, *The 103rd Ballot: Democrats and the Disaster in Madison Square Garden*, 52, 169, 203–5.

21. Garrettson, *Hubert H. Humphrey*, 78, 86; Sherrill and Ernst, *Drugstore Liberal*, 183–86; Humphrey, *The Man and His Dream*, 128; Ryskind, *Hubert: An Unauthorized Biography*, 118, 206; Colby and Dennett, *Thy Will Be Done*, 217, 307; Levinson, *Vodka-Cola*, 131–32.

22. Humphrey, *Education of a Public Man*, 218–20, 376; Thomas Ferguson and Joel Rogers, *Right Turn: The Decline of the Democrats and the Future of American Politics*, 164, 166; Morris, *Partners in Power*, 262–63; Stanley G. Hilton, *Senator for Sale: An Unauthorized Biography of Senator Bob Dole*, 180–84; Sklar, ed., *Trilateralism*.

23. Smith, *Thomas E. Dewey*, 601, 626–39, 289–90, 301–3; Schlafly, *Choice Not an Echo*, 45–50; Ferguson and Rogers, *Right Turn*, 143; George Will, "Strauss Wrong Choice as Instructor in Capitalism," *Columbia (Mo.) Daily Tribune*, June 19, 1991, 6A; Horowitz, "Operators Make Their Play."

24. Cohen, *Undefeated: The Life of Hubert Humphrey*, 219, 305, 437; "Committee Hails Humphrey," *New York Times*, April 12, 1968, 22; Solberg, *Humphrey: A Biography*, 153; "Humphrey Backers Form Eastern Unit," *New York Times*, January 13, 1960, 13; Lundberg, *America's Sixty Families*, 12, 36, 153–54, 222–23, 439–40; Rudy Abramson, *Spanning the Century: The Life of W. Averell Harriman, 1891–1986*, 236; Walter Isaacson and Evan Thomas, *The Wise Men: Six Friends and the World They Made*.

25. Humphrey, *The Man and His Dream*, 106–9, 209; "They're Off—How They'll Run," *Newsweek*, January 11, 1960, 20; Ryskind, *Hubert: An Unauthorized Biography*, 266; Thayer, *Who Shakes the Money Tree? American Campaign Financing Practices from 1789 to the Present*, 84; Herbert E. Alexander, *Financing the 1968 Election*, 9; Lippmann, "Goldwater Movement," 13; White, *Making of the President, 1964*, 364, 369–70; Kevin Phillips, *The Politics of Rich and Poor: Wealth and the American Electorate in the Reagan Aftermath*, 38; Solberg, *Humphrey: A Biography*, 260; Burch, *Elites in American History*, 3:195–96.

26. Humphrey, *Education of a Public Man*, 218–20; Sherrill and Ernst, *Drugstore Liberal*, 183–84.

27. Solberg, *Humphrey: A Biography*, 279–80.

28. Coletta, *Progressive Politician*, 38; Solberg, *Humphrey: A Biography*, 326; Berman, *Hubert: The Triumph and Tragedy*, 76, 161, 170, 212; "Henry Ford for Humphrey, Saying Country Needs Him," *New York Times*, August 22, 1968, 3; G. William Domhoff, *Fat Cats and Democrats: The Role of the Big Rich in the Party of the Common Man*, 38–39, 58, 44; Allen, "They Run America," 35; Robert E. Bedingfield, "Wall St. Leader Backs Humphrey: Weinberg to Seek 'Millions' in One-Man Fund Drive," *New York Times*, April 30, 1968, 1; Alexander, *Financing the 1968 Election*, 63, 341–42; Ben A. Franklin, "Humphrey Names Donors: 121 Gave $1,000 or More," *New York Times*, March 15, 1972, 33.

29. "Mrs. Lehman for Humphrey," *New York Times*, May 8, 1968, 31; Alexander, *Financing the 1968 Election*, 180–81; Lundberg, *America's Sixty Families*, 179–80, 38–39, 223–24; Sutton, *Wall Street and FDR*, 111–12; Joseph Wechsberg, *The Merchant Bankers*, 219–61; Isaacson and Thomas, *Wise Men*, 710–12; Abramson, *Spanning the Century*, 654, 666–67, 671, 686–87; "'Weak' Nixon Lead Found among Top Businessmen," *New York Times*, May 20, 1968, 38; "Humphrey Meets with Executives," *New York Times*, May 7, 1968, 24.

30. Morton Mintz and Jerry S. Cohen, *America, Inc.: Who Owns and Operates the United States*, 210; Alexander, *Financing the 1968 Election*, 151, 341–42; Domhoff, *Fat Cats and Democrats*, 43; "Humphrey is Backed by One Hundred Businessmen," *New York Times*, November 3, 1968, 80; Quigley, *Tragedy and Hope*, 138, 499–500, 520–21, 581, 950–54; Hoar, "Humphrey: The Dark Horse Is at the Gate," 73; Solberg, *Humphrey: A Biography*, 387; English et al., *Divided They Stand*, 174, 386; Thayer, *Who Shakes the Money Tree?* 101.

31. Cohen, *Undefeated: The Life of Hubert Humphrey*, 391, 436–39; Solberg, *Humphrey: A Biography*, 425, 428, 429, 432, 445–46; Franklin, "Humphrey Names Donors," 33; Barbara D. Paul et al., eds., *CRF Listing of Political Contributors and Lenders of $10,000 or More in 1972*; Hoar, "Humphrey: The Dark Horse Is at the Gate," 71, 73.

32. "Humphrey Repays Debts 4c on Dollar," *Des Moines Register*, December 30, 1975, 5A; "Forgive Us Our Debts," *Review of the News*, November 1, 1975; "Humphrey's Backers Ready for Big Push: Nationwide Draft Effort to Open This Week," *Des Moines Register*, April 4, 1976, 1A; Loye Miller Jr., "Humphrey Draft Call Revived; Carter Still Favorite," *Des Moines Register*, May 20, 1976, 13A; Cohen, *Undefeated: The Life of Hubert Humphrey*, 479–80; Ferguson and Rogers, *Right Turn*, 162–63.

33. Solberg, *Humphrey: A Biography*, 437; Morris, *Partners in Power*, 260; Shoup, *Carter Presidency and Beyond*, 255; "Businessmen Behind the Democrats," *Fortune*, November 14, 1983, 46; Ferguson and Rogers, *Right Turn*, 162–64; Herbert E. Alexander and Brian A. Haggerty, *Financing the 1984 Election*, 160.

34. Shoup and Minter, *Imperial Brain Trust*, 4–5; Ferdinand Lundberg, *The Rockefeller Syndrome*, 289–93; Allen, *Rockefeller File*, 51–56; James Perloff, *The Shadows of Power: The Council on Foreign Relations and the American Decline*, 7–9.

35. Quigley, *Tragedy and Hope*, 130–75, 580–85, 950–54, 939; Carroll Quigley, *The Anglo-American Establishment: From Rhodes to Cliveden;* Shoup and Minter, *Imperial Brain Trust*, 11–20, 103–7, 23; Schulzinger, *Wise Men of Foreign Affairs*, 2–6; Abraham, *Call It Conspiracy*, 92–93; Perloff, *Shadows of Power*, 104.

36. Abraham, *Call It Conspiracy*, 97–102, 314–15; Perloff, *Shadows of Power*, 178–90; "Shadows across the Land: Current CFR Dominance over Government, Foundations, Media, and Industry," *The New American*, September 16, 1996, 16–19; "Lengthening Shadows: From 1929 to the Present," *The New American*, September 16, 1996, 20–21; *Council on Foreign Relations: 2003 Annual Report*, 124. CFR members have included Eisenhower and Stevenson (1952 and 1956), Nixon and Kennedy (1960), Nixon and Humphrey (1968), Nixon and McGovern (1972), Ford and Carter (1976), Bush Sr. and Dukakis (1988), and Bush Sr. and Clinton (1992).

37. Domhoff, *The Higher Circles: The Governing Class in America*, 112, 118; Barnes, *Chickens of the Interventionist Liberals*, 10; Rovere, *American Establishment*, 18; Chester Ward and Phyllis Schlafly, *Kissinger on the Couch;* Richard J. Barnet, *Roots of War*, 49; Shoup and Minter, *Imperial Brain Trust*, 45–46, 258; Schulzinger, *Wise Men of Foreign Affairs*, 210–11, 236.

38. Thomas Fleming, "The Illusions of Democracy," 11; Noam Chomsky, *The Culture of Terrorism*, 32; Chomsky, *Language and Politics*, 699; Zinn, *People's History of the United States*, 546–48.

39. Barnet, *Roots of War*, 49, 182; Bill Kauffman, "Who Can We Shoot?" *Chronicles*, March 1996, 18; Isaacson and Thomas, *Wise Men*, 677–78, 681, 707; Noam Chomsky, *Towards a New Cold War: Essays on the Current Crisis and How We Got There*, 77–79; Leonard Mosley, *Dulles: A Biography of Eleanor, Allen, and John Foster Dulles and Their Family Network;* Gary Allen, "Insiders of the Great Conspiracy," *American Opinion*, September 1982, 77–78; Perloff, *Shadows of Power*, 129.

40. Charles Morrow Wilson, *The Commoner: William Jennings Bryan*, 218; Leopold, *Elihu Root*, 45–46, 101–2; Johnson, *Diary Letters of Hiram Johnson*, 1:2–2–18, 3:6–22–19, 5:2–15–30.

41. Southwick, *Presidential Also-Rans and Running Mates*, 471–73; Levine, *Defender of the Faith*, 299–300, 315–21; Koenig, *Bryan: A Political Biography*, 622–25; Tansill, *America Goes to War*, 162–69, 210; Bernstein, *Towards a New Past*, 202–31; Williams, *Contours of American History*, 419–24.

42. Schulzinger, *Wise Men of Foreign Affairs*, 17–19, 24.

43. Craig, *After Wilson*, 58–59, 67; Lovett, "American Foreign Policy: A Progressive View," 49–60; Levine, *Defender of the Faith*, 299–300, 315–21; Koenig, *Bryan: A Political Biography*, 622–23, 625; Murray, *103rd Ballot*, 251, 238–40; Burgchardt, *La Follette Sr.: The Voice of Conscience*, 111; Perloff, *Shadows of Power*, 46–47; Johnson, *Diary Letters of Hiram Johnson*, 4:7–10–24; Schulzinger, *Wise Men of Foreign Affairs*, 12.

44. Falk, *End of World Order*, 122, 124; Shoup and Minter, *Imperial Brain Trust*, 105; Leopold, *Elihu Root;* Schulzinger, *Wise Men of Foreign Affairs*, 10.

45. Freidel, *Franklin D. Roosevelt*, 2:17–18, 73, 122–24, 235–40; Schulzinger, *Wise Men of Foreign Affairs*, 11–12, 60–61, 122–24, 135–36; Perloff, *Shadows of Power*, 54–55, 60–61, 81–100, 120–40; Shoup and Minter, *Imperial Brain Trust*, 25–29, 62–64, 118–22, 193–94, 199–205; *Council on Foreign Relations: A Record of Twenty-Five Years;* Abraham, *Call It Conspiracy*, 99–101.

46. Shoup and Minter, *Imperial Brain Trust*, 94; Dan Smoot, *The Invisible Government*, 148.

47. Shoup, *Carter Presidency and Beyond*, 9; Quigley, *Tragedy and Hope*, 73–74, 945, 1244; Sherrill and Ernst, *Drugstore Liberal*, 53. See also Allen, *Richard Nixon*, 79–80.

48. *Council on Foreign Relations: 2003 Annual Report,* 136; Zakaria, "The Vision Thing," *New York Times,* August 21, 1996, A17.

49. Davison, *Secret Government,* 84–85; Allen, *Richard Nixon,* 82. See also Barry M. Goldwater, "Barry Goldwater Talks About 'Liberals' and 'Liberalism.'"

CHAPTER 8: POSITIONS ON DEMOCRACY

1. William Morris, ed., *The American Heritage Dictionary of the English Language,* 351.

2. Arthur A. Rouner Jr., *The Congregational Way of Life;* Manfred Waldemar Kohl, *Congregationalism in America;* Joshua Miller, "Direct Democracy and the Puritan Theory of Membership," *Journal of Politics* 53 (February 1991): 57–74; Leonard Verduin, *The Anatomy of a Hybrid: A Study in Church-State Relationships.*

3. Zinn, *People's History of the United States,* 76–101; Jensen, *New Nation;* Black, *Our Constitution;* Beard, *Economic Interpretation;* Burch, *Elites in American History,* vol. 1; Will Durant and Ariel Durant, *The Age of Voltaire,* 682–92; Rousseau, *Social Contract;* Hanna Fenichel Pitkin, "Representation and Democracy: Uneasy Alliance," *Scandinavian Political Studies* 27 (September 2004): 335–42.

4. Parenti, *Democracy for the Few,* 60–75; Thomas R. Dye and L. Harmon Zeigler, *The Irony of Democracy: An Uncommon Introduction to American Politics,* 26–56; Lundberg, *Myth of Democracy,* 11–14; Matthews, *If Men Were Angels;* Wiltse, *Jeffersonian Tradition in American Democracy,* 22, 99.

5. Matthews, *Radical Politics of Thomas Jefferson,* 4–5, 8, 26–27, 98–99, 103–4; Miller, *Alexander Hamilton,* 15, 123–25, 227–28; Hamilton, Madison, and Jay, *Federalist Papers,* 300–303, 83–84, 100–102; John Locke, *Two Treatises of Government;* Durant and Durant, *Age of Voltaire,* 346–60; Storing, *What the Anti-Federalists Were For,* 53–63, 15–23; Black, *Our Constitution,* 50.

6. Wiltse, *Jeffersonian Tradition in American Democracy,* 46, 47–50; Matthews, *Radical Politics of Thomas Jefferson,* 9–10, 17–18, 24–29, 63–64, 119–26.

7. Mills, *Power Elite;* Parenti, *Democracy for the Few;* Herman and Chomsky, *Manufacturing Consent;* Roy C. Macridis and Bernard E. Brown, *Comparative Politics: Notes and Readings,* 93, 95.

8. Dankwart A. Rustow and Kenneth Paul Erickson, eds., *Comparative Political Dynamics: Global Research Perspectives,* 173; Sørensen, *Democracy and Democratization: Processes and Prospects in a Changing World,* 29–30, 47–50, 57–60, 80–85.

9. Bryan, *Bryan: Selections,* 31; Coletta, *Political Evangelist,* 390; Bryan, *Speeches,* 2:100–119; Johnson and Porter, comps., *National Party Platforms,* 144, 150–51; Hardy, *Government in America,* 346–47; Bryan, *Under Other Flags,* 238–39; "The Candidates and Their Platforms," *Locomotive Engineers Journal,* September 1924, 653.

10. Lundberg, *Myth of Democracy,* 29–30.

11. Johnson and Porter, comps., *National Party Platforms,* 170; Bryan, *The Commoner,* 280; Bryan, *Under Other Flags,* 52–53; Glad, ed., *Bryan: A Profile,* 134, 152.

12. Croly, *Promise of American Life,* 159; Johnson and Porter, comps., *National Party Platforms,* 105; Bryan, *Speeches,* 2:254–55; Werner, *Bryan,* 157; Coletta, *Political Evangelist,* 402; Koenig, *Bryan: A Political Biography,* 437–38; William Howard Taft and William Jennings Bryan, *World Peace,* 75; Clements, *Bryan: Missionary Isolationist,* 117, 139; Kauffman, *America First!* 54–55, 225.

13. Walter T. K. Nugent, *The Tolerant Populists: Kansas Populism and Nativism,* 123–24, 152, 158–65; Thomas R. Burkholder, "Kansas Populism, Woman Suffrage, and the

Agrarian Myth: A Case Study in the Limits of Mythic Transcendence"; Koenig, *Bryan: A Political Biography*, 48, 64, 95–96, 317, 358, 559, 570–72; Bryan, *Bryan: Selections*, 47–49, 71; Levine, *Defender of the Faith*, 128–30.

14. Bryan, *The Commoner*, 85, 32; Bryan, *Credo of the Commoner*, 94–95; Johnson and Porter, comps., *National Party Platforms*, 170, 106, 115, 149, 118; Bryan, *Bryan: Selections*, 31–35; Bryan, *Under Other Flags*, 237; A. Bower Sageser, *Joseph L. Bristow: Kansas Progressive*, 100–102; Springen, *Bryan: Orator*, 160; Werner, *Bryan*, 152.

15. Bryan, *Credo of the Commoner*, 69–70; Johnson and Porter, comps., *National Party Platforms*, 100, 170; Bryan, *The Commoner*, 15, 258–60; Werner, *Bryan*, 258.

16. Werner, *Bryan*, 25, 37; Bryan, *Under Other Flags*, 307; Bryan, *The Commoner*, 312; Johnson and Porter, comps., *National Party Platforms*, 150.

17. Bryan, *Bryan: Selections*, 45; Bryan and Bryan, *Memoirs of William Jennings Bryan*, 174–75.

18. Johnson and Porter, comps., *National Party Platforms*, 114, 145, 169–70; Smith, *Social and Religious Thought of Bryan*, 34–35; Koenig, *Bryan: A Political Biography*, 418; Coletta, *Political Evangelist*, 412; Levine, *Defender of the Faith*, 305.

19. Bryan, *Second Battle*, 205, 183, 228; Johnson and Porter, comps., *National Party Platforms*, 114, 146, 169; Bryan, *Speeches*, 2:120–42; Smith, *Social and Religious Thought of Bryan*, 9–10; Koenig, *Bryan: A Political Biography*, 413–17; Springen, *Bryan: Orator*, 153–55; Kolko, *Triumph of Conservatism*, 255–78; Coletta, *Progressive Politician*, 140–43; Schaffer, *America in the Great War*, xv, 46, 59; Keating, *Gentleman from Colorado*, 349–53, 474–75.

20. Wiltse, *Jeffersonian Tradition in American Democracy*, 220–21; Garson, *Power and Politics in the United States*, 284; Werner, *Bryan*, 31–32; Bryan, *Credo of the Commoner*, 78–79; Bryan, *Second Battle*, 213, 243, 523; Johnson and Porter, comps., *National Party Platforms*, 98, 146; Bryan, *Under Other Flags*, 105. See also Taylor, *Inquiry into the Principles and Policy*, 488; and Taylor, *Construction Construed*, 247.

21. Bryan, *Credo of the Commoner*, 68, 77–78; Coletta, *Political Evangelist*, 56–57; Bryan, *Second Battle*, 164–67; Bryan, *The Commoner*, 225; Johnson and Porter, comps., *National Party Platforms*, 147, 169; Levine, *Defender of the Faith*, 98–100; Koenig, *Bryan: A Political Biography*, 597.

22. Werner, *Bryan*, 27; Coletta, *Progressive Politician*, 143; Curti, *Bryan and World Peace*, 120; Koenig, *Bryan: A Political Biography*, 447; Bryan, *Second Battle*, 523, 542; Bryan, *The Commoner*, 17, 49–50, 322–23; Cook, Harris, and Radosh, *Past Imperfect*, 30–31.

23. Clements, *Bryan: Missionary Isolationist*, 67–68; Robert S. Maxwell, ed., *La Follette*, 46; Johnson and Porter, comps., *National Party Platforms*, 173; Leopold, *Elihu Root*, 101; Claudius O. Johnson, *Borah of Idaho*, 190–91; Ollie James, "The Tolls Question," *Congressional Record*, April 15, 1914, 6723–25; Ruth Warner Towne, *Senator William J. Stone and the Politics of Compromise*, 136–40.

24. Bryan, *Second Battle*, 229, 285; Bryan, *Speeches*, 2:162, 59–60, 91, 100–119; Johnson and Porter, comps., *National Party Platforms*, 150; Bryan, *The Commoner*, 268–69, 73; Werner, *Bryan*, 279–80; Bryan, *Credo of the Commoner*, 53.

25. Pettigrew, *Imperial Washington*, 118; Osnes, *Charles W. Bryan*, 377–78; Tierney, *Darrow: A Biography*, 427–34; T. Harry Williams, *Huey Long*; Alan Brinkley, *Voices of Protest: Huey Long, Father Coughlin, and the Great Depression*; Meriwether, *Jim Reed*, 259.

26. Humphrey, "The American System: The Great Society," 682, 685.

27. Thelen, *La Follette and the Insurgent Spirit*, 104–32, 176–94; Schaffer, *America in the Great War*, 212; Gibbs, *Great Silent Majority*, 109–20; Chomsky, *Culture of Terrorism*, 32–33; Robert H. Wiebe, *Self-Rule: A Cultural History of American Democracy*.

28. Schlesinger, *Vital Center,* 178–79; Barnes, *Chickens of the Interventionist Liberals,* 8–9; Francis, *Beautiful Losers,* 95–117; Chomsky, *Culture of Terrorism,* 33; Macdonald, *Henry Wallace,* 180–81.

29. Humphrey, *Political Philosophy of the New Deal,* 31–34; Humphrey, *Cause is Mankind,* 14–15, 47–48, 52–53.

30. Rae, *Decline and Fall,* 17, 20–23, 43–44, 119; Christopher Lasch, *The Revolt of the Elites and the Betrayal of Democracy,* 166–67; Forcey, *Crossroads of Liberalism,* 125–27; Pinchot, *History of the Progressive Party,* 146; Berman, *Hubert: The Triumph and Tragedy,* 47, 279; Chomsky, *American Power,* 74; English et al., *Divided They Stand,* 82, 84; Alsop, *Nixon and Rockefeller,* 164–66.

31. Robert S. Maxwell, *La Follette and the Rise of the Progressives in Wisconsin,* 12; Fleming, "Illusions of Democracy," 11; Sklar, ed., *Trilateralism,* 35–39, 293–307; Chomsky, *Culture of Terrorism,* 32; and Chomsky, *Language and Politics,* 699; Zinn, *People's History of the United States,* 546–48.

32. Kolko, *Triumph of Conservatism,* 206; Thelen, *La Follette and the Insurgent Spirit,* 130–32; Lundberg, *America's Sixty Families,* 112; Rae, *Decline and Fall,* 21; Griffith, ed., *Major Problems in American History,* 185, 188; Louis L. Ludlow, "Should a War Referendum Amendment be Added to the Constitution?" *Congressional Digest,* February 1938, 44–47; Ludlow, "Vision of Jefferson," 479; Kauffman, *America First!* 196–97, 225–27; Henry L. Stimson, "Should a War Referendum Amendment Be Added to the Constitution?" *Congressional Digest,* February 1938, 59–62; Cole, *Senator Gerald P. Nye,* 120–22; "State Amendments: No on Recall, Yes on Bonuses," *Minneapolis Star Tribune,* October 30, 1996, A16.

33. Berman, *Hubert: The Triumph and Tragedy,* 248–51.

34. William Langer, "Proposed Change in Method of Election of President and Vice President," *Congressional Record,* February 1, 1950, 1268; Theodore H. White, *The Making of the President, 1960,* 36–42; W. H. Lawrence, "Johnson's Big Problem: How Texan's Congressional Support Has Failed Him in Delegate Quests," *New York Times,* June 19, 1960, 40; Ralph G. Martin, *Ballots and Bandwagons,* 419; Schlesinger, ed., *History of American Presidential Elections,* 8:3239–40; Solberg, *Humphrey: A Biography,* 200.

35. Ryskind, *Hubert: An Unauthorized Biography,* 251; Scammon and Wattenberg, *Real Majority,* 123, 126–42, 327; Berman, *Hubert: The Triumph and Tragedy,* 162; Solberg, *Humphrey: A Biography,* 327, 345; English et al., *Divided They Stand,* 218.

36. Solberg, *Humphrey: A Biography,* 428, 429, 452; Rowland Evans and Robert Novak, "Non-Candidate Strategy Worries Humphrey Pals," *Sioux City Journal,* January 22, 1976; James Flansburg, "Hughes Chides Humphrey for 'Non-Campaign,'" *Des Moines Register,* April 6, 1976, 2B; Tom Wicker, "Humphrey Seen as Spoiler Splitting the Party," *Des Moines Register,* April 24, 1976, 18A.

37. Solberg, *Humphrey: A Biography,* 141; Humphrey, "Proposed Change in Method of Election of President and Vice President," *Congressional Record,* February 1, 1950, 1261–63; "The Senate: Slingshot and a Giant," *Newsweek,* March 2, 1959, 19; Sherrill, *Accidental President,* 53–54.

38. Johnson and Porter, comps., *National Party Platforms,* 170; Caro, *Johnson: Path to Power,* 566–67; "An Ominous Nomination," *The Christian Century,* July 31, 1940, 942–44.

39. Robert A. Caro, *The Years of Lyndon Johnson: Means of Ascent,* xxxii–iii, 191–93, 296–97, 403; Vance Packard, *The Hidden Persuaders,* 156; Berman, *Hubert: The Triumph and Tragedy,* 55.

40. Schlesinger, *Vital Center,* 24, 44; Depoe, *Arthur M. Schlesinger Jr.,* 38–39;

Humphrey, *Education of a Public Man,* 130, 329; Ryskind, *Hubert: An Unauthorized Biography,* 45; Schlesinger, ed., *History of American Presidential Elections,* 8:3162–65, 3173.

41. Link, *Woodrow Wilson and the Progressive Era;* Lundberg, *America's Sixty Families,* 109–48; Kolko, *Triumph of Conservatism;* Cook, Harris, and Radosh, *Past Imperfect,* 127–58; Schaffer, *America in the Great War;* Burch, *Elites in American History,* 2:201–44.

42. Craig, *After Wilson;* Sutton, *Wall Street and FDR,* 106–14, 119; Levine, *Defender of the Faith,* 299; Lundberg, *America's Sixty Families,* 178–81; Lundberg, *Rich and the Super-Rich,* 172, 793; "Political Note: Warrior to War," *Time,* February 3, 1936, 14–15; Wolfskill, *Revolt of the Conservatives,* 142–43, 149–52; Jules Archer, *The Plot to Seize the White House,* 30–32, 160–61, 228–29.

43. Sutton, *Wall Street and FDR;* Freidel, *Franklin D. Roosevelt,* 2:92–93, 248, 255, 259; Lundberg, *America's Sixty Families,* 452–89; Lundberg, *Rich and the Super-Rich,* 172–73, 214, 649–50; Hofstadter, *Age of Reform,* 310–14; Collins, "Positive Business Responses to the New Deal," 369–91; Bernstein, *Towards a New Past,* 263–99; Ferguson and Rogers, *Right Turn,* 37–38, 46–48; Moss, *Moving on,* 16–18; Burch, *Elites in American History,* 3:13–122.

44. Fleming, "Illusions of Democracy," 11; Bernstein, *Towards a New Past,* 300–321; Frank Kofsky, *Harry S. Truman and the War Scare of 1948: A Successful Campaign to Deceive the Nation;* Burch, *Elites in American History,* 3:80–122; Griffith, ed., *Major Problems in American History,* 152–55.

45. Dye and Zeigler, *Irony of Democracy,* 121; Shoup and Minter, *Imperial Brain Trust,* 37; Quigley, *Tragedy and Hope,* 988–89; Moss, *Moving On,* 112–13.

46. Quigley, *Tragedy and Hope,* 1245; Colby and Dennett, *Thy Will Be Done,* 337–39; Lundberg, *Rich and the Super-Rich,* 173–74; Burch, *Elites in American History,* 3:169–230.

47. Schlafly, *Choice Not an Echo,* 101; Domhoff, *Fat Cats and Democrats,* 42–44, 53; Lundberg, *Rich and the Super-Rich,* 174–76, 258, 261, 512–19, 772, 785–86; Sherrill, *Accidental President,* 56–58, 74–78; Caro, *Johnson: Path to Power,* 33–49, 79–99, 272–74, 663–64; Caro, *Johnson: Means of Ascent,* 5–8, 78, 253; Burch, *Elites in American History,* 3:192–230.

48. Herbert E. Alexander, *Financing the 1976 Election,* 235, 237; Christopher Lydon, "Jimmy Carter Revealed: He's a Rockefeller Republican"; Roger Morris, "Jimmy Carter's Ruling Class"; Sklar, ed., *Trilateralism,* 197–211; Shoup, *Carter Presidency and Beyond,* 39–64, 237; Zinn, *People's History of the United States,* 548–62; Abraham, *Call It Conspiracy,* 189–207; Burch, *Elites in American History,* 3:307–58.

49. Solberg, *Humphrey: A Biography,* 119; Ryskind, *Hubert: An Unauthorized Biography,* 118, 206; Humphrey, *The Man and His Dream,* 128.

50. Schattschneider, *Semisovereign People,* 70–80; Hollingsworth, *Whirligig of Politics,* 57; Levine, *Defender of the Faith,* 321–23; Eisele, *Almost to the Presidency,* 87–107; Sherrill and Ernst, *Drugstore Liberal,* 92–97; Sherrill, *Accidental President,* 85–89; Humphrey, *The Man and His Dream,* 144; Lundberg, *Rich and the Super-Rich,* 482–87, 490–91; Solberg, *Humphrey: A Biography,* 135; Domhoff, *Fat Cats and Democrats,* 79–82, 103.

51. Solberg, *Humphrey: A Biography,* 259; "The Presidency: History Repeats," *Time,* January 20, 1936, 11–12; "Campaign: Money, Money, Money," *Time,* November 2, 1936, 11; Morris, *Partners in Power,* 260.

52. Kolko, *Triumph of Conservatism,* 206–7, 255–67, 278; Johnson and Porter, comps., *National Party Platforms,* 169; Coletta, *Progressive Politician,* 140–43; Craig, *After Wilson,* 140–41; Lundberg, *America's Sixty Families,* 460; Tierney, *Darrow: A Biography,* 427–34; Bennett Champ Clark, "Is the Increasing Power of the President Improving the American Government?" *Congressional Digest,* November 1933, 275.

53. Humphrey, *Education of a Public Man,* 24, 73; Solberg, *Humphrey: A Biography,* 89,

150, 165–66, 142–43; Garrettson, *Hubert H. Humphrey,* 78, 86; Sherrill and Ernst, *Drugstore Liberal,* 183–86; Humphrey, "Should the American People Reject the 'Welfare State'?" *Congressional Digest,* August–September 1950, 205; Bowen, "What's New?" 144; Amrine, *This is Humphrey,* 137.

54. Ryskind, *Hubert: An Unauthorized Biography,* 15–16, 297–98; Sherrill, *Accidental President,* 56, 128; Humphrey, *Cause is Mankind,* 48; Solberg, *Humphrey: A Biography,* 261, 280.

55. Cole, *Roosevelt and the Isolationists,* 95, 106–10; David L. Porter, *Congress and the Waning of the New Deal,* 45–47, 51; Arthur Capper, "Reciprocal Trade Agreements: Markets Depend upon Purchasing Power," *Vital Speeches of the Day,* February 1, 1940, 232–33; Shoup and Minter, *Imperial Brain Trust,* 24–27, 104–6, 119, 125; Beard, *Giddy Minds and Foreign Quarrels,* 27–42, 70–73, 78–87; Amrine, *This is Humphrey,* 75; Solberg, *Humphrey: A Biography,* 170–71.

56. Solberg, *Humphrey: A Biography,* 146–47; Sherrill and Ernst, *Drugstore Liberal,* 98; G. William Domhoff, *The Powers That Be: Processes of Ruling-Class Domination in America,* 27–28; Gerard Colby Zilg, *Du Pont: Behind the Nylon Curtain,* 394–96; Nancy Gager Clinch, *The Kennedy Neurosis,* 247–50; Bruce Miroff, *Pragmatic Illusions: The Presidential Politics of John F. Kennedy,* 203–22; Colby and Dennett, *Thy Will Be Done,* 401–2; Humphrey, *The Man and His Dream,* 280.

57. Lustig, *Corporate Liberalism;* Craig, *After Wilson,* 140–47; Domhoff, *Who Rules America Now?* 90–91; Domhoff, *Higher Circles,* 156–250.

58. Humphrey, "Should the American People Reject the 'Welfare State'?" 203–7; Humphrey, *The Man and His Dream,* 47–48; Johnson, *Diary Letters of Hiram Johnson,* 6:9–22–36, 7:1–21–39; Domhoff, *Higher Circles,* 286; Lokos, *Hysteria 1964,* 120; Lundberg, *Rich and the Super-Rich,* 174; David R. Carlin, "The Withering of the Working Class and Who's Letting It Happen," *Commonweal,* October 7, 1994, 14.

59. Schaffer, *America in the Great War,* xii; Thomas H. Walz and Gary Askerooth, *The Upside-Down Welfare State;* Zinn, *Declarations of Independence,* 150–58; "Corporate Welfare Battle: Left and Right Form Odd Coalition to End Subsidies for Business," *Pittsburgh Post-Gazette,* January 29, 1997, A8; "Right-Left Coalition Denounces Boeing Corporate Welfare Deal," *U.S. Newswire,* December 20, 2001, 1.

60. Garrettson, *Hubert H. Humphrey,* 331–36; Humphrey, "The Question of the Effectiveness of the Administration's Poverty Program," *Congressional Digest,* March 1966, 76, and Humphrey, "Should the American People Reject the 'Welfare State'?" 205.

61. Isaacson and Thomas, 219–20; Cobbs, *Rich Neighbor Policy;* Burch, *Elites in American History,* 3:97–101; Gregory A. Fossedal, *Our Finest Hour: Will Clayton, the Marshall Plan, and the Triumph of Democracy;* Gannon, *Biographical Dictionary of the Left,* 1:368–70.

62. Kofsky, *Truman and the War Scare of 1948;* Mills, *Power Elite;* Lundberg, *Rich and the Super-Rich,* 174; Dye and Zeigler, *Irony of Democracy,* 114–20.

63. Kolko, *Triumph of Conservatism,* 275–76; Leonard P. Liggio and James J. Martin, eds., *Watershed of Empire: Essays on New Deal Foreign Policy;* Joyce Kolko and Gabriel Kolko, *The Limits of Power: The World and United States Foreign Policy, 1945–1954;* Justus D. Doenecke, *Not to the Swift: The Old Isolationists in the Cold War Era;* Griffith, "Old Progressives and the Cold War"; Colby and Dennett, *Thy Will Be Done,* 189, 237, 376–81, 396–402; Quigley, *Tragedy and Hope,* 1129–35; Shoup and Minter, *Imperial Brain Trust;* Sklar, ed., *Trilateralism.*

64. Guy Gillette, "Title to Certain Submerged Lands," *Congressional Record,* April 23, 1953, 3643; Stanford M. Mirkin, ed., *Conventions and Elections, 1960: A Complete Handbook Prepared by CBS News,* 35; Sherrill and Ernst, *Drugstore Liberal,* 99.

65. Solberg, *Humphrey: A Biography*, 432; George D. Moffett III, *The Limits of Victory: The Ratification of the Panama Canal Treaties*, 49–53, 144–67, 112–37; Burch, *Elites in American History*, 3:314–21, 330–31, 352; Richard A. Viguerie, *The Establishment vs. the People: Is a New Populist Revolt on the Way*, 58–59; Shoup, *Carter Presidency and Beyond*, 139–40; Sklar, ed., *Trilateralism*, 407–9; Phillips, *Arrogant Capital*, 123; Smith, "Humphrey Gone."

66. Raymond Arsenault, *The Wild Ass of the Ozarks: Jeff Davis and the Social Bases of Southern Politics*, 230–31; Humphrey, *Beyond Civil Rights*, 64–66; Sherrill and Ernst, *Drugstore Liberal*, 92–119; Eisele, *Almost to the Presidency*, 87–107; Pettigrew, *Imperial Washington*, 269–76, 277.

67. Morris, *Partners in Power*, 354; David R. Carlin, "Casey for President?" *America*, September 17, 1994, 21; Carlin, "Withering of the Working Class."

CHAPTER 9: POSITIONS ON DOMESTIC POLICY

1. Henry Steele Commager, *The American Mind: An Interpretation of American Thought and Character since the 1880s*, 217–18; 337–38; Kazin, *A Godly Hero*; Gerstle, "Protean Character of American Liberalism," 1047; Bryan, *Bryan: Selections*, 99–100; Graham, *Encore for Reform*, 7, 4, 116; Benson, *Concept of Jacksonian Democracy*; Wilson, *Presidency of Martin Van Buren*.

2. Curti, *Bryan and World Peace*, 139; Bryan, *Under Other Flags*, 258, 107, 249, 266, 75; Bryan, *Bryan: Selections*, 85–86, 88–89; Bryan, *The Commoner*, 274–77; Werner, *Bryan*, 151; Coletta, *Political Evangelist*, 319; Kolko, *Triumph of Conservatism*, 281–82.

3. Johnson and Porter, comps., *National Party Platforms*, 97, 146, 169; Hamilton, Madison, and Jay, *Federalist Papers*, 292–93; Bryan, *Speeches*, 2:398–99, 181–87; Bryan, *The Commoner*, 21, *Second Battle*, 214–15; Bryan, *The Commoner*, 203–4; Bryan, *Bryan: Selections*, 83–84; Bryan, *Under Other Flags*, 70–71; Koenig, *Bryan: A Political Biography*, 413–17, 575; Levine, *Defender of the Faith*, 195–96; Smith, *Social and Religious Thought of Bryan*, 9–10; Croly, *Promise of American Life*, 158–59.

4. Cohen, *Undefeated: The Life of Hubert Humphrey*, 13–14; Flynn, *As We Go Marching*; "Dictator Feared by Amos Pinchot," *New York Times*, February 15, 1937, 3; Johnson, *Diary Letters of Hiram Johnson*, 6:2–6–37, 3–20–37, 7:7–27–41, 8–1–43; Hamilton, Madison, and Jay, *Federalist Papers*, 262–64, 497; Solberg, *Humphrey: A Biography*, 463; Humphrey, *Political Philosophy of the New Deal*, 71; John F. McManus, "'General Welfare' vs. Welfare," *The New American*, January 20, 1997, 44.

5. Humphrey, *Political Philosophy of the New Deal*, 60; Humphrey, *The Man and His Dream*, 7, 267; Humphrey, *Education of a Public Man*, 213, 355; Sherrill and Ernst, *Drugstore Liberal*, 98; Humphrey, *Cause is Mankind*, 78, 80; Scammon and Wattenberg, *Real Majority*, 120; Solberg, *Humphrey: A Biography*, 388; Johnson and Porter, comps., *National Party Platforms*, 648–49.

6. Humphrey, *Education of a Public Man*, 26; Kolko, *Triumph of Conservatism*, 285; Humphrey, "Should the American People Reject the 'Welfare State'?" *Congressional Digest*, August–September 1950, 203–7; Humphrey; *Cause is Mankind*, 89; Humphrey, *Political Philosophy of the New Deal*, ix–x, 87–90; Polsby, *Citizen's Choice*, 13; Humphrey, *The Man and His Dream*, 178.

7. Cabell Phillips, "A.D.A. is Target of Republicans: Humphrey Linked to Group Described as Subversive," *New York Times*, October 11, 1964, 74; Quigley, *Tragedy and Hope*, 956; "Ask Probe of Campaigning by Kissinger," *Des Moines Register*, March 14,

1976, 7A; "Humphrey: Americans Want Strong Government," *Des Moines Register,* March 21, 1976; Humphrey, "Should Congress Adopt the Proposed Humphrey-Hawkins Employment Bill?" *Congressional Digest,* June–July 1976, 170–78; Solberg, *Humphrey: A Biography,* 450–51.

8. Sherrill, *Accidental President,* 150; Joseph Sobran, "Semantic Fog, Euphemisms Blur Reality of Government"; Solberg, *Humphrey: A Biography,* 451; James Risser, "Humphrey Jabs at Criticism of Social Programs," *Des Moines Register,* March 25, 1976, 5A; Tom Mathews, "The Happy Warrior," *Newsweek,* January 23, 1978, 18.

9. Sherrill and Ernst, *Drugstore Liberal,* 170–71; Allen, *Richard Nixon,* 302–6; Smoot, *The Invisible Government,* 98, 208; Levinson, *Vodka-Cola,* 183.

10. Commager, *American Mind,* 338; Forcey, *Crossroads of Liberalism,* 28; Croly, *Promise of American Life,* 158; Bryan, *The Commoner,* 8–9; Bryan, *Speeches,* 2:398; Bryan, *Under Other Flags,* 238; Bryan, *Bryan: Selections,* 33, 197.

11. Berman, *Hubert: The Triumph and Tragedy,* 56; Humphrey, "Controversy over the Nixon Administration Proposal for a Federal Spending Ceiling"; Humphrey, *Political Philosophy of the New Deal,* 63, 67–74, 78; Meriwether, *Jim Reed,* 259–60; Caroline Thomas Harnsberger, *A Man of Courage: Robert A. Taft,* 128; "The Presidency: History Repeats," *Time,* January 20, 1936, 12; Donald R. McCoy, *The Presidency of Harry S. Truman,* 293; Bowen, "What's New?" 143.

12. Bowers, *Jefferson and Hamilton,* 74–79, 87–90; Nock, *Mr. Jefferson,* 163; Taylor, *Inquiry into the Principles and Policy,* xx–xxi, xxvi, 215, 240–41, 244, 339, 434; Taylor, *Construction Construed,* 79–201; Charles Sellers, ed., *Andrew Jackson, Nullification, and the State-Rights Tradition,* 172; Bernstein, *Towards a New Past,* 67–68; Wilson, *Presidency of Martin Van Buren,* 202–3; Shepard, *Martin Van Buren,* 342–43, 446.

13. Wiltse, *Jeffersonian Tradition in American Democracy,* 220; Lasch, *Revolt of the Elites,* 56–57; Johnson and Porter, comps., *National Party Platforms,* 89–90, 97–98, 104–5; Koenig, *Bryan: A Political Biography,* 129; Coletta, *Political Evangelist,* 93–96; Allen, "Speeches at a Jacksonian Banquet," 1539–42; Bryan, *Second Battle,* 203–7, 285, 170; Bryan, *Under Other Flags,* 89, 70; Long, *Bryan, the Great Commoner,* 187, 46, 48; Werner, *Bryan,* 47–53, 66, 86; Jeffrey Ostler, "The Rhetoric of Conspiracy and the Formation of Kansas Populism"; Bryan, *Bryan: Selections,* 46, 51–58.

14. Coletta, *Political Evangelist,* 94; Bryan, *Second Battle,* 11, 173–75, 243, 249; Bryan, *Bryan: Selections,* 41–42; Bryan, *The Commoner,* 8–9, 226; Bryan, *Credo of the Commoner,* 66–67; Johnson and Porter, comps., *National Party Platforms,* 98, 114–15; Francis Cockrell and Charles Culberson, "Extension of National-Bank Charters," *Congressional Record,* February 17, 1902, 1827.

15. Bryan, *Second Battle,* 176; Bryan, *The Commoner,* 355–56; La Follette and La Follette, *Robert M. La Follette,* 1:245–56; Johnson and Porter, comps., *National Party Platforms,* 171; Coletta, *Political Puritan,* 124–25; Kolko, *Triumph of Conservatism,* 219–20, 253; Koenig, *Bryan: A Political Biography,* 475–78, 491, 525, 616–17; Levine, *Defender of the Faith,* 156, 160, 299; Burch, *Elites in American History,* 2:206–9, 220, 231–33; Craig, *After Wilson,* 30–50.

16. Coletta, *Progressive Politician,* 126–39; Werner, *Bryan,* 226–28; Link, *Woodrow Wilson and the Progressive Era,* 47–50; Kolko, *Triumph of Conservatism,* 217–54; Meriwether, *Jim Reed,* 47–50; Keith L. Bryant Jr., *Alfalfa, Bill Murray,* 109–11; Larson, *Lindbergh of Minnesota,* 159–66.

17. Burch, *Elites in American History,* 2:213–15; Lundberg, *America's Sixty Families,* 122–23; "Owen Criticizes Reserve Board," *New York Times,* July 25, 1921, 12; Craig, *After Wilson,* 68; Bryan, *Bryan: Selections,* 202; Levine, *Defender of the Faith,* 192–94.

18. Bryan and Bryan, *Memoirs of William Jennings Bryan*, 174–75; Bryan, *Bryan: Selections*, 131–32; Quigley, *Tragedy and Hope*, 938–40; Bryan, *Second Battle*, 175; Johnson and Porter, comps., *National Party Platforms*, 91, 105, 147; Robert Owen, "Postal Savings Depositories," *Congressional Record*, March 5, 1910, 2763–65; Springen, *Bryan: Orator*, 153; Bryan, *The Commoner*, 377, 127–28, 142; Werner, *Bryan*, 105, 112, 267; Coletta, *Political Evangelist*, 388–89.

19. Eisele, *Almost to the Presidency*, 22; Humphrey, *Education of a Public Man*, 12–13; Amrine, *This is Humphrey*, 251; Griffith, *Humphrey: A Candid Biography*, 101.

20. Schulzinger, *Wise Men of Foreign Affairs;* Isaacson and Thomas, *Wise Men;* Shoup and Minter, *Imperial Brain Trust;* Sklar, ed., *Trilateralism*, 35–39, 293–307; Brzezinski, *Between Two Ages*, 215; Barnet, *Roots of War*, 49; Kauffman, "Who Can We Shoot?" 17–19.

21. Humphrey, *Education of a Public Man*, 29; Voorhis, *Out of Debt, Out of Danger;* Jerry Voorhis, *Confessions of a Congressman*, 161–82; Allen, *Richard Nixon*, 128–33; "The Last Populist," *Newsweek*, January 14, 1963, 57–58; "Wright Patman: A Lonely 'Populist,'" *Business Week*, July 23, 1966, 51–54; Sherrill, *Accidental President*, 75–78; Nancy Beck Young, *Wright Patman: Populism, Liberalism, and the American Dream.*

22. Bryan, *The Commoner*, 41, 51; Bryan, *Credo of the Commoner*, 89–89; Croly, *Promise of American Life*, 159; Springen, *Bryan: Orator*, 161; Clements, *Bryan: Missionary Isolationist*, 123; Smith, *Social and Religious Thought of Bryan*, 149.

23. Schlesinger, *Imperial Presidency*, 205; Solberg, *Humphrey: A Biography*, 463.

24. Humphrey, *Political Philosophy of the New Deal*, 74–76; Porter, *Congress and the Waning of the New Deal*, 48, 53–54; Solberg, *Humphrey: A Biography*, 170–71; Humphrey, *Education of a Public Man*, 98–100; Francis, "Principalities and Powers: Where the Buck Really Stops," *Chronicles*, October 1995, 8; Harnsberger, *Man of Courage*, 169; Kirk and McClellan, *Political Principles of Robert A. Taft*, 96–98; McCoy, *Presidency of Truman*, 57–60, 291–93.

25. "The Month in Congress: Bricker Amendment Holds Spotlight," *Congressional Digest*, March 1954 and April 1954, 65–66 and 97–98; Doenecke, *Not to the Swift*, 235–38; Allen, *Richard Nixon*, 183–84; Humphrey, *Education of a Public Man*, 99; Jay G. Sykes, *Proxmire*, 125–26.

26. Humphrey, *Education of a Public Man*, 140–41; Cohen, *Undefeated: The Life of Hubert Humphrey*, 433–34; "Humphrey: Choose Able, Trusted Leader," *Des Moines Register*, January 12, 1976.

27. Remini, *Andrew Jackson and the Course of American Democracy*, 340; Matthew J. Franck, *Against the Imperial Judiciary: The Supreme Court vs. the Sovereignty of the People;* Destler, *American Radicalism*, 197; Johnson and Porter, comps., *National Party Platforms*, 106, 118, 99, 115; Beard, *Economic Basis of Politics*, 220; Bryan, *The Commoner*, 400–401; Bryan, *Bryan: Selections*, 41, 121–22; Werner, *Bryan*, 152; Allen, "Speeches at a Jacksonian Banquet," 1539; Pettigrew, *Imperial Washington*, 163–95.

28. Humphrey, *Political Philosophy of the New Deal*, 62–63; Seymour Martin Lipset and Earl Raab, *The Politics of Unreason: Right-Wing Extremism in America, 1790–1970*, 257–60; Allen, *Richard Nixon*, 156–57; John J. Synon, ed., *George Wallace: Profile of a Presidential Candidate*, 104–6; Johnson and Porter, comps., *National Party Platforms*, 702.

29. Burch, *Elites in American History*, 3:522–34; Hamilton, Madison, and Jay, *Federalist Papers*, 77–84; Black, *Our Constitution*, 50–51; Matthews, *If Men Were Angels;* John B. Gates and Charles A. Johnson, eds., *The American Courts: A Critical Assessment*, 290; Dye, *Who's Running America? The Reagan Years*, 128; Lazere, *American Media and Mass Culture*, 84; Bob Woodward and Scott Armstrong, *The Brethren: Inside the Supreme Court*, 288–89.

30. Bryan, *Bryan: Selections*, 195–96, 86; Bryan, *The Commoner*, 257, 330–33, 359–62;

Bryan and Bryan, *Memoirs of William Jennings Bryan,* 458–60, 485–86; Levine, *Defender of the Faith,* 95–98.

31. Bryan, *Bryan: Selections,* 196, 198; Clements, *Bryan: Missionary Isolationist,* 122–23.

32. Schaffer, *America in the Great War,* 13; Gerstle, "Protean Character of American Liberalism," 1052–53; Loewen, *Lies My Teacher Told Me,* 19–21; Noam Chomsky, *Necessary Illusions: Thought Control in Democratic Societies,* 347–49; Oswald Garrison Villard, "Issues and Men: A Letter to the President," *The Nation,* May 21, 1938, 589; Macdonald, *Henry Wallace,* 123; Cole, *Senator Gerald P. Nye,* 209–11.

33. "Senate, 55–4, Votes New Alien Control," *New York Times,* June 1, 1940, 6; Charles A. Beard, *The Republic: Conversations on Fundamentals,* 160–62; Ronald Radosh, *Prophets on the Right: Profiles of Conservative Critics of American Globalism,* 290–94; Zinn, *Declarations of Independence,* 217; J. Garry Clifford and Samuel R. Spencer Jr., *The First Peacetime Draft.*

34. Philip Jenkins, "Defenders of Democracy: Covert Policing and Dirty Tricks," *Chronicles,* December 1995, 13; Victor Lasky, *It Didn't Start with Watergate,* 161–67; Eugene Lyons, "Our Totalitarian 'Liberals,'" *The American Mercury,* April 1939, 385–87; Macdonald, *Discriminations: Essays,* 400–401; Moss, *Moving On,* 17–18; Samuel Francis, "Enemies of the State," *Chronicles,* February 1996, 39; Kauffman, *America First!* 19; Barnes, *Chickens of the Interventionist Liberals,* 3.

35. Barnes, *Chickens of the Interventionist Liberals,* 12, 33–34; Doenecke, *Not to the Swift,* 212, 216; Zinn, *People's History of the United States,* 420–27; Solberg, *Humphrey: A Biography,* 118–19; Peterson, *Prophet without Honor;* Kofsky, *Truman and the War Scare of 1948;* Sherrill and Ernst, *Drugstore Liberal,* 69.

36. Dye and Zeigler, *Irony of Democracy,* 155; Baltzell, *Protestant Establishment,* 285–92; Isaacson and Thomas, *Wise Men,* 563–73; Lipset and Raab, *Politics of Unreason,* 224–29, 236, 257–60; Burch, *Elites in American History,* 3:133, 149, 165; Quigley, *Tragedy and Hope,* 935–56, 1244–46; Doenecke, *Not to the Swift,* 213–16; Allen, *Richard Nixon,* 176–79; Perloff, *Shadows of Power,* 106–7; Alan Crawford, *Thunder on the Right: The "New Right" and the Politics of Resentment,* 303; Miles, *Odyssey of the American Right,* 211–12, 217; Francis, *Beautiful Losers,* 15–16, 101–2, 105–6, 139–51.

37. Lasky, *It Didn't Start with Watergate;* Lundberg, *Rockefeller Syndrome,* 373–74; Kauffman, "Mighty Long Fall," 17; Griffith, ed., *Major Problems in American History,* 368–70, 455–59; Chomsky, *Radical Priorities,* 169–72.

38. Solberg, *Humphrey: A Biography,* 118–19, 159; Humphrey, *The Man and His Dream,* 33, 64–65, 79–80; Sherrill and Ernst, *Drugstore Liberal,* 71–73, 87–91; Gorey, "'I'm a Born Optimist,'" 62; Ryskind, *Hubert: An Unauthorized Biography,* 190, 196–97, 200–203; Clifton Brock, *Americans for Democratic Action: Its Role in National Politics,* 156–57.

39. Solberg, *Humphrey: A Biography,* 283, 311, 388, 370; Thompson, *Fear and Loathing,* 89; "Humphrey Doubts M'Govern Power," *New York Times,* August 12, 1968, 24. For traditional liberal perspectives on Hoover, see Chomsky, *Radical Priorities,* 172; Wheeler, *Yankee from the West,* 227–28; "Senate, 55–4, Votes New Alien Control," 6; and Edwin C. Johnson, "Administration of Central Intelligence Agency," *Congressional Record,* May 27, 1949, 6954.

40. Glad, ed., *Bryan: A Profile,* 139–40; Bryan and Bryan, *Memoirs of William Jennings Bryan,* 106; D. Joy Humes, *Oswald Garrison Villard, Liberal of the 1920s,* 87–88; Werner, *Bryan,* 108, 216; Coletta, *Political Evangelist,* 283, 152; Coletta, *Political Puritan,* 94; Coletta, *Progressive Politician,* 143; Koenig, *Bryan: A Political Biography,* 447; Craig, *After Wilson,* 25–26; Smith, *Social and Religious Thought of Bryan,* 45–47; Bryan, *The Commoner,* 17, 49–50, 322–23; Cook, Harris, and Radosh, *Past Imperfect,* 30–31; Samuel Francis, "Immigration's Real Victims," *The New American,* November 11, 1996, 31; Bryan, *Credo of the*

Commoner, 83; Bryan, *Under Other Flags,* 275, 319; Storing, *What the Anti-Federalists Were For,* 19–20, 45; Bryan, *Second Battle,* 522–23, 542, 97, 371, 383–84, 513–14.

41. Glad, ed., *Bryan: A Profile,* 115; Bryan, *Under Other Flags,* 89; Coletta, *Political Puritan,* 113, 131, 162–64, 188, 236; Levine, *Defender of the Faith,* 299.

42. Ostler, "Rhetoric of Conspiracy," 26; Hofstadter, *Age of Reform.* See also Glad, ed., *Bryan: A Profile,* 115; Koenig, *Bryan: A Political Biography,* 246; Cook, Harris, and Radosh, *Past Imperfect,* 28–31; Robert M. Collins, "The Originality Trap: Richard Hofstadter on Populism," *Journal of American History* 76 (June 1989): 163.

43. Bryan, *First Battle,* 581; Koenig, *Bryan: A Political Biography,* 246, 447–48, 494; Coletta, *Political Puritan,* 112–13, 131; Werner, *Bryan,* 208; Levine, *Defender of the Faith,* 258, 300; Smith, *Social and Religious Thought of Bryan,* 42–44; Glad, ed., *Bryan: A Profile,* 116.

44. Bryan and Bryan, *Memoirs of William Jennings Bryan,* 10; Koenig, *Bryan: A Political Biography,* 76, 334–35, 357–58, 448–50; Smith, *Social and Religious Thought of Bryan,* 55–59; Bryan, *The Commoner,* 288–94; Bryan, *Bryan: Selections,* 70–71; Thelen, *La Follette and the Insurgent Spirit,* 120.

˒ 45. Roger C. Storms, *Partisan Prophets: A History of the Prohibition Party, 1854–1972,* 4; Rayford W. Logan, *The Betrayal of the Negro from Rutherford B. Hayes to Woodrow Wilson,* 44, 66, 94–95; Schattschneider, *Semisovereign People,* 70–80; Levine, *Defender of the Faith,* 299; Craig, *After Wilson,* 174–77, 241, 293–98, 367–68; Morgan, *Redneck Liberal,* 2–4, 47, 50–52, 169, 228, 237, 241–43, 249, 251; Ryskind, *Hubert: An Unauthorized Biography,* 44–45.

46. Smith, *Social and Religious Thought of Bryan,* 58–64; Bryan, *The Commoner,* 289–90, 393; Bryan, *Bryan: Selections,* 71–74, 217–24; Bryan, *Credo of the Commoner,* 72–74; Emma Lou Thornbrough, "The Brownsville Episode and the Negro Vote," *Mississippi Valley Historical Review* 44 (December 1957): 487–92; Manning Marable, *W. E. B. Du Bois: Black Radical Democrat,* 69; Levine, *Defender of the Faith,* 309–10.

47. Clara NiiSka, "Green Candidate McGaa Launches Campaign in Tight Three-Way Senate Race," *Native American Press/Ojibwe News* (Minn.) June 7, 2002; Humphrey, *The Man and His Dream,* 273–77, 110, 63, 138, 329–30; Humphrey, *Stranger at Our Gate,* 2, 10–14; Humphrey, *Cause is Mankind,* 100–104; Amrine, *This is Humphrey,* 93; Cohen, *Undefeated: The Life of Hubert Humphrey,* 123; Scammon and Wattenberg, *Real Majority,* 65; Schlesinger, ed., *History of American Presidential Elections,* 9:3751.

48. Berman, *Hubert: The Triumph and Tragedy,* 29–30, 56–57, 79; Solberg, *Humphrey: A Biography,* 160, 125, 133; Humphrey, *The Man and His Dream,* 3–5, 260; Humphrey, *Beyond Civil Rights,* 34–35, 40–41; Humphrey, *Education of a Public Man,* 76–79, 198–212; Amrine, *This is Humphrey,* 247; Polsby, *Citizen's Choice,* 7; Mirkin, ed., *Conventions and Elections, 1960,* 89–90; "Periscoping the Nation: Inside Politics," *Newsweek,* June 27, 1960, 17; Lokos, *Hysteria 1964,* 130–31, 133–36; Robert Mann, *The Walls of Jericho: Lyndon Johnson, Hubert Humphrey, Richard Russell, and the Struggle for Civil Rights.*

49. Humphrey, *Cause is Mankind,* 19, 20, 27; Humphrey, *Beyond Civil Rights,* 4, 47, 112, 174–75; Solberg, *Humphrey: A Biography,* 343, 418; H. Rap Brown, *Die Nigger Die!* 51–54; Sherrill, *Accidental President,* 165; Meehan, "Housecleaning for American Liberals"; David J. Garrow, *Bearing the Cross: Martin Luther King Jr. and the Southern Christian Leadership Conference, 1955–1968,* 545, 575, 592, 604; Scammon and Wattenberg, *Real Majority,* 140–41; White, *Making of the President, 1972,* 41, 126–27.

50. Ferguson and Rogers, *Right Turn,* 55–56; Domhoff, *Fat Cats and Democrats,* 126–36; Solberg, *Humphrey: A Biography,* 198, 235–36; Morgan, *Redneck Liberal,* 241–43; Berman, *Hubert: The Triumph and Tragedy,* 50; Ryskind, *Hubert: An Unauthorized Biography,* 211, 320; James Forman, *The Making of Black Revolutionaries: A Personal Account,* 386–406; Brown, *Die Nigger Die!* 60–63; Sherrill and Ernst, *Drugstore Liberal,* 136–40.

51. Johnson and Porter, comps., *National Party Platforms,* 91, 99, 115, 144–45, 171; Bryan and Bryan, *Memoirs of William Jennings Bryan,* 302; Bryan, *The Commoner,* 42, 389; Bryan, *Second Battle,* 498, 18, 542, 175, 499; Charles Culberson, "Amendment of National Banking Laws," *Congressional Record,* May 29, 1908, 7156–61; Werner, *Bryan,* 222; Beard, *Economic Basis of Politics,* 187; Bryan, *Speeches,* 2:19; Bryan, *Under Other Flags,* 309; Levine, *Defender of the Faith,* 99.

52. Schaffer, *America in the Great War;* La Follette, *Political Philosophy of Robert M. La Follette,* 218–19, 419; John H. Makin and Norman J. Ornstein, *Debt and Taxes,* 84; "Congress Prepares to Consider the Growing National Debt," *Congressional Digest,* January 1940, 3–4; Barnes, *Perpetual War.*

53. Humphrey, "Should the American People Reject the 'Welfare State'?" 203–7; Zinn, *Declarations of Independence,* 150–58; Solberg, *Humphrey: A Biography,* 143; Kenneth Wherry, "Voting Records on Economy Proposals," *Congressional Record,* August 29, 1949, 12441–62; Ryskind, *Hubert: An Unauthorized Biography,* 178, 279, 281; Porter, *Congress and the Waning of the New Deal,* 94, 100–101; Byrd, "Comment on New Federal Spending," *Congressional Digest,* February 1958, 56–57; Wayne Morse, "Should the Amount of U.S. Foreign Aid be Decreased?" *Congressional Digest,* August–September 1957, 204, 206, 208; Sykes, *Proxmire,* 127–32.

54. Griffith, ed., *Major Problems in American History,* 222–24; Solberg, *Humphrey: A Biography,* 463; Humphrey, "The Question of Mandatory Balancing of the Federal Budget," *Congressional Digest,* March 1976, 83; Ryskind, *Hubert: An Unauthorized Biography,* 280; Americans for Democratic Action, "Comment on New Federal Spending," February 1958, 59; Bruce Miroff, *Pragmatic Illusions: The Presidential Politics of John F. Kennedy,* 205, 210; Humphrey, *Cause is Mankind,* 32; Humphrey, "Controversy over the Nixon Administration Proposal," 299–305.

55. Humphrey, *Education of a Public Man,* 105, 46; Garrettson, *Hubert H. Humphrey,* 227; "McGovern: Carter Forgetting his Promises," *Des Moines Register,* May 8, 1977, 2A; Solberg, *Humphrey: A Biography,* 451; "Ask Probe of Campaigning by Kissinger."

56. Thomas Gore, "Amendment of National Banking Laws," *Congressional Record,* May 30, 1908, 7253; Johnson and Porter, comps., *National Party Platforms,* 91, 147, 169, 99, 115, 144–45, 171; Bryan, *Second Battle,* 249, 164–67; Coletta, *Political Evangelist,* 56–57; Werner, *Bryan,* 51–52; Bryan, *Under Other Flags,* 268–69.

57. Bryan, *Second Battle,* 13, 18, 121–22; Bryan, *The Commoner,* 389; Springen, *Bryan: Orator,* 151; Makin and Ornstein, *Debt and Taxes,* 84; Werner, *Bryan,* 279; Moss, *Moving On,* 5; Craig, *After Wilson,* 18–19, 23, 57–58, 125; Johnson, *Diary Letters of Hiram Johnson,* 4:1–6–24, 5–27–24; Wolfskill, *Revolt of the Conservatives.*

58. Moss, *Moving on,* 5; Bernstein, *Towards a New Past,* 295; Griffith, ed., *Major Problems in American History,* 157.

59. Mirkin, *Conventions and Elections, 1960,* 96; Garrettson, *Hubert H. Humphrey,* 227; Colby and Dennett, *Thy Will Be Done,* 400–402; Koenig, *Bryan: A Political Biography,* 597; Johnson and Porter, comps., *National Party Platforms,* 254; Lundberg, *America's Sixty Families,* 164–68; Clinch, *Kennedy Neurosis,* 247–50; Miroff, *Pragmatic Illusions,* 203–22; Burch, *Elites in American History,* 3:209.

CHAPTER 10: POSITIONS ON FOREIGN POLICY

1. Bryan, *Under Other Flags,* 334, 318; Bryan, *Credo of the Commoner,* 82; Curti, *Bryan and World Peace,* 114, 134; Coletta, *Political Puritan,* 57–58; Levine, *Defender of the Faith,*

90–95; Smith, *Social and Religious Thought of Bryan,* 65, 129, 81–82, 116, 150–54; Macdonald, *Henry Wallace,* 178; Johnson and Porter, comps., *National Party Platforms,* 58, 113–14; Allen, "Speeches at a Jacksonian Banquet," 1541–42; Bryan, *Second Battle,* 12, 82, 121–22, 187, 499; Bryan, *The Commoner,* 6, 25–26, 38–40, 8–9; Bryan, *Under Other Flags,* 68, 242–43, 309, 317–18; Taft and Bryan, *World Peace,* 76–78, 50, 114; Clements, *Bryan: Missionary Isolationist,* 138–39; Levine, *Defender of the Faith,* 163.

2. Robert W. Cherny, *A Righteous Cause: The Life of William Jennings Bryan,* 75–77; Koenig, *Bryan: A Political Biography,* 276, 272–88; Curti, *Bryan and World Peace,* 116–17, 114, 135–36; Bryan, *Second Battle,* 82, 85–86, 95, 388, 490–91, 529; Cook, Harris, and Radosh, *Past Imperfect,* 74–107; Coletta, *Political Evangelist,* 318; Johnson and Porter, comps., *National Party Platforms,* 113; Bryan, *The Commoner,* 14, 123; Bryan, *Under Other Flags,* 323, 96; Smith, *Social and Religious Thought of Bryan,* 71–76; Bryan and Bryan, *Memoirs of William Jennings Bryan,* 460–61.

3. Bryan, *Under Other Flags,* 345; Bryan, *Speeches,* 2:50–62; Glad, ed., *Bryan: A Profile,* 164–82; Curti, *Bryan and World Peace,* 175–76, 181–83, 248; Clements, *Bryan: Missionary Isolationist,* 84–94, 72, 115, 121; Levine, *Defender of the Faith,* 3–90; Smith, *Social and Religious Thought of Bryan,* 88–128; Macdonald, *Discriminations: Essays,* 379; Tansill, *America Goes to War,* 69–113, 464–84; Ray H. Abrams, *Preachers Present Arms,* 23–24, 40; Taft and Bryan, *World Peace,* 28–29, 39, 50, 67–68, 78, 114; Lundberg, *America's Sixty Families,* 265.

4. Bryan, *Bryan: Selections,* 187–88; Levine, *Defender of the Faith,* 89–102; Stone, "War with Germany," *Congressional Record,* April 4, 1917, 210; Vardaman, "War with Germany," *Congressional Record,* April 4, 1917, 208–10; Pettigrew, *Imperial Washington,* 369–83; Keating, *Gentleman from Colorado,* 420–22; Tolstoy, *Christianity and Patriotism, with Pertinent Extract From Other Essays;* Clements, *Bryan: Missionary Isolationist,* 122–23.

5. Smith, *Social and Religious Thought of Bryan,* 70, 76–77, 95; Bryan, *Under Other Flags,* 68; Bryan, *The Commoner,* 6–7; Taft and Bryan, *World Peace,* 78, 140–41.

6. Humphrey, *Cause is Mankind,* 142, 122–31, 51; Polsby, *Citizen's Choice,* 13; Amrine, *This is Humphrey,* 208–25; English et al., *Divided They Stand,* 218; Humphrey, *Education of a Public Man,* 185–87; Johnson and Porter, comps., *National Party Platforms,* 650–51; Solberg, *Humphrey: A Biography,* 448; Humphrey, *The Man and His Dream,* 315, 56–60.

7. Solberg, *Humphrey: A Biography,* 182; Robert Bendiner, "Men Who Would Be President: V. Burton K. Wheeler," *The Nation,* April 27, 1940, 534; Humphrey, *The Man and His Dream,* 101–4; Humphrey, *Cause is Mankind,* 32; Sherrill and Ernst, *Drugstore Liberal,* 171–72; Humphrey, "American System," 684; Johnson and Porter, comps., *National Party Platforms,* 649–50; Cohen, *Undefeated: The Life of Hubert Humphrey,* 415–16; White, *Making of the President, 1972,* 134.

8. Solberg, *Humphrey: A Biography,* 182, 67, 79–80, 85, 275–76; Garrettson, *Hubert H. Humphrey,* 208, 204; Barnes, *Chickens of the Interventionist Liberals,* 3–10; Amrine, *This is Humphrey,* 76, 82–83; Humphrey, *The Man and His Dream,* 315–16; Macdonald, *Memoirs of a Revolutionist,* 64, 72–74; Sobran, "Questioning Myths of 'The Good War' Still Forbidden," 6A; Quigley, *Tragedy and Hope,* 1129–31; Sherrill, *Accidental President,* 188; Humphrey, "American System," 684; Ryskind, *Hubert: An Unauthorized Biography,* 322–23.

9. Eisele, *Almost to the Presidency,* 228–29; Sherrill and Ernst, *Drugstore Liberal,* 167–68, 173–78; "Background of U.S. Southeast Asia Policy," *Congressional Digest,* April 1966, 101; Solberg, *Humphrey: A Biography,* 269; Humphrey, *Cause is Mankind,* 172, 221–22; Noam Chomsky, *Rethinking Camelot: JFK, the Vietnam War, and U.S. Political Culture;* Solberg, *Humphrey: A Biography,* 263, 275–76, 281–90, 426; Berman, *Hubert: The Triumph and Tragedy,* 93.

10. Solberg, *Humphrey: A Biography*, 292, 312.

11. Berman, *Hubert: The Triumph and Tragedy*, 94, 181–82; Sherrill and Ernst, *Drugstore Liberal*, 174–78; Humphrey, "Humphrey Talk Transcript," *New York Times*, April 28, 1968, 66; Solberg, *Humphrey: A Biography*, 301, 448; Crawford, "It's Not Tough Sledding Anymore," 10.

12. Berman, *Hubert: The Triumph and Tragedy*, 155, 180–82, 215–20, 24, 102–4, 182, 209, 229; Stephen C. Shadegg, *Winning's a Lot More Fun*, 232–33, 169; Solberg, *Humphrey: A Biography*, 320–21, 348–54, 375–85, 408, 448, 417; Humphrey, *Education of a Public Man*, 236–42, xviii; Sherrill and Ernst, *Drugstore Liberal*, 170–71.

13. Humphrey, *Education of a Public Man*, 99, 139, 349–50; Brock, *Americans for Democratic Action*, 91; Schlesinger, ed., *History of American Presidential Elections*, 8:3103–04; Allen, *Richard Nixon*, 109–11; Ryskind, *Hubert: An Unauthorized Biography*, 127–28; Garrettson, *Hubert H. Humphrey*, 247–73; Swanberg, *Norman Thomas*, 288–90; Barnes, *Chickens of the Interventionist Liberals*, 5–6; Solberg, *Humphrey: A Biography*, 80; H. C. Engelbrecht and F. C. Hanighen, *Merchants of Death: A Study of the International Armament Industry;* Cole, *Senator Gerald P. Nye*, 65–96; Cohen, *Undefeated: The Life of Hubert Humphrey*, 479–80; Ferguson and Rogers, *Right Turn*, 162–64; Alexander and Haggerty, *Financing the 1984 Election*, 160.

14. Doenecke, *Not to the Swift*, 11–13; Clements, *Bryan: Missionary Isolationist*, 39.

15. Coletta, *Political Evangelist*, 299; Coletta, *Political Puritan*, 146; Taft and Bryan, *World Peace*, 98–100, 89–90, 101–2; Clements, *Bryan: Missionary Isolationist*, xii, 57, 96, 110–11, 143, 32–35, 41–44, 68–70, 79, 131–32, 77–95; Johnson and Porter, comps., *National Party Platforms*, 112; Pettigrew, *Imperial Washington*, 307–19; Richard F. Pettigrew, "Annexation of the Hawaiian Islands," *Congressional Record*, July 6, 1898, 6693–6702; William Allen, "Annexation of the Hawaiian Islands," *Congressional Record*, July 6, 1898, 6702–07; Bryan, *Under Other Flags*, 166–67, 274, 311–16, 325, 360–61, 368; Bryan, *Second Battle*, 86–102, 126–33, 151, 397, 511–12; Bryan, *The Commoner*, 29–42, 58, 143–53, 186, 308–11, 434–54; Werner, *Bryan*, 154, 216, 151, 230–31; Glad, ed., *Bryan: A Profile*, 58–63, 74–75, 85–86, 171, 162, 175–78; Smith, *Social and Religious Thought of Bryan*, 67, 74, 92–93; Curti, *Bryan and World Peace*, 165–77.

16. Ostler, "Rhetoric of Conspiracy"; Johnson and Porter, comps., *National Party Platforms*, 104; Werner, *Bryan*, 46–47, 66; Bryan, *Under Other Flags*, 70; Coletta, *Political Evangelist*, 299; Bryan, *Bryan: Selections*, 46, 51–58; Clements, *Bryan: Missionary Isolationist*, 24–25; Allen, "Speeches at a Jacksonian Banquet," 1539, 1543–44; Bryan, *Second Battle*, 97, 170, 171, 172, 202; Pettigrew, *Imperial Washington*, 393–94; Keating, *Gentleman from Colorado*, 413, 441, 446–50; Tansill, *Back Door to War*, 3; Quigley, *Tragedy and Hope*, 52–53, 326–27, 945, 951–54; Quigley, *Anglo-American Establishment*.

17. Taft and Bryan, *World Peace;* Levine, *Defender of the Faith*, 63, 135–47, 163–64; Ralph Stone, *The Irreconcilables: The Fight against the League of Nations*, 16–17, 140–42; Clements, *Bryan: Missionary Isolationist*, xii, 127, 131–35; Bryan, *Second Battle*, 12–13, 86, 500–501; Bryan, *The Commoner*, 8–9; Springen, *Bryan: Orator*, 161–62; Griffith, "Old Progressives and the Cold War," 336; Meriwether, *Jim Reed*, 62–65; Pettigrew, *Imperial Washington*, 389–95; Keating, *Gentleman from Colorado*, 441; Coletta, *Political Puritan*, 184.

18. Clements, *Bryan: Missionary Isolationist*, 13, 136, 140, xiii–iv, 49; Taft and Bryan, *World Peace*, 37, 50, 78–79, 113–14, 154–55, 89; Smith, *Social and Religious Thought of Bryan*, 155–56, 71–73, 76, 107; Coletta, *Political Puritan*, 146–47; George M. Marsden, *Fundamentalism and American Culture: The Shaping of Twentieth-Century Evangelicalism, 1870–1925*, 132–35; Koenig, *Bryan: A Political Biography*, 37–38, 303; Glad, *Trumpet*

Soundeth, 30–32; Curti, *Bryan and World Peace,* 114–15, 135–36; Bryan, *The Commoner,* 281; Glad, ed., *Bryan: A Profile,* 162, 186.

19. Solberg, *Humphrey: A Biography,* 78, 155; Humphrey, *Cause is Mankind,* 106–7; Humphrey, *Education of a Public Man,* 119–20, 146; Humphrey, *The Man and His Dream,* 7, 48–49, 131; Chomsky, *American Power,* 300; Schlesinger, *Vital Center,* 30–31, 222; Steven M. Gillon, "Hubert H. Humphrey: The Politics of Joy," *Society,* March/April 1994, 87; Garrettson, *Hubert H. Humphrey,* 225; Brzezinski, *Between Two Ages,* 32–33, 307; Sherrill and Ernst, *Drugstore Liberal,* 170–71; Macdonald, *Henry Wallace,* 31–35, 63–72; Barnes, *Perpetual War,* 34–35, 58–59; Sobran, "Semantic Fog."

20. Humphrey, *Political Philosophy of the New Deal,* 24–25; Humphrey, *Education of a Public Man,* 101, 221; Ryskind, *Hubert: An Unauthorized Biography,* 39–40; Amrine, *This is Humphrey,* 75–76; Solberg, *Humphrey: A Biography,* 78, 82, 85, 166, 170–71; "Humphrey: Policy Statements," *Congressional Quarterly Weekly Report,* April 19, 1968, 887.

21. Amrine, *This is Humphrey,* 150; Thomas C. Kennedy, *Charles A. Beard and American Foreign Policy;* Radosh, *Prophets on the Right;* Barnes, *Perpetual War;* Sanders, *Peddlers of Crisis;* Cobbs, *Rich Neighbor Policy,* 2–3, 65, 244; Domhoff, *Who Rules America?* 97–98; Peterson, *Prophet without Honor,* 156; Viguerie, *Establishment vs. the People,* 38.

22. Humphrey, *The Man and His Dream,* 197–98, 315, 16, 133; Humphrey, *Cause is Mankind,* 108, 116; Humphrey, "Foreign Assistance Act of 1974," 38123–24; Cohen, *Undefeated: The Life of Hubert Humphrey,* 473; Humphrey, *Education of a Public Man,* 189, 318–20; Humphrey, "Is Present United States Cuban Policy Adequate?" 276, 278, 280; "Major U.S. Foreign Defense Commitments"; Oswald Garrison Villard, "Are We to Rule the World?" *The Christian Century,* March 26, 1941, 421–22; Isaacson and Thomas, *Wise Men,* 349.

23. Humphrey, *Cause is Mankind,* 144; Humphrey, *Education of a Public Man,* 98–99, 322, 326; Amrine, *This is Humphrey,* 126, 129; Griffith, *Humphrey: A Candid Biography,* 184–85; Humphrey, "The North Atlantic Treaty," 9777–79; Cohen, *Undefeated: The Life of Hubert Humphrey,* 12.

24. Humphrey, *The Man and His Dream,* 302; Ryskind, *Hubert: An Unauthorized Biography,* 25; Johnson, *Diary Letters of Hiram Johnson,* 3:7–24–19; Quigley, *Anglo-American Establishment,* 257–59; Quigley, *Tragedy and Hope,* 130–33, 581–83, 936–56.

25. Clarence K. Streit, *Union Now: The Proposal for Inter-Democracy Federal Union (Shorter Version);* "Proposed Union of the World's Democracies," *Congressional Digest,* June–July 1941, 163–64; Jensen, *New Nation,* xi–xii; Allen, *Richard Nixon,* 298–300; Smoot, *Invisible Government,* 86–87, 93–96; Quigley, *Anglo-American Establishment,* 260, 282–84; Quigley, *Tragedy and Hope,* 582–83; Johnson, *Diary Letters of Hiram Johnson,* 7:9–20–43, 10–14–43.

26. Julia E. Johnsen, comp., *United Nations or World Government,* 131, 139, 211, 225; Allen, *Richard Nixon,* 289–98, 300–313; Smoot, *Invisible Government,* 96–105, 177–205; John F. Kennedy, *Public Papers of the Presidents of the United States: John F. Kennedy, 1962,* 537–39; Nelson A. Rockefeller, *The Future of Federalism,* 59–83; Levinson, *Vodka-Cola,* 183; "Multilateral Trade Policy Developments," *Congressional Digest,* October 1962, 226–28; Sklar, ed., *Trilateralism;* Ralph Nader et al., *The Case against Free Trade: GATT, NAFTA, and the Globalization of Corporate Power,* 14–15, 16–18.

27. C. Wright Mills, *Power, Politics, and People: The Collected Essays of C. Wright Mills,* 120; Smith, *Thomas E. Dewey,* 276–77, 395; Barnet, *Roots of War,* 204; Brzezinski, *Between Two Ages,* 56; Falk, *End of World Order;* Falk, *Promise of World Order.*

28. Humphrey, *The Man and His Dream,* 16, 48–49, 59, 99–100, 131; Humphrey, *Cause is Mankind,* 106–7, 116, 142, 144; Solberg, *Humphrey: A Biography,* 112, 114; Isaacson and

Thomas, *Wise Men,* 323; Robert A. Divine, *Foreign Policy and U.S. Presidential Elections, 1940–1948,* 92; Johnsen, *United Nations,* 131, 139, 225; Brzezinski, *Between Two Ages,* 3–5, 32–33, 56, 274–75, 295–97, 305–8; Strobe Talbott, "America Abroad: The Birth of the Global Nation," *Time,* July 20, 1992, 70–71; Humphrey, "Should the U.S.A. Retain the Connally Reservation to the Jurisdiction of the World Court?"

29. Schaffer, *America in the Great War,* xv; Villard, *Prophets: True and False,* 174–75; Burns, *Roosevelt: The Lion and the Fox;* Zinn, *Declarations of Independence,* 19–20; Chomsky, *Necessary Illusions,* 17; Garrettson, *Hubert H. Humphrey,* 247–73; Williams, *Contours of American History,* 472–73; Victor Marchetti and John D. Marks, *The CIA and the Cult of Intelligence,* 8–9; David Wise and Thomas B. Ross, *The Invisible Government,* 92–97, 350–51; Humphrey, *Education of a Public Man,* 139, 319; Eisele, *Almost to the Presidency,* 49–64, 94, 268, 431; Sherrill and Ernst, *Drugstore Liberal,* 110–11, 112–13; Domhoff, *Higher Circles,* 269–71.

30. James A. Bill, *The Eagle and the Lion: The Tragedy of American-Iranian Relations,* 136–37, 169, 176, 228–30, 333, 367, 375, 502; Noam Chomsky and Edward S. Herman, *The Washington Connection and Third World Fascism: The Political Economy of Human Rights-Volume I.*

31. "Recent Congress Action on Trade Policy," *Congressional Digest,* February 1964, 45, 64; Humphrey, "The Question of Encouraging Expansion of Trade with the Red-Bloc Nations at the Present Time"; Sherrill and Ernst, *Drugstore Liberal,* 169; Ryskind, *Hubert: An Unauthorized Biography,* 313–14; Polsby, *Citizen's Choice,* 13; Humphrey, *Cause is Mankind,* 135–41; Humphrey, *Education of a Public Man,* xx, 195–96, 329; Crawford, "It's Not Tough Sledding Anymore," 10.

32. Solberg, *Humphrey: A Biography,* 166; Bertram Gross, *Friendly Fascism: The New Face of Power in America,* 134; Jesse Helms, "Export Administration Act Amendments," *Congressional Record,* February 29, 1984, S1937–66; Antony C. Sutton, *The Best Enemy Money Can Buy;* Joseph Finder, *Red Carpet;* James J. Drummey, "Let's Unmask the Red Traders," *The New American,* October 24, 1988, 10; George Orwell, *Animal Farm: A Fairy Story,* 123–28; Levinson, *Vodka-Cola;* George Athan, "Advice from Butz Aids Ford in Bid for Illinois Farmers' Votes," *Des Moines Register,* March 14, 1976, 11A.

CHAPTER 11: THE POST-HUMPHREY ERA AND JEFFERSONIAN
TRANSCENDENCE

1. Smith, "Humphrey Gone"; Cohen, *Undefeated: The Life of Hubert Humphrey,* 472–73; Berman, *Hubert: The Triumph and Tragedy,* 21; "McGovern: Carter Forgetting his Promises," *Des Moines Register,* May 8, 1977, 2A; George Carpozi Jr., *Clinton Confidential: The Climb to Power: The Unauthorized Biography of Bill and Hillary Clinton,* 19–20, 30–49, 92, 106, 110, 208, 424–31; Morris, *Partners in Power,* 98–106, 130–31; Quigley, *Anglo-American Establishment,* 33–50; Quigley, *Tragedy and Hope,* 129–33, 581–83, 950–56, 937; Isaacson and Thomas, *Wise Men.*

2. Martin L. Gross, *The Great Whitewater Fiasco: An American Tale of Money, Power, and Politics,* 62–64, 122–48, 90–106; Charles Lewis, Alejandro Benes, and Meredith O'Brien, *The Buying of the President,* 34–39; Alexander Cockburn and Ken Silverstein, *Washington Babylon,* 250–55.

3. John Vinson, "The Trojan Chicken," *Chronicles,* February 1997, 39–40; Mike McGraw, "Cheep Labor," *Mother Jones,* January/February 1996, 13; Morris, *Partners in Power,*

311, 449, 451–53; Jennifer Bleyer, "Buchanan, Nader Take on Big Ag at FarmAid," *csindy.com,* September 21, 2000, http://www.csindy.com/csindy/2000–09–21/news3 .html; Norman Solomon, *False Hope: The Politics of Illusion in the Clinton Era,* 10; Bill Quinn, *How Wal-Mart Is Destroying America.*

4. Evan Thomas, "The Lady Has a Midas Touch," *Newsweek,* June 15, 1987, 32; Sally Bedell Smith, *Reflected Glory: The Life of Pamela Churchill Harriman.*

5. John B. Judis, "Clinton and the Lobbyists: Who is Paying the Bill?" *In These Times,* March 11–17, 1992, 3; Leah Nathans Spiro and Paula Dwyer, "Bill Clinton, the Terror and Toast of Wall Street," *Business Week,* April 6, 1992, 83; Jack Wardlaw, "Corporate Lobbyists Picking Up Party Tab," *New Orleans Times-Picayune,* July 16, 1992, A4.

6. Robert Scheer, "Brown Sees National Need for Economic Reorientation," *Los Angeles Times,* June 1, 1992, A18; Michael Krasny, "Let's Talk Clinton," *Mother Jones,* November/December 1994, 54; James Petras, "President Clinton, Wall Street Populist," *Z Magazine,* April 1993, 18–22; Cockburn and Silverstein, *Washington Babylon,* 255–301; David S. Broder and Michael Weisskopf, "Business Prospered in 103rd Congress: Despite Democratic Leadership, Labor Had a Sparse Two Years on Hill," *Washington Post,* September 25, 1994, A1, A28, A29; Stephen Labaton, "Big Business is Sharply Shifting Its 1994 Campaign Donations to Democrats," *New York Times,* October 21, 1994, A11.

7. Ferguson and Rogers, *Right Turn;* Lenni Brenner, *The Lesser Evil;* Greider, *Who Will Tell the People;* Morris, *Partners in Power,* 153–54, 262–63; Jill Abramson and Phil Kuntz, "Antitrust Probe of Archer-Daniels Puts Spotlight on Chairman Andreas's Vast Political Influence"; Frank Greve, "Corn King"; Eugene McCarthy, "Chicago, 1996," *The Progressive Populist,* August 1996; Jerry Brown, "Party Has Forgotten Populist Roots."

8. John F. McManus, "Establishment Dittohead," *The New American,* July 10, 1995, 23–32; Walter Shapiro, "Whose Hillary is She, Anyway?" *Esquire,* August 1993, 86.

9. Bill Kauffman, "Come Home, America," *The American Conservative,* January 30, 2006, 12–15.

10. Sam Tanenhaus, "When Left Turns Right, It Leaves the Middle Muddled," *New York Times,* September 16, 2000, 7; John Laughland, "Flirting with Fascism," *The American Conservative,* June 30, 2003, 13–15; Patrick J. Buchanan, *Where the Right Went Wrong: How Neoconservatives Subverted the Reagan Revolution and Hijacked the Bush Presidency;* Stanley I. Kutler, "The Vision Thing," *Washington Post,* August 15, 2004, T5; Thomas Omestad, "Fixin' for a Fight," *U.S. News and World Report,* October 25, 2004, 51–55.

11. Max Boot, "George W. Bush: The 'W' Stands for Woodrow," *Wall Street Journal,* July 1, 2002, A14; William F. Jasper, "Bush's Wilsonian Internationalism," *The New American,* September 9, 2002, 19–22.

12. Joseph Sobran, "Age of Feelings Has Voided Legitimate Political Debate," *Columbia (Mo.) Daily Tribune,* August 22, 1996, 6A; Joseph Sobran, "Big Government Has Given Way to 'Big Family' in 1996," *Columbia (Mo.) Daily Tribune,* September 5, 1996, 6A; Katharine Q. Seelye, "Gingrich's Life: The Complications and Ideals," *New York Times,* November 24, 1994, A14; William F. Jasper, "Speaking for Whom?" *The New American,* December 12, 1994, 5–10; Jerry Gray, "Kemp Courts Harlem Voters with Open Arms, Little Hope," *New York Times,* September 7, 1996, 10.

13. G. R. Anderson Jr., "United They Sit," *City Pages,* January 16, 2002; Steven Dornfeld, "Wellstone Ad Campaign Paid for with the Money He Loves to Hate," *St. Paul Pioneer Press,* August 12, 2002, 8A; Mark Brunswick, "Wellstone Gets Down to Business," *Minneapolis Star Tribune,* August 14, 2002, 1B; David Schimke, "Chickenshit, Inter-

rupted," *City Pages,* September 18, 2002; Alexander Cockburn and Jeffrey St. Clair, eds., *Dime's Worth of Difference: Beyond the Lesser of Two Evils,* 153–68.

14. Doug Grow, "Coleman Attempts a Difficult Illusion," *Minneapolis Star Tribune,* June 10, 1996, 2B; Anthony Lonetree, "Coleman Staying Neutral on U.S. Senate Race," *Minneapolis Star Tribune,* October 26, 1996, 1B.

15. Langer, "Proposed Investigation of Republican National Convention of 1940," *Congressional Record,* January 17, 1944, 287; and Langer, "Wartime Method of Voting by Members of the Armed Forces," *Congressional Record,* February 4, 1944, 1250; Griffith, "Old Progressives and the Cold War," 347; Kauffman, *America First!* 204; Rothbard, "Conservative Movement R.I.P.?" 20.

16. Falk, *End of World Order,* 122.

17. Michael Oreskes, "Alienation from Government Grows, Poll Finds," *New York Times,* September 19, 1990, A26; Ralph Z. Hallow, "Right Seems Right to Americans in Survey," *Washington Times,* May 23, 1996, A1.

18. Falk, *Promise of World Order,* 34; John McClaughry, "Jefferson's Vision," *New York Times,* April 13, 1982, A27; Makin and Ornstein, *Debt and Taxes,* 87; Paul, "Rep. Ron Paul Quits Republican Party," *The American,* January 1987, 1. For the less conservative, less Jeffersonian side of President Reagan, see John B. Judis, "The Right and the Wrongs of Reagan: Two Years That Didn't Shake the World," *The Progressive,* January 1983, 22–27; Richard A. Viguerie, "Hello Baker, Bye-Bye Reagan: In the End, the Washington Establishment Always Wins," *Washington Post,* March 15, 1987, C5; Joshua Green, "Reagan's Liberal Legacy," *The Washington Monthly,* January/February 2003, 28–33.

19. "Bush to Tell Congress of 'a New World Order,'" *Columbia (Mo.) Daily Tribune,* September 11, 1990, 1; Rich Hood, "Bush Takes on 'Isolationists,'" *Kansas City Star,* November 14, 1991, A1, A20; Carroll J. Doherty, "Democrats Aim to Strike Chord Playing 'America First' Tune," *Congressional Quarterly Weekly Report,* November 16, 1991, 3393–95; "Quayle Calls Buchanan a Closet Liberal," *Columbia (Mo.) Daily Tribune,* February 27, 1992, 7A; "Many Favor Cutting Military, Foreign Affairs," *USA Today,* June 18, 1992, 4A.

20. Albright interview, *Today Show* broadcast, NBC-TV, February 19, 1998; Bob Herbert, "Snug in our Living Rooms While the Bombs Drop Afar," *New York Times,* February 23, 1998.

21. Falk, *End of World Order,* 124; Henry Kissinger and Cyrus Vance, "Bipartisan Objectives for American Foreign Policy," 899; Quigley, *Tragedy and Hope,* 1247–48.

22. Gregory A. Fossedal, *The Democratic Imperative: Exporting the American Revolution;* Ken Silverstein, "Gore's Oil Money," *The Nation,* May 22, 2000, 11–15.

23. Arthur Schlesinger Jr., "Back to the Womb? Isolationism's Renewed Threat," *Foreign Affairs* 74 (July/August 1995): 8; William Kristol and Robert Kagan, "Toward a Neo-Reaganite Foreign Policy," *Foreign Affairs* 75 (July/August 1996): 23, 32.

24. James R. Schlesinger and Thomas R. Pickering, "Keep Iraq above Politics," *Los Angeles Times,* March 30, 2004, B13.

25. "Gannett and Pinchot Decline," *New York Times,* December 18, 1937, 2; Pinchot, *History of the Progressive Party,* 80–84; Johnson, *Diary Letters of Hiram Johnson,* 1:67; Wheeler, *Yankee from the West,* 389; Radosh, *Prophets on the Right,* 116; Taft, "Future of the Republican Party"; "Taft Hits Stassen on 'Liberal' Issue," *New York Times,* April 22, 1948, 14; Quigley, *Tragedy and Hope,* 1244–45; "Hamilton Stays," *The Literary Digest,* 26 December 1936, 5.

26. Shoup, *Carter Presidency and Beyond,* 10.

27. Lipset and Raab, *Politics of Unreason,* 342–77, 394–98, 413–27, 513–14; Michael

Kazin, *The Populist Persuasion: An American History*, 220–42; Stephan Lesher, *George Wallace: American Populist*.

28. Allen, *Richard Nixon*, 92–95, 115–16; Kenneth Crawford, "Taft the Presidential Candidate," *The American Mercury*, June 1948, 647–53; Robert A. Taft, "Reply by Senator Taft," *The American Mercury*, June 1948, 654–58; Radosh, *Prophets on the Right*, 119–95; Murray N. Rothbard, "The Foreign Policy of the Old Right," 85–96.

29. Sykes, *Proxmire*, 132; Warden Moxley, "Brown: Striving for a New Political Coalition," 2329–34; "Are We Ready to Face Up to Jerry Brown's Visions?" *Madison (Wis.) Capital Times*, March 24, 1980; Phil Haslanger, "Jerry Brown," *Madison (Wis.) Capital Times*, March 31, 1980; Michael Bauman, "Brown Uses La Follette Approach," *Milwaukee Journal*, March 16, 1980.

30. Matthews, "Jerry Brown in Right on Target"; Alexander Cockburn, "The Jerry Brown Hate Campaigners," *The Nation*, April 20, 1992, 511; Scheer, "Brown Sees National Need for Economic Reorientation"; Jerry Brown, "Democrats' Platform is Toothless," *Los Angeles Times*, July 5, 1992, M5; Richard Reeves, "Jerry Brown's Never-Ending Campaign," *Kansas City Star*, August 8, 1992, C7.

31. Macdonald, *Discriminations: Essays*, 36, 302; Mills, *Politics*, 120, 337; Lee Edwards, *Goldwater: The Man Who Made a Revolution*, 10, 28–29, 53, 116; Goldwater, *With No Apologies*, 22, 44–45, 281–82; Viguerie, *Establishment vs. the People*, 14, 179; Crawford, *Thunder on the Right*; Charlene Spretnak and Fritjof Capra, with Rüdiger Lutz, *Green Politics*, 227–28; Rensenbrink, *Greens and the Politics of Transformation*; Jonathan Alter, "Jerry's Date With History," *Newsweek*, April 13, 1992, 31; Gloria Borger and Jerry Buckley, "Perot Keeps Going and Going," *U.S. News and World Report*, May 17, 1993, 37; Walter Berns, "On Hamilton and Popular Government," *The Public Interest*, Fall 1992, 112.

32. Domhoff, *Higher Circles*, 281–308; Samuel Francis, "From Household to Nation: The Middle American Populism of Pat Buchanan," *Chronicles*, March 1996, 12–16; Kauffman, *America First!*; Jeffrey Bell, *Populism and Elitism: Politics in the Age of Equality*; Allen D. Hertzke, *Echoes of Discontent: Jesse Jackson, Pat Robertson, and the Resurgence of Populism*; Phillips, *Boiling Point*; Kazin, *Populist Persuasion*; Karl G. Trautman, ed., *The New Populist Reader*.

33. Steve Hirsch, ed., *Memo Two: Soviets Examine Foreign Policy for a New Decade*, 21; Burkholder, "Kansas Populism," 292; Schattschneider, *Semisovereign People*, 70–80; Thelen, *La Follette and the Insurgent Spirit*, 192.

34. Of course, even in 1924, some populists voted for the Davis-Bryan ticket and some for Coolidge and the standard bearers of smaller parties.

35. Kauffman, *America First!* 11; Mary Meehan, "Abortion: The Left Has Betrayed the Sanctity of Life," *The Progressive*, September 1980, 32–34; David R. Carlin, "The Suicide of Contemporary Liberalism"; Lasch, *Revolt of the Elites*, 6–7, 28–29, 176–77, 184–87; Wayne S. Cole, *America First: The Battle against Intervention, 1940–1941*; Radosh, *Prophets on the Right*, 116.

36. Cole, *Senator Gerald P. Nye*, 223; Gerald P. Nye, "Interventionist Madness," *The American Mercury*, Fall 1966, 26–29; Kauffman, *America First!* 213–14; Teodori, ed., *New Left*, 454–55; Kauffman, "Don't Underrate Isolationism," 759; Goldwater, "Goldwater Talks"; Lipset and Raab, *Politics of Unreason*, 364–65, 513–14; Eisele, *Almost to the Presidency*, 303; Carlson, *George*, 146; Perry, *Us and Them*, 68; Elizabeth O. Colton, *The Jackson Phenomenon: The Man, the Power, the Message*, 179.

37. Charley Reese, "Brown Stood Alone among Manipulators of America"; William P. Hoar, "Extra-Spicy Conservatism," *The New American*, July 7, 1997, 35.

38. William Greider, "Buchanan Rethinks the American Empire"; Joseph Sobran, "Chomsky's Innocence Gives a Radical View of U.S. Policy"; "Mr. President, Bring the Troops Home!" *The New American,* January 15, 1991, 22–23; Falk, *End of World Order,* 124.

39. Patrick J. Buchanan, "Business a Poor Ally for GOP," *Chicago Tribune,* December 12, 1976, sec. 2, 6; Francis, *Revolution,* 11–14, 133–47, 244–50; Bill Turque, "Maverick's Playground: Will Perot Be the Next 'Outsider' to Run?" *Newsweek,* March 30, 1992, 32; E. J. Dionne Jr., "This Season's Political Mavericks See Perot's Rise as Validation"; Goldman et al., *Quest for the Presidency, 1992;* Phillips, *Boiling Point;* Kauffman, *America First!;* Reese, "Buchanan Won't Score Points with American Establishment," 4A; Charley Reese, "Jerry Brown Only Candidate Who Can Save the Country," *Columbia (Mo.) Daily Tribune,* March 12, 1992, 6A.

40. Richard L. Berke, "Brown or Perot? Former 'Boy Wonder' of Politics Isn't Sure Whom to Help," *New York Times,* April 16, 1992, A10; Henry Muller and Richard Woodbury, "Working Folks Say 'We're Not Interested in Your Damn Positions, Perot, We're Interested in Your Principles,'" *Time,* May 25, 1992, 36–38, 43; Alexander Cockburn, "Perot: How I Learned to Love Him," *The Nation,* November 9, 1992, 530; Albert J. Menendez, *The Perot Voters and the Future of American Politics.*

41. Ralph Nader, "Treaty Would Tie Down U.S.," *Columbia (Mo.) Daily Tribune,* August 21, 1994, 3D; Phillips, *Arrogant Capital,* 125, 178; David Barsamian, "Super Power: John Stockwell Interviewed by David Barsamian," *Z Magazine,* March 1991, 51; Nader et al., *Case against Free Trade,* 3, 11, 13–22, 69, 160–62; Noam Chomsky, *Keeping the Rabble in Line: Interviews with David Barsamian,* 11–12, 47–48, 55; Alexander Cockburn, "Neither 'Left' nor 'Right.'"

42. Bryan, *Second Battle,* 523, 542; Burton K. Wheeler, "The American People Want No War: We Must Act Now before It Is Too Late," *Vital Speeches of the Day,* June 1, 1941, 490; Porter, *Congress and the Waning of the New Deal,* 45–58; "Hull's Victory," *Newsweek,* March 4, 1940, 16; Frank Church, "Foreign Assistance Act of 1974," *Congressional Record,* December 4, 1974, 38107–08.

43. Jim Christie, "Jerry Brown Talks"; Lee Walczak, "Populism: A Diverse Movement Is Shaking America—and May Imperil its Role in the Global Economy"; "Buchanan: Put Our People and Our Country First," *Des Moines Register,* November 19, 1995, 2C; Alexander Cockburn, "The People's Pit Bull"; "Who's Who in the 'Halloween Coalition,'" *Newsweek,* March 25, 1996, 32; Wesley J. Smith, "Nobody's Nader: The Tough Activist Has Some Kind Words for Buchanan, But None for Clinton."

44. Barbara Ehrenreich, "Who's on Main Street?" *Mother Jones,* July/August 1992, 42; "'Radical' Caucus: Politicians Discuss Third Party Possibilities," *Columbia (Mo.) Daily Tribune,* November 27, 1995, 10A; Michael Lind, "The Radical Center or the Moderate Middle?"; Kauffman, "Who Can We Shoot?" 17–18.

45. Kevin Phillips, "The Unexpected Quest"; Jacqueline Salit, "Buchanan Fights for New Life," *San Francisco Chronicle,* October 7, 1999, A29.

46. Alexander Cockburn and Jeffrey St. Clair, "The Left's 'Silver Lining,'" *Counter-Punch,* December 4, 2001, http://www.counterpunch.org/silverlining.html; Jill Lawrence, "Conservative Favorites to Join ACLU," *USA Today,* November 25, 2002, 2A; Sabrina Eaton, "Diverse Groups Fighting New Security Act," *Cleveland Plain Dealer,* March 4, 2003, A2; Nat Hentoff, "Conservatives Rise for the Bill of Rights!" *Village Voice,* April 30–May 6, 2003, 33; Norman Mailer, "I Am Not for World Empire," *The American Conservative,* December 2, 2002, 8–18; Neil Clark, "A Necessary Alliance," *The American Conservative,* March 10, 2003, 8–11.

47. Miles Benson, "Nader Commands Small But Loyal Following," *Newhouse News Service,* March 8, 2004, 1.

48. Ralph Nader, "Dear Conservatives Upset with the Policies of the Bush Administration"; Pat Buchanan, "Ralph Nader: Conservatively Speaking"; Justin Raimondo, "Old Right Nader."

CHAPTER 12: DEMOCRATIC POLITICS TODAY AND TOMORROW

1. Rob Gurwitt, "1986 Elections Generate GOP Power Struggle: Christian Right vs. Party Establishment," *Congressional Quarterly Weekly Report,* April 12, 1986, 802–5; "Bush-Dole Nomination Contest is No Watershed Event for GOP," *Congressional Quarterly Weekly Report,* January 23, 1988, 155–57; Tamar Jacoby, "Populist Pat's Outreach Program," *Newsweek,* February 29, 1988, 18–19; Gerald M. Boyd, "Bush Says He Has Earned Support of Right Wing," *New York Times,* June 2, 1988, A1, D25.

2. For an historical range of evangelical critiques of "shallow Christianity," see Søren Kierkegaard, *Attack Upon "Christendom";* Dietrich Bonhoeffer, *The Cost of Discipleship;* A. W. Tozer, *Of God and Men,* 11–13; Jeanne Guyon, *Experiencing the Depths of Jesus Christ,* 143–64; Jacques Ellul, *The Subversion of Christianity.*

3. C. I. Scofield, ed., *The Scofield Reference Bible,* 1342; Luke 4:5–8; John 16:7–11, 17:6–16; 2 Cor. 4:3–4; Gal. 5:16–24; Eph. 2:1–3, 6:10–17; James 1:27, 3:13–18, 4:1–7; 1 John 2:14–28, 5:18–21; Rev. 13; Watchman Nee, *Love Not the World;* A. W. Tozer, *The Divine Conquest,* 110–20; A. W. Tozer, *God Tells the Man Who Cares,* 22–25; Donald Grey Barnhouse, *The Invisible War,* 189–95, 230–48.

4. Clarence Larkin, *Dispensational Truth, or, God's Plan and Purpose in the Ages;* George M. Marsden, *Understanding Fundamentalism and Evangelicalism,* 39–41; Alan Cooperman, "Openly Religious, to a Point," *Washington Post,* September 16, 2004, A1; Bill Broadway, "Backing Israel for Different Reasons," *Washington Post,* March 27, 2004, B9; George Monbiot, "Their Beliefs are Bonkers, But They Are at the Heart of Power," *London Guardian,* April 20, 2004; Bill Moyers, "There is No Tomorrow," *Minneapolis Star Tribune,* January 30, 2005, AA1, AA5.

5. Matt. 22:15–22; Leonard Verduin, *The Reformers and Their Stepchildren;* Edwin S. Gaustad, *Liberty of Conscience: Roger Williams in America;* Douglas Gwyn, *Apocalypse of the Word: The Life and Message of George Fox.*

6. Judy Keen, "Strain of Iraq War Showing on Bush, Those Who Known Him Say," *USA Today,* April 2, 2003, A1.

7. Matt Born, "God Told Me to Fight Terrorists," *London Daily Mail,* October 7, 2005, 19; "'Road Map is a Life Saver for Us,' PM Abbas Tells Hamas," *Haaretz (Israel),* June 26, 2003; Jack Brubaker, "Did George Bush Really Say, 'I Trust God Speaks through Me'?" *Lancaster (Pa.) New Era,* July 23, 2004, 1.

8. Richard Cohen, "The Crude Crusader," *Washington Post,* February 11, 2003, A21; Georgie Anne Geyer, "You're Invited to the War Party," *The American Conservative,* January 13, 2003; Matt. 7:21–23.

9. W. T. Stead, *Life of Mrs. Booth,* 195–204; Stephen Hobhouse, *William Law and Eighteenth Century Quakerism,* 333–40; Angus I. Kinnear, *Against the Tide: The Story of Watchman Nee,* 117.

10. Bryan, *Second Battle,* 196–97; Will Durant, *Caesar and Christ,* 564–67, 654–58; Gene Edwards, *Our Mission,* 81–106; C. S. Lewis, *Mere Christianity,* 78–83; Cal Thomas and Ed Dobson, *Blinded by Might: Can the Religious Right Save America?;* J. Budziszewski,

The Revenge of Conscience: Politics and the Fall of Man; Dan Balz, "Team Bush," *Washington Post,* July 23, 1999, C1; Tracy Warner, "The Real Story behind Rove, McKinley, and 'Dollar Mark,'" *Ft. Wayne Journal-Gazette,* November 11, 2004, 7A.

11. Timothy P. Carney, "A Specter Haunts the GOP," *The American Conservative,* June 7, 2004, 20–21.

12. Bryan, *Second Battle,* 194–96.

13. Bryan, *Speeches,* 2:6–8, 261–90; Matt. 12:30; Rom. 8:18–25; Col. 1:24–29; John 1:1–14; C. S. Lewis, *The Screwtape Letters,* 119–20, 126; A. W. Tozer, *The Root of the Righteous,* 23–26; Francis A. Schaeffer, *The Church at the End of the Twentieth Century,* 81–83; John H. Yoder, *The Original Revolution: Essays on Christian Pacifism;* Jim Wallis, "Dangerous Religion," *Sojourners Magazine,* September–October 2003, 20–26.

14. Marsden, *Fundamentalism and American Culture,* 124–38, 184–88.

15. Marsden, *Understanding Fundamentalism and Evangelicalism,* 46–50.

16. John Nichols, "The Lone Dissenter," *The Progressive,* November 2001, 28.

17. Bryan, *Second Battle,* 227–28.

18. Al From and Bruce Reed, "Get the Red Out," *Wall Street Journal,* December 8, 2004, A12; Donna Brazile and Timothy Bergreen, "What Would Scoop Do?" *Wall Street Journal,* May 21, 2003, A12; John Rensenbrink, "Two Myths the Facts Dismantle," *Green Horizon Quarterly,* Spring/Summer 2005, 37; Charles M. Sennott, "Clinton Finds Favor with Blair, Labor Party," *Boston Globe,* October 3, 2002, A17.

19. Patrick Healy, "Kerry Says He'd Still Vote to Authorize Iraq War," *Boston Globe,* August 10, 2004, A1; William Safire, "Kerry, Newest Neocon," *New York Times,* October 4, 2004, A25.

20. Humphrey, *Education of a Public Man,* 189; Kolko, *Another Century of War?;* "Majority of Americans Now Feel Iraq War was Wrong: Poll," *Agence France Presse,* October 25, 2005; Meg Bortin, "Americans Are More Isolationist, Poll Finds," *International Herald Tribune,* November 18, 2005, 2; Linda Feldmann, "Why Iraq War Support Fell So Fast," *Christian Science Monitor,* November 21, 2005, 1.

21. Marc Humbert, "Sheehan Opposes Clinton for Not Being against War," *Buffalo News,* October 26, 2005.

22. From and Reed, "Get the Red Out"; Al From and Bruce Reed, "What We Stand For," *Blueprint,* March 16, 2005.

23. Mike Madden, "Thune Hit Daschle as Out of Touch to Win South Dakota Victory," *Gannett News Service,* November 4, 2004; Christopher Lee, "Dole Played a Key Role in Recruiting Former Senator," *Washington Post,* March 14, 2005, A17; Trautman, ed., *New Populist Reader,* 71–79.

24. David Crary, "Conservatives, Gay Rights Groups Gird for Next Round after Sweeping Setback for Gay Marriage," *Bismarck (N.Dak.) Tribune,* November 4, 2004, 10; Robert Tanner, "New England an Outpost of Support for Gay Couples," *Providence (R.I.) Journal,* April 7, 2005, A11.

25. Mark Stricherz, "Public's View on Roe Depends on the Question," *Chicago Tribune,* October 2, 2005, 4.

26. Mary Krane Derr, Linda Naranjo-Huebl, and Rachel MacNair, eds., *Prolife Feminism: Yesterday and Today;* Zillah R. Eisenstein, ed., *Capitalist Patriarchy and the Case for Socialist Feminism,* 107–50; Germaine Greer, *Sex and Destiny: The Politics of Human Fertility;* Angela Y. Davis, *Women, Race and Class,* 202–21; Andrea Dworkin, *Right-Wing Women,* 88–105, 148–52; Catharine A. MacKinnon, *Feminism Unmodified: Discourses on Life and Law,* 93–102, 144–45, 248–51, 261; Lindsy Van Gelder, "Playboy's Charity: Is It Reparations or Rip-Off?" *Ms.,* June 1983, 78–81.

27. Bryan, *Bryan: Selections,* 190; Smith, *Social and Religious Thought of Bryan,* 129; "Humphrey Offers Views on Abortion," *New York Times,* April 25, 1976, 39.

28. Ralph Z. Hallow, "Carter Condemns Abortion Culture," *Washington Times,* November 4, 2005, A6.

29. Kolko, *Another Century of War?* 45–50; Bill, *Eagle and the Lion;* Chomsky, *Towards a New Cold War,* 337–70; Don Oberdorfer, "Deep Differences Mixed with Air of Tolerance," *Washington Post,* June 19, 1979, A16; "Chinese Vice Premiers Deng Xiaoping and Fang Yi Visit the United States," *Department of State Bulletin,* March 1979, 1–5; Levinson, *Vodka-Cola,* 260–61; Sklar, ed., *Trilateralism;* Shoup, *Carter Presidency and Beyond;* Allen, "1976 Democrat Convention," 51; Victor Lasky, *Jimmy Carter: The Man and the Myth,* 220–25, 234–38.

30. Beth Joyner Waldron, "Why Avoid Using 'Merry Christmas'?" *Christian Science Monitor,* December 1, 2005, 9; Samuel P. Huntington, *Who Are We? The Challenges to America's National Identity.*.

31. "The American Ethnic Experience as it Stands in the Nineties," *The Public Perspective,* 9 (February/March 1998): 52.

32. Michael J. Behe, *Darwin's Black Box: The Biochemical Challenge to Evolution.*

33. Jefferson, *Life and Selected Writings,* 558.

34. Martha Raffaele, "Judge Bars the Teaching of 'Intelligent Design,'" *St. Louis Post-Dispatch,* December 21, 2005.

35. "Poll: Evolution Rejected by Most in Survey," *UPI,* October 24, 2005.

36. Sam Smith, "False Faith Defeats Lousy Works."

37. Frank, *What's the Matter with Kansas?;* Ostler, "Rhetoric of Conspiracy"; Burkholder, "Kansas Populism."

38. Taylor, *Inquiry into the Principles and Policy,* 382–83.

39. Logan, *Betrayal of the Negro,* 54–55, 94–95; Palmer, *"Man over Money,"* 50–66, 171–81; George Brown Tindall, ed., *A Populist Reader: Selections from the Works of American Populist Leaders,* 118–28.

40. The states that Bryan carried in 1896, 1900, and/or 1908 that have since become reliably Republican in presidential elections are Louisiana, Arkansas, Mississippi, Alabama, Georgia, Florida, South Carolina, North Carolina, Virginia, Tennessee, Nevada, Kentucky, Missouri, Idaho, Montana, Nebraska, Oklahoma, Colorado, Utah, Wyoming, Kansas, and South Dakota.

41. Lance Morrow, "George Wallace Overcomes," *Time,* October 11, 1982, 15–16; Viguerie, *Establishment vs. the People,* 216.

42. Allen, "1976 Democrat Convention."

43. Samuel G. Freedman, *The Inheritance: How Three Families and the American Political Majority Moved from Left to Right;* Mark Stricherz, "Who Killed Archie Bunker?: Working-Class Television and the Democratic Party," *Doublethink,* Fall 2005; Malcolm X, *The Autobiography of Malcolm X,* 373–74.

44. Gary Olson, "Democrats Need to Return to Their Populist Roots," *Allentown (Pa.) Morning Call,* November 8, 2004, A13; W. James Antle III, "The People's Party," *The American Conservative,* January 31, 2005, 15–17.

BIBLIOGRAPHY

Abraham, Larry, and Gary Allen. *Call It Conspiracy.* Seattle: Double A Publications, 1985.

Abrams, Ray H. *Preachers Present Arms.* New York: Round Table Press, 1933.

Abramson, Jill, and Phil Kuntz. "Antitrust Probe of Archer-Daniels Puts Spotlight on Chairman Andreas's Vast Political Influence." *Wall Street Journal,* July 11, 1995, A16.

Abramson, Rudy. *Spanning the Century: The Life of W. Averell Harriman, 1891–1986.* New York: William Morrow, 1992.

Ahlstrom, Sydney E. *A Religious History of the American People.* Garden City, N.Y.: Image Books, 1975.

Aldrich, Nelson W., Jr. *Old Money: The Mythology of America's Upper Class.* New York: Vintage Books, 1989.

Alexander, Herbert E. *Financing the 1968 Election.* Lexington, Mass.: Lexington Books, 1971.

———. *Financing the 1972 Election.* Lexington, Mass.: Lexington Books, 1976.

———. *Financing the 1976 Election.* Washington, D.C.: Congressional Quarterly Press, 1979.

Alexander, Herbert E., and Brian A. Haggerty. *Financing the 1984 Election.* Lexington, Mass.: Lexington Books, 1987.

Allen, Gary. "The 1976 Democrat Convention." *American Opinion,* September 1976, 39–54, 107–10.

———. *Richard Nixon: The Man Behind the Mask.* Boston: Western Islands, 1971.

———. *The Rockefeller File.* Seal Beach, Calif.: '76 Press, 1976.

Allen, Gary, and Larry Abraham. *None Dare Call It Conspiracy.* Rossmoor, Calif.: Concord Press, 1972.

Allen, William. "Speeches at a Jacksonian Banquet." *Congressional Record,* February 7, 1899, 1535–44.

Alsop, Stewart. *Nixon and Rockefeller: A Double Portrait.* Garden City, N.Y.: Doubleday, 1960.

The American Heritage Book of the Presidents and Famous Americans. Vol. 2. New York: Dell, 1967.

Amrine, Michael. *This is Humphrey: The Story of the Senator.* Garden City, N.Y.: Doubleday, 1960.

Antle, W. James, III. "The People's Party." *The American Conservative,* January 31, 2005, 15–17.

Archer, Jules. *The Plot to Seize the White House.* New York: Hawthorn Books, 1973.

Aristotle. *The Politics.* Translated by T. A. Sinclair and Trevor J. Saunders. Harmondsworth: Penguin Books, 1981.

Arnove, Robert F., ed. *Philanthropy and Cultural Imperialism: The Foundations at Home and Abroad.* Bloomington: Indiana University Press, 1982.

Arsenault, Raymond. *The Wild Ass of the Ozarks: Jeff Davis and the Social Bases of Southern Politics.* Philadelphia: Temple University Press, 1984.

Ashby, LeRoy. *William Jennings Bryan: Champion of Democracy.* Boston: Twayne, 1987.

Ashworth, John. *"Agrarians" and "Aristocrats": Party Political Ideology in the United States, 1837–1846.* Cambridge: Cambridge University Press, 1987.

Bacevich, Andrew J. *American Empire: The Realities and Consequences of U.S. Diplomacy.* Cambridge: Harvard University Press, 2002.

———. *The New American Militarism: How Americans Are Seduced by War.* New York: Oxford University Press, 2005.

Bailey, Thomas A., and David M. Kennedy. *The American Pageant: A History of the Republic.* 6th ed. Lexington, Mass.: D. C. Heath, 1979.

Baltzell, E. Digby. *The Protestant Establishment: Aristocracy and Caste in America.* New York: Random House, 1964.

———. *Puritan Boston and Quaker Philadelphia: Two Protestant Ethics and the Spirit of Class Authority and Leadership.* Boston: Beacon Press, 1982.

Banning, Lance. *The Jeffersonian Persuasion: Evolution of a Party Ideology.* Ithaca: Cornell University Press, 1978.

Barnes, Harry Elmer. *The Chickens of the Interventionist Liberals Have Come Home to Roost: The Bitter Fruits of Globaloney.* Brooklyn: Herbert C. Roseman, 1954.

———. *In Quest of Truth and Justice: De-Bunking the War-Guilt Myth.* Colorado Springs: Ralph Myles, 1972.

———, ed. *Perpetual War for Perpetual Peace: A Critical Examination of the Foreign Policy of Franklin Delano Roosevelt and its Aftermath.* Caldwell, Idaho: Caxton Printers, 1953.

Barnes, James A. "Myths of the Bryan Campaign." *Mississippi Valley Historical Review* 34 (December 1947): 367–404.

Barnet, Richard J. *Roots of War.* New York: Pelican Books, 1973.

Barnhouse, Donald Grey. *The Invisible War.* Grand Rapids, Mich.: Zondervan, 1965.

Barry, William T. S., comp. *Journal of the State Convention.* Jackson, Miss.: E. Barksdale, 1861.

Barta, Carolyn. *Perot and His People: Disrupting the Balance of Political Power.* Fort Worth: Summit Group, 1993.

Bates-Froiland, Lisa. "Forgetting Hubert Humphrey: Rhetorical Dimensions of American Public Memory." PhD diss., Indiana University, 2003.

Beard, Charles A. *American Foreign Policy in the Making, 1932–1940: A Study in Responsibilities.* New Haven: Yale University Press, 1946.

———. *The American Party Battle.* New York: Book League of America, 1929.

———. *The Economic Basis of Politics and Related Writings.* Compiled by William Beard. New York: Vintage Books, 1957.

———. *An Economic Interpretation of the Constitution of the United States.* New York: Macmillan, 1913.

———. *Giddy Minds and Foreign Quarrels: An Estimate of American Foreign Policy.* New York: Macmillan, 1939.

———. *President Roosevelt and the Coming of the War, 1941: A Study in Appearances and Realities.* New Haven: Yale University Press, 1948.

———. *The Republic: Conversations on Fundamentals.* New York: Viking Press, 1943.

Behe, Michael J. *Darwin's Black Box: The Biochemical Challenge to Evolution.* New York: Free Press, 1996.

Bell, Jeffrey. *Populism and Elitism: Politics in the Age of Equality.* Washington, D.C.: Regnery Gateway, 1992.

Benson, Lee. *The Concept of Jacksonian Democracy: New York as a Test Case.* Princeton: Princeton University Press, 1970.

Berman, Edgar. *Hubert: The Triumph and Tragedy of the Humphrey I Knew.* New York: G. P. Putnam's Sons, 1979.

Bernstein, Barton J., ed. *Politics and Policies of the Truman Administration.* Chicago: Quadrangle Books, 1970.

———. *Towards a New Past: Dissenting Essays in American History.* New York: Vintage Books, 1969.

Bernstein, R. B. *Thomas Jefferson.* New York: Oxford University Press, 2003.

Berry, Wendell. *Sex, Economy, Freedom, and Community: Eight Essays.* New York: Pantheon Books, 1993.

Bill, James A. *The Eagle and the Lion: The Tragedy of American-Iranian Relations.* New Haven: Yale University Press, 1988.

Black, David. *The King of Fifth Avenue: The Fortunes of August Belmont.* New York: Dial Press, 1981.

Black, Eric. *Our Constitution: The Myth That Binds Us.* Boulder, Colo.: Westview Press, 1988.

Boggs, Carl. *The End of Politics: Corporate Power and the Decline of the Public Sphere.* New York: Guilford Press, 2000.

Bonhoeffer, Dietrich. *The Cost of Discipleship.* New York: Collier, 1963.

Bowen, William. "What's New about the New Hubert Humphrey?" *Fortune,* August 1965, 142–45, 238–41.

Bowers, Claude G. *Jefferson and Hamilton: The Struggle for Democracy in America.* Boston: Houghton Mifflin, 1925.

———. *Jefferson in Power: The Death Struggle of the Federalists.* Boston: Houghton Mifflin, 1936.

Branch, Taylor. *Parting the Waters: America in the King Years, 1954–1963.* New York: Simon and Schuster, 1988.

Brenner, Lenni. *The Lesser Evil.* Secaucus, N.J.: Lyle Stuart, 1988.

Brinkley, Alan. *Voices of Protest: Huey Long, Father Coughlin, and the Great Depression.* New York: Vintage Books, 1983.

Brock, Clifton. *Americans for Democratic Action: Its Role in National Politics.* Washington, D.C.: Public Affairs Press, 1962.

Brodie, Fawn M. *Thomas Jefferson: An Intimate History.* New York: Bantam Books, 1975.

Brommel, Bernard J. *Eugene V. Debs: Spokesman for Labor and Socialism.* Chicago: Charles H. Kerr Publishing, 1978.

Brown, H. Rap. *Die Nigger Die!* New York: Dial Press, 1969.

Brown, Jerry. "Party Has Forgotten Populist Roots." *San Francisco Chronicle,* March 26, 1998, A25.

Bryan, William Jennings. *The Commoner: Condensed.* New York: Abbey Press, 1902.

———. *The Credo of the Commoner: William Jennings Bryan.* Edited by William Jennings Bryan Jr. and Franklin Modisett. Los Angeles: Occidental College, 1968.

———. *The First Battle: A Story of the Campaign of 1896.* Chicago: W. B. Conkey, 1896.

———. *The Second Battle, or, the New Declaration of Independence, 1776–1900: An Account of the Struggle of 1900.* Chicago: W. B. Conkey, 1900.

———. *Speeches of William Jennings Bryan.* Vol. 2. New York: Funk and Wagnalls, 1909.

————. *Under Other Flags: Travels, Lectures, Speeches.* Lincoln, Neb.: Woodruff-Collins Printing, 1904.

————. *William Jennings Bryan: Selections.* Edited by Ray Ginger. Indianapolis: Bobbs-Merrill, 1967.

Bryan, William Jennings, and Mary Baird Bryan. *The Memoirs of William Jennings Bryan.* Chicago: John C. Winston, 1925.

Bryant, Keith L., Jr. *Alfalfa Bill Murray.* Norman: University of Oklahoma Press, 1968.

Brzezinski, Zbigniew. *Between Two Ages: America's Role in the Technetronic Era.* New York: Viking Press, 1970.

Buchanan, Pat. "Ralph Nader: Conservatively Speaking." *The American Conservative,* June 21, 2004, 6–10.

————. *Where the Right Went Wrong: How Neoconservatives Subverted the Reagan Revolution and Hijacked the Bush Presidency.* New York: Thomas Dunne, 2004.

Budziszewski, J. *The Revenge of Conscience: Politics and the Fall of Man.* Dallas: Spence, 1999.

————. *What We Can't Not Know: A Guide.* Dallas: Spence, 2004.

————. *Written on the Heart: The Case for Natural Law.* Downers Grove, Ill.: InterVarsity, 1997.

Bugg, James L., Jr., ed., *Jacksonian Democracy: Myth or Reality?* Hinsdale, Ill.: Dryden Press, 1962.

Bullock, Paul. *Jerry Voorhis: The Idealist as Politician.* New York: Vantage Press, 1978.

Burch, Philip, H., Jr. *Elites in American History.* 3 vols. New York: Holmes and Meier, 1981.

Burgchardt, Carl R. *Robert M. La Follette Sr.: The Voice of Conscience.* New York: Greenwood Press, 1992.

Burke, Robert E. "A Friendship in Adversity: Burton K. Wheeler, Hiram W. Johnson." *Montana, the Magazine of Western History* (Winter 1986): 12–25.

Burkholder, Thomas R. "Kansas Populism, Woman Suffrage, and the Agrarian Myth: A Case Study in the Limits of Mythic Transcendence." *Communication Studies* 40 (Winter 1989): 292–307.

Burns, James MacGregor. *Roosevelt: The Lion and the Fox.* New York: Harcourt, Brace, 1956.

Burns, Rex. *Success in America: The Yeoman Dream and the Industrial Revolution.* Amherst: University of Massachusetts Press, 1976.

Campbell, Norine Dickson. *Patrick Henry: Patriot and Statesman.* Old Greenwich, Conn.: Devin-Adair, 1969.

Capers, Gerald M. *John C. Calhoun, Opportunist: A Reappraisal.* Gainesville: University of Florida Press, 1960.

Carlin, David R. "The Suicide of Contemporary Liberalism." *America,* September 24, 1994, 9–11.

Carlson, Jody. *George C. Wallace and the Politics of Powerlessness: The Wallace Campaigns for the Presidency, 1964–1976.* New Brunswick, N.J.: Transaction Books, 1981.

Caro, Robert A. *The Years of Lyndon Johnson: Means of Ascent.* London: Bodley Head, 1990.

———. *The Years of Lyndon Johnson: The Path to Power.* New York: Knopf, 1982.

Carpozi, George, Jr. *Clinton Confidential: The Climb to Power: The Unauthorized Biography of Bill and Hillary Clinton.* Del Mar, Calif.: Emery Dalton Books, 1995.

Chamberlin, William Henry. *America's Second Crusade.* Chicago: Henry Regnery, 1950.

Cherny, Robert W. *A Righteous Cause: The Life of William Jennings Bryan.* Boston: Little, Brown, 1985.

Chester, Lewis, Godfrey Hodgson, and Bruce Page. *An American Melodrama: The Presidential Campaign of 1968.* New York: Viking Press, 1969.

Chomsky, Noam. *American Power and the New Mandarins.* New York: Pantheon Books, 1969.

———. *The Culture of Terrorism.* Boston: South End Press, 1988.

———. *Keeping the Rabble in Line: Interviews with David Barsamian.* Monroe, Maine: Common Courage Press, 1994.

———. *Language and Politics.* Edited by Carlos P. Otero. Montreal: Black Rose Books, 1988.

———. *Necessary Illusions: Thought Control in Democratic Societies.* Boston: South End Press, 1989.

———. *Radical Priorities.* Edited by Carlos P. Otero. Montreal: Black Rose Books, 1984.

———. *Rethinking Camelot: JFK, the Vietnam War, and U.S. Political Culture.* Boston: South End Press, 1993.

———. *Towards a New Cold War: Essays on the Current Crisis and How We Got There.* New York: Pantheon Books, 1982.

Chomsky, Noam, and Edward S. Herman. *The Washington Connection and Third World Fascism: The Political Economy of Human Rights, Volume I.* Boston: South End Press, 1979.

Christie, Jim. "Jerry Brown Talks." *Chronicles,* November 1994, 17–20

Clements, Kendrick A. *William Jennings Bryan: Missionary Isolationist.* Knoxville: University of Tennessee Press, 1982.

Clifford, J. Garry, and Samuel R. Spencer Jr. *The First Peacetime Draft.* Lawrence: University Press of Kansas, 1986.

Clinch, Nancy Gager. *The Kennedy Neurosis.* New York: Grosset and Dunlap, 1973.

Coates, Eyler Robert, Sr., ed. *The Jefferson-Hemings Myth: An American Travesty.* Charlottesville: Jefferson Editions, 2001.

Cobbs, Elizabeth Anne. *The Rich Neighbor Policy: Rockefeller and Kaiser in Brazil.* New Haven: Yale University Press, 1992.

Cockburn, Alexander. "Neither 'Left' nor 'Right,'" *The Nation,* July 17 and 24, 1995, 80.

———. "The People's Pit Bull." *Salon Magazine,* February 10, 1996. http://archive.salon.com/07/features/buchanan.html.

Cockburn, Alexander, and Jeffrey St. Clair, eds. *Dime's Worth of Difference: Beyond the Lesser of Two Evils.* Petrolia, Calif.: CounterPunch, 2004.

Cockburn, Alexander, and Ken Silverstein. *Washington Babylon.* London: Verso, 1996.

Cohen, Dan. *Undefeated: The Life of Hubert H. Humphrey.* Minneapolis: Lerner Publications, 1978.

Colby, Gerard, and Charlotte Dennett. *Thy Will Be Done: The Conquest of the Amazon: Nelson Rockefeller and Evangelism in the Age of Oil.* New York: Harper Collins, 1995.

Cole, Wayne S. *America First: The Battle against Intervention, 1940–1941.* Madison: University of Wisconsin Press, 1953.

———.*Roosevelt and the Isolationists, 1932–1945.* Lincoln: University of Nebraska Press, 1983.

———. *Senator Gerald P. Nye and American Foreign Relations.* Minneapolis: University of Minnesota Press, 1962.

Coletta, Paolo E. *William Jennings Bryan, vol. 1: Political Evangelist, 1860–1908.* Lincoln: University of Nebraska Press, 1964.

———. *William Jennings Bryan, vol. 2: Progressive Politician and Moral Statesman, 1909–1915.* Lincoln: University of Nebraska Press, 1969.

———. *William Jennings Bryan, vol. 3: Political Puritan, 1915–1925.* Lincoln: University of Nebraska Press, 1969.

Collins, Robert M. "Positive Business Responses to the New Deal: The Roots of the Committee for Economic Development, 1933–1942." *Business History Review* 52 (Autumn 1978): 369–91.

Colton, Elizabeth O. *The Jackson Phenomenon: The Man, the Power, the Message.* New York: Doubleday, 1989.

Commager, Henry Steele. *The American Mind: An Interpretation of American Thought and Character since the 1880s.* New Haven: Yale University Press, 1950.

Cook, Blanche Wiesen, Alice Kessler Harris, and Ronald Radosh, eds. *Past Imperfect: Alternative Essays in American History, Volume 2: From Reconstruction to the Present.* New York: Knopf, 1973.

Cooper, William J., Jr., and Thomas E. Terrill. *The American South: A History.* New York: McGraw-Hill, 1991.

Copleston, Frederick. *A History of Philosophy.* New York: Image Books, 1985.

Council on Foreign Relations: 2003 Annual Report. New York: Council on Foreign Relations, 2003.

Council on Foreign Relations: A Record of Twenty-Five Years. New York: Council on Foreign Relations, 1947.

Crackel, Theodore J. *Mr. Jefferson's Army: Political and Social Reform of the Military Establishment, 1801–1809.* New York: New York University Press, 1987.

Craig, Douglas B. *After Wilson: The Struggle for the Democratic Party, 1920–1934.* Chapel Hill: University of North Carolina Press, 1992.

Crawford, Alan. *Thunder on the Right: The "New Right" and the Politics of Resentment.* New York: Pantheon, 1980.

Crawford, Clare. "It's Not Tough Sledding Anymore for the New Serene Hubert Humphrey." *People,* February 9, 1976, 8–11.

Croly, Herbert. "The Eclipse of Progressivism." *The New Republic,* October 27, 1920, 210–16.

———. *The Promise of American Life.* New York: Macmillan, 1909.

Cunningham, Noble E., Jr. *In Pursuit of Reason: The Life of Thomas Jefferson.* New York: Ballantine Books, 1988.

———. *The Jeffersonian Republicans: The Formation of Party Organization, 1789–1801.* Chapel Hill: University of North Carolina Press, 1957.

Curti, Merle Eugene. *Bryan and World Peace.* Smith College Studies in History, vol. 16, nos. 3–4. Northampton, Mass.: Smith College, 1931.

Daniels, Josephus. *Editor in Politics.* Chapel Hill: University of North Carolina Press, 1941.

Darrow, Clarence. *The Story of My Life.* New York: Charles Scribner's Sons, 1932.

Daugherty, Harry M. *The Inside Story of the Harding Tragedy.* New York: Churchill Company, 1932.

Davis, Angela Y. *Women, Race, and Class.* New York: Vintage, 1983.

Davison, Mary M. *The Secret Government of the United States.* Omaha: Greater Nebraskan, 1962.

Dayton, Donald W. *Discovering an Evangelical Heritage.* New York: Harper and Row, 1976.

Depoe, Stephen P. *Arthur M. Schlesinger Jr. and the Ideological History of American Liberalism.* Tuscaloosa: University of Alabama Press, 1994.

Derr, Mary Krane, Linda Naranjo-Huebl, and Rachel MacNair, eds. *Prolife Feminism: Yesterday and Today.* New York: Sulzburger and Graham, 1995.

Destler, Chester McArthur. *American Radicalism: 1865–1901.* Chicago: Quadrangle Paperbacks, 1966.

Dionne, E. J., Jr. "This Season's Political Mavericks See Perot's Rise as Validation." *Washington Post,* May 31, 1992, A16.

———. *Why Americans Hate Politics.* New York: Simon and Schuster, 1992.

Divine, Robert A. *Foreign Policy and U.S. Presidential Elections, 1940–1948.* New York: New Viewpoints, 1974.

Doan, Edward N. *The La Follettes and the Wisconsin Idea.* New York: Rinehart, 1947.

Doenecke, Justus D., ed. *In Danger Undaunted: The Anti-Interventionist Movement of 1940–1941 as Revealed in the Papers of the America First Committee.* Stanford: Hoover Institution Press, 1990.

———. *Not to the Swift: The Old Isolationists in the Cold War Era.* Lewisburg, Pa.: Bucknell University Press, 1979.

Domhoff, G. William. *Fat Cats and Democrats: The Role of the Big Rich in the Party of the Common Man.* Englewood Cliffs, N.J.: Prentice-Hall, 1972.

———. *The Higher Circles: The Governing Class in America.* New York: Vintage Books, 1971.

———. *The Powers That Be: Processes of Ruling-Class Domination in America.* New York: Vintage Books, 1979.

———. *Who Rules America?* Englewood Cliffs, N.J.: Prentice-Hall, 1967.

———. *Who Rules America Now? A View for the '80s.* New York: Touchstone, 1986.

Donald, David. *Charles Sumner and the Coming of the Civil War.* New York: Fawcett Columbine, 1989.

———. *Charles Sumner and the Rights of Man.* New York: Knopf, 1970.

Douglas, Paul H. *In the Fullness of Time: The Memoirs of Paul H. Douglas.* New York: Harcourt, Brace, Jovanovich, 1972.

Douglass, Elisha P. *Rebels and Democrats: The Struggle for Equal Political Rights and Majority Rule during the American Revolution.* Chicago: Quadrangle Paperbacks, 1965.

Downs, Anthony. *An Economic Theory of Democracy.* New York: Harper and Row, 1957.

Durant, Will. *Caesar and Christ.* New York: Simon and Schuster, 1944.

Durant, Will, and Ariel Durant. *The Age of Faith.* New York: Simon and Schuster, 1950.

———. *The Age of Voltaire.* New York: Simon and Schuster, 1965.

Dworkin, Andrea. *Right-Wing Women.* New York: Perigee, 1983.

Dye, Thomas R. *Who's Running America? Institutional Leadership in the United States.* Englewood Cliffs, N.J.: Prentice-Hall, 1976.

———. *Who's Running America? The Reagan Years.* Englewood Cliffs, N.J.: Prentice-Hall, 1983.

Dye, Thomas R., and L. Harmon Zeigler. *The Irony of Democracy: An Uncommon Introduction to American Politics.* 2nd ed. Belmont, Calif.: Duxbury Press, 1972.

Edsall, Thomas B. "Voter Values Determine Political Affiliation." *Washington Post,* March 26, 2001, A1.

Edwards, Gene. *Our Mission.* Augusta, Maine: Christian Books, 1984.

Edwards, Lee. *Goldwater: The Man Who Made a Revolution.* Washington, D.C.: Regnery, 1997.

Eisele, Albert. *Almost to the Presidency: A Biography of Two American Politicians.* Blue Earth, Minn.: Piper, 1972.

Eisenstein, Zillah R., ed. *Capitalist Patriarchy and the Case for Socialist Feminism.* New York: Monthly Review Press, 1979.

Ekirch, Arthur A., Jr. *The Civilian and the Military: A History of the American Antimilitarist Tradition.* Colorado Springs: Ralph Myles, 1972.

Elazar, Daniel J. *American Federalism: A View from the States.* New York: Thomas Y. Crowell, 1966.

Elazar, Daniel J., and Joseph Zikmund II, eds. *The Ecology of American Political Culture: Readings.* New York: Thomas Y. Crowell, 1975.

Ellis, Joseph J. *American Sphinx: The Character of Thomas Jefferson.* New York: Knopf, 1997.

Ellul, Jacques. *The Subversion of Christianity.* Grand Rapids, Mich.: Eerdmans, 1986.

Engelbrecht, H. C., and F. C. Hanighen. *Merchants of Death: A Study of the International Armament Industry.* New York: Dodd, Mead, 1934.

English, David, et al. *Divided They Stand.* Englewood Cliffs, N.J.: Prentice-Hall, 1969.

Exoo, Calvin F., ed. *Democracy Upside Down: Public Opinion and Cultural Hegemony in the United States.* New York: Praeger, 1987.

Faber, Harold, ed. *The Road to the White House: The Story of the 1964 Election by the Staff of the New York Times.* New York: McGraw-Hill, 1965.

Falk, Richard. *The End of World Order: Essays on Normative International Relations.* New York: Holmes and Meier, 1983.

———. *The Promise of World Order: Essays in Normative International Relations.* Philadelphia: Temple University Press, 1987.

Feinman, Ronald L. *Twilight of Progressivism: The Western Republican Senators and the New Deal.* Baltimore: Johns Hopkins University Press, 1981.

Ferguson, Thomas. "The Lost Crusade of Ross Perot." *The Nation,* August 17 and 24, 1992, 168–76.

Ferguson, Thomas, and Joel Rogers. *Right Turn: The Decline of the Democrats and the Future of American Politics.* New York: Hill and Wang, 1986.

Finder, Joseph. *Red Carpet.* Fort Worth: American Bureau of Economic Research, 1987.

Finkelman, Paul. *Slavery and the Founders: Race and Liberty in the Age of Jefferson.* Armonk, N.Y.: M. E. Sharpe, 1996.

Fleming, Dan B., Jr. *Kennedy vs. Humphrey, West Virginia, 1960: The Pivotal Battle for the Democratic Presidential Nomination.* Jefferson, N.C.: McFarland, 1992.

Fleming, Thomas. "From Bryan to Buchanan." *Chronicles,* March 1996, 8–11.

———. "The Illusions of Democracy." *Chronicles,* January 1996, 8–11.

———. "The New Fusionism." *Chronicles,* May 1991, 10–12.

Flynn, John T. *As We Go Marching.* New York: Free Life Editions, 1973.

———. *The Roosevelt Myth.* Garden City, N.Y.: Garden City Publishing, 1949.

Forcey, Charles. *The Crossroads of Liberalism: Croly, Weyl, Lippmann, and the Progressive Era, 1900–1925.* London: Oxford University Press, 1967.

Førland, Tor Egil. "Bringing It All Back Home or Another Side of Bob Dylan: Midwestern Isolationist." *Journal of American Studies* 26 (December 1992): 337–55.

Forman, James. *The Making of Black Revolutionaries: A Personal Account.* New York: Macmillan, 1972.

Fossedal, Gregory A. *The Democratic Imperative: Exporting the American Revolution.* New York: Basic Books, 1989.

———. *Our Finest Hour: Will Clayton, the Marshall Plan, and the Triumph of Democracy.* Stanford: Hoover Institution Press, 1993.

Francis, Samuel. *Beautiful Losers: Essays on the Failure of American Conservatism.* Columbia: University of Missouri Press, 1993.

———. *Revolution from the Middle.* Raleigh, N.C.: Middle American Press, 1997.

Franck, Matthew J. *Against the Imperial Judiciary: The Supreme Court vs. the Sovereignty of the People.* Lawrence: University Press of Kansas, 1996.

Frank, Thomas. *What's the Matter with Kansas? How Conservatives Won the Heart of America.* New York: Metropolitan Books, 2004.

Freedman, Samuel G. *The Inheritance: How Three Families and the American Political Majority Moved from Left to Right.* New York: Simon and Schuster, 1998.

Freidel, Frank. *Franklin D. Roosevelt.* 2 vols. Boston: Little, Brown, 1952–1954.

Fresia, Jerry. *Toward an American Revolution: Exposing the Constitution and Other Illusions.* Boston: South End Press, 1988.

Fried, Albert, ed. *The Jeffersonian and Hamiltonian Traditions in American Politics: A Documentary History.* Garden City, N.Y.: Anchor, 1968.

Gannon, Francis X. *Biographical Dictionary of the Left.* Boston: Western Islands, 1969–1973.

Garrettson, Charles Lloyd, III. *Hubert H. Humphrey: The Politics of Joy.* New Brunswick, N.J.: Transaction Publishers, 1993.

Garrow, David J. *Bearing the Cross: Martin Luther King Jr. and the Southern Christian Leadership Conference, 1955–1968.* New York: Morrow, 1986.

Garson, G. David. *Power and Politics in the United States: A Political Economy Approach.* Lexington, Mass.: D. C. Heath, 1977.

Gates, John B., and Charles A. Johnson, eds. *The American Courts: A Critical Assessment.* Washington, D.C.: CQ Press, 1991.

Gaustad, Edwin S. *Liberty of Conscience: Roger Williams in America.* Grand Rapids, Mich.: Eerdmans, 1991.

Gerring, John. *Party Ideologies in America, 1828–1996.* New York: Cambridge University Press, 1998.

Gerstle, Gary. "The Protean Character of American Liberalism." *American Historical Review* 99 (October 1994): 1043–73.

Gibbs, Christopher C. *The Great Silent Majority: Missouri's Resistance to World War I.* Columbia: University of Missouri Press, 1988.

Gieske, Millard L. *Minnesota Farmer-Laborism: The Third-Party Alternative.* Minneapolis: University of Minnesota Press, 1979.

Girvetz, Harry K. *The Evolution of Liberalism.* New York: Collier, 1966.

Glad, Paul W. *McKinley, Bryan, and the People.* Philadelphia: J. B. Lippincott, 1964.

———. *The Trumpet Soundeth: William Jennings Bryan and His Democracy, 1896–1912.* Westport, Conn.: Greenwood Press, 1986.

———, ed. *William Jennings Bryan: A Profile.* New York: Hill and Wang, 1968.

Goddard, Arthur, ed. *Harry Elmer Barnes, Learned Crusader: The New History in Action.* Colorado Springs: Ralph Myles, 1968.

Goldman, Peter, et al. *Quest for the Presidency, 1992.* College Station: Texas A & M University Press, 1994.

Goldwater, Barry M. "Barry Goldwater Talks about 'Liberals' and 'Liberalism.'" *U.S. News and World Report,* July 8, 1963, 44–45.

———. *The Conscience of a Conservative.* Shepherdsville, Ky.: Victor Publishing, 1960.

———. *With No Apologies: The Personal and Political Memoirs of United States Senator Barry M. Goldwater.* New York: William Morrow, 1979.

Gompers, Samuel. *Seventy Years of Life and Labor: An Autobiography.* Edited by Nick Salvatore. Ithaca: ILR Press, 1984.

Goodman, Mitchell, comp. *The Movement toward a New America: The Beginnings of a Long Revolution.* Philadelphia: Pilgrim Press, 1970.

Goodwyn, Lawrence. *The Populist Moment: A Short History of the Agrarian Revolt in America.* New York: Oxford University Press, 1978.

Gorey, Hays. "'I'm a Born Optimist': The Era of Hubert H. Humphrey." *American Heritage,* December 1977, 58–68.

Gottfried, Paul E. *After Liberalism: Mass Democracy in the Managerial State.* Princeton: Princeton University Press, 1999.

———. "Conservative Crack-Up Continued." *Society,* January/February 1994, 23–29.

Gould, Stephen Jay. "William Jennings Bryan's Last Campaign." *Natural History,* November 1987, 16–26.

Graham, Otis L., Jr. *An Encore for Reform: The Old Progressives and the New Deal.* New York: Oxford University Press, 1967.

Greenbaum, Fred. *Robert Marion La Follette.* Boston: Twayne, 1975.

Greer, Germaine. *Sex and Destiny: The Politics of Human Fertility.* New York: Harper and Row, 1984.

Gregory, Dick. *No More Lies: The Myth and the Reality of American History.* Edited by James R. McGraw. New York: Harper and Row, 1971.

———. *Write Me In!* Edited by James R. McGraw. New York: Bantam Books, 1968.

Greider, William. "Buchanan Rethinks the American Empire." *Rolling Stone,* February 6, 1992, 37–39.

———. *Who Will Tell the People: The Betrayal of American Democracy.* New York: Simon and Schuster, 1992.

Greve, Frank. "Corn King." *Columbia (Mo.) Daily Tribune,* February 26, 1995, 1D.

Griffith, Robert. "Old Progressives and the Cold War." *Journal of American History* 66 (September 1979): 334–47.

———, ed. *Major Problems in American History since 1945: Documents and Essays.* Lexington, Mass.: D. C. Heath, 1992.

Griffith, Winthrop. *Humphrey: A Candid Biography.* New York: William Morrow, 1965.

Gross, Bertram. *Friendly Fascism: The New Face of Power in America.* Boston: South End Press, 1980.

Gross, Martin L. *The Great Whitewater Fiasco: An American Tale of Money, Power, and Politics.* New York: Ballantine Books, 1994.

Guyon, Jeanne. *Experiencing the Depths of Jesus Christ.* Edited by Gene Edwards. Goleta, Calif.: Christian Books, 1975.

Gwyn, Douglas. *Apocalypse of the Word: The Life and Message of George Fox.* Richmond, Ind.: Friends United Press, 1986.

Hamby, Alonzo L. *Beyond the New Deal: Harry S. Truman and American Liberalism.* New York: Columbia University Press, 1973.

Hamilton, Alexander. *The Basic Ideas of Alexander Hamilton.* Edited by Richard B. Morris. New York: Pocket Books, 1957.

Hamilton, Alexander, James Madison, and John Jay. *The Federalist Papers.* Edited by Clinton Rossiter. New York: Mentor, 1961.

Hardy, Richard J. *Government in America.* Teacher's ed. Boston: Houghton Mifflin, 1991.

Harnsberger, Caroline Thomas. *A Man of Courage: Robert A. Taft.* Chicago: Wilcox and Follett, 1952.

Hartz, Louis. *The Liberal Tradition in America: An Interpretation of American Political Thought since the Revolution.* New York: Harcourt, Brace, 1955.

Haynes, Fred Emory. *James Baird Weaver.* New York: Arno Press, 1975.

Herman, Edward S., and Noam Chomsky. *Manufacturing Consent: The Political Economy of the Mass Media.* New York: Pantheon Books, 1988.

Herrick, Genevieve Forbes, and John Origen Herrick. *The Life of William Jennings Bryan.* Chicago: Grover C. Buxton, 1925.

Hertzke, Allen D. *Echoes of Discontent: Jesse Jackson, Pat Robertson, and the Resurgence of Populism.* Washington, D.C.: CQ Press, 1993.

Hess, Stephen. *America's Political Dynasties: From Adams to Kennedy.* Garden City, N.Y.: Doubleday, 1966.

Hettle, Wallace. *The Peculiar Democracy: Southern Democrats in Peace and War.* Athens: University of Georgia Press, 2001.

Hibben, Paxton. *The Peerless Leader: William Jennings Bryan.* New York: Farrar and Rinehart, 1929.

Hicks, John D. *The Populist Revolt: A History of the Farmers' Alliance and the People's Party.* Lincoln: University of Nebraska Press, 1961.

Hill, C. William, Jr. *The Political Theory of John Taylor of Caroline.* Rutherford, N.J.: Fairleigh Dickinson University Press, 1977.

Hilton, Stanley G. *Senator for Sale: An Unauthorized Biography of Senator Bob Dole.* New York: St. Martin's Press, 1995.

Hirsch, Steve, ed. *Memo Two: Soviets Examine Foreign Policy for a New Decade.* Washington, D.C.: Bureau of National Affairs, 1991.

Hoar, William P. "Hubert Humphrey: The Dark Horse Is at the Gate." *American Opinion,* April 1976, 7–12, 71–74.

Hobhouse, Stephen. *William Law and Eighteenth Century Quakerism.* London: G. Allen and Unwin, 1927.

Hofstadter, Richard. *The Age of Reform: From Bryan to F.D.R.* New York: Knopf, 1955.

———. *The American Political Tradition and the Men Who Made It.* New York: Knopf, 1948.

———. *Anti-Intellectualism in American Life.* New York: Vintage Books, 1963.

———. *The Paranoid Style in American Politics and Other Essays.* New York: Vintage Books, 1967.

Hollingsworth, J. Rogers. *The Whirligig of Politics: The Democracy of Cleveland and Bryan.* Chicago: University of Chicago Press, 1963.

Holmes, William F. *The White Chief: James Kimble Vardaman.* Baton Rouge: Louisiana State University Press, 1970.

Horowitz, Irving Louis. "The Operators Make Their Play." *The Nation,* January 15, 1973, 72–75.

Humes, D. Joy. *Oswald Garrison Villard, Liberal of the 1920s.* Syracuse: Syracuse University Press, 1960.

Humphrey, Hubert H. "The American System: The Great Society." *Vital Speeches of the Day,* September 1, 1964, 682–85.

———. *Beyond Civil Rights: A New Day of Equality.* New York: Random House, 1968.

———. *The Cause is Mankind: A Liberal Program for Modern America.* New York: Frederick A. Praeger, 1964.

———. "Controversy over the Nixon Administration Proposal for a Federal Spending Ceiling." *Congressional Digest,* December 1972, 299–305.

———. "Director and Deputy Director, Office of Management and Budget, Veto." *Congressional Record,* May 22, 1973, 16506.

———. *The Education of a Public Man: My Life and Politics.* Edited by Norman Sherman. Minneapolis: University of Minnesota Press, 1991.

———. "Foreign Assistance Act of 1974." *Congressional Record,* December 4, 1974, 38123–24

———. *Hubert Humphrey: The Man and His Dream.* Edited by Sheldon D. Engelmayer and Robert J. Wagman. New York: Methuen, 1978.

———. "Is Present United States Cuban Policy Adequate?" *Congressional Digest,* November 1962, 276–82.

———. "Is the Impoundment of Appropriated Funds a Valid Exercise of the Executive Power?" *Congressional Digest,* April 1973, 119–23.

———. "Major U.S. Foreign Defense Commitments," *Congressional Digest,* August–September 1969, 199–200, 224.

———. "The North Atlantic Treaty." *Congressional Record,* July 20, 1949, 9777–79.

———. *The Political Philosophy of the New Deal.* Baton Rouge: Louisiana State University Press, 1970.

————. "The Question of Encouraging Expansion of Trade with the Red-Bloc Nations at the Present Time." *Congressional Digest,* February 1964, 52–58.

————. Should Development of Nuclear Weapons be Prohibited by International Agreement?" *Congressional Digest,* October 1958, 236–42.

————. "Should the U.S.A. Retain the Connally Reservation to the Jurisdiction of the World Court?" *Congressional Digest,* January 1961, 11–13.

————. *The Stranger at Our Gate: America's Immigration Policy.* New York: Public Affairs Committee, 1954.

————. "War Powers of Congress and the President-Veto." *Congressional Record,* November 7, 1973, 36190–91.

Hunter, James Davison, and Carl Bowman. *The State of Disunion: 1996 Survey of American Political Culture.* Charlottesville: Post-Modernity Project (University of Virginia), 1996.

Huntington, Samuel P. *Who Are We? The Challenges to America's National Identity.* New York: Simon and Schuster, 2004.

I'll Take My Stand: The South and the Agrarian Tradition, by Twelve Southerners. New York: Harper and Brothers, 1930.

Isaacson, Walter, and Evan Thomas. *The Wise Men: Six Friends and the World They Made.* New York: Touchstone, 1988.

Jaffa, Harry V. *A New Birth of Freedom: Abraham Lincoln and the Coming of the Civil War.* Lanham, Md.: Rowman and Littlefield, 2000.

Javits, Jacob K. *Javits: The Autobiography of a Public Man.* Boston: Houghton Mifflin, 1981.

————. *Order of Battle: A Republican's Call to Reason.* New York: Atheneum, 1964.

Jefferson, Thomas. *Letters and Addresses.* Edited by William B. Parker and Jonas Viles. New York: Sun Dial Classics, 1908.

————. *The Life and Selected Writings of Thomas Jefferson.* Edited by Adrienne Koch and William Peden. New York: Modern Library, 1944.

————. *The Political Writings of Thomas Jefferson: Representative Selections.* Edited by Edward Dumbauld. Indianapolis: Bobbs-Merrill, 1955.

————. *The Portable Thomas Jefferson.* Edited by Merrill D. Peterson. New York: Penguin, 1977.

————. *Thomas Jefferson on Democracy.* Edited by Saul K. Padover. New York: Mentor, 1946.

Jensen, Merrill. *The New Nation: A History of the United States during the Confederation, 1781–1789.* New York: Vintage Books, 1950.

Johnsen, Julia E., comp. *United Nations or World Government.* New York: H. W. Wilson, 1947.

Johnson, Claudius O. *Borah of Idaho.* New York: Longmans, Green, 1936.

Johnson, Donald Bruce, and Kirk H. Porter, comps. *National Party Platforms, 1840–1972.* Urbana: University of Illinois Press, 1973.

Johnson, Evans C. *Oscar W. Underwood: A Political Biography.* Baton Rouge: Louisiana State University Press, 1980.

Johnson, Hiram W. *The Diary Letters of Hiram Johnson, 1917–1945.* 7 vols. Edited by Robert E. Burke. New York: Garland, 1983.

Johnson, Roger T. *Robert M. La Follette Jr. and the Decline of the Progressive Party in Wisconsin.* Hamden, Conn.: Archon Books, 1970.

Jonas, Manfred. *Isolationism in America, 1935–1941.* Ithaca: Cornell Paperbacks, 1969.

Jones, Stanley L. *The Presidential Election of 1896.* Madison: University of Wisconsin Press, 1964.

Judis, John B. "Libertarianism: Where the Left Meets the Right." *The Progressive,* September 1980, 36–38.

Karnow, Stanley. *Vietnam: A History.* New York: Viking Press, 1983.

Katz, Irving. *August Belmont: A Political Biography.* New York: Columbia University Press, 1968.

Kauffman, Bill. *America First! Its History, Culture, and Politics.* Amherst, N.Y.: Prometheus Books, 1995.

———. "Bigger Isn't Always Better." *Wall Street Journal,* July 8, 2003, D8.

———. "Don't Underrate Isolationism." *The Nation,* June 6, 1987, 758–60.

———. "A Mighty Long Fall: An Interview with Eugene McCarthy." *Chronicles,* July 1996, 14–17.

———. "Who Can We Shoot?" *Chronicles,* March 1996, 17–19.

Kazin, Michael. *A Godly Hero: The Life of William Jennings Bryan.* New York: Knopf, 2006.

———. *The Populist Persuasion: An American History.* New York: Basic Books, 1995.

Keating, Edward. *The Gentleman from Colorado: A Memoir.* Denver: Sage, 1964.

Kennedy, John F. *Public Papers of the Presidents of the United States: John F. Kennedy, 1962.* Washington, D.C.: U.S. Government Printing Office, 1963.

Kennedy, Thomas C. *Charles A. Beard and American Foreign Policy.* Gainesville: University Presses of Florida, 1975.

Ketcham, Ralph, ed. *The Anti-Federalist Papers and the Constitutional Convention Debates.* New York: Mentor, 1986.

Kierkegaard, Søren. *Attack Upon "Christendom."* Princeton: Princeton University Press, 1968.

King, Martin Luther, Jr. *The Words of Martin Luther King Jr.* Compiled by Coretta Scott King. New York: Newmarket Press, 1983.

Kinnear, Angus I. *Against the Tide: The Story of Watchman Nee.* Fort Washington, Pa.: Christian Literature Crusade, 1973.

Kirk, Russell, and James McClellan. *The Political Principles of Robert A. Taft.* New York: Fleet Press, 1967.

Kirkland, Richard I., Jr. "Today's GOP: The Party's Over for Big Business." *Fortune,* February 6, 1995, 50–62.

Kissinger, Henry, and Cyrus Vance. "Bipartisan Objectives for American Foreign Policy." *Foreign Affairs* 66 (Summer 1988): 899–921.

Koenig, Louis W. *Bryan: A Political Biography of William Jennings Bryan.* New York: G. P. Putnam's Sons, 1971.

Kofsky, Frank. *Harry S. Truman and the War Scare of 1948: A Successful Campaign to Deceive the Nation.* New York: St. Martin's Press, 1993.

Kohl, Manfred Waldemar. *Congregationalism in America.* Oak Creek, Wis.: Congregational Press, 1977.

Kohn, Richard H. *Eagle and Sword: The Federalists and the Creation of the Military Establishment in America, 1783–1802.* New York: Free Press, 1975.

Kolkey, Jonathan Martin. *The New Right, 1960–1968: With Epilogue, 1969–1980.* Washington, D.C.: University Press of America, 1983.

Kolko, Gabriel. *Another Century of War?* New York: New Press, 2002.

———. *The Triumph of Conservatism: A Reinterpretation of American History, 1900–1916.* New York: Free Press, 1977.

Kolko, Joyce, and Gabriel Kolko. *The Limits of Power: The World and United States Foreign Policy, 1945–1954.* New York: Harper Collins, 1972.

Kunen, James Simon. *The Strawberry Statement: Notes of a College Revolutionary.* New York: Avon Books, 1970.

La Follette, Belle Case, and Fola La Follette. *Robert M. La Follette: June 14, 1855–June 18, 1925.* 2 vols. New York: Macmillan, 1953.

La Follette, Philip. *Adventure in Politics: The Memoirs of Philip La Follette.* Edited by Donald Young. New York: Holt, Rinehart, and Winston, 1970.

La Follette, Robert M. *La Follette's Autobiography: A Personal Narrative of Political Experiences.* Madison: University of Wisconsin Press, 1960.

———. *The Political Philosophy of Robert M. La Follette as Revealed in His Speeches and Writings.* Compiled by Ellen Torelle. Madison: Robert M. La Follette, 1920.

Larkin, Clarence. *Dispensational Truth, or, God's Plan and Purpose in the Ages.* Glenside, Pa.: Larkin Est., 1920.

Larson, Bruce L. *Lindbergh of Minnesota: A Political Biography.* New York: Harcourt, Brace, Jovanovich, 1973.

Lasch, Christopher. *The Agony of the American Left*. New York: Knopf, 1969.
———. *The Revolt of the Elites and the Betrayal of Democracy*. New York: W. W. Norton, 1996.
Lasky, Victor. *It Didn't Start with Watergate*. New York: Dell, 1978.
———. *Jimmy Carter: The Man and the Myth*. New York: Richard Marek, 1979.
Lause, Mark A. *The Civil War's Last Campaign: James B. Weaver, the Greenback-Labor Party, and the Politics of Race and Section*. Lanham, Md.: University Press of America, 2001.
Lawson, R. Alan. *The Failure of Independent Liberalism, 1930–1941*. New York: G. P. Putnam's Sons, 1971.
Lazere, Donald, ed. *American Media and Mass Culture: Left Perspectives*. Berkeley: University of California Press, 1987.
Leopold, Richard W. *Elihu Root and the Conservative Tradition*. Boston: Little, Brown, 1954.
Lesher, Stephan. *George Wallace: American Populist*. Reading, Mass.: Addison-Wesley, 1994.
Levine, Lawrence W. *Defender of the Faith: William Jennings Bryan: The Last Decade, 1915–1925*. Cambridge: Harvard University Press, 1987.
Levinson, Charles. *Vodka-Cola*. London: Gordon and Cremonesi, 1978.
Levy, Leonard W. *Jefferson and Civil Liberties: The Darker Side*. Cambridge: Harvard University Press, 1963.
Lewis, C. S. *The Abolition of Man, or, Reflections on Education with Special Reference to the Teachings of English in the Upper Forms of Schools*. New York: Macmillan, 1965.
———. *Mere Christianity*. New York: Macmillan, 1960.
———. *The Screwtape Letters*. New York: Macmillan, 1959.
———. *That Hideous Strength: A Modern Fairy-Tale for Grown-Ups*. New York: Macmillan, 1965.
Lewis, Charles, Alejandro Benes, and Meredith O'Brien. *The Buying of the President*. New York: Avon Books, 1996.
Liggio, Leonard P., and James J. Martin, eds. *Watershed of Empire: Essays on New Deal Foreign Policy*. Colorado Springs: Ralph Myles, 1976.
Lind, Michael. "The Radical Center or the Moderate Middle?" *New York Times*, December 3, 1995, sec. 6, 72.
Lindbergh, Charles A. *Banking and Currency, and the Money Trust*. Washington, D.C.: National Capital Press, 1913.
———. *The Economic Pinch*. Philadelphia: Dorrance, 1923.
———. *Why is Your Country at War, and What Happens to You after the War, and Related Subjects*. Washington, D.C.: Lindbergh, 1917.

Link, Arthur S. *Woodrow Wilson and the Progressive Era, 1910–1917.* New York: Harper and Brothers, 1954.

Lippmann, Walter. "The Goldwater Movement." *Newsweek,* August 5, 1963, 13.

Lipset, Seymour Martin, and Earl Raab. *The Politics of Unreason: Right-Wing Extremism in America, 1790–1970.* New York: Harper and Row, 1970.

Livermore, Shaw, Jr. *The Twilight of Federalism: The Disintegration of the Federalist Party, 1815–1830.* Princeton: Princeton University Press, 1962.

Locke, John. *Two Treatises of Government.* Edited by Peter Laslett. Cambridge: Cambridge University Press, 1990.

Loewen, James W. *Lies My Teacher Told Me: Everything Your American History Textbook Got Wrong.* New York: New Press, 1995.

Logan, Rayford W. *The Betrayal of the Negro from Rutherford B. Hayes to Woodrow Wilson.* New York: Collier Books, 1965.

Lokos, Lionel. *Hysteria 1964: The Fear Campaign against Barry Goldwater.* New Rochelle, N.Y.: Arlington House, 1967.

Long, J. C. *Bryan, the Great Commoner.* New York: D. Appleton, 1928.

Lovett, Robert Morss. "American Foreign Policy: A Progressive View." *Foreign Affairs* 3 (September 15, 1924): 49–60.

Lowi, Theodore J. *The End of Liberalism: Ideology, Policy, and the Crisis of Public Authority.* New York: W. W. Norton, 1969.

Ludlow, Louis L. "The Vision of Jefferson: Lessons He Taught Us." *Vital Speeches of the Day,* May 15, 1940, 479–80.

Lundberg, Ferdinand. *America's Sixty Families.* New York: Halcyon House, 1939.

———. *Imperial Hearst: A Social Biography.* New York: Equinox Cooperative Press, 1936.

———. *The Myth of Democracy.* Secaucus, N.J.: Carol Publishing Group, 1989.

———. *The Rich and the Super-Rich: A Study in the Power of Money Today.* New York: Lyle Stuart, 1968.

———. *The Rockefeller Syndrome.* New York: Zebra Books, 1976.

Lustig, R. Jeffrey. *Corporate Liberalism: The Origins of Modern American Political Theory, 1890–1920.* Berkeley: University of California Press, 1986.

Lydon, Christopher. "Jimmy Carter Revealed: He's a Rockefeller Republican." *The Atlantic Monthly,* July 1977, 50–57.

———. "McGovern Gibes at 'Park Ave. Populism.'" *New York Times,* February 26, 1972, 14.

Lynd, Staughton. *Intellectual Origins of American Radicalism.* Cambridge: Harvard University Press, 1982.

Macdonald, Dwight. *Discriminations: Essays and Afterthoughts.* New York: Da Capo Press, 1985.

————. *Henry Wallace: The Man and the Myth.* New York: Vanguard Press, 1948.

————. *Memoirs of a Revolutionist: Essays in Political Criticism.* New York: Farrar, Straus, and Cudahy, 1957.

Machiavelli, Niccolò. *The Prince and the Discourses.* Translated by Luigi Ricci, E. R. P. Vincent, and Christian E. Detmold. New York: Modern Library, 1950.

MacKay, Kenneth Campbell. *The Progressive Movement of 1924.* New York: Octagon Books, 1966.

MacKinnon, Catharine A. *Feminism Unmodified: Discourses on Life and Law.* Cambridge: Harvard University Press, 1987.

Macridis, Roy C., and Bernard E. Brown. *Comparative Politics: Notes and Readings.* 7th ed. Pacific Grove, Calif.: Brooks/Cole, 1990.

Madison, Charles A. *Critics and Crusaders: A Century of American Protest.* New York: Frederick Ungar Publishing, 1959.

Main, Jackson Turner. *The Antifederalists: Critics of the Constitution, 1781–1788.* Chicago: Quadrangle Paperbooks, 1964.

Makin, John H., and Norman J. Ornstein. *Debt and Taxes.* New York: Times Books, 1994.

Malcolm X. *The Autobiography of Malcolm X.* New York: Ballantine, 1973.

Malone, Dumas. *Jefferson and His Time.* 5 vols. Boston: Little, Brown, 1948–1974.

Mann, Robert. *The Walls of Jericho: Lyndon Johnson, Hubert Humphrey, Richard Russell, and the Struggle for Civil Rights.* New York: Harcourt, Brace, 1996.

Marable, Manning. *W. E. B. Du Bois: Black Radical Democrat.* Boston: Twayne, 1986.

Marchetti, Victor, and John D. Marks. *The CIA and the Cult of Intelligence.* New York: Knopf, 1974.

Marsden, George M. *Fundamentalism and American Culture: The Shaping of Twentieth-Century Evangelicalism, 1870–1925.* Oxford: Oxford University Press, 1982.

————. *Understanding Fundamentalism and Evangelicalism.* Grand Rapids, Mich.: Eerdmans, 1991.

Martin, James J. *American Liberalism and World Politics, 1931–1941: Liberalism's Press and Spokesmen on the Road Back to War between Mukden and Pearl Harbor.* 2 vols. New York: Devin-Adair, 1964.

————. *Men against the State: The Expositors of Individualist Anarchism in America, 1827–1908.* Colorado Springs: Ralph Myles, 1970.

Martin, Ralph G. *Ballots and Bandwagons.* Chicago: Rand McNally, 1964.

Matthews, Christopher. "Jerry Brown is Right on Target." *San Francisco Examiner,* December 19, 1991.

Matthews, Richard K. *If Men Were Angels: James Madison and the Heartless Empire of Reason.* Lawrence: University Press of Kansas, 1995.

———. *The Radical Politics of Thomas Jefferson: A Revisionist View.* Lawrence: University Press of Kansas, 1984.

Maude, Aylmer. *The Life of Tolstoy.* Oxford: Oxford University Press, 1987.

Maxwell, Robert S. *La Follette and the Rise of the Progressives in Wisconsin.* Madison: State Historical Society of Wisconsin, 1956.

———, ed. *La Follette.* Englewood Cliffs, N.J.: Prentice-Hall, 1969.

Mayer, David N. "The Misunderstood Mr. Jefferson." *Liberty* 10, no. 5 (May 1997): 29–39.

McCarthy, Eugene. *Up 'til Now: A Memoir.* San Diego: Harcourt, Brace, Jovanovich, 1987.

McClaughry, John. "Jefferson's Vision." *New York Times,* April 13, 1982, A27.

McCoy, Donald R. *The Presidency of Harry S. Truman.* Lawrence: University Press of Kansas, 1984.

McDonald, Forrest. *The Presidency of Thomas Jefferson.* Lawrence: University Press of Kansas, 1976.

McNall, Scott G. *The Road to Rebellion: Class Formation and Kansas Populism, 1865–1900.* Chicago: University of Chicago Press, 1988.

Means, Russell, and Marvin J. Wolf. *Where White Men Fear to Tread: The Autobiography of Russell Means.* New York: St. Martin's, 1995.

Meehan, Mary. "A Housecleaning for American Liberals." *America,* February 16, 1974, 106–9.

Menendez, Albert J. *The Perot Voters and the Future of American Politics.* Amherst, N.Y.: Prometheus Books, 1996.

Meriwether, Lee. *Jim Reed, "Senatorial Immortal": A Biography.* Webster Groves, Mo.: International Mark Twain Society, 1948.

Meyers, Marvin. *The Jacksonian Persuasion: Politics and Belief.* Stanford: Stanford University Press, 1960.

Miles, Michael W. *The Odyssey of the American Right.* New York: Oxford University Press, 1980.

Miller, John C. *Alexander Hamilton and the Growth of the New Nation.* New York: Harper Torchbooks, 1964.

Miller, John E. *Governor Philip F. La Follette, the Wisconsin Progressives, and the New Deal.* Columbia: University of Missouri Press, 1982.

Miller, Karen A. J. *Populist Nationalism: Republican Insurgency and American Foreign Policy Making, 1918–1925.* Westport, Conn.: Greenwood Press, 1999.

Miller, Nathan. *FDR: An Intimate History.* Garden City, N.Y.: Doubleday, 1983.

Miller, Richard Lawrence. *Truman: The Rise to Power.* New York: McGraw-Hill, 1986.

Mills, C. Wright. *The Power Elite.* New York: Oxford University Press, 1956.

————. *Power, Politics, and People: The Collected Essays of C. Wright Mills.* Edited by Irving Louis Horowitz. London: Oxford University Press, 1967.

Mintz, Morton, and Jerry S. Cohen. *America, Inc.: Who Owns and Operates the United States.* New York: Dial Press, 1971.

Mirken, Stanford M., ed. *Conventions and Elections, 1960: A Complete Handbook Prepared by CBS News.* Great Neck, N.Y.: Channel Press, 1960.

Miroff, Bruce. *Pragmatic Illusions: The Presidential Politics of John F. Kennedy.* New York: David McKay, 1976.

Moffett, George D., III. *The Limits of Victory: The Ratification of the Panama Canal Treaties.* Ithaca, N.Y.: Cornell University Press, 1985.

Morgan, Chester M. *Redneck Liberal: Theodore G. Bilbo and the New Deal.* Baton Rouge: Louisiana State University Press, 1985.

Morgenstern, George. *Pearl Harbor: The Story of the Secret War.* New York: Devin-Adair, 1947.

Morlan, Robert L. *Political Prairie Fire: The Nonpartisan League, 1915–1922.* St. Paul: Minnesota Historical Society Press, 1985.

Morris, Roger. "Jimmy Carter's Ruling Class." *Harper's,* October 1977, 37–45.

————. *Partners in Power: The Clintons and Their America.* New York: Henry Holt, 1996.

Morris, William, ed. *The American Heritage Dictionary of the English Language.* Boston: Houghton Mifflin, 1976.

Moseley-Braun, Carol. "Statement on the Extension of the Patent of the Insignia of the United Daughters of the Confederacy." *Vital Issues* 4, nos. 1 and 2 (1994): 20–27.

Mosley, Leonard. *Dulles: A Biography of Eleanor, Allen, and John Foster Dulles and Their Family Network.* New York: Dial Press/James Wade, 1978.

Moss, George Donelson. *Moving On: The American People since 1945.* Englewood Cliffs, N.J.: Prentice Hall, 1994.

Moxley, Warden. "Brown: Striving for a New Political Coalition." *Congressional Quarterly Weekly Report,* October 20, 1979, 2329–34.

Mulder, Ronald A. *The Insurgent Progressives in the United States Senate and the New Deal, 1933–1939.* New York: Garland, 1979.

Murray, Robert K. *The 103rd Ballot: Democrats and the Disaster in Madison Square Garden.* New York: Harper and Row, 1976.

Nader, Ralph. "Dear Conservatives Upset with the Policies of the Bush Administration." *voteNader.org,* April 2, 2004. http://www.votenader.org /why;ralph/index.php?cid=14.

Nader, Ralph, et al. *The Case against Free Trade: GATT, NAFTA, and the Globalization of Corporate Power.* San Francisco: Earth Island Press, 1993.

Neal, Steve. *Dark Horse: A Biography of Wendell Willkie.* Garden City, N.Y.: Doubleday, 1984.

Nee, Watchman. *Love Not the World.* Wheaton, Ill.: Tyndale/CLC, 1978.

Newfield, Jack. *A Prophetic Minority.* New York: Signet, 1970.

Nichols, Roy Franklin. *Franklin Pierce: Young Hickory of the Granite Hills.* Philadelphia: University of Pennsylvania Press, 1958.

Nicolosi, Terry Hitchins, and Jose L. Ceballos, eds. *Official Proceedings of the 1992 Democratic National Convention.* Washington, D.C.: Democratic National Committee, 1992.

Niven, John. *Martin Van Buren: The Romantic Age of American Politics.* New York: Oxford University Press, 1983.

Nock, Albert Jay. *Mr. Jefferson.* Tampa, Fla.: Hallberg Publishing, 1983.

Norris, George W. "Bryan as a Political Leader." *Current History,* September 1925, 859–67.

Nugent, Walter T. K. *The Tolerant Populists: Kansas Populism and Nativism.* Chicago: University of Chicago Press, 1963.

Olasky, Marvin N., and John Perry. *Monkey Business: The True Story of the Scopes Trial.* Nashville: Broadman and Holman, 2005.

Onuf, Peter S. *Jefferson's Empire: The Language of American Nationhood.* Charlottesville: University Press of Virginia, 2000.

Ornstein, Norman, Andrew Kohut, and Larry McCarthy. *The People, the Press, and Politics: The Times Mirror Study of the American Electorate.* Reading, Mass.: Addison-Wesley, 1988.

Orwell, George. *Animal Farm: A Fairy Story.* New York: Signet, n.d.

Osnes, Larry G. *Charles W. Bryan: Latter-Day Populist and Rural Progressive.* Master's thesis, University of Cincinnati, 1970.

Ostler, Jeffrey. "The Rhetoric of Conspiracy and the Formation of Kansas Populism." *Agricultural History* 69 (Winter 1995): 1–27.

Packard, Vance. *The Hidden Persuaders.* New York: Pocket Cardinal, 1958.

Paine, Thomas. *The Political Works of Thomas Paine.* 2 vols. London: W. T. Sherwin, 1817.

———. *Political Writings.* Edited by Bruce Kuklick. Cambridge: Cambridge University Press, 1989.

Palmer, Bruce. *"Man over Money": The Southern Populist Critique of American Capitalism.* Chapel Hill: University of North Carolina Press, 1980.

Parenti, Michael. *Democracy for the Few.* 4th ed. New York: St. Martin's Press, 1983.

Parrington, Vernon Louis. *Main Currents in American Thought: An Interpretation of American Literature from the Beginnings to 1920.* New York: Harcourt, Brace, 1930.

Patterson, James T. *Congressional Conservatism and the New Deal: The Growth of the Conservative Coalition in Congress, 1933–1939.* Lexington: University of Kentucky Press, 1967.

———. *Mr. Republican: A Biography of Robert A. Taft.* Boston: Houghton Mifflin, 1972.

Paul, Barbara D., et al., eds. *CRF Listing of Political Contributors and Lenders of $10,000 or More in 1972.* Princeton: Citizens' Research Foundation, 1975.

Perloff, James. *The Shadows of Power: The Council on Foreign Relations and the American Decline.* Boston: Western Islands, 1988.

Perry, James. *Us and Them: How the Press Covered the 1972 Election.* New York: Clarkson N. Potter, 1973.

Perry, Lewis. *Radical Abolitionism: Anarchy and the Government of God in Antislavery Thought.* Ithaca: Cornell University Press, 1973.

Peterson, F. Ross. *Prophet without Honor: Glen H. Taylor and the Fight for American Liberalism.* Lexington: University Press of Kentucky, 1974.

Peterson, Merrill D. *The Jefferson Image in the American Mind.* New York: Oxford University Press, 1962.

———. *Thomas Jefferson and the New Nation: A Biography.* New York: Oxford University Press, 1970.

Pettigrew, Richard F. *Imperial Washington: The Story of American Public Life from 1870 to 1920.* Chicago: Charles H. Kerr, 1922.

Phillips, Kevin. *Arrogant Capital: Washington, Wall Street, and the Frustration of American Politics.* Boston: Little, Brown, 1994.

———. *Boiling Point: Republicans, Democrats, and the Decline of Middle-Class Prosperity.* New York: Random House, 1993.

———. *The Politics of Rich and Poor: Wealth and the American Electorate in the Reagan Aftermath.* New York: Harper Perennial, 1991.

———. "The Unexpected Quest." *Los Angeles Times,* September 19, 1999, M1.

Piccone, Paul. "The Crisis of American Conservatism." *Telos,* Winter 1987–1988, 3–29.

Pinchot, Amos R. E. *History of the Progressive Party, 1912–1916.* Edited by Helene Maxwell Hooker. New York: New York University Press, 1958.

Plato. *Great Dialogues of Plato.* Translated by W. H. D. Rouse. New York: Mentor, 1956.

————. *The Republic of Plato.* Translated by Allan Bloom. New York: Basic Books, 1968.

————. *Statesman.* Edited by Martin Ostwald. Translated by J. B. Skemp. Indianapolis: Bobbs-Merrill, 1957.

Pollack, Norman. *The Populist Response to Industrial America: Midwestern Populist Thought.* Cambridge: Harvard University Press, 1962.

Polsby, Nelson W. *The Citizen's Choice: Humphrey or Nixon.* Washington, D.C.: Public Affairs Press, 1968.

————. "What Hubert Humphrey Wrought." *Commentary,* November 1984, 47–50.

Popper, Karl R. *The Open Society and Its Enemies, Volume 1: The Spell of Plato.* Princeton: Princeton University Press, 1971.

Porter, David L. *Congress and the Waning of the New Deal.* Port Washington, N.Y.: Kennikat Press, 1980.

Quarles, Benjamin, and Sterling Stuckey, eds. *Separate and Unequal, 1865–1910.* Chicago: Encyclopædia Britannica, 1969.

Quigley, Carroll. *The Anglo-American Establishment: From Rhodes to Cliveden.* New York: Books in Focus, 1981.

————. *Tragedy and Hope: A History of the World in Our Time.* New York: Macmillan, 1966.

Quinn, Bill. *How Wal-Mart Is Destroying America.* Berkeley: Ten Speed Press, 1998.

Quirk, William J. "The Earth Belongs to the Living." *Chronicles,* April 1997, 47–48.

Radosh, Ronald. *Prophets on the Right: Profiles of Conservative Critics of American Globalism.* New York: Free Life Editions, 1978.

Rae, Nicol C. *The Decline and Fall of the Liberal Republicans: From 1952 to the Present.* New York: Oxford University Press, 1989.

Raimondo, Justin. "Old Right Nader." *American Conservative,* November 8, 2004, 10–11.

Randall, Willard Sterne. *Thomas Jefferson: A Life.* New York: Holt, 1993.

Reese, Charley. "Brown Stood Alone among Manipulators of America." *Columbia (Mo.) Daily Tribune,* July 26, 1992, 2D.

————. "Buchanan Won't Score Points with American Establishment." *Columbia (Mo.) Daily Tribune,* December 21, 1991, 4A.

————. "Conservative Movement R.I.P.?" *Chronicles,* May 1991, 18–19.

Reeves, Thomas C. *A Question of Character: A Life of John F. Kennedy.* Rocklin, Calif.: Prima Publishing, 1992.

Remini, Robert V. *Andrew Jackson and the Course of American Democracy, 1833–1845.* New York: Harper and Row, 1984.

————. *Andrew Jackson and the Course of American Freedom, 1822–1832.* New York: Harper and Row, 1981.

Rensenbrink, John. *The Greens and the Politics of Transformation.* San Pedro, Calif.: R. and E. Miles, 1992.

Riker, William H. *Liberalism against Populism: A Confrontation between the Theory of Democracy and the Theory of Social Choice.* Prospect Heights, Ill.: Waveland Press, 1988.

Robertson, James Oliver. *No Third Choice: Progressives in Republican Politics, 1916–1921.* New York: Garland, 1983.

Rockefeller, Nelson A. *The Future of Federalism.* Cambridge: Harvard University Press, 1962.

————. "National Economic Growth: Factors Controlling It." *Vital Speeches of the Day,* January 15, 1963.

————. "A Way to Bind Free Africa to the Free World." *Newsweek,* July 25, 1960, 33.

Rockwell, Llewellyn H., Jr. "Paleos, Neos, and Libertarians." *The New American,* February 26, 1990, 5–7.

Romm, Ethel Grodzins. *The Open Conspiracy: What America's Angry Generation Is Saying.* Harrisburg, Pa.: Stackpole Books, 1970.

Root, Oren. *Persons and Persuasions.* New York: W. W. Norton, 1974.

Roske, Ralph J. *His Own Counsel: The Life and Times of Lyman Trumbull.* Reno: University of Nevada Press, 1979.

Rothbard, Murray N. "Conservative Movement R.I.P.?" *Chronicles,* May 1991, 20–21.

————. "The Conspiracy Theory of History Revisited." *Reason,* April 1977, 39–40.

————. "The Foreign Policy of the Old Right." *Journal of Libertarian Studies* 2 (1978): 85–96.

Rouner, Arthur A., Jr. *The Congregational Way of Life.* Milwaukee: Hammond Publishing, 1972.

Rousseau, Jean Jacques. *The Social Contract.* Translated by Maurice Cranston. Middlesex: Penguin Books, 1968.

Rovere, Richard H. *The American Establishment and Other Reports, Opinions, and Speculations.* New York: Harcourt, Brace, 1962.

Rustow, Dankwart A., and Kenneth Paul Erickson, eds. *Comparative Political Dynamics: Global Research Perspectives.* New York: Harper Collins, 1991.

Ryskind, Allan H. *Hubert: An Unauthorized Biography of the Vice President.* New Rochelle, N.Y.: Arlington House, 1968.

Sageser, A. Bower. *Joseph L. Bristow: Kansas Progressive.* Lawrence: University Press of Kansas, 1968.

Salit, Jacqueline. "Buchanan Fights for New Life." *San Francisco Chronicle,* October 7, 1999, A29.

Salter, J. T., ed. *Public Men In and Out of Office.* Chapel Hill: University of North Carolina Press, 1946.

Salvatore, Nick. *Eugene V. Debs: Citizen and Socialist.* Urbana: University of Illinois Press, 1982.

Sanders, Jerry W. *Peddlers of Crisis: The Committee on the Present Danger and the Politics of Containment.* Boston: South End Press, 1983.

Scammon, Richard M., and Ben J. Wattenberg. *The Real Majority.* New York: Coward-McCann, 1970.

Schaeffer, Francis A. *The Church at the End of the Twentieth Century.* Downers Grove, Ill.: InterVarsity, 1970.

Schaffer, Ronald. *America in the Great War: The Rise of the War Welfare State.* New York: Oxford University Press, 1991.

Schattschneider, E. E. *The Semisovereign People: A Realist's View of Democracy in America.* Hinsdale, Ill.: Dryden Press, 1975.

Schlafly, Phyllis. *A Choice Not an Echo.* 3rd ed. Alton, Ill.: Pere Marquette Press, 1964.

Schlesinger, Arthur M., Jr. *The Age of Jackson.* Boston: Houghton Mifflin, 1945.

———. *The Age of Roosevelt.* 3 vols. Boston: Houghton Mifflin, 1957–1962.

———, ed. *History of American Presidential Elections.* 10 vols. New York: Chelsea House, 1986.

———. "Ideology vs. Democracy." *Vital Speeches and Documents of the Day,* March 1, 1962, 246–50.

———. *The Imperial Presidency.* New York: Popular Library, 1974.

———. *The Vital Center: The Politics of Freedom.* Boston: Houghton Mifflin, 1949.

Scofield, C. I. *The Scofield Reference Bible.* New York: Oxford University Press, 1917.

Schulzinger, Robert D. *The Wise Men of Foreign Affairs: The History of the Council on Foreign Relations.* New York: Columbia University Press, 1984.

Schwartz, Michael, ed. *The Structure of Power in America: The Corporate Elite as a Ruling Class.* New York: Holmes and Meier, 1987.

Sellers, Charles, ed. *Andrew Jackson, Nullification, and the State-Rights Tradition.* Chicago: Rand McNally, 1963.

Shadegg, Stephen C. *Winning's a Lot More Fun.* London: Macmillan, 1969.

Sharkansky, Ira. "The Utility of Elazar's Political Culture: A Research Note." *Polity* 2 (Fall 1969): 66–83.

Shatz, Adam. "Ross Perot and Anti-Politics." *New Politics* (Winter 1993): 13–16.

Sheehan, Bernard W. *Seeds of Extinction: Jeffersonian Philanthropy and the American Indian.* Chapel Hill: University of North Carolina Press, 1973.

Sheehan, Colleen A. "Madison v. Hamilton: The Battle over Republicanism and the Role of Public Opinion," *American Political Science Review* 98, no. 3 (August 2004): 405–24.

Sheldon, Garrett W. *The Political Philosophy of Thomas Jefferson.* Baltimore: Johns Hopkins University Press, 1991.

Shelton, Robert. *No Direction Home: The Life and Music of Bob Dylan.* New York: Ballantine, 1987.

Shepard, Edward M. *Martin Van Buren.* Boston: Houghton Mifflin, 1916.

Sherrill, Robert. *The Accidental President.* New York: Pyramid Books, 1968.

Sherrill, Robert, and Harry W. Ernst. *The Drugstore Liberal.* New York: Grossman Publishers, 1968.

Shields, James M. *Mr. Progressive: A Biography of Elmer Austin Benson.* Minneapolis: T. S. Denison, 1971.

Shoup, Laurence H. *The Carter Presidency and Beyond: Power and Politics in the 1980s.* Palo Alto, Calif.: Ramparts Press, 1980.

Shoup, Laurence H., and William Minter. *Imperial Brain Trust: The Council on Foreign Relations and United States Foreign Policy.* New York: Monthly Review Press, 1977.

Sifry, Micah L. "GOPulism." *The Nation,* March 4, 1996, 4–7.

Silverman, Henry J., ed. *American Radical Thought: The Libertarian Tradition.* Lexington, Mass.: D. C. Heath, 1970.

Silverstein, Ken. "D.L.C. Dollars." *The Nation,* June 20, 1994, 858.

Simkins, Francis Butler. *Pitchfork Ben Tillman: South Carolinian.* Baton Rouge: Louisiana State University Press, 1944.

Simon, James F. *What Kind of Nation: Thomas Jefferson, John Marshall, and the Epic Struggle to Create a United States.* New York: Simon and Schuster, 2002.

Skaggs, William H. *The Southern Oligarchy: An Appeal in Behalf of the Silent Masses of Our Country against the Despotic Rule of the Few.* New York: Devin-Adair, 1924.

Sklar, Holly, ed. *Trilateralism: The Trilateral Commission and Elite Planning for World Management.* Boston: South End Press, 1980.

Smith, Hedrick. "Humphrey Gone, Carter Loses Key Ally in Senate." *Des Moines Register,* January 16, 1978, 5A.

Smith, Richard Norton. *Thomas E. Dewey and His Times.* New York: Simon and Schuster, 1984.

Smith, Sally Bedell. *Reflected Glory: The Life of Pamela Churchill Harriman.* New York: Simon and Schuster, 1996.

Smith, Sam. "False Faith Defeats Lousy Works." *Progressive Review,* November 6, 2004. http://prorev.com/faithworks.htm.

Smith, Wesley J. "Nobody's Nader: The Tough Activist Has Some Kind Words for Buchanan, But None for Clinton." *Mother Jones,* July/August 1996, 61, 63.

Smith, Willard H. *The Social and Religious Thought of William Jennings Bryan.* Lawrence, Kans.: Coronado Press, 1975.

Smoot, Dan. *The Invisible Government.* Boston: Western Islands, 1977.

Sobran, Joseph. "Chomsky's Innocence Gives a Radical View of U.S. Policy." *Columbia (Mo.) Daily Tribune,* March 27, 1991, 6A.

——— . "Questioning Myths of 'The Good War' Still Forbidden." *Columbia (Mo.) Daily Tribune,* December 9, 1991, 6A.

——— . "Semantic Fog, Euphemisms Blur Reality of Government." *Columbia (Mo.) Daily Tribune,* November 13, 1995, 4A.

Solberg, Carl. *Hubert Humphrey: A Biography.* New York: W. W. Norton, 1984.

Solomon, Norman. *False Hope: The Politics of Illusion in the Clinton Era.* Monroe, Maine: Common Courage Press, 1994.

Sørensen, Georg. *Democracy and Democratization: Processes and Prospects in a Changing World.* Boulder, Colo.: Westview Press, 1993.

Southwick, Leslie H. *Presidential Also-Rans and Running Mates, 1788–1980.* Jefferson, N.C.: McFarland, 1984.

Spano, Wy. "Why Rudy Boschwitz Never had a Chance to Beat Paul Wellstone." *Minneapolis Star Tribune,* November 6, 1996, A25.

Spretnak, Charlene, and Fritjof Capra, with Rüdiger Lutz. *Green Politics.* Santa Fe: Bear, 1986.

Springen, Donald K. *William Jennings Bryan: Orator of Small-Town America.* New York: Greenwood Press, 1991.

Stead, W. T. *Life of Mrs. Booth.* New York: Revell, 1900.

Stone, Ralph. *The Irreconcilables: The Fight against the League of Nations.* New York: W. W. Norton, 1973.

Storing, Herbert J., ed. *The Anti-Federalist: An Abridgment, by Murray Dry, of the Complete Anti-Federalist, edited by Herbert J. Storing.* Chicago: University of Chicago Press, 1985.

——— , ed. *What Country Have I? Political Writings by Black Americans.* New York: St. Martin's Press, 1970.

——— . *What the Anti-Federalists Were For.* Chicago: University of Chicago Press, 1981.

Storms, Roger C. *Partisan Prophets: A History of the Prohibition Party, 1854–1972.* Denver: National Prohibition Foundation, 1972.

Streit, Clarence K. *Union Now: The Proposal for Inter-Democracy Federal Union (Shorter Version)*. New York: Harper, 1940.

———. *Union Now with Britain*. New York: Harper, 1941.

Sumner, Charles. *The Selected Letters of Charles Sumner*. Edited by Beverly Wilson Palmer. Boston: Northeastern University Press, 1990.

Sutton, Antony C. *The Best Enemy Money Can Buy*. Billings, Mont.: Liberty House Press, 1986.

———. *Wall Street and FDR*. New Rochelle, N.Y.: Arlington House, 1975.

Swanberg, W. A. *Citizen Hearst: A Biography of William Randolph Hearst*. New York: Bantam Books, 1971.

———. *Norman Thomas: The Last Idealist*. New York: Charles Scribner's Sons, 1976.

Sykes, Jay G. *Proxmire*. Washington, D.C.: Robert B. Luce, 1972.

Synon, John J., ed. *George Wallace: Profile of a Presidential Candidate*. Kilmarnock, Va.: Ms Inc., 1968.

Taft, Robert A. "The Future of the Republican Party." *The Nation*, December 13, 1941, 611–12.

Taft, William Howard, and William Jennings Bryan. *World Peace*. New York: Kraus Reprint, 1970.

Tansill, Charles Callan. *America Goes to War*. Boston: Little, Brown, 1938.

———. *Back Door to War: The Roosevelt Foreign Policy, 1933–1941*. Chicago: Henry Regnery, 1952.

Tate, Adam L. *Conservatism and Southern Intellectuals, 1789–1861: Liberty, Tradition, and the Good Society*. Columbia: University of Missouri Press, 2005.

Taylor, George Rogers, ed. *Jackson versus Biddle: The Struggle over the Second Bank of the United States*. Boston: D. C. Heath, 1949.

Taylor, Jeffrey L. *From Radical to Respectable*. Ann Arbor: UMI, 1998.

Taylor, John. *Construction Construed and Constitutions Vindicated*. Richmond: Shepherd and Pollard, 1820.

———. *An Inquiry into the Principles and Policy of the Government of the United States*. Edited by Loren Baritz. Indianapolis: Bobbs-Merrill, 1969.

Teodori, Massimo, ed. *The New Left: A Documentary History*. Indianapolis: Bobbs-Merrill, 1969.

Thayer, George. *The Farther Shores of Politics: The American Political Fringe Today*. New York: Simon and Schuster, 1968.

———. *Who Shakes the Money Tree? American Campaign Financing Practices from 1789 to the Present*. New York: Simon and Schuster, 1973.

Thelen, David P. *Robert M. La Follette and the Insurgent Spirit*. Madison: University of Wisconsin Press, 1985.

Thomas, Cal, and Ed Dobson. *Blinded by Might: Can the Religious Right Save America?* Grand Rapids, Mich.: Zondervan, 1999.

Thompson, Hunter S. *Fear and Loathing: On the Campaign Trail '72.* New York: Warner Books, 1983.

Thurber, Timothy N. *The Politics of Equality: Hubert H. Humphrey and the African American Freedom Struggle.* New York: Columbia University Press, 1999.

Tierney, Kevin. *Darrow: A Biography.* New York: Thomas Y. Crowell, 1979.

Tilman, Rick. *C. Wright Mills: A Native Radical and His American Intellectual Roots.* University Park: Pennsylvania State University Press, 1984.

Tindall, George Brown, ed. *A Populist Reader: Selections from the Works of American Populist Leaders.* Gloucester, Mass.: Peter Smith, 1976.

Tise, Larry E. *Proslavery: A History of the Defense of Slavery in America, 1701–1840.* Athens: University of Georgia Press, 1987.

Tobin, Eugene M. *Organize or Perish: America's Independent Progressives, 1913–1933.* New York: Greenwood Press, 1986.

Tolstoy, Leo. *Christianity and Patriotism, with Pertinent Extract from Other Essays.* Translated by Paul Borger et al. Chicago: Open Court Publishing, 1905.

———. *Tolstoy's Letters.* Translated by R. F. Christian. New York: Charles Scribner's Sons, 1978.

———. *Writings on Civil Disobedience and Nonviolence.* Translated by Aylmer Maude and Ronald Sampson. Philadelphia: New Society Publishers, 1987.

Towne, Ruth Warner. *Senator William J. Stone and the Politics of Compromise.* Port Washington, N.Y.: Kennikat Press, 1979.

Tozer, A.W. *The Divine Conquest.* Harrisburg, Pa.: Christian Publications, 1950.

———. *God Tells the Man Who Cares.* Harrisburg, Pa.: Christian Publications, 1970.

———. *Of God and Men.* Harrisburg, Pa.: Christian Publications, 1960.

———. *The Root of the Righteous.* Harrisburg, Pa.: Christian Publications, 1955.

Trautman, Karl G., ed. *The New Populist Reader.* Westport, Conn.: Praeger, 1997.

Truman, Harry S. "A Year of Challenge: Liberalism or Conservatism." *Vital Speeches of the Day,* March 1, 1948, 290–93.

Trumpbour, John, ed. *How Harvard Rules: Reason in the Service of Empire.* Boston: South End Press, 1989.

Tucker, Robert W., and David C. Hendrickson. *Empire of Liberty: The State-craft of Thomas Jefferson.* New York: Oxford University Press, 1990.

Turner, Robert F., ed., *The Jefferson-Hemings Controversy: Report of the Scholars Commission.* Durham: Carolina Academic Press, 2006.

Verduin, Leonard. *The Anatomy of a Hybrid: A Study in Church-State Relationships.* Grand Rapids, Mich.: Eerdmans, 1976.

———. *The Reformers and Their Stepchildren.* Grand Rapids, Mich.: Eerdmans, 1964.

Vidal, Gore. *Homage to Daniel Shays: Collected Essays, 1952–1972.* New York: Vintage Books, 1973.

———. *Inventing a Nation: Washington, Adams, Jefferson.* New Haven: Yale University Press, 2003.

———. *Matters of Fact and of Fiction: Essays, 1973–1976.* New York: Vintage Books, 1978.

———. *The Second American Revolution, and Other Essays (1976–1982).* New York: Random House, 1982.

———. *United States: Essays, 1952–1992.* New York: Random House, 1993.

Viguerie, Richard A. *The Establishment vs. the People: Is a New Populist Revolt on the Way?* Chicago: Regnery Gateway, 1984.

Villard, Oswald Garrison. *Prophets: True and False.* New York: Knopf, 1928.

Volkomer, Walter E., ed. *The Liberal Tradition in American Thought: An Anthology.* New York: Putnam, 1969.

Voorhis, Jerry. *Confessions of a Congressman.* Garden City, N.Y.: Doubleday, 1947.

———. *Out of Debt, Out of Danger: Proposals for War Finance and Tomorrow's Money.* New York: Devin-Adair, 1943.

Walczak, Lee. "Populism: A Diverse Movement Is Shaking America—and May Imperil its Role in the Global Economy." *Business Week,* March 13, 1995, 72–80.

Wallace, George C. *What I Believe: Governor Wallace Lays It Out Straight.* Belmont, Mass.: American Opinion, 1971.

Ward, Chester, and Phyllis Schlafly. *Kissinger on the Couch.* New Rochelle, N.Y.: Arlington House, 1975.

Watkins, William J., Jr. *Reclaiming the American Revolution: The Kentucky and Virginia Resolutions and Their Legacy.* New York: Palgrave Macmillan, 2004.

Wayman, Dorothy G. *David I. Walsh: Citizen-Patriot.* Milwaukee: Bruce Publishing, 1952.

Wechsberg, Joseph. *The Merchant Bankers.* New York: Pocket Books, 1966.

Weisberger, Bernard A. *The La Follettes of Wisconsin: Love and Politics in Progressive America.* Madison: University of Wisconsin Press, 1994.

Werner, M. R. *Bryan.* New York: Harcourt, Brace, 1929.

Wheeler, Burton K. "Nominations of Henry L. Stimson and Frank Knox." *Congressional Record,* June 20, 1940, 8693–96.

———. *Yankee from the West.* New York: Octagon Books, 1977.

Whicher, George F., ed. *William Jennings Bryan and the Campaign of 1896.* Boston: D. C. Heath, 1953.

White, John Kenneth, and John C. Green, eds. *The Politics of Ideas: Intellectual Challenges Facing the American Political Parties.* Albany: State University of New York Press, 2001.

White, Theodore H. *The Making of the President, 1960.* New York: Atheneum, 1961.

———. *The Making of the President, 1964.* New York: Atheneum, 1965.

———. *The Making of the President, 1968.* New York: Atheneum, 1969.

———. *The Making of the President, 1972.* New York: Atheneum, 1973.

White, William Allen. "The End of an Epoch: The Passing of the Apostles of Liberalism in the United States." *Scribner's Magazine,* June 1926, 561–70.

Whitfield, Stephen J. *A Critical American: The Politics of Dwight Macdonald.* Hamden, Conn.: Archon Books, 1984.

Wiebe, Robert H. *Self-Rule: A Cultural History of American Democracy.* Chicago: University of Chicago Press, 1995.

Williams, Leonard. *American Liberalism and Ideological Change.* DeKalb: Northern Illinois University Press, 1998.

Williams, T. Harry. *Huey Long.* New York: Knopf, 1969.

Williams, Wayne C. *William Jennings Bryan: A Study in Political Vindication.* New York: Fleming H. Revell, 1923.

Williams, William Appleman. *The Contours of American History.* Chicago: Quadrangle Paperbacks, 1966.

Willkie, Wendell L. *One World.* New York: Simon and Schuster, 1943.

Wilson, Charles Morrow. *The Commoner: William Jennings Bryan.* Garden City, N.Y.: Doubleday, 1970.

Wilson, Clyde. "Conservative Movement R.I.P.?" *Chronicles,* May 1991, 19–20.

———. *From Union to Empire: Essays in the Jeffersonian Tradition.* Columbia, S.C.: Foundation for American Education, 2003.

———. "The Jeffersonian Conservative Tradition." *Modern Age,* Winter 1969–1970, 36–48.

———. "Why They Hate Jefferson." *Chronicles,* August 1997, 29–30.

Wilson, Major L. *The Presidency of Martin Van Buren.* Lawrence: University Press of Kansas, 1984.

Wiltse, Charles Maurice. *The Jeffersonian Tradition in American Democracy.* New York: Hill and Wang, 1960.

Wise, David, and Thomas B. Ross. *The Invisible Government.* New York: Vintage Books, 1974.

Wiseman, John B. *The Dilemmas of a Party Out of Power: The Democrats, 1904–1912.* New York: Garland, 1988.

Witcover, Jules. *Marathon: The Pursuit of the Presidency, 1972–1976.* New York: Viking Press, 1977.

Wolfskill, George. *The Revolt of the Conservatives: A History of the American Liberty League, 1934–1940.* Westport, Conn.: Greenwood Press, 1974.

Woodcock, George. *Anarchism: A History of Libertarian Ideas and Movements.* Cleveland: Meridian Books, 1962.

Woodward, Bob, and Scott Armstrong. *The Brethren: Inside the Supreme Court.* New York: Avon, 1981.

Wreszin, Michael. *Oswald Garrison Villard: Pacifist at War.* Bloomington: Indiana University Press, 1965.

―――. *A Rebel in Defense of Tradition: The Life and Politics of Dwight Macdonald.* New York: Basic Books, 1994.

Yarbrough, Jean M. *American Virtues: Thomas Jefferson on the Character of a Free People.* Lawrence: University Press of Kansas, 1998.

Yoder, John H. *The Original Revolution: Essays on Christian Pacifism.* Scottdale, Pa.: Herald Press, 1977.

Young, James P. *Reconsidering American Liberalism: The Troubled Odyssey of the Liberal Idea.* Boulder, Colo.: Westview Press, 1996.

Young, Nancy Beck. *Wright Patman: Populism, Liberalism, and the American Dream.* Dallas: Southern Methodist University Press, 2000.

Youngdale, James M., ed. *Third Party Footprints: An Anthology from Writings and Speeches of Midwest Radicals.* Minneapolis: Ross and Haines, 1966.

Zilg, Gerard Colby. *Du Pont: Behind the Nylon Curtain.* Englewood Cliffs, N.J.: Prentice-Hall, 1974.

Zinn, Howard. *Declarations of Independence: Cross-Examining American Ideology.* New York: Harper Perennial, 1991.

―――. *A People's History of the United States.* New York: Perennial Library, 1980.

INDEX

PERMISSIONS

Quotations from *The Political Philosophy of the New Deal* by Hubert H. Humphrey reprinted by permission of Louisiana State University Press. Copyright © 1970 by Hubert H. Humphrey.

Quotations from *The Education of a Public Man: My Life and Politics* by Hubert H. Humphrey (edited by Norman Sherman) reprinted by permission of University of Minnesota Press. Copyright © 1991 by the Regents of the University of Minnesota.

Quotations from *Hubert: The Triumph and Tragedy of the Humphrey I Knew* by Edgar Berman reprinted by permission of Don Congdon Associates. Copyright © 1979 by Edgar Berman.

ABOUT THE AUTHOR

Jeff Taylor teaches political science at the community college in Rochester, Minnesota.